InterSections   Over the last decade, critical theories of different kinds have had an enormous impact on many different disciplines and practices. *InterSections* is the first book to comprehensively survey this impact on architecture, providing sixteen chapters that intersect a particular critical theory with specific architectural ideas, projects and events. An extended essay by the editors gives an in-depth introduction to the subject. Essays range from psychoanalysis and interiors; colonialism and modern urbanism; gender and the Renaissance; to heterotopia and Las Vegas. Contributors come from Europe and the USA and include Iain Borden, Zeynep Çelik, Sarah Chaplin, Beatriz Colomina, Darell W. Fields, Murray Fraser, Diane Ghirardo, Joe Kerr, Clive R. Knights, Neil Leach, Barbara Penner, Jane Rendell, Katherine Shonfield, Helen Thomas, Jeremy Till, Henry Urbach and Sarah Wigglesworth.

Iain Borden and **Jane Rendell** both lecture in architectural history and theory at The Bartlett, University College London, UK.

D1609824

Inter**Sections**

Architectural Histories

and

Critical Theories

Iain Borden and Jane Rendell

London and New York

First published 2000
by Routledge
11 New Fetter Lane, London EC4P 4EE

Simultaneously published in the USA and Canada
by Routledge
29 West 35th Street, New York, NY 10001

Routledge is an imprint of the Taylor & Francis Group

Typeset in Akzidenz Grotesk by Keystroke, Jacaranda Lodge, Wolverhampton
Printed and bound in Great Britain by Biddles Ltd, Guildford and King's Lynn

British Library Cataloguing in Publication Data
A catalogue record for this book is available from the British Library

Library of Congress Cataloging in Publication Data
A catalog record for this book has been requested

ISBN 0-415-23179-5 (pbk)
ISBN 0-415-232-929 (hbk)

History is not merely a therapy. By questioning its own materials, it reconstructs them and continuously reconstructs itself.

Manfredo Tafuri

Contents

Illustrations

Notes on contributors

Iain Borden

Iain Borden is Reader in Architecture and Urban Culture at The Bartlett, University College London, where he is Director of Architectural History and Theory. He is author of *Architecture in Motion: Skateboarding and Urban Experience* (forthcoming) and, with Jane Rendell, co-author of *DoubleDecker: Architecture through History, Politics and Poetics* (forthcoming). He is also co-editor of *Architecture and the Sites of History: Interpreting Buildings and Cities* (1995), *Strangely Familiar: Narratives of Architecture in the City* (1996), *The Unknown City: Contesting Architecture and Social Space* (2000), *Gender Space Architecture: an Interdisciplinary Introduction* (2000) and *The City Cultures Reader* (2000).

Zeynep Çelik

Zeynep Çelik is Professor of Architecture at the New Jersey Institute of Technology. She is the author of *The Remaking of Istanbul* (1986/1993), *Displaying the Orient: Architecture of Islam at Nineteenth Century World's Fairs* (1992), and *Urban Forms and Colonial Confrontations: Algiers under French Rule* (1997) and co-editor of *Streets: Critical Perspectives on Public Space* (1993/1996).

Sarah Chaplin

Sarah Chaplin trained as an architect at Nottingham and Oxford Brookes universities, and has a Masters in Architecture and Critical Theory. She is currently programme leader for the MA Digital Architecture at Middlesex University and teaches across two departments: Visual Culture and Media, and the Centre for Electronic Arts. She is also a director of the design consultancy *evolver*. Her publications include articles in the *Journal of Architecture*, *Leonardo*, *Space and Culture*, *Urban Design International* and *Architecture*. She is the co-author, with John A. Walker, of *Visual Culture, an Introduction* and co-editor, with Eric Holding, of *Consuming Architecture* (1998).

Beatriz Colomina

Beatriz Colomina is Professor in the School of Architecture at Princeton University, and has also taught at the Escuela Técnica Superior de Arquitectura de Barcelona and Columbia University. An architectural historian and theorist, she is editor of

Sexuality and Space (1992) and *Architectureproduction* (1988) and the author of *Privacy and Publicity: Modern Architecture as Mass Media* (1993). She is currently working on a book on the relationships between war and modern architecture.

Darell W. Fields

Darell W. Fields teaches design studios and seminars on architectural theory and criticism. He received his BS in architecture from the University of Texas at Arlington and his Master of Architecture from Harvard's Graduate School of Design, receiving the school's AIA Gold Medal in 1988. He received his PhD from Harvard University in 1995. He has initiated and participated in various projects in Dallas, New York, Boston and Tokyo. In 1993, his serial video montage of New York City, entitled "Co-Lateral Damage," was presented at the Whitney Museum of American Art. He is a founding editor of *Appendx*, an interdisciplinary publication providing a link to vital cultural realities affecting the discipline of architecture.

Murray Fraser

Murray Fraser trained as an architect and architectural historian at The Bartlett, University College London, where he taught briefly before taking up his current post in the School of Architecture at Oxford Brookes University. He has written widely on the theme of cultural imperialism and hybridisation, focusing on Anglo-Irish and Anglo-American relationships. He is currently preparing two books, one on the work of Eero Saarinen, and one, with Joe Kerr, entitled *The Special Relationship: the Influence of America on British Architecture since 1945*.

Diane Ghirardo

Diane Ghirardo is a Professor in the School of Architecture at the University of Southern California. She is editor of *Out of Site: a Social Criticism of Architecture* (1991) and author of *Building New Communities: New Deal America and Fascist Italy* (1989), *Mark Mack* (1994) and *Architecture After Modernism* (1996). She is also executive editor of the *Journal of Architectural Education*. Her present research concerns women's spaces in Renaissance Italy.

Joe Kerr

Joe Kerr is Senior Tutor at the Royal College of Art, London. A founding member of Strangely Familiar, he is co-editor of *Strangely Familiar: Narratives of Architecture in the City* (1996) and *The Unknown City: Contesting Architecture and Social Space* (2000). He is currently writing, with Murray Fraser, a book entitled *The Special Relationship: the Influence of America on British Architecture since 1945*.

Clive R. Knights

Clive R. Knights studied architectural design at Portsmouth Polytechnic and architectural history and theory at Cambridge University. He has taught design studio and architectural theory at Portsmouth Polytechnic and Sheffield University, and is presently an Associate Professor at the Department of Architecture, Portland State University, Oregon. He has presented papers on design pedagogy, aesthetics and cultural theory at many international conferences and has been both guest lecturer and critic at institutions on both sides of the Atlantic. He is currently struggling to release himself from the seduction of words and rediscover the sensuality of matter through making.

Neil Leach

Neil Leach is Reader in Architecture and Critical Theory at Nottingham University. He is author of *The Anaesthetics of Architecture* (1999) and editor of *Rethinking Architecture* (1997), and *Architecture and Revolution: Contemporary Perspectives on Central and Eastern Europe* (1999). He is co-translator (with Joseph Rykwert and Robert Tavernor) of Leon Battista Alberti, *On the Art of Building in Ten Books* (1988). His forthcoming books include *The Hieroglyphics of Space: Reading and Experiencing the Modern Metropolis* and *Millennium Culture*.

Barbara Penner

Barbara Penner is a Lecturer at the University of East London and at University College London. She has co-edited *Gender Space Architecture* (1999) and presented a radio programme on the history of women's public lavatories, "The Ladies' Room," for the BBC. She is currently working on her doctoral thesis, "Alone at Last: Honeymooning in America, 1830–1910."

Jane Rendell

Jane Rendell is Lecturer in architectural History and Theory at The Bartlett, University College London. She is author of *The Pursuit of Pleasure* (forthcoming) and, with Iain Borden, co-author of *DoubleDecker: Architecture through History, Politics and Poetics* (forthcoming). She is also co-editor with Borden of *Strangely Familiar: Narratives of Architecture in the City* (1996), *The Unknown City: Contesting Architecture and Social Space* (2000) and *Gender Space Architecture: an Interdisciplinary Introduction* (2000).

Katherine Shonfield

Katherine Shonfield studied sociology and worked as a local authority planner before qualifying as an architect. She is Senior Lecturer in Architecture at South Bank University, author of the influential Commedia/Demos urban policy document *At Home*

With Strangers: Public Space and the New Urbanity (1998) and *Walls Have Feelings: Architecture, Film and the City* (2000). She has a weekly column in the *Architects' Journal*, is deputy editor of the *Journal for Architecture* and is a member of the Royal Society of Art's "Art for Architecture Committee" and of the governing council of the Architectural Association. She is a principal in the practice Shonfield and Williams, and is consultant to Muf Architects.

Helen Thomas

Helen Thomas trained as an architect at Liverpool University and graduated in architectural history from The Bartlett, University College London. She has worked as an architect in London and Seville and has taught architectural history, theory and design at The Bartlett and University of North London. She has published various articles and chapters on spatial theory and Latin American architecture, and is currently researching her doctorate on post-colonial imaginations at the University of Essex.

Jeremy Till

Jeremy Till is Head of School and Professor of Architecture at Sheffield University. His work investigates the social and political aspects of architecture, and in particular the relationship to the everyday. He is in practice with Sarah Wigglesworth Architects where he pursues design as a research activity. He and Wigglesworth are the only architects to have been awarded the Fulbright Arts Fellowship.

Henry Urbach

Henry Urbach teaches, exhibits and writes about architecture in New York. His gallery, Henry Urbach Architecture, presents works by artists and architects that offer new possibilities for interpreting and representing contemporary space. Currently completing a PhD in architectural history and theory at Princeton University, he teaches architectural theory at Parsons School of Design. Henry has published in *Assemblage*, *Sites*, *ANY*, *Journal of Architecture*, *Regarding the Proper* and *Desiring Practices: Architecture, Gender and the Interdisciplinary*. A contributing editor to *Interior Design*, he has also written architectural criticism for the *Village Voice*, *Metropolis*, *New York Times* and *Artforum*.

Sarah Wigglesworth

Sarah Wigglesworth heads her own architectural practice in London. The practice is best known for its Strawbale House and Office, a research project into sustainable mixed use in an urban environment. She is co-editor of *Desiring Practices: Architecture, Gender and the Interdisciplinary* (1996) and, with Jeremy Till, is co-editor of a special issue of *Architectural Design* on *The Everyday and Architecture* (1998). She is currently Professor of Architecture at Sheffield University.

Illustration credits

The authors and the publishers would like to thank the following individuals and institutions for giving permission to reproduce illustrations. We have made every effort to contact copyright holders, but if any errors have been made we would be happy to correct them at a later printing.

Architects' Journal, The 17.7, 17.8
Archivio di Stato, Ferrara 11.11
Archivio Fotografico del Comune di Ferrara 8.5, 11.1, 11.6, 11.12
Beinecke Rare Book and Manuscript Library, Yale University 11.9
Borden, I. 13.1–13.12
Canal + Image UK Ltd 17.4
Cezar, M. *Sanatta Batiya Açilis ve Osman Hamdi*, (Istanbul: Is Bankasi Yayinlari, 1971) 10.2
Chantiers, (March 1935) 10.1
Collection Dieter Bogner, Vienna 4.1
Egan, P. *Life in London*, (London: Sherwood, Neely and Jones, 1820–1) 14.1, 14.3, 14.5
Euro London Films Ltd 17.5
Gemaci 17.6
Frank O. Gehry & Associates 8.9, 8.13
Fraser, M./Kerr, J. 8.1, 8.2, 8.4, 8.6–8.8, 8.10–8.12, 8.14
Frederick Kiesler Archives, New York 4.2–4.5
Ghirardo, D. 11.3–11.5
HMSO 17.3
Holding, E. 12.1–12.10
Kim, M. 3.1
National Gallery of Ireland 11.2
Rendell, J. 14.2, 14.4, 14.6
Richard Meier & Partners 8.3, 8.5
Sandri, A. *Origine delle chiese di Ferrara e luoghi della provincia* 11.7, 11.10
Shaw, C. 17.2
Thomas, H. 7.1 – 7.3
Till, J. 16.1
Vecellio, C. *Habiti antichi et moderni di tutto il mondo*, (Venice, 1598) 11.8
Vickery, R./Architectural Association 6.1–6.8
Vittone, B. 17.1

Preface

Architectural history has, necessarily, always had theory at its heart. From the German aesthetics of Wölfflin and Schmarsow, to the empiricism of Hitchcock and Summerson, to the Hegelian histories of Giedion and Pevsner, to the neo-marxism of Tafuri and Cacciari, such formulations have carried a theoretical model within them. Yet it is in the 1990s that critical theory has exploded within architectural history, embedding itself into the discipline in a myriad of different shapes and means. As a result, poststructuralism, feminism, psychoanalysis, (post)marxism, postmodern cultural theory and a multitude of other formulations have changed not only the interpretative categories but also the very epistemological foundations on which architectural history is grounded.

It is in this context that *InterSections* has been produced. Although far from being the first book in architectural history to engage with critical theory, *InterSections* is, nonetheless, the first attempt to systematically explore the nature of that engagement. It delineates some of the great range of theories to which those interested in the history of architecture might refer, giving an indication of the possibilities for interpretation and speculation. Its seventeen chapters all offer, in their own way, a particular intersection with architecture, thus showing how architecture and theory, history and criticism, are (re)produced in their creative interplay. And it suggests how the very grounds of historical thinking in relation to architecture are now being profoundly restructured.

Acknowledgements

We wish to thank all the contributors for their efforts, patience and commitment to the project. And we wish to thank our students, colleagues and friends for conversations past, present and future. This book is dedicated to all those who intersect history and theory, scholarship and passion.

Iain Borden and Jane Rendell
London
May 2000

Introduction

Chapter 1
From chamber to transformer: epistemological challenges
and tendencies in the intersection of architectural histories and
critical theories
Iain Borden and Jane Rendell

*In the summer of 1985, I lay on a beach on Crete, struggling to read a text whose
pages and words seemed to me to be wholly resistant to offering up their meaning.
The book, Raymond Williams'* Marxism and Literature,[1] *had been "suggested reading"
for a course in architectural history that I was about to start in London the following
September. And I struggled with it for a number of reasons. First, and perhaps
understandably, it was my first real introduction to marxist thought, and for anyone's
initial forays into that conceptual schema, any book, no matter how well written (and
Williams' script is a model of reasoned clarity), was always going to be hard work.
Second, and though I barely knew it, this was also my first real introduction to the
realm of critical theory in general. Up to that juncture, my education had been in
history of various kinds − architecture, art, ancient world − but none of it held much
truck with ideas beyond the world of its own objects of study, still less with general
cultural abstractions of this ilk. Third, therefore, was a growing unease not just with
the difficulty of the text, but also with its very relevance to the course on which I was
about to embark. "Base and Superstructure," "Hegemony," "Typification and
Homology," "Ideology," "From Reflection to Mediation" − of what possible relevance
were these chapters for the historical study of Le Corbusier, Mies van der Rohe and
Ebenezer Howard? Why the hell, my sun-soaked brain demanded, was I reading
this?*

*In the autumn of 1985, a first year student of architectural design, I entered a world
of seductive forms (glass boxes, white villas) and earnest politics (ugly housing).
Although drawn to the latter, the social issues seemingly only got in the aesthetic
way. The two bore a strange and uneasy relation. Later and deeper into the world
of architectural education, this relationship was torn entirely asunder. I was told that
because I liked thinking about theory I would never have any architectural idea. For,
as the Master carefully explained to me, those who were interested in thinking
theoretically could never be architects. Then came my entry into history, into
historiography, into, therefore, a place where one could think − that is think
"architecturally" as something at once ideational and material. Here arose the central*

question: through exploring the workings of architectural history in terms of both epistemology and methodology, how would it be possible for my politics to inform theoretically creative practices?

In any historical or critical field – whether concerning the interpretation of architecture, planning history, social events, art, medicine and so forth – there is a danger that the methodology of the investigating author will conflate or conspire with the ostensible objects of study. Rather than taking an independent critical line, the interpretation consequently takes the form of an excavation that can repeat only what it unearths, say only what it is allowed to say.

Nowhere, perhaps, has this process been more readily apparent in the field of historical and critical studies of the built environment – architecture, urbanism, landscape, planning[2] – where the perpetual trend among historians has been to conduct their lines of enquiry less upon their own theoretical or political agendas and more on the internal concerns of the spatial professions and the intricacies of their procedural practices. The discourse around architecture is particularly redolent of this kind of approach, where very often architecture is understood simply to be "what the architect does."

This much is, perhaps, not in itself a bad thing, for the recording and explanation of the practices of urban professionals according to their own concerns is certainly of some historical worth: what architects think, what they have done (or what they think they have done), and what they themselves have considered to be the most important ideas and influences on their operations are all things which deserve to be recorded, assessed and communicated. And, of course, many architectural historians have concentrated on exactly this kind of study, typified by the work of those such as Kenneth Frampton, who, for example, notes in his *Modern Architecture: a Critical History*, that in this text, and despite a professed "affinity for the critical theory of the Frankfurt School," he has tried "whenever possible to let the protagonists speak for themselves."[3]

One other point worth making here is that many of these architectural historians have also either trained as, and/or continue to work as, architects in their own right. Their concerns are, therefore, necessarily and perhaps rightly directed at the operative functions of the architectural practitioner. Nonetheless, as all of the chapters in this book in some way demonstrate – including many by those who are both historians and design practitioners – it is not only the internal matters of architecture with which the architect/historian need be concerned.

The machinations of the drawing board are not the only things that ought to be addressed. There is life outside of the studio, the building site and the private library, and, of course, architects and everyone involved in architecture (which is, in fact, simply everyone) is absolutely implicated in this wider world of architecture – inescapably, everyday, we all live in and through architecture.

The problem, however, is that resisting the gravitational pull of the object is particularly difficult in the case of histories concerned with the built environment. First, there is the perplexing nature of the objectival object, that is of the material character of the city and its multifarious buildings. A more complex, dynamic and opaque entity than the (post)modern metropolis would be hard to imagine. Second, there is the problem of the inextricably implicated relation that architecture (as with planning) holds with this city-entity, being both challenged and constrained by a set of institutional practices that draw their power from as diverse a range of sources as capital and economies, national and municipal governments, dominant classes, smaller yet mobilised interest groups, territorialised zones and cultural conventions.

Architecture's problem – that of the physical and social complexity of its arena of action, compounded by the multifaceted negotiations it has to undertake in order to act at all – is then replicated in the representations made of it in history. Unable to see the wood for the trees, historians are constantly tempted to focus on the minutiae of architecture, on individual agents, individual projects, individual codes as the constituting elements of their histories. Too often, they closely follow architects such as Richard Meier who earnestly believe that "[a]rchitecture is the subject of my architecture,"[4] and that, consequently there is no need to look beyond the internalised concerns of the discipline in order to understand it historically. Hence certain monographs on the single architect or architectural practice, special publications on the single building, or focused studies of a particular aspect of architectural practice. All these provide glimpses or partial views of architecture, but ultimately do little more than record the general character of architecture, yielding a textual snapshot of particular objects and surfaces. Not so much hidden away as lost altogether are the forgotten peoples, the alternative practices, the imagined representations that fall outside of the hegemonic realm. Similarly struck off from the political agenda are the wider concerns, the mobilising forces that provide both the occasion and much of the substance for city development and architectural activity. What these studies lack is an explicit framework in which to situate their objects of study. As a result, the apparent implication is too often that the given subject is, at best, an isolated arena of activity, and, at worst, the only one really worth studying.

Alternatively, unable to see the trees for the wood, historians are tempted to throw what they intend to be a catch-net over their objects, seeking to cover all peoples, all things, all activities under one banner. Here, encyclopaedic historical volumes attempt to survey such things as the whole of twentieth century architecture,[5] the whole of Indian architecture,[6] or, in the case of the magisterial Banister Fletcher, the whole of everything.[7]

If architecture is the conception, design and construction of the spaces of the city, then it is important to realise that this creative system occurs neither solely in the ways in which the great projects purport to operate (that is, architectural activities have discursive content and meaning far beyond their avowed intentions and surface appearance), nor indeed only through these great projects. There are not only hidden meanings, but also hidden practices to architecture.

How then is the historian to cut through this dense swathe of money, power and ideology? How to make sense of its concomitant spatial existence, the city, and of the creative practice of architecture? The aim must be, first of all, to recognise the grounds on which the historical interpretation is being made, by which is meant not so much the meanings that can be located *within* the historical object as the *questions that may be asked* of it according to an explicit historian-centred agenda. It is to this problematic which we now turn.

NINE CHALLENGES

Although antiquarian historians such as Deborah Howard may believe that "good history does not need methodology,"[8] the notion that history can or should be written "without methodology" or "without theory" is an absurdity; it is impossible to approach history using the old ideas and minds of those who have gone before. "Theory is indispensable. It is how we make sense of the world."[9] How else are we to construct history except through our own contemporary concerns? And how are we to translate those concerns into interpretative questions to be asked of the past? Conversely, how are we to use the past as the grounds upon which to conduct our own interpretative enquiries? Any consideration of the past must then use some kind of mediating concept to negotiate between its specific substance and the present condition of the historian – "all history is theoretical."[10] Furthermore, that mediating concept can no longer be simply the language-manipulation of literary technique or writerly prowess; discussions about architectural historical methodology cannot remain simply within the remit of narrative style or communicability.[11] This "crisis in narrative or storytelling history,"[12] is, as Hayden White succinctly states, true of *all* kinds of history whether theorised (what he calls "philosophy of history") or empirical ("history" or "history proper"):

> Those historians who draw a firm line between history and philosophy of history fail to recognize that every historical discourse contains within it a full-blown, if only implicit, philosophy of history . . . the principal difference between history and philosophy of history is that the latter brings the conceptual apparatus by which the facts are ordered in the discourse to the surface of the text, while history proper (as it is called) buries it in the interior of the narrative, where it serves as a hidden or implicit shaping device.[13]

As Keith Jenkins concludes, the choice is not whether history should be theoretical or not, but rather between "a history that is aware of what it is doing and a history that is not."[14] Theory then is, on one level, the making explicit of the historian's negotiation, of setting out the interpretative agenda not as an implicit, invisible subterfuge, but as a necessarily implicated set of thought processes.

The question of whether to use theory or not is an irrelevance. Rather the questions must be, first, which theory to use, and second, how to relate it to the ostensible objects of study?

To consider the first of these questions, if architecture is, as already stated, inextricably implicated in the material and ideological practices that conduct and control city affairs, then it makes sense that for any architectural history to provide a critical interpretation of architecture, its theoretical grounding *must* come not just from within the architectural discourse. "For the master's tools will never dismantle the master's house."[15] Instead, it is necessary to look at other arenas, other theoretical territories. Furthermore, just as historians should not be slaves to the internal concerns of architecture, nor should they be driven solely by the classifications and limited scopes of particular kinds of theories. To do so would be to be sealed within the chamber of philosophy. Therefore, in *InterSections* we take "critical theory" not only to mean the work of the Frankfurt School (Adorno, Benjamin, Habermas, Horkheimer, Marcuse *et al.*), but also to encompass any self-reflexive emancipatory theory (various feminisms, marxisms, psychoanalysis etc.) together with any theoretically informed academic discipline (such as historical and cultural studies, anthropology, geography, sociology etc.). Critical theory is any mental schema which abstracts a model, explanation, speculation, hypothesis or method of action for any aspect of social life. It is our contention, therefore, that some of the best works in architectural history – best that is both for architectural historians to consider in relation to their own research, and for those who wish to understand and confront the received history in which we live each day – do not in fact necessarily have the label "architectural history" on their back cover. They are, however, of direct relevance to architectural and city history, such that it is possible to speak of the "difference that theory makes."[16]

This, in turn, raises the secondary question of how theory relates to the historical and critical study of architecture. What difference does theory indeed make? It occurs in nine ways.

Theory as objects of study

First, theory can be the object of study for histories of architecture. This can occur as an historical discourse about particular theories, describing their content and development and intimating at their relevance to architecture. Here, critics and historians change their primary focus from architecture to theory, often using the former as a way in to the latter. Alternatively, historians may study the ways in which architects have deployed theory in order to inform their design practices. Here, instead of "architectural theory" being viewed as the autonomous realm in which architects discuss their design methodologies, such theory can also be seen to encompass abstract ideas from outside of architecture. Finally, historians may, while accepting the centrality of the figure of the architect, interpret the architect's design process through the lens of critical theory.

New architectures

Second, critical theory in itself has the potential to tell us something different about the way people go about their lives other than through the conventional architectural history discourse. Simply put, the range of ideas in critical theory offers the chance to see architecture as something other than buildings, compositional techniques or architect-based practices. This theory is a space of imaginative abstraction outside of the immediate remits and dictates of *architectural practice*, and it is therefore here that the conventional objects of study may be displaced out of their normative arena, such that they are challenged, made wider, more varied, less predictable. Theorised history thus, to transpose Fredric Jameson's account of materialist history, "does its work ultimately by undermining the very foundations, framework, constitutive presuppositions, of the specialized disciplines themselves" not in order to erase such disciplines but to disclose "an *Other* of the discipline, an outside, a limit, the revelation of the *extrinsic*, which it is felt to be scandalous and unscholarly to introduce into a carefully regulated traditional debate."[17] Architecture is not, then, lost or reduced in the process of theorised interpretations but, conversely, is found once again and made richer, more significant to the world in general.

Framing questions

While finding new objects to study is an important part of theorised history, as Griselda Pollock[18] and, more recently, Leonie Sandercock point out, "simply adding new stories is not enough. There is a difference between rewriting history by adding the forgotten or repressed contributions of (for example) women and retheorizing history by using gender or race as categories of analysis."[19] Third, therefore, critical theory can provide a theoretical outside from which to challenge conventional representations. Seemingly conventional subjects, such as a particular building, can be given a new meaning and a new lease of life by posing different questions. Here, the questions asked of architecture are challenged. This theory is a space of imaginative abstraction outside of the immediate remits and dictates of the *historical discourse*, and it is therefore here that the questions most commonly asked of architecture may be revised, such that they too, like the objects of study in architectural history, are also made wider, more varied, less predictable.

Critical history

However, in any intersection of architectural history and critical theory the latter cannot say anything it likes of the former. Rather, there is an interplay between critical theory and the architectural history which, epistemologically, is not a freely associative criticism, one which simply uses architecture from which to spring in to open speculation that, in Barthes' terms, "has in its favour the right of the signifier to spread out where it will,"[20] but which instead calls upon history in order to limit the terms of engagement while at the same time posing questions of it.

> To criticize . . . is to put into crisis, something which is not possible without evaluating the conditions of the crisis (its limits), without considering its historical moment.[21]

Critical theorised history is then a form of "criticism" which is determined by methodology rather than by a temporal distance from its objects of study. Architectural histories of this kind can be histories of the present as well as of the past.

Interdisciplinary debates

Fifth, the audience or readership of architectural history can also be developed. Too often architectural history is directed either at an audience seen to be comprised solely of architects and/or of architectural "tourists" concerned more with simply seeing constructions than understanding architecture according to the full range of its interpretative potentialities. The task here, then, is to put across the meaning, the relevance of architecture to those who are either too immersed or, alternatively, not immersed enough in its culture. And the way to do this is not to present architecture as an autonomous activity, which can be appreciated only by being fully engaged in its ways or by watching respectively from afar, but as something capable of being inserted and understood in wider comprehensions of cultural production.

Such a task, can, of course, be achieved by showing the economic, social and political contexts of architecture, and a large number of architectural histories do exactly this. However, as Manfredo Tafuri has argued, such contexts are not unitary formations:

> to displace the investigation from a text . . . to a context is not sufficient. The context binds together . . . [b]ut it is constantly broken up by "technical accidents:" . . . tactical manoeuvers that obscurely intersect larger strategies . . . subterranean ideologies that nevertheless act on an intersubjective level . . . diverse techniques of domination, each of which possess its own untranslatable language.[22]

If architectural histories are to consider context as part of their subject matter, they must also confront and develop the various theorisations and interpretative methods that others have already used to analyse them. The fifth challenge, therefore, is not only that architecture must be placed as an historical subject within various historical contexts, but also that architectural history should engage in the interdisciplinary debates centred on different theorisations of the cultural. Here, the "audience" is seen to include academic and intellectual debates, themselves wrestling with the turbulent nexus of society, space and time in the context of critical theories of all kinds.

Disclosing methodology

Sixth, by engaging with critical theory historians can make explicit their own method-ologies to the readers, allowing the latter to more fully comprehend (and hence question) what they are reading. To use a theatrical analogy here, this means disclosing not just the stage scene itself, but also all of the various pulleys, ropes, screens and trapdoors, as well as performative staging effects such as music, lighting and narrative, that help make up the staging and theatrical process. This, then, and to continue the theatrical analogy, is a Brechtian approach, one which deliberately deploys distancing effects (or Brecht's *V-Effekte*) in order to disclose the constructed nature of history.

It is important to realise that this is more than just a technical operation, but an attack on the epistemology (from the Greek *episteme* = knowledge) of history as the narration of past events. Such a history is one where the historical object is explicitly seen to be as much produced by historical writing as being the starting point from which historical writing springs.

> The problem arises of knowing whether the unity of a discourse is based not so much on the permanence and uniqueness of an object as on the space in which various objects emerge and are continuously transformed.[23]

In other words, architecture is seen to be produced by architectural history as much as architectural history is founded on architecture. Epistemologically, therefore, the reader is encouraged to consider the very grounds on which historical representations are formed, as well as to consider the events of history, and hence is encouraged to think about the constructed nature of all events, from history to the present day.

Self-reflexivity

Seventh, critical theory makes historians themselves conscious of what they are doing, and so able to consider not only the ostensible object of study, but also the development of the critical field that focuses on and helps to create that object. As

Henri Lefebvre and Roland Barthes both point out, this is essential, for all intellectual enterprises must be self-critical in order to properly exist.

> There can be no philosophy without a critique of philosophy and a refusal to "philosophize." Equally, there can be no science without a critique of the scientific canon and science in general, no psychology without a critique of psychologism, no history without a critique of historicism. And so on and so forth.[24]

> All criticism must include in its discourse an implicit reflection on itself; every criticism is a criticism of the work and a criticism of itself. In other words, criticism is not at all a table of results or a body of judgements, it is essentially an activity.[25]

Just as the reader is encouraged to consider the constructed nature of history, so too must the historian also consider the procedures and assumptions by which they operate. For architectural history, this means that the discipline is forever, in Tafuri's terms, in crisis:

> History is . . . an analytical construction that is never definite and always provisional; an instrument of deconstruction of ascertainable realities . . . With the fading away of the dream of knowledge as a means to power, the constant struggle between the analysis and its objects – their irreducible tension – remains. Precisely this tension is "productive:" the historical "project" is always the "project of a crisis."[26]

Once again, this historical endeavour is always and already an epistemological one, seeking to continually revise the grounds of knowledge as well as what historical knowledge might say of particular architectural events, actions and spaces.

Re-engagement with theory

Eighth, and as the last quotation implies, it is not just architectural history that is to be rethought through an encounter with critical theory. Critical theory is not just another arena in which to think architecture – simply writing or reading such texts at this level of abstraction is not enough. One common approach within theorised architectural history is to follow Gilles Deleuze in treating theory as "exactly like a box of tools."[27] Well, this is both true and not true. On the one hand, considering critical theories in relation to architecture provides many advantages, as argued above, enabling those within architecture to extend and validate their choice of subject matter, to engage with other disciplines, and to import in new interpretations and speculations. Texts and ideas from the realm of critical theory allow the possibility for this to happen – they are that "box of tools."

On the other hand, there is, of course, far more to rethinking architecture than reading and contemplating; it cannot be the simple setting of critical theory alongside architecture, or of just using critical theory as an operative procedure that is itself left unmodified. Such technicity runs the risk of producing an architectural history that although pretending to be polemical, argumentative, political and transgressive is, in reality, a toothless and endless reiteration of other people's ideas – and here one might recall F.H. Bradley's denigration of Hegel's idealist logic as "a ghostly ballet of bloodless categories."[28] Instead, then, of treating the "tool" of critical theory against architecture in the manner of a simple application of a device against a remote object (comparable to Martin Heidegger's *Vorhandenheit*, or "presentness-at-hand" of the object "out there"), the architectural historian should consider the tool-object in relation to themselves and their object of study (cf. Heidegger's *Zuhandenheit*, or "readiness-to-hand").[29]

Hence, for example, the concern of the editors of *Architecture and Feminism* to avoid the more contingent relation of "architecture *if* feminism" or the more additive relation of "architecture *plus* feminism" in favour of the more "strategic and speculative" conjuncture of "architecture *and* feminism," a relation that not only exchanges concepts but also seeks to open up a new ground for both conceptual schema.[30] Those concerned with the engagement with critical theory must, therefore, also *return* architecture to critical theories, not only showing architecture's value to external theories that seek to understand the cultural world, but also altering and modifying (in effect, producing) those theories accordingly. To quote marxist historian E.P. Thompson, arguing against what he viewed as the overly theorised formulations of structuralist marxists such as Louis Althusser,

> Historical practice is above all engaged in this kind of dialogue; with an argument between received, inadequate, or ideologically-informed concepts of hypotheses on the one hand, and fresh or inconvenient evidence on the other; with the elaboration of hypotheses; with the testing of these hypotheses against the evidence, which may involve interrogating existing evidence in new ways, or renewed research to confirm or disprove the new notions; with discarding those hypotheses which fail these tests, and refining or revising those which do, in the light of this engagement.[31]

The rethinking of theory and history must be a two-way process – not an application of one to the other, but a true intersection, an inter-production of both at once.

There is also another dimension to this intersection. If explicitly theorised history is concerned with the return to theory, and is also concerned with interdisciplinarity, then, *a fortiori*, it must also provide a challenge not only to itself and to theory but also to those other disciplines. To quote Tafuri once again, history "calls into question the problem of 'limit:' it confronts the division of labor in general; it tends to go outside of its own boundaries; *it projects the crisis of techniques already given.*"[32] History does not simply contextualise or link together different disciplines, but situates itself in the discontinuities between them in order to further complexify that interrelation.

Praxis

History has always been implicated in the development of the city and its architecture, a relationship that has become increasingly complicated and fractured from the nineteenth century onward.[33] So in this sense we know that whatever architectural historians write will, in some way, make a difference to architecture. This means that historians should take an interest in and responsibility for the potential ramifications of their thoughts and actions; historians should consider not only *what* they might want the world to be but also *on what grounds* their work might relate to that possible world.

In constructing a critical and theorised history, this engagement, these grounds, necessarily take on a particular form. Any critical theory aims not only at the understanding of the world but also at a simultaneous transformation of both itself and that world "beyond" theory.[34] Critical theory is in this sense always aimed at liberation and emancipation – not just social and political liberation of the kind associated with class revolution and new economic systems, but with the creation of a total revolution that encompasses the full scope of productive creativity, in the fullest sense of that term, including not only architecture and art, forms of making and writing, but also emotions and desires, loves and actions of all kinds.

To undertake this process in architecture does not, therefore, mean finding one overarching metatheory that is capable of explaining everything at one fell swoop – as Sandercock recognises:

> The search for such a totalizing theory seems a misguided one, pushing us toward some kind of universal generalizing in our work, predetermining what we are going to find in our researches, ignoring the Foucauldian insight that power begins in little places and in terms of little things, and closing off the possibilities of human agency.[35]

Nor does it mean what Tafuri calls "operative criticism," that kind of architectural history (from James Fergusson to Nikolaus Pevsner, Morton Shand and Bruno Zevi) which seeks to explicitly support and promote a particular kind of architectural design practice, i.e. that kind of history which "has as its objective the planning of a precise poetical tendency, anticipated in its structures and derived from historical analyses programmatically distorted and finalised."[36] And nor does it mean constructing scientific relations between cause and effect, between the knowable past, plannable present and predictable future[37] – architectural history is not about certainty. Above all, it does not mean saying what is good or bad (a Kantian project of justifying historical discourse in terms of what ought to be),[38] correct or erroneous – architectural ideology is not an error or a slippage between illusion and reality,[39] but is always a negotiation of different external contexts, internal procedures, possible meanings and potential occurrences. Architectural history is as much in the realm of the perhaps and the maybe as in the therefore and the consequently.

Rather, the kind of theoretically informed praxis we seek here is one that is far more open, more fractured, more provisional in its tasks – a praxis which is about possibility as much as about prescription. We need, therefore, theorised histories of all kinds, those that deal with issues of gender and race, those that deal with mind and body, those that deal with materiality and idealism, those that bewitch and those that puzzle. We need theorised histories that will inform the ever-changing range of practices that intersect with cities and their spaces, with architecture. We need theorised histories that help us to think and act critically, now and in the future. As Jonathan Charley has argued,

> If critical theory is to become truly critical and not simply a means of giving academic weight to traditional debates over aesthetic hierarchies, it must at some point return to the critique of revolution, to the rethinking of how the built environment is produced, to the continuation of the assault on capital, and to the maintenance of a belief in social progress and human emancipation that is not defined by the reproduction of bourgeois utopias.[40]

Such a critical, theorised architectural history will share the intensity of intellectual energy and the concern for the provisional nature of historical knowledge that Jameson finds in "dialectical history" (and of which he cites Tafuri's *Architecture and Utopia* as an exceedingly rare example),[41] but will be distinguished from dialectical history in not sharing its sense of inevitable failure and unresolvable contradictions, offering instead a utopian impulse that is forever awash with the incessant waves of human creativity. Such theorised history is a transformer, a constant movement toward achieving new forms and contents of thought and action, an activity that perpetually speculates on the varied differences both of architecture as it now is and of architecture as it is yet to become. Then, and only then, is architecture rethought.[42]

It is this nine-fold challenge – to theory as the object of study, to new architectures, to the framing of interpretative questions, to the critical nature of history, to interdisciplinary debates, to the opening of methodological procedures, to self-critical development of the discipline, to re-engagement with critical theory, to praxis – that constitutes critical theory's most important potential contributions to architectural history.

Some voice *a priori* objections to such intentions. The architectural historian Gavin Stamp, for example, has described one of these kinds of theorisations, poststructuralism, as "an irrelevant masturbation."[43] But if there is going to be any onanism in architectural history, then it is going to be done by those who get on with it only by themselves. If architectural history ignores the kinds of theoretical explorations undertaken by other disciplines, it runs the risk of doing something that, while perhaps perfectly enjoyable, will be meaningful only as a self-referential exercise and thus irrelevant to anyone else. Architecture, the social art, should surely be rendered relevant and enjoyable to everyone, and not just to architects and architectural historians. The history of architecture is something to share.

Of course, discussing theoretical concepts like deconstruction and post-modernism may not be the best things with which, for example, to commence an introductory study of architecture – they certainly need to be introduced carefully and intelligently into the discourse – but neither are they quite the "virus" or "disease" that those like Stamp would have us believe. Such things enable historians, practitioners, students and non-academics alike to address other disciplines and current conditions and preoccupations, and thus to diversify the significance of architecture. This kind of intellectual contemplation enriches both historical and other ways of conceiving of architecture. Dealing with matters of race, sexuality, class, psychoanalysis, social space, of how meanings are created and transferred, with experience, political action, gender and so on, dealing with these kinds of things in both architectural production specifically and cultural production in general maximises the opportunity to learn all that architecture is and might be capable of. It maximises the opportunity to learn from the past, and so to relate history to the present. To speak about architectural history without reference to these things, without reference to other disciplines, without reference to theory, is not only to dismiss architecture's relevance to the world in general, but also to trivialise current conditions and preoccupations. And, to quote Sandercock once again, "to understand these systematic exclusions, we need theory."[44] Only then will we realise that architecture is present everywhere, that our lives are necessarily architectural in ways that we are only just beginning to comprehend, and that consequently, if I might reverse one of the most Lefebvrian of sentiments from the events of 1968, beneath the beach, lies the pavement.[45]

THREE TENDENCIES

When we first began this project, it was our intention to structure the text according to the kinds of theories that different authors deployed in their intersection with architecture. There were to be sections on theories of language, theories of social categories, theories of action, theories of knowledge, and so forth. This, however, proved impossible for a number of reasons, not least the resistance (rightly so) of many contributors to being pigeon-holed in such a manner. And just as importantly, their work indeed supports this resistance through its determinedly interdisciplinary and intertheoretical nature: most if not all of the chapters draw on not one but several kinds of critical theory, using it not as a singular reference point but as a varied terrain in which to reconfigure architecture and its theorised interpretations.

Nor can this text be a comprehensive review of all kinds of critical theories which might relate to architecture. The continuous invention of new social concerns, new arenas of architectural action and the extraordinary acceleration of all manner of critical theory means that such an encyclopaedic approach not only would run contrary to the very nature of critical theory (which is itself an historical production, forever changing in relation to contemporary conditions) but also would in any case be impossible in any practical manner.

The structuring of this book does not, therefore, follow the *kinds* of theories with which contributors engage, but rather the strategies and tactics they have used in this engagement. This, therefore, is a book structured around neither architectural subject nor interpretative theory, but around epistemology – around the different grounds by which contributors seek to know the subject of which they speak and by which they construct their histories. If, as is argued above, the relation of critical theory to architectural theory is one which poses epistemological challenges, then it is indeed appropriate to respond along similar epistemological grounds.

We should point out straight away that this, too, is a kind of pigeon-holing, in that many contributors may easily fall in to more than one of the three strategies that we identify here. Therefore we prefer to identify not strategies *per se* but *tendencies* of methodology, where contributors tend to move towards a particular mode of intersecting history and theory rather than adopting it solely as a prescriptive operational system.

Tendency 1 Theory as objects of study

Perhaps the most obvious intersection of critical theory and architectural history is to treat the former as an object of study in its own right, as an entity to be described and interpreted autonomously as well as in relation to architecture. Neil Leach, in Chapter 2, undertakes such a task in using Walter Benjamin's thoughts on photography as a starting point from which to spring off into a more lengthy exegesis of, successively, Benjamin's theory of mimesis, James George Frazer's anthropological consideration of sympathetic magic, Sigmund Freud's psychoanalytical concerns and Theodor Adorno's marxism. Leach then returns briefly to photography, reinterpreting photographs less as representations of particular figures or buildings and more as means by which one might identify creatively and imaginatively with the world. In a close interweaving of theory and architecture, Darell W. Fields, in Chapter 3, seeks to deliberately "mis-read" the philosophy of history and ideas on aesthetics in the work of the nineteenth century philosopher G.W.F. Hegel. Through a highly intense and logical methodological procedure, Fields shows how the concept of race and blackness is embedded both in Hegel's texts and within the notion of architecture that such texts set up. Partly transgressive, partly hermeneutical, Fields uses theory on theory to reconsider a foundational concept of architecture.

Another approach to the treatment of theory as an object of study in its own right is to consider the way in which critical theories of various kinds might be used directly or indirectly by architects themselves in their designs for architecture. In Chapter 4, Beatriz Colomina considers the work of the architect Frederick Kiesler and, in particular, his project for the "Space House." In Colomina's careful interpretation of architectural design, theory and published reactions, Kiesler's notions of eroticism, seduction and psychosexuality are brought to the fore. Such concepts are shown to exist as ideational architectural entities, in relation to particular architectural elements such as walls and doors, and through architectural materials like rubber, sponge, straw, rayon and oiled silk. An even more explicit exemplar of critical theory used in design is provided by Chapter 5. Here, Clive R. Knights takes on one of the most notorious intersections of theory and architecture, that of deconstruction in the work of Peter Eisenman and Jacques Derrida. Knights shows that both architect (Eisenman) and philosopher (Derrida) fail to account for the human subject, and, in terms of architecture, how Eisenman fails to realise that his work is a representation of a representation. Significantly, Knights works here both *within* the logic of deconstruction and *outside* of that logic, deploying Ricoeurian hermeneutics to sustain his own argument.

Tendency 2 Theorised interpretation

As the above intimate, it is not just inside or outside of architecture that critical theory may be seen to exist. It is in the interplay between the two that historians can focus their interpretative efforts, using theory to reinterpret architecture and architecture to reinterpret theory. It is the epistemological category, therefore, of "interpretation" that is important here, that intellectual and active space in-between the historian and their subject, that space which is neither purely subjective nor objective, that space which distinguishes history from the disciplines of science, social science and the arts.[46]

One of the most fruitful arenas for this kind of intellectual labour has come in the rethinking of the modernist condition, and, in Chapter 6, Sarah Wigglesworth confronts one of the seminal buildings of architectural modernism, that of the Maison de Verre designed by Pierre Chareau and Bernard Bijvoet. Focusing in particular on ideas of medicine, surgery and fetishism, Wigglesworth draws on alternatively feminism, marxism, psychoanalysis and film theory in order to wrench the building out of a conventional architectural historical discourse on form and technology into another about disavowal and patriarchy within architectural practice. A somewhat different revision of a canonic modernist architect is provided by Helen Thomas in Chapter 7, where Thomas considers the Los Jardines del Pedregal de San Ángel by Mexican architect Luis Barragán. Part architecture and part property development, the Jardines del Pedregal is considered by Thomas under different conceptions of time, drawn from the poet T.S. Eliot, the eighteenth century philosopher Immanuel Kant and the historian Fernand Braudel. If Thomas' interpretation is partly driven by postcolonial techniques of breaking down universalist narratives, then Chapter 8, by Murray Fraser and Joe Kerr, is even more explicitly postcolonialist in its identification of themes of hybridity and otherness in (post)modern architecture. Although informed by theories of cultural theorists Jean Baudrillard and Umberto Eco and historian Edward Said, Fraser and Kerr consider two building projects, the Getty Center in Los Angeles by architect Richard Meier and the Guggenheim Museum in Bilbao by architect Frank Gehry, to show how a specifically architectural contribution might be made to the postcolonial debate. Here, architecture is seen to be not a resultant effect of difference but a mechanism for its creation.

Two other chapters in this part likewise consider modernity, but move away from the deliberate architectural modernism as artefacts consciously designed by architects. In Chapter 9, Henry Urbach turns his attention not only to the Maison de la Publicité by Oscar Nitzchke but also to the quotidian streets and electric lighting of Paris. Using concepts of gender and the psychoanalytic concerns of Julia Kristeva and Freud as his guides, Urbach shows how neon and electric light was seen as feminised and hence at once seductive yet threatening. Historians of architectural modernism, such as Henry Russell Hitchcock, Pevsner and Zevi, consequently demonstrated their own photophobia by excluding such discussions from their histories. Zeynep Çelik, in Chapter 10, confronts a rather different kind of non-architect modernism in the form of the French colonialist interventions in the city of al-Jaza'ir (Algiers) during the nineteenth century. Comparing these events with Orientalist scene paintings by Osman Handi, and drawing on the ideas of Said and postcolonialist theoretician Gayatri Spivak, Çelik shows how not only new objects but also new interpretations must be made if architectural history as the history of both the Western canon and of previously repressed peoples is to be rewritten.

It is not, of course, only modernity that can be reconsidered in this way. In the final chapter of this part, Chapter 11, Diane Ghirardo considers the history of women and space in the Italian Renaissance city of Ferrara. Using detailed empirical and archival work alongside more theoretical ideas drawn from the sociologist Pierre Bourdieu and (implicitly) historian Michel Foucault, Ghirardo discloses how concerns of eroticism, the spatial control of bodies, and power pervaded women's relation to the streets, laundries, property, convents and other architectures of the city. In doing so, Ghirardo shows how archival sources, architectural historians and architecture in general are all implicated in a patriarchal exclusion of women.

Tendency 3 Theorising historical methodology

As the chapters by Çelik and Ghirardo in particular make clear, it is not just the interpreting categories of architectural history that become modified in the intersection with architectural history – the epistemological foundations, procedures and political objectives of architectural history become challenged, twisted and reworked. Here, architectural history stops being just the history of architecture, but becomes a different kind of history and maybe even not a "history" at all – it becomes that procedure, partly theoretical, partly historical and partly speculative, which refers to things architectural in order to construct its arguments and speculations.

A stimulating exemplar of this kind of procedure is provided by Chapter 12, in which Sarah Chaplin directs her attention toward Las Vegas. Referring to Foucault, Baudrillard, the Situationist provocateur Guy Debord and to cultural theorists Gianni Vattimo and Arthur Kroker, it is the concept of heterotopia in particular that Chaplin uses not just to drive her interpretation of Las Vegas but also to construct her chapter. Categories of naming, taming, saming and gaming lead to a consideration not just of past events but also of the "irruption of possibilities," and hence of the future as much as of the present. In Chapter 13, Iain Borden provides a similarly close intersection of critical theory and object, this time looking at three different kinds of boundary (exclusionary, identity-challenging, commodified) in contemporary London. Referring to sociologist Georg Simmel, anthropologist Marc Augé, philosophers Maurice Merleau-Ponty, Lefebvre and Heidegger, Borden reconceptualises architecture not as a thing but as a production formed out of physicality, politics and social experience.

The next pair of chapters, as with many of the other contributions to this volume, both confront the category of gender, although to rather different effect. Jane Rendell, in Chapter 14, looks at "rambling texts" and prostitution in nineteenth century London. Rendell uses the psychoanalytic theories of Freud, Jacques Lacan and, in particular, Luce Irigaray in order to consider issues of sexuality, movement, masculinity, class, exchange, consumption and mimicry. This is not so much a history of Regency London as, in Rendell's own terms, a "starting point for considering the gendering of public space through the pursuit of pleasure" and, in particular, a problematisation of the conventional trope of the "separate spheres" of public and private. Barbara Penner in Chapter 15 similarly looks at a text, this time *Mrs Dalloway* by Virginia Woolf. Penner's concern here, however, is with the processes of identity formation, arguing alternatively with and against the ideas of historians Joan Scott and Elizabeth Wilson and literary critic Toril Moi. Rather than treating Woolf's writings as historical evidence or proof of women's experiences in the city, Penner shows how they represent the production and reproduction of such different gendered urban experiences. Architectural history here is concerned not with evidential facts, buildings or events, but with processes, social constructions and formations.

It is perhaps significant that the last pair of chapters in this book (as with many of the others in this book) are both written by those who are active architectural educationalists and designers. If we are indeed "in an era where discourse is as important as design,"[47] then it is important to realise how each may be implicated in the other, not just as mutual referents but as a simultaneous project. In Chapter 16, Jeremy Till provides an intersection between the architectural projects and writings of Le Corbusier, Eisenman, Giedion and high-tech architects, and the philosophy of Kant and Lefebvre. The literature of James Joyce, particularly *Ulysses*, provides an additional triangulation point. Focusing on the nature of (spatialised) time, Till's concern here is not with causal links between philosophy and architecture, but the very distinction between them. His aim, in doing so, is to help "administer the practice of architecture" – a way of thinking which is simultaneously historical, theoretical and practical. Katherine Shonfield, in the concluding Chapter 17, also has similar epistemological complexifications in mind. Moving successively from the marxism of urban geographer David Harvey to the anthropology of Mary Douglas to the role of the fiction, Shonfield seeks to posit interpretation as a kind of architectural theory in its own right, and hence to blur the boundaries between criticism, history and design. As Shonfield concludes, this is of particular relevance to urban development, transgressing the categories of specialisation, expertise, professional and other practices which restrict the potential culture of architecture and the city.

References

This introductory chapter has been written by Iain Borden; the content is based on a two-way exchange of ideas between him and Jane Rendell.

1   Raymond Williams, *Marxism and Literature* (Oxford: Oxford University Press, 1977).

2   For a review of publications specifically in the context of planning discourse, and on which this introduction is partly based, see Iain Borden, Jane Rendell and Helen Thomas, "Knowing Different Cities: Reflections on Recent European City History and Planning,"

Leonie Sandercock (ed.), *Making the Invisible Visible: Insurgent Planning Histories* (Berkeley, CA: University of California Press, 1998), pp. 135–49.

3   Kenneth Frampton, *Modern Architecture: a Critical History* (London: Thames and Hudson, 1980), p. 9.

4   Richard Meier, quoted in *Seeing the Getty Center* (Los Angeles: John Paul Getty Trust, undated, *c.* 1997), p. 20.

5   See, for example, William J.R. Curtis, *Modern Architecture Since 1900* (London: Phaidon, 3rd edition, 1996).

6   See, for example, Christopher Tadgell, *The History of Architecture in India: From the Dawn of Civilization to the End of the Raj* (London: Architecture Design and Technology Press, 1990).

7   Dan Cruickshank (ed.), *Sir Banister Fletcher's A History of Architecture* (London: Architectural Press, 20th edition, 1996).

8   Deborah Howard, paper delivered at the Annual Conference of Teachers of Architectural History at Schools of Architecture, Nottingham University (June 1993). For a review of this conference, see Iain Borden, "Learning to Read the Past," *Building Design*, n. 1130 (25 June 1993), pp. 28–9.

9   Leonie Sandercock, "Framing Insurgent Historiographies," Sandercock (ed.), *Making the Invisible Visible*, p. 20.

10 Keith Jenkins, *Re-thinking History* (London: Routledge, 1991), p. 70.

11 Réjean Legault, "Architecture and Historical Representation," *Journal of Architectural Education*, v. 44 n. 4 (August 1991), pp. 200–5. See also Hayden White, *Metahistory: the Historical Imagination in Nineteenth-Century Europe* (Baltimore, MD: Johns Hopkins University Press, 1973).

12 Fredric Jameson, "Architecture and the Critique of Ideology," *The Ideologies of Theory: Essays 1971–1986. Volume 2 Syntax of History* (London: Routledge, 1988), p. 39.

13 Hayden White, *Tropics of Discourse: Essays in Cultural Criticism* (Baltimore, MD: Johns Hopkins University Press, 1978), pp. 126–7.

14 Jenkins, *Re-thinking History*, p. 69.

15 Audre Lorde, "The Master's Tools Will Never Dismantle the Master's House," *The Audre Lorde Compendium* (London: Pandora, 1996), p. 160.

16 Sandercock, "Framing Insurgent Historiographies," p. 14. See also Leonie Sandercock, *Towards Cosmopolis: Planning for Multicultural Cities* (Chichester: Wiley, 1998), pp. 85–104; Edward W. Soja and Barbara Hooper, "The Spaces that Difference Makes: Some Notes on the Geographical Margins of the New Cultural Politics," Michael Keith and Steve Pile (eds), *Place and the Politics of Identity* (London: Routledge, 1993), pp. 183–205.

17 Jameson, "Architecture and the Critique of Ideology," pp. 42–3.

18 Griselda Pollock, *Visions and Difference: Femininity, Feminism and Histories of Art*

(London: Routledge, 1988), pp. 1–2. Pollock is following here Elizabeth Fox-Genovese, "Placing Women's History in History," *New Left Review*, n. 133 (1982), p. 6.

19 Sandercock, "Framing Insurgent Historiographies," p. 14. Sandercock is following here Joan Gadol Kelly, *Women, History, and Theory* (Chicago: University of Chicago Press, 1984), and Gerda Lerner, "Placing Women in History: a 1975 Perspective," Berenice Carroll (ed.), *Liberating Women's History: Theoretical and Critical Essays* (Urbana, IL: University of Illinois Press, 1976).

20 Roland Barthes, "Writers, Intellectuals, Teachers," *Image Music Text* (London: Fontana, 1977), p. 207.

21 Barthes, "Writers, Intellectuals, Teachers," p. 208.

22 Manfredo Tafuri, *The Sphere and the Labyrinth: Avant-Gardes and Architecture from Piranesi to the 1970s* (Cambridge, MA: MIT Press, 1987), p. 5.

23 Michel Foucault, *The Archaeology of Knowledge* (New York: Pantheon, 1972), p. 32.

24 Henri Lefebvre, *Introduction to Modernity: Twelve Preludes September 1959 – May 1961* (London: Verso, 1995), p. 4.

25 Roland Barthes, "What is Criticism?," *Critical Essays* (Evanston, IL: Northwestern University Press), quoted in Beatriz Colomina, "On Architecture, Production and Reproduction," Beatriz Colomina (ed.), *Architectureproduction* (New York: Princeton Architectural Press, 1988), p. 23.

26 Tafuri, *Sphere and the Labyrinth*, pp. 2–3.

27 Gilles Deleuze and Michel Foucault, "Intellectuals and Power," Donald Bouchard (ed.), *Language, Counter-Memory, Practice* (Ithaca, NY: Cornell University Press, 1977), p. 206, quoted in Neil Leach (ed.), *Rethinking Architecture: a Reader in Cultural Theory* (London: Routledge, 1997), p. xx.

28 Quoted in W.H. Walsh, *An Introduction to the Philosophy of History* (London: Hutchinson University Library, 3rd edition, 1967), pp. 137–8.

29 George Steiner, *Heidegger* (London: Fontana, 1992), p. 89.

30 Debra Coleman, "Introduction," Debra Coleman, Elizabeth Danze and Carol Henderson (eds), *Architecture and Feminism* (New York: Princeton Architectural Press, 1996), p. xiv.

31 E.P. Thompson, *The Poverty of Theory* (London: Merlin, 1978), p. 235.

32 Tafuri, *Sphere and the Labyrinth*, p. 13 (emphasis in the original).

33 M. Christine Boyer, *The City of Collective Memory: Its Historical Imagery and Architectural Entertainments* (Cambridge, MA: MIT Press, 1994), p. 4.

34 Raymond Geuss, *The Idea of a Critical Theory: Habermas and the Frankfurt School* (Cambridge: Cambridge University Press, 1981), pp. 55–95; and David Held, *Introduction to Critical Theory: Horkheimer to Habermas* (Berkeley, CA: University of California Press, 1980), pp. 24–6.

35 Sandercock, "Framing Insurgent Historiographies," p. 20.

36   Manfredo Tafuri, *Theories and History of Architecture* (New York: Harper and Row, 1980), pp. 141–70.

37   Boyer, *City of Collective Memory*, p. 22.

38   Tomas Lorens, "On Making History," Joan Ockman, Deborah Berke and Mary McLeod (eds), *Architecture Criticism Ideology* (Princeton, NJ: Princeton University Press, 1985), pp. 29–34.

39   Demetri Porphyrios, "On Critical History," Ockman, Berke and McLeod (eds), *Architecture Criticism Ideology*, pp. 16–18.

40   Jonathan Charley, "The Business of Thought," *Building Design*, n. 1315 (11 July 1997), p. 13.

41   Jameson, "Architecture and the Critique of Ideology," pp. 39–40. The other texts cited by Jameson are Roland Barthes, *Writing Degree Zero*, and Theodor Adorno, *Philosophy of Music*.

42   Charley, "Business of Thought," p. 13.; and Iain Borden, review of Leach (ed.), *Rethinking Architecture*, *Environment and Planning B: Planning and Design*, v. 25 n. 3 (May 1998), pp. 467–8.

43   Gavin Stamp, paper delivered at the Annual Conference of Teachers of Architectural History at Schools of Architecture, Nottingham University (June 1993). See also Borden, "Learning to Read the Past."

44   Sandercock, "Framing Insurgent Historiographies," p. 13.

45   "Au dessous les pavés, la plage" – beneath the pavement, the beach. Rob Shields, *An English Précis of Henri Lefebvre's "La Production de l'espace"* (University of Sussex: Urban and Regional Studies Working Paper n. 63, 1988), p. 2. Rem Koolhaas, in *S,M,L,XL* (New York: Monacelli, 1995), p. 965, gives an alternative version: "Sous le pavé, la plage."

46   See, for example, Thompson, *Poverty of Theory*, pp. 229–42; Jenkins, *Re-thinking History*, pp. 27–57; Roland Barthes, "The Discourse of History," Derek Attridge, Geoff Bennington and Robert Young (eds), *Post-Structuralism and the Question of History* (Cambridge: Cambridge University Press, 1987).

47   Diane Agrest, Patricia Conway and Leslie Kanes Weisman, "Introduction," Diane Agrest, Patricia Conway and Leslie Kanes Weisman (eds), *The Sex of Architecture* (New York: Harry N. Abrams, 1996), p. 11.

Tendency 1

Theory as objects of study

Chapter 2
Walter Benjamin, mimesis and the dreamworld of photography
Neil Leach

Walter Benjamin wrote extensively on photography. Aside from his "A Small History of Photography," there are references to photography throughout his works. Much of his famous essay, "The Work of Art in an Age of Mechanical Reproduction," is devoted to film and photography. Indeed, for Benjamin, photography captures the very essence of the age of mechanical reproduction, even if, as he acknowledges, film is better suited to grasp its transitory, fleeting character. Moreover, Benjamin's writings are peppered with photographic allusions. Not only do we find references to the "snapshot" throughout his *oeuvre* – as in the piece, "Surrealism: The Last Snapshot of the European Intelligentsia" – but also the very flash of recognition that forms the core of the "dialectics of seeing" seems to have been drawn as much from the burning magnesium paper of photography as it is from the lightning flash of nature.

It is as though human beings – in an age increasingly dominated by photography – have taken on the attributes of the camera. Just as workers in the factory, as Benjamin observes, are conditioned by the jolting, jarring, repetitive actions of the machine, such that their own behaviour begins to replicate those actions, so too human beings in general have adapted to the world of the camera. They now see the world in terms of the "snapshot," and according to the mechanism of the camera itself. Indeed Benjamin makes an explicit reference to the "flash bulb" and the mechanism of photographic exposure when describing the way that various architectural spaces are imprinted onto the mind by events that take place there:

> Anyone can observe that the duration for which we are exposed to impressions has no bearing on their fate in memory. Nothing prevents our keeping rooms in which we have spent twenty-four hours more or less clearly in our memory, and forgetting others in which we passed months. It is not, therefore, due to insufficient exposure time if no image appears on the plate of remembrance. More frequent, perhaps, are the cases when the half-light of habit denies the plate the necessary light for years, until one day from an alien source it flashes as if from burning magnesium powder, and now a snapshot transfixes the room's image on the plate. Nor is this very mysterious, since such moments of sudden illumination are at the same time moments when we are beside ourselves, and while our waking, habitual, everyday self is involved actively or passively in what is happening, our deeper

self rests in another place and is touched by the shock, as is the little heap of magnesium powder by the flame of the match.[1]

Here the mind acts like some form of *camera obscura*. This provocative analogy establishes a connection between the mind and the architectural environment via a form of "photographic" image. And the image plays a vital role in Benjamin's way of thinking, especially in Benjamin's two autobiographical pieces about Berlin, "A Berlin Childhood around 1900" and "A Berlin Chronicle."[2] Memories are constructed as images, and his whole recollection of childhood memories in pieces such as "A Berlin Chronicle" is presented as a tableau of largely architectural vignettes – "street images" as he terms them. Descriptions of buildings such as his old school with its frosted glass and "carved wooden battlements over the doors" are presented as brief, verbal portraits, that develop a form of "unconscious optics," highlighting often overlooked features with their close-up details.[3] These are snapshots of the physical fabric of Berlin, on to which has been etched, as though through some photosensitive process, a deeply personal sense of meaning. Thus the classrooms are haunted by Benjamin's fear of the *Arbitur* examination, and by "dreamlike memories" of the damp odour of sweat from having to rush up the stone steps into the school several times a day. Otherwise insignificant places have been charged with a special significance as part of a mental "map," as Benjamin calls it, of his early childhood experiences in Berlin.[4]

If the mind stores these images, as though in some photo album, to recollect one's youth is, as it were, to leaf through the pages of that album, which constitutes the visual archive of the mind. Each image is charged with the capacity to retrieve a past. Like Proust and his tale of the Madeleine cakes, these snapshots trigger off unconscious associations of a bygone world, and in the flash of recognition past and present become conjoined for a fleeting moment. But might not the corollary also hold true? If the mind can act as a repository of images of past events like some vast photographic album, cannot actual photographs in an exhibition act as a register of potential events? In this sense the image – especially the photographic image – may have some privileged role in summoning up an entirely new world. In this process the mind might play an active part. In order to fully appreciate a photograph, the mind must work in creative and imaginative ways so as to engage *through the medium of the photograph* with the world which it represents. This chapter addresses this question. It does so in the context of Benjamin's autobiographical writings of Berlin, and the insights they offer as to how photographs might act as a form of window to the architecture that they depict.

BENJAMIN AND THE PICTURE POSTCARD

Benjamin makes few references to actual photographs in his possession, but he does claim to have been an avid collector of picture postcards. In "A Berlin Chronicle" he describes how as a young boy he started this collection, much of it supplied by his maternal grandmother, who was an inveterate traveller. These postcards had a magnetic effect on the young Benjamin. They seemed to have the capacity to transport him to the places they depicted, as though by some form of magic carpet:

> For I was there – in Tabarz, Brindisi, Madonna di Campiglio, Westerland, when I gazed, unable to tear myself away, at the wooded slope of Tabarz covered with glowing red berries, the yellow-and-white-daubed quays of Brindisi, the cupolas of Madonna di Campiglio printed bluish on blue, and the bows of the "Westerland" slicing high through the waves.[5]

This seemingly "throw-away" comment – "I was there, . . . when I gazed" – is one which merits further investigation. It is, arguably, part of a consistent and highly sophisticated theory of representation that adds a certain crucial gloss to Benjamin's overall aesthetic theory in general and to his approach towards photography in particular. Nor is the observation of this phenomenon an isolated remark by Benjamin, which should be overlooked as insignificant. In "The Work of Art" essay there is a further enigmatic reference on a similar theme:

> A man who concentrates before a work of art is absorbed by it. He enters into this work of art the way that legend tells of the Chinese painter when he viewed his finished painting.[6]

This comment, seemingly overlooked by mainstream commentators on Benjamin, is explained by a fuller version contained in the obscure fragment, "*Die Mummerehlen*," to be found in Benjamin's other autobiographical text of his childhood in Berlin, "A Berlin Childhood," which has yet to be published in English. This tells the tale of the young Benjamin being absorbed into the world depicted on some porcelain vase:

> [The story] comes from China and tells of an old painter who gave his newest painting to friends to look at. The painting was of a park, a narrow path along the water and through some foliage, to end at a small door offering entry in the back to a little house. The friends looked around for the painter, but he was gone and in the picture. He walked along the narrow path to the door, stopped in front of it, turned around, smiled, and disappeared through the crack. So was I, with my little bowls and brushes, suddenly in the picture. I became similar to the porcelain, into which I moved with a cloud of colour.[7]

MIMESIS

The process by which Benjamin's concept of ... ed either within the world of the porcelain vase or the scenes depicting on the picture postcards can be explained, I would argue, by engaging with Benjamin's provocative theory of *mimesis*, which suggests a way in which children in particular have the ability to identify with and assimilate to another world. Moreover, once Benjamin's use of the concept of mimesis has been examined, and its relevance to the visual arts articulated, it can be recognised as possibly one of Benjamin's most important contributions to aesthetic theory.

BENJAMIN AND MIMESIS

In *One Way Street* Walter Benjamin offers a telling description of a child hiding:

> Standing behind the doorway curtain, the child becomes himself something floating and white, a ghost. The dining table under which he is crouching turns him into the wooden idol in a temple whose four pillars are the carved legs. And behind a door he is himself a door, wears it as his heavy mask and as a shaman will bewitch all those who unsuspectingly enter. At no cost must he be found. When he pulls faces, he is told, the clock need only strike and he will remain so. The element of truth in this he finds out in his hiding place. Anyone who discovers him can petrify him as an idol under the table, weave him for ever as a ghost into the curtain, banish him for life into the heavy door. And so, at the seeker's touch he drives out with a loud cry the demon who has transformed him – indeed, without waiting for the moment of discovery, he grabs the hunter with a shout of self-deliverance.[8]

What is striking about this story is the way in which the child becomes one with the environment. Behind the curtain, the child turns into the curtain, "floating and white, a ghost." Under the dining table the child becomes a wooden idol in a temple, and behind a door "he is himself a door." The child has become so perfectly at one with the environment that he fears that he may never escape. Just as he might carry the burden of the face he is pulling, if caught making the expression when the clock strikes, so he risks remaining camouflaged and absorbed into the environment. He needs to offer a shriek of self-deliverance so as to free himself from the spell under which he had made himself identical to the interior landscape around him.

What Benjamin is alluding to here is his theory of mimesis, a theory that he developed in two short writings, "Doctrine of the Similar" and "On the Mimetic Faculty," the latter being a condensed reworking of the former.[9] Mimesis here should not be understood in the terms used, say, by Plato, as simple "imitation." Rather mimesis in Adorno, as indeed in Walter Benjamin's writings, is a psychoanalytic term – taken from Freud – that refers to a creative engagement with an object. Freud writes about the term in the context of jokes. Mimesis is ideational. It operates through the medium of the idea, and is what allows one to empathise with the subject of a joke. In listening to the tale about the unfortunate individual who slips up on a banana skin, one puts oneself in the position of that individual, and imagines oneself also slipping up, drawing upon memories of similar experiences. One thereby identifies with that individual. But the implications of the term extend beyond empathising with the subject of a joke. Mimesis is a term, as Freud himself predicted, of great potential significance for aesthetics.[10]

For Benjamin the concept of mimesis allows for an identification with the external world. It facilitates the possibility of forging a link between self and other. The principle behind mimesis is the urge to seek similarities in the world as a means of relating to it. "Every day," writes Benjamin, "the urge grows stronger to get hold of an object at very close range by way of its likeness, its reproduction."[11] To understand the meaning of mimesis in Benjamin we must recognise its origin in the process of modelling, of "making a copy of." In essence it refers to an interpretative process that relates either to modelling oneself on an object, or to making a model of that object. Likewise mimesis may come into operation as a third party engages with that model, and the model becomes the vehicle for identifying with the original object. In each case the aim is to assimilate to the original object. Mimesis is therefore a form of imitation that may be evoked both by the artist who makes a work of art, and also by the person who views it.

Mimesis for Benjamin is a linguistic concept. It offers a way of finding meaning in the world, through the discovery of similarities. These similarities become absorbed and then rearticulated in language. As such, language becomes a repository of meaning, and writing bec[...] [...] the process of writing writers [...] not be aware. Indeed writing [...] ling. Likewise the reader must [...] ation which exceeds the purel[...] the principles of mimesis, serving as the vehicle for some revelatory moment. For Benjamin the meaning becomes apparent in a constellatory flash, a dialectics of seeing, in which subject and object become one for a brief moment. Mimesis can also be observed, according to Benjamin, in dance movements. Here he opens up the possibility, which Adorno goes on to explore, that the principle of mimesis can extend to all forms of aesthetic expression. So it is that photography and the visual arts might be included within the range of its scope.

The point here is that to reproduce something may step beyond mere imitation. Benjamin reverses the hierarchy between object and its representation. He challenges the earlier Platonic notion of mimesis as an essentially compromised form of imitation that necessarily loses something of the original. For Benjamin mimesis alludes to a

[handwritten annotation: "constellatory flash / Subject/object become one / For brief moment"]

EMPATHY

constructive reint. . . . . act in itself. Furthermore, it potentially becomes a way of empathising with the world, and it is through empathy that we can – if not fully understand the other – at least assimilate to the other. In mimesis imagination is at work, and serves to reconcile the subject with the object. This imagination operates at the level of fantasy, which mediates between the unconscious and the conscious, dream and reality. Here fantasy is used as a positive term. Fantasy creates its own fictions not as a way of escaping reality, but as a way of accessing reality, a reality that is ontologically charged, and not constrained by an instrumentalised view of the world.

CHILDREN AND MIMESIS

The urge to seek similarities leads one to read similarities into the other, and – ultimately – to read oneself into the other. Thus, for example, in "The Berlin Chronicle" Benjamin tells the story of a child trying to hunt a butterfly. The butterfly begins to take on human characteristics, while the child takes on characteristics of the butterfly:

> The old rules of hunting took over between us: the more my being, down to its very fibres, adapted to my prey (the more I got butterflies in my stomach), the more the butterfly took on in all it did (and didn't do) the color of the human resolution, until finally it was as if capturing it was the price, was the only way I would regain my humanity.[12]

It is precisely through children's play, as Walter Benjamin has observed, that one can best see the principle of mimesis at work. For Benjamin "play" is for many the "school" of mimesis: "Children's play is everywhere permeated by mimetic modes of behaviour, and its realm is by no means limited to what one person can imitate in another."[13] The child therefore has a form of privileged access to mimetic processes. Much depends on the child's creative imagination, and it is this that allows the child to invest discarded objects with a special significance. As Benjamin observes:

> [In the child's bureau] drawers must become arsenal and zoo, crime museum and crypt. "To tidy up" would be to demolish an edifice full of prickly chestnuts that are spiky clubs, tin foil that is hoarded silver, bricks that are coffins, cacti that are totem poles, and copper pennies that are shields.[14]

It is as though the creative imagination of the child – the capacity for indulging in make-believe – gives the child a greater ability to assimilate. And if mimesis is the key to understanding the principle of representation in art, children's play might offer us some insight into that question. This is precisely the viewpoint taken by Kendall Walton: "In order to understand paintings, plays, films and novels, we must look first at dolls, hobbyhorses, toy trucks and teddy bears. The activities in which representational works of art are embedded and which give them their point are best seen as continuous with children's games of make-believe."[15]

Mimesis involves the capacity to mimic and identify with not only the animate world, but also the inanimate. Benjamin notes that children may equally play at being inanimate objects. "The child plays at being not only a shopkeeper or teacher but also a windmill and a train," he notes, as though the windmill or train has some animate life force that the child can appropriate.[16] The play between the animate and the inanimate, between life and death, is crucial to understanding the force of mimesis. The origins of this adaptation to the inanimate may be found in instinctual mechanisms of self-defence. Animals, when threatened with life-endangering situations, will often freeze, so as to blend in with their environment, and escape the gaze of the predator. These instincts may also be traced in human responses. But this "surrendering" of life in the moment of becoming one with the inanimate world serves ultimately to reinforce life. These gestures of surrender are in fact predicated on survival.

It is this ability to assimilate with the inanimate world which makes Benjamin's observations so relevant to the question of architecture. It suggests a capacity to read oneself into the environment, and to see oneself reflected in that environment.[17] If, moreover, we are to understand mimesis as offering the possibility of assimilation not only by modelling oneself on an object, but also by engaging with the model of that object, we can see how photographic representation may provide that mechanism of identification. Photography becomes the model, and architecture the object of assimilation. Through the architectural photograph we may read ourselves into the architecture, just as the young Benjamin found himself within the scenes depicted in his picture postcards, as though transported there by some magic carpet.

MIMESIS AND SYMPATHETIC MAGIC

But what exactly can one understand by the expression "as though transported there by some magic carpet?" Can one make a direct comparison between mimesis and magic? We might reflect here on the world of voodoo dolls, effigies, models and other types of representation which attempt to establish some link between an originary object and its miniaturised representation through a form of sympathetic magic.[18]

There are clear parallels between mimesis and magic. Both appear to operate within the same conceptual orbit, and both establish an ideational relationship between subject and object. In the context of architectural photography, the photograph appears to stand in a not dissimilar relation to the architecture that it depicts as the figurine does to the originary object in sympathetic magic. Just as the viewer of a photograph may *imagine* him or herself within that scene, so too the primitive *imagines* a relationship between the voodoo doll or image and the intended victim. One might point also to a more direct connection between magical practices and the domain of art and architecture. Freud acknowledges the affinities between the world of art and sympathetic magic. Citing Reinach who observes that the "primitive artists who left behind the carvings and paintings in the French cave did not seek to 'please' but to 'evoke' and conjure up," Freud traces parallels between the two:

> In only a single field of civilisation has the omnipotence of thoughts been retained, and that is in the field of art. Only in art does it still happen that a man who is consumed by desires performs something resembling the accomplishments of those desires and that what he does in play produces emotional effects – thanks to artistic illusion – just as though it were something real. People speak with justice of the "magic of art" and compare artists to magicians. But the comparison is perhaps more significant than it claims to be. There can be no doubt that art did not begin as art for art's sake. It worked originally in the service of impulses which are for the most part extinct today. And among them we may suspect the presence of many magical processes.[19]

It would be wrong, however, to equate art – as a form of mimesis – with magic. Certainly, even if Freud is happy to bracket them together, Benjamin always resists this temptation. There is a clear genealogy to art. Benjamin acknowledges that at one stage pictures were indeed connected with magic. "The elk," he notes, "portrayed by the man of the Stone Age on the walls of his cave was an instrument of magic."[20] But equally he adds that there has been a shift, as the work of art later became recognised in its own right, and a further shift, within the age of mechanical reproduction, when the accent on "cult value" has been replaced by one of "exhibition value," such that its status as a work of art is perhaps incidental:

> With the different methods of technical reproduction of a work of art, its fitness for exhibition increased to such an extent that the quantitative shift between its two poles turned into a qualitative transformation of its nature. This is comparable to the situation of the work of art in prehistoric times when, by the absolute emphasis on its cult value, it was, first and foremost, an instrument of magic. Only later did it come to be recognised as a work of art. In the same way today, by the absolute emphasis on its exhibition value the work of art becomes a creation with entirely new functions, among which the one we are conscious of, the artistic function, later may be recognised as incidental.[21]

We can therefore detect in Benjamin's thought a sympathy for mimesis that extends to new forms of representation such as photography, but which distances itself increasingly from magic. As Susan Buck-Morss explains:

> [Benjamin] holds open the possibility of a future development of mimetic expression, the potentialities for which are far from exhausted. Nor are they limited to verbal language – as the new technologies of camera and film clearly demonstrate. These technologies provide human beings with unprecedented perceptual acuity, out of which, Benjamin believed, a less magical, more scientific form of the mimetic faculty was developing in his own era.[22]

Indeed Adorno, who subsequently develops Benjamin's thesis on mimesis, explicitly distances art from magic. While Adorno acknowledges a certain affinity between the two, in that the artist, like the magician, exerts a form of "organised control" that has parallels in the conjurer plotting a trick, art does not follow the same project as magic. Although both are grounded in the human imagination, art does not lay claim to some truth in the same way as magic. While art operates in the domain of the "as if," magic claims to operate within the domain of the actual. "Art," notes Adorno, "is magic delivered from the lie of being truth."[23]

Nonetheless, through the process of mimesis – an imaginary identification with a representation of an object – the original object can be invoked. And the process applies equally to photography. Photographs can be seen in the same light as mimetic representations of actual buildings, which might, as it were, "conjure up" those buildings for the beholder. Photographs can therefore be seen to charged with the potential to open up a "world." Although the mimetic impulse should not be equated with sympathetic magic, there are clear affinities between the two. The photograph therefore plays out its role as an object of wish-fulfilment. It is as though we might entertain the wish of entering another world through the medium of the photograph itself, as though stepping through some window.

CONCLUSION

What then is the consequence of this? Above all it highlights an important aspect of what it is to be human. According to Ridley Scott's film *Blade Runner* (1982), one of the features which distinguish replicants from humans is their need for photographs. Without a natural memory imprinted on to their minds as though on to some photographic plate, as Benjamin describes it, replicants need to construct an artificial memory for themselves through photographs of someone else's childhood.

Yet it could be argued that it is precisely the capacity to gaze at a photograph and to imagine oneself in the picture that marks out the very essence of what it is to be human. The capacity to recognise similarities is one of humankind's distinguishing features. As Benjamin comments: "Nature creates similarities. One need only think of mimicry. The highest capacity for producing similarities, however, is man's."[24] Moreover, Theodor Adorno once claimed on the subject of mimesis, "The human is indissolubly linked with imitation: a human being becomes human at all by imitating other human beings."[25] If we extend Adorno's comments from a mimesis of other individuals to a mimesis of architectural environments through representations of that environment, we might argue that what defines human beings as being human is their capacity to identify with those representations and through them to conjure up whole environments which they depict. And so it would appear that while human beings have adapted to the camera, and have assimilated themselves to its technological mechanisms, such that they now read the world in terms of the snapshot, it is also *through* the camera – and the images that it produces – that they can understand precisely what it is to be human.

But what is crucial is the manner in which one gazes at these representations – photographic or otherwise. The action of mimesis is dependent upon a state of mind. One has to be receptive, and alert to the possibilities of the creative imagination. And it is children above all who would appear to be the most receptive to images, and the most capable of reading themselves into them, so as to imagine other possible worlds. One has to be open to the realm of fantasy, and the fantasy of the creative genius, as Freud himself observes, is born of the play and games of children.[26]

Perhaps, then, there is something to be said for viewing photographs with a certain childish imagination, while not overlooking, of course, the negative side of childish behaviour – the threat of regression into some fascistic tantrum. To gaze with a childish imagination in front of a photograph – or indeed any pictorial image – is to be, as it were, absorbed by it. It is to dream oneself into another place, like Benjamin being transported into his postcards, or like the Chinese painter disappearing into his painting, or indeed like Alice stepping through the looking glass.

References

1   Walter Benjamin, *One-Way Street* (London: Verso, 1997), pp. 342–3.
2   "A Berlin Childhood around 1900" appears as "Berliner Kinderheit um Neunzehn-hundert," *Gesammelte Schriften*, IV: 1, but has yet to be published in English. "A Berlin Chronicle" appears in Benjamin, *One-Way Street*, pp. 293–346.

3   For Benjamin "unconscious optics" are the visual equivalent of the Freudian "slip of the tongue." "By close-ups of the world around us," Benjamin notes, "by exploring commonplace milieus under the ingenious guidance of the camera, the film, on the one hand extends our comprehension of the necessities which rule our lives; on the other hand, it manages to assure us of an immense and unexpected field of action." Benjamin, *Illuminations* (London: Fontana, 1973), p. 229. Hence, Benjamin concludes, "The camera introduces us to unconscious optics as does psychoanalysis to unconscious impulses." Benjamin, *Illuminations*, p. 230.

4   Benjamin, *One-Way Street*, p. 295.

5   Benjamin, *One-Way Street*, p. 328.

6   Benjamin, *Illuminations*, p. 232.

7   Benjamin, "Berliner Kinderheit um Neunzehnhundert," *Gesammelte Schriften*, IV:1, pp. 262–3, quoted in Gunter Gebauer and Christoph Wulf, *Mimesis: Culture, Art, Society* (Berkeley and Los Angeles: University of California Press, 1995), p. 277.

8   Benjamin, *One-Way Street*, p. 74.

9   Benjamin, "On the Mimetic Faculty," *Reflections* (New York: Schocken, 1986), pp. 333–6.

10   "I believe that if ideational mimetics are followed up, they may be as useful in other branches of aesthetics." Sigmund Freud, *Jokes and their Relation to the Unconscious* (1905) (London: Routledge, 1960), p. 193. For further reading on *mimesis*, see Erich Auerbach, *Mimesis* (Princeton, NJ: Princeton University Press, 1953); Michael Taussig, *Mimesis and Alterity* (London: Routledge, 1993); Gebauer and Wulf, *Mimesis*.

11   Benjamin, *Illuminations*, p.217.

12   Benjamin, *Gesammelte Schriften*, IV: 1, 262–3, quoted in Gebauer and Wulf, *Mimesis*, pp. 277–8.

13   Benjamin, *Reflections*, p. 333.

14   Benjamin, *One Way Street*, p. 74, quoted in Susan Buck-Morss, *The Dialectics of Seeing: Walter Benjamin and the Arcades Project* (Cambridge, MA: MIT Press, 1991), p. 263.

15   Kendall Walton, *Mimesis as Make-Believe* (Cambridge, MA: Harvard University Press, 1990), p. 11.

16   Benjamin, *Reflections*, p. 333.

17   Identification can therefore be seen as a narcissistic form of identification. Narcissistic identification with others has been explored by many theorists, including Laura Mulvey in the context of film theory, but the notion of identification with an inanimate object remains relatively unexplored.

18   These practices have fascinated anthropologists for some time. *The Golden Bough* by James George Frazer, for example, is full of such examples. "When an Obejway Indian desires to work evil on any one," writes Frazer, "he makes a little wooden image of his

enemy and runs a needle into its head or heart, or he shoots an arrow into it, believing that wherever the needle pierces or the arrow strikes the image, his foe will the same instant be seized with a sharp pain in the corresponding part of his body; but if he intends to kill the person outright, he burns or buries the puppet, uttering certain magic words as he does so." James George Frazer, *The Golden Bough* (Harmondsworth: Penguin, 1996), p. 15. Significantly, in terms of any discussion of photography, the representation of the victim need not be a three-dimensional model, but may equally be a two-dimensional drawing: "Thus the North American Indians, we are told, believe that by drawing the figure of a person in sand, ashes, or clay, or by considering any object of his body, and then pricking it with a sharp stick or doing it any other injury, they inflict a corresponding injury on the person represented." Frazer, *The Golden Bough*, p. 15. Of course these gestures need not be malignant. Magic can also be used for more benign purposes such as medicine and hunting.

19   Sigmund Freud, *The Origins of Religion* (Harmondsworth: Penguin, 1990), pp. 148–9.

20   Benjamin, *Illuminations*, p. 218.

21   Benjamin, *Illuminations*, p. 219.

22   Buck-Morss, *Dialectics of Seeing*, p. 267.

23   Theodor Adorno, *Minima Moralia* (London: Verso, 1978), p. 222.

24   Benjamin, *Reflections*, p. 332.

25   Adorno, *Minima Moralia*, p. 154.

26   Sigmund Freud, "Creative Writers and Day-Dreaming", Peter Gay (ed.), *The Freud Reader* (London: Vintage, 1995), p. 437.

Chapter 3
Historical errors and black tropes
Darell W. Fields

Hegel called architecture the mother of all arts: architecture was deemed autonomous and inclusive of all other fields such as music, fine art, and theater performance.[1]

Arata Isozaki

A hut and the house of god presuppose inhabitants, men, images of gods, etc. and have been constructed for them. Thus in the first place a need is there, lying outside art, and its appropriate satisfaction has nothing to do with fine art and does not evoke any works of art . . . [W]e . . . have on our hands a division in the case of art and architecture.[2]

G.W.F. Hegel

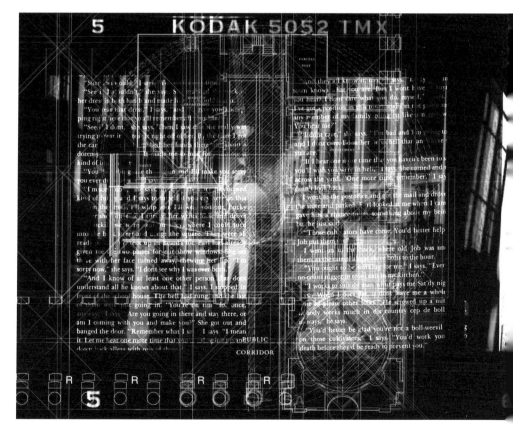

3.1 'April 6, 1928c' (Photo Montage) © 1997 Michael Kim

The citations chosen to begin this text represent the conundrum of historical writing in the context of architecture. Isozaki's statement signifies a popular architectural myth – that architecture is the sum-total of the fine arts. Hegel, the father of modern history, debunks this myth and places architecture in its proper aesthetic place – a place outside art. Architecture overcomes this dilemma by skilfully misquoting and mis-apprehending Hegel's system of aesthetics. But before placing Hegel's statement in an absolute position of historical/aesthetic truth, let us assume that it too consciously constructs and conceals a similar error-making technique. In Hegel's case, however, the technique is used to represent philosophy as history, and his aesthetic system signifies his idealized version of history. When architecture, as demonstrated by the first citation, erroneously embraces Hegel's system aesthetics (a philosophical/aesthetic system that is against the contingencies of architecture), the resulting relationship produces a logical and seductive series of historical and/or aesthetic errors.

Even though the statements of the "architect" and the "philosopher" represent confrontational logics they also represent a rare opportunity to suspend disbelief. Let us suppose I am a black author (I am), and I write about blackness (I do). Let us also suppose I have succumbed to a certain state of dementia causing me to see blackness everywhere – in history, in aesthetics, in architecture, in et cetera. What if I wanted to do some misreading and establish some black methodological errors of my own? How can I make sense of these two oppositional statements in terms of my black state of mind? Is it possible to construct a methodological intersection to demonstrate that Hegel's aesthetic problem with architecture is, in reality, a philosophical problem with blackness?

To answer these questions I will first proceed with a close reading of Hegel's construction of history to verify the presence of historical anomalies. Second, I will demonstrate that these anomalies are, in fact, black racial tropes that Hegel constructs and places outside art and alongside architecture.

Georg Wilheim Friedrich Hegel (1770–1831), at the University of Berlin, delivered two sets of lectures that are of particular interest in establishing more concrete representations of history and aesthetics. An analysis of these texts is necessary to understand the comprehensive nature of Hegel's ideas and reveals a distinct textual structure. This structure, independent of the content found within it, represents the same methodological device existing in both texts. The first text, *Lectures on the Philosophy of World History*, was given from the winter semester of 1822–3 through the winter semester of 1830–1. Similarly, *Aesthetics: Lectures on the Fine Arts* was delivered in 1823, 1826, and 1828–9. These dates are important for three reasons. First, *The Philosophy of History* and *Aesthetics* demonstrate sustained levels of argument, scholarship, and intellectual inquiry maintained, respectively, for nine and six years. Because these texts were constructed as lectures, their respective arguments evolved concurrently and became more refined during the years in which they were presented. Second, because they were produced by the same mind of the same individual at the same time, they can be conceptually described as simultaneous texts, one conveying explicit notions about blackness (*The Philosophy of History*) and the other, about the fine arts and architecture (*Aesthetics*). The internal logics of both texts, as will be demonstrated, are highly complementary. One text (*Aesthetics*) represents the methodological/formal extension of the other (*The Philosophy of History*). Finally, although the lectures are discussed here in isolation, they must also be considered as significant examples of a broader range of historical and philosophical activity, including the rise of racial determinism characteristic of intellectual, philosophical and historical discourse in the nineteenth century.[3] Given the comprehensive scheme of representation initiated by these texts, it is difficult for any potential historical or aesthetic subject to escape their definitions or categories.

In the *Philosophy of History*, Hegel defines three categories of history: "original history," "reflective history" and "philosophical history." These categories are actually representations of history formulated through Hegel's dialectic. The process can be summarized as follows: "It is this dialectic between the subject (man in society) and object (the material world), in which men progressively subordinate the material world to their purposes, and thereby transform those purposes and generate new needs."[4] In Hegel's context, "original history" describes a material world placed against the object of man (and man's self-image) in society. A conflict emerges between this material world and the ideal possibility (again, the self-image). For the sake of clarifying the self-image, the material world must be ordered and reordered. This model, although distinct, remains highly abstract unless these categories can be personified in some way: Hegel begins this personification of "original history" with the following elaboration:

> As to the first mode, the mention of a few names should give a definite picture of what I mean. Herodotus, Thucydides and their like belong to this class – that is, to the class of historians who have themselves witnessed, experienced and lived through the deeds, events and situations they describe . . . and in the spirit which informed them. They have compiled a written record of these deeds and events, thereby transferring what was previously mere extraneous happenings into the realm of intellectual representation . . . Admittedly, such historians also make use of the narratives and reports of others; but these are simply the more scattered.
>
> From this category of original history I would exclude all legends, folksongs, traditions, and poems; for legends and traditions are but obscure records [of actual events], and are the product of nations . . . whose consciousness is still obscure.[5]

These citations have been extracted not only because they provide an indication of what Hegel sees as "original history," but also because they represent what Hegel considers not to be history at all. For example, a document or part of a document written by Herodotus (c. 484–424 BC) about legends cannot be considered historical; other literary constructs such as "folksongs, traditions, and poems" are acknowledged as records but, for Hegel, they are "obscure records" and are not by definition historical records.[6]

Hegel continues to refine his point as he discusses the appropriate role of the historian:

> individuals and nations themselves . . . express their aspirations and their awareness of what their aspirations are. [The historian] has no need to explain their motives (and emotions) on his own initiative, or to assimilate them into his personal consciousness. He does not put his words or those of others into their mouths . . . The historian has left himself little or no room for personal reflections, and what he makes his characters say is not the expression of an alien consciousness projected into them, but of their own culture and consciousness.[7]

For Hegel, the original historian who breaks this code of historical ethics and who is referred to explicitly in the formulation of original history is, principally, Herodotus. Hegel specifically defines Herodotus as the "father" or "originator" of history, thereby placing him in the original position. While calling Herodotus the "greatest historian" and admiring his "masterpieces," Hegel, seemingly contradicting himself, also cautions that

> such works are not the exclusive prerogative of antiquity. For a nation to possess historians, it must not only enjoy a high level of culture; it must also have a culture which is not just the isolated privilege of clerics, scholars, and the like, but which is shared by the leaders of the state and the armed forces . . . For those classes which are more or less excluded from political activity console themselves with moral principles which they use to compensate for their position and to set themselves up as superior to the higher classes.[8]

Hegel's exclusion of other types of historicity, now coupled with notions of privilege, moral compensation, "alien" subjectivity, as well as high and low/high culture, characterize a thoughtful rendition of history for a predetermined audience. My efforts here do not concern the identification of the audience, but what subject or subjects Hegel removes from Herodotus' history to make history more presentable. In other words, what needs to be negated by Hegel so that his philosophy of history conforms to his idea of self-image? To understand this conceptualization more fully, it is necessary to move to a discussion of Hegel's second type of history – reflective history.

The concept of reflective history is itself subdivided by Hegel into three categories: reflective/pragmatic,[9] critical and specialized. Reflective/pragmatic history is seen as a historical moment as called forth in the present. This mechanism allows him to revise original history for the sake of the human self-image and the present. It is not initiated to cancel out entire documents – the process of cancellation is thoughtfully considered, well argued, and strategic.

The next sub-category of reflective history is that of "critical history," described as an evaluation of historical narratives that "examines their authenticity and credibility. Its distinguishing characteristic and intention are to be found not so much in the subject it deals with, but rather in the acuteness with which the writer wrests new information from the narratives he examines."[10] One might think that Hegel would condone this type of scholarship because its methods of scrutiny are in line with his argument for the exclusion of narratives as a viable component of history. This is not the case, however, because he sees it as a method for distorting historical facts in terms of the present.

The final category within reflective history is defined as specialized history. This historical type constitutes a methodological intersection between *The Philosophy of History* and Hegel's other text, *Aesthetics*. For example, consider the following precautionary citation from *The Philosophy of History* in his description of "specialized history:"

> Such branches of national activity are directly related to the history of the nation as a whole, and everything depends on whether this wider context is brought fully to light, or merely glossed over in favour of external relationships. But it must be emphasised that, if reflective history has reached the stage of adopting general perspectives [i.e., the arts, law, etc.] and if these perspectives are valid ones, such activities appear not just as an external thread, a superficial sequence, but as the inward guiding spirit of the events and deed themselves.[11]

Now consider the following remarks on art from *Aesthetics*:

> But while on the one hand we give this high position to art, it is on the other hand just as necessary to remember that neither in content nor form is art the highest and absolute mode of bringing to our minds the true interests of the spirit. For precisely on account of its form, art is limited to a specific content. Only one sphere and stage of truth is capable of being represented in the element of art . . . This is the case, for example, with the gods of Greece.[12]

Considering these statements simultaneously, it is obvious that Hegel accepts art as an "external relationship" or "form" of the spirit. However, he also states specifically in both citations that such representations are "superficial" or "limited" in discussing the truth acknowledged by the spirit-making activity of the mind. Not only do we have a concise description of the limitations of art, but also Hegel presents us with an idea as to where the pure combination of mind and art existed in history: ancient Greece. It is this same subject that constitutes the legitimizing force in Hegel's category of "original history." In essence *The Philosophy of History* and *Aesthetics* are simultaneous texts invented to create and sustain an ideal cultural form in Hegel's present – ancient Greece.

The final overarching category of history presented by Hegel is "philosophical history." It is in this category that we find an initiation of a "general perspective of philosophical world history . . . [that] is concrete and absolutely present."[13] The description of this category is extremely brief. In fact, in his introduction of the second draft presented in 1830, Hegel states that "there is no need for me to spend time refuting and correcting the individual misconceptions and mistaken reflections . . . I can omit all of this entirely, or merely touch on it in passing."[14] For the purpose of showing how Hegel's categorical descriptions apply to his idealization of the (or his) present, I too will omit a strict critical reading of the main body of *The Philosophy of History* and move directly to the appendix of his text. In this section the explicit and sustained use of race in the construction of world history is introduced. Most important, it is within this particular section, and no other, that the concept of race is personified and given a particular black identity.

Before engaging Hegel's rendition of this other identity, we must first situate it in terms of its "original" formulation. We first encounter this significant alien other in Herodotus' text, where the author relates the following:

> The Egyptians . . . were the first to discover the solar year, and to portion out its course into twelve parts. They obtained this knowledge from the stars. (To my mind they contrive their year much more cleverly than the Greeks . . . dividing the year into twelve months of thirty days each.)
>
> The Egyptians . . . first brought into use the names of the twelve gods, which the Greeks adopted from them; and first erected altars, images, and temples to the gods.
>
> Besides these which have been here mentioned, there are many other practices whereof I shall speak hereafter, which the Greeks have borrowed from the Egyptians.
>
> [A]t Dodona, the women who deliver the oracles relate the matter as follows, "Two black doves flew away from Egyptian Thebes . . . The Dodonaeans called the women doves because they were foreigners, and seemed to them to make a noise like birds. After a

while the dove spoke with a human voice, because the woman, whose foreign talk had previously sounded to them like the chattering of a bird, acquired the power of speaking what they could understand . . . Lastly, by calling the dove black the Dodonaeans indicated that the woman was an Egyptian."

The Egyptians were also the first to introduce solemn assemblies, processions, and litanies to the gods; of all which the Greeks were taught the use by them. It seems to me a sufficient proof of this, that in Egypt these practices have been established from remote antiquity, while in Greece they are only recently known.

There can be no doubt that Colchians are an Egyptian race . . . Still the Egyptians said that they believed the Colchians to be descended from the army of Sesostris. My own conjectures were founded, first on the fact that they are black skinned and have woolly hair; which certainly amounts to but little, since several other nations are so too; but further and more especially, on the circumstance that the Colchians, the Egyptians, and the Ethiopians, are the only nations to have practised circumcision from the earliest times . . . With respect to the Ethiopians, indeed, I cannot decide whether they learnt the practice of the Egyptians, or the Egyptians from them.[15]

These accounts signify a distinct, black racial presence within ancient Greek history and culture. This presence is not limited to the Egyptians, but is extended specifically to the Ethiopians and Colchians. Also, it is important to note that race as a concept for Herodotus, as opposed to its "modern" version, is not simply a monolithic representation of attitudes and behaviors made evident by skin color. Other sociocultural practices such as religious beliefs, rituals, and so on are necessary in distinguishing patterns of behavior. Thus the relationship between Egypt, the Colchians and the Ethiopians is not based purely on the characteristics of "dark skin and woolly hair," but on the fact that they practised circumcision.

Regardless of the realities revealed by Herodotus, Hegel's historical prerequisites eliminate them. A significant number, if not all, of the references to the Egyptians, Ethiopians and others are cancelled out because they are found within the narrative accounts of others, myth, folklore and (even) personal observation – all of which fail to meet Hegel's historical criteria. Because of its consistent and persistent presence in all the available categories of historical documentation, however, it is impossible to dismiss Egypt. Such a description, within the context of the nineteenth century in general and Hegel's philosophy of history in particular, is paramount in understanding the emerging Greek ideal adjacent to Egypt (a black race).[16]

We return now to consider Hegel's own vehicle of expedition against Egypt: *The Philosophy of History*. We will proceed from Hegel's Appendix, where his racial state of mind is clearly presented, to the main body of lectures entitled "The Natural Context or the Geographical Basis of World History." To stabilize his version of world history, Hegel shifts his discourse from a geopolitical description to one that is more anthropological and more negative in its formal attempt to deal with the African intrusion and all it signifies:

> Africa, generally speaking, is the continent in which the upland principle, the principle of cultural backwardness, predominates.
>
> Generally speaking, Africa is a continent enclosed within itself, and this closedness remained its chief characteristic.
>
> We shall attempt to define the universal spirit and form of the African character in the light of particular traits which such accounts enumerate.

Now, with this consciousness firmly situated strictly within the continent of Africa, he produces a anthropomorphic projection – a projection defining the undeniable characteristics of a black (racial) consciousness.

> The characteristic feature of the Negroes is that their consciousness has not yet reached an awareness of any substantial activity – for example, of God or the law.
>
> All our observations of African man show him as living in a state of savagery and barbarism, and he remains in that state to the present day. The Negro is an example of an animal man in all his savagery and lawlessness. If we wish to understand him at all, we must put aside our European attitudes. We must not think of a spiritual God or of moral laws . . . for we can only feel that which is akin to our own feelings.
>
> Thus, in Africa as a whole, we encounter what has been called the state of innocence . . . This primitive state of nature is in fact a state of animality.
>
> Religion begins with the awareness that there is something higher than man. But this kind of religion is unknown to Negroes . . . In this condition, man sees himself and nature as opposed to one another, but with himself in the commanding position; this is the situation in Africa, as Herodotus was first to testify.
>
> Since human beings are valued so cheaply, it is easily explained why slavery is the basis legal relationship in Africa. The only significant relationship between the Negroes and the Europeans has been – and still is – that of slavery. The Negroes see nothing improper about it.
>
> The Negroes are enslaved by the Europeans and sold to America. Nevertheless, their lot in their own country, where slavery is equally absolute, is almost worse than this; for the basis principle of all slavery is that man is not yet conscious of his freedom. In all the African kingdoms known to the Europeans, this slavery is endemic and accepted as natural.
>
> The Negroes have no sentiments of regret at this condition of slavery. When the Negro slaves have laboured all day, they are perfectly contented and will dance with the most violent convulsions throughout the night.

> Men sell their wives, parents sell their children, and children sell their parents whenever they have it in their power to do so.

These observations counter, on a point-by-point basis, those presented by Herodotus. Even in the midst of this overwhelming negative "evidence," however, Hegel must pause and give special consideration to Egypt. His discursive technique not only isolates Egypt but also relocates it from Africa to Asia:

> Carthage, while it lasted, represented an important phase; but as a Phoenician colony, it belongs to Asia. Egypt will be considered as a stage in the movement from the east to the west, but it is no part of the spirit of Africa. What we understand as Africa proper is that unhistorical and undeveloped land which is still enmeshed in the natural spirit, and which had to be mentioned here before we cross the threshold of history itself.
>
> Having disposed of these preliminary matters, we now at last find ourselves on the real theatre of world history. Among the Negroes, the natural will of the individual is not yet negated; but it is through its negation that a consciousness of being in and for itself will arise.[17]

This reformation of Africa combined with the Egypt's "relocation" brings us to the threshold of understanding the proximity of blackness and architecture. First, there must be an explicit discussion of how the term "Egypt" is to be understood in the remainder of this text. "Egypt" is a black racial trope now suspended somewhere between Africa and Asia. By signifying "Egypt" as "Asian" and not "African", Hegel resolves the historical relationship between Egypt and Greece while reaffirming the strictly closed consciousness of Africa. The original relationship between Egypt (as black) and Greece is transformed into an altogether different (reflective) relationship between Egypt (as Asian) and Greece. This strategy is useful in confirming the ability of particular climatic zones and geographical territories to nurture the appropriate consciousness. Even with climatic and geographical repositioning, however, Hegel is still unable to eradicate Herodotus' simple description that the Egyptians are "black skinned and have woolly hair."

To reconfirm the relationship between race (blackness) and architecture, it is important to show direct methodological links between *The Philosophy of History* and *Aesthetics*. Second, the relative definition and function of the philosophical and aesthetic categories must be conceptually compatible. This is the only way to be certain that the same definition of the black subject exists in both texts. Finally, at least one of the established categories must result in an "identity" construction that is inclusive of blackness and architecture.

In Hegel's *Philosophy of History* a threefold categorical scheme (original history, reflective history, and philosophical history) demonstrates a precise use of the dialectical process in which original history was negated (perfected) by reflective history, producing a philosophical version of history. This process represents a historical equivalent of thesis, antithesis, and synthesis. Similarly, Hegel's *Aesthetics* is constituted around a three-part categorical schema in which the notion of art is subdivided into symbolic, classical and romantic forms. "These forms find their origin in the different ways of grasping the Idea as content, whereby a difference in the configuration in which the Idea appears is conditioned."[18] For Hegel this issue of grasping (or the inability to grasp) is encountered immediately in the first category – the symbolic form of art. Similar to the category of original history, Hegel defines the symbolic category as lacking the ability to conceptualize an ideal present.

> First, art begins with the Idea, still in its indeterminacy and obscurity, or in bad and untrue determinacy, is made content of artistic shapes. Being indeterminate, it does not yet possess in itself the individuality which the Ideal demands; its abstraction and one-sidedness leave its shape externally defective and arbitrary. The [symbolic] form of art is therefore rather a mere search for portrayal than a capacity for true presentation; the Idea has not found the form even in itself and therefore remains struggling and striving after it.[19]

Considering this statement in the context of Hegel's definition of original history as formulated in his *Philosophy of History*, one finds similar objections to "mundane content" and arbitrary or defective forms of historical writing. Just as Hegel considered Herodotus' use of narrative, folk tales and personal observation an obstruction to a true understanding of history, he devalued the symbolic form of art because of its "defective and arbitrary" representation.

The second form of art as defined by Hegel is the classical form, in which

> the double defect of the symbolic form is extinguished. The symbolic shape is imperfect because (i) in it the Idea is presented to consciousness only as indeterminate or determined abstractly, and (ii) for this reason the correspondence of meaning and shape is always defective and must itself remain purely abstract. The classical art-form clears up the double defect.[20]

Here the symbolic definition of art is negatively affirmed in "classical" terminology. Again, in this transitional category the two opposing forces are subjected to one another within the dialectical process. This idea is a consistent rendition of how Hegel defines "reflective history" in *The Philosophy of History*. For example, he states the events constituting reflective history are "various, but their general significance, their inner quality and coherence, are one. This circumstance cancels out the past and raises the event into the present."[21]

In terms of methodology, it is clear that the "middle" category of both the historical and aesthetic schemes function in the same way: the opposing constituencies are defined, redefined, and characterized in an effort to maintain them as perfect opposites. In essence, reflective history equals the classical form of art. Therefore the first category of both schemes is used to identify defective and arbitrary agents; the second category of both schemes represents a realm of purification in which these defective and arbitrary constituencies are cancelled.

The final form of art in *Aesthetics* is defined as "romantic." This category is seen as a continuation of perfection initiated in the classical form. As such, "the romantic form of art cancels again the completed unification of the Idea and its reality, and reverts, even if in a higher way, to that difference and opposition of the two sides which in symbolic art remained unconquered."[22] As with the other two forms, the definition of the romantic form already resides in Hegel's definition of philosophical history. Philosophical world history is not "abstractly general, but concrete and absolute present; for it is the spirit which is eternally present itself and for which it has no past."[23] This absolute object, the dissolution of the past, is both the implied and explicit function of the final third of Hegel's scheme. This dissolution is far more absolute, as has been shown, in the context of Hegel's *Philosophy of History* and more specifically in the "philosophical category" in which racial reasoning is used to reconstruct the origin of Egypt, relocating it out of Africa and to the East.

The artistic forms discussed as "romantic arts" are painting, music, and poetry. Unlike the previous categories, these "forms" of art are not restricted by criteria falling outside Hegel's spiritual sentiment. For example, poetry represents for Hegel the ultimate artistic endeavor, the highest form of art in his system of arts.

> Poetry, the art of speech, the third term, the totality, which unites in itself, within the province of the spiritual inner life and on a higher level, the two extremes, i.e. the visual arts and music. For on the one hand, poetry, like music, contains that principle of the self-apprehension of the inner life as inner, which architecture, sculpture, and painting lack.[24]

There has yet to be a definitive categorizing of architecture, forcing us to double back on our argument to find exactly where architecture fits in Hegel's hierarchy of the arts. It is also important to consider, within the context of our argument, whether "Egypt," the racially defined subject, is confined to a similar category.

The previous discussion has demonstrated the transparent nature of Hegel's threefold categorical schemes relative to the texts discussed here. In essence, *Aesthetics* repeats and extrapolates the method represented in *The Philosophy of History*. The reconstituted subjects' original identities are altered as they pass from category to category, from text to text. As elsewhere in his writings, Hegel relies on techniques of personifying the more abstract notions of his logic by using concrete examples. If my argument as to the relationship between architecture and blackness is compelling, their concretized images, as presented by Hegel, would coexist in the same aesthetic category and, regardless of their obvious differences in form, be defined in the same way. This is exactly the case in terms of "Egypt" (read: a black race) and architecture. As Hegel elaborates on the characteristics of the symbolic form of art, he fixes "Egypt" within his model of aesthetics.

> But the complete example of the thorough elaboration of symbolic art, both in its special content and in its form, we have to seek in Egypt. Egypt is the country of symbols, the country which sets itself the spiritual task of the self-deciphering of the spirit, without actually attaining the decipherment. The problems remain unresolved ... For this reason the Egyptian, amongst the peoples hitherto mentioned, are the properly artistic people. But their works remain mysterious and dumb, mute and motionless because here spirit itself has still not really found its inner life and still cannot speak the clear and distinct language of the spirit.[25]

"Egypt," for Hegel, is *the* example of the symbolic form of art. Furthermore, this definition of symbolic art is compatible with the definition given for "original" history. Herodotus was described not only as the "father of history," but also as being historically "naive." Similarly, "Egypt" is defined as "artistic," but its art is "mysterious and dumb, mute and motionless." Much later in the text, Hegel is more explicit about such characterizations: "It is common prejudice that art made its beginning with the natural and the simple ... Those beginnings which are simple and natural have nothing to do with art and beauty ... Beauty, as a work of the spirit, requires on the contrary even for its beginnings a developed technique, many sorts of experiment and practice."[26] Again, these descriptions not only identify the subject in question, but also superimpose definitions onto the subject – a preparation that will allow for its negation in the categories to follow.

Having shown Hegel situating "Egypt" within the symbolic category of art, architecture must now be evaluated in a similar fashion. Hegel describes architecture specifically in his "System of the Individual Arts" and gives it the following artistic definition:

> In the case of a house and a temple and other buildings the essential feature which interests us here is that such erections are mere means, presupposing a purpose external

to them. A hut and the house of god presuppose inhabitants, men images of gods, etc. and have been constructed for them. Thus in the first place a need is there, lying outside art, and its appropriate satisfaction has nothing to do with fine art and does not evoke any works of art. Men also take pleasure in leaping and singing and they need the medium of speech, but speaking, jumping, screaming, and singing are not yet, for this reason, poetry, dance, or music. But even if, within architecture's adaptability to satisfaction of particular needs . . . the urge for artistic form and beauty becomes conspicuous, we nevertheless have on our hands a division in the case of art and architecture.

In this connection . . . architecture corresponds to the symbolic form of art, and, as a particular art . . . [it] is distinguished again from sculpture by reason of the fact that, as architecture, it does not produce constructions the meaning of which is the inherently spiritual and subjective . . . On the contrary, what this architecture produces is works which stamp the meaning on their external shape only symbolically. For this reason, then this kind of architecture is of a strictly symbolic kind both in its content and in its mode of presenting it.[27]

This reading of architecture by Hegel is consistent with the prerequisites of the symbolic category and the type of language used to define "Egypt." It is clear that Hegel believes architecture to be less than adequate in fulfilling the notions of the spirit. Architecture, as defined within the symbolic category, is subdivided, by Hegel, into three sub-categories. Although architecture has symbolic (Egyptian), classical (Greek) and Romantic (Gothic) distinctions, all of these divisions are permanently situated beneath sculpture (classical), music and poetry (romantic). Unlike sculpture, painting and music, architecture is perpetually limited (as is blackness) and unable to produce a pure formation of Hegel's "spirit."

What is most important is to understand architecture as existing within the symbolic category that has already been defined as signifying "Egypt." If the symbolic category is "Egypt," and "Egypt" is defined in the context of *The Philosophy of History* as a negatively affirmed black racial trope, and architecture is placed within the same category, it is difficult to continue to maintain that blackness has nothing to do with architecture.

Given the loaded circumstance (Africa) surrounding this new construction of "Egypt," it is easy to discern why architecture is relegated to its "symbolic" status. By Hegel's own admission, the beginning of architecture (i.e., the primitive hut) is an infinitely accessible form of architecture. If Hegel allowed the definition of architecture to compete with that of poetry (and the Greeks), for example, he would need an infinite number of qualifiers to maintain his position. On the other hand, the Egyptians were eloquently versed in the construction of architectural monuments. It is difficult, even for Hegel, to deny the initial wonder produced by these works. However, because of this very association with "Egypt," the country of symbols, even the most perfected version of architecture (the Gothic cathedral) is beneath sculpture, painting, and poetry. It is not possible to discern where architecture would be ranked in Hegel's scheme if its Egyptian lineage were not so prominent. In any case, the mere fact that architecture, as an art, is ranked perpetually beneath other forms of the fine arts is evidence of this fundamental relationship. It is clear, given the inherent logic of his texts and categories that, in Hegel's spirit-making state of mind, architecture signifies blackness.

It could be argued that the architecture of "Egypt" is the only "art" that prevented Egypt from being concealed altogether by Hegel's refined historical technique. The Pyramids and the Labyrinths, even in Hegel's terms, are legitimate historical artefacts that resisted the same form of negation constructed in *The Philosophy of History*. In *Aesthetics*, Hegel resurrects "Egypt" only to subject it to a more refined form of negation housed within aesthetic characterizations and definitions. In essence, the "double defect" (read: the black subject and its architecture) of "Egypt" and the symbolic category is given a double dose of the dialectic. Without repeating these symbolic, classical and romantic divisions, it would not be possible for Hegel to even speak of Greek temples and Gothic cathedrals as more ideal forms of architecture. Once these more appropriate manifestations of the "spirit" (in architecture) are firmly situated in Hegel's total system of representation, the philosophical and aesthetic problem of "Egypt" is finally put to rest. Even in a relatively brief argument such as this, the black racial subject is buried within a complex matrix of at least twelve dialectical categories and sub-categories. The result of these techniques and terminologies is the construction of the symbolic category – a category fundamentally composed of "Egypt" (read: a black race) and architecture (read: a questionable art).

If architecture saved Egypt, the inverse is also true. It is argued here that Hegel considers the possibility of architecture as art necessary only because of his continuing racial conflict with Egypt. "Egypt" maintains a place in Hegel's world through its architecture, but it is Hegel who sets a new trajectory for the development of architecture. Because of his opposition to Egypt, he reinvigorates the very question of architecture by challenging its legitimacy in the realm of the true arts. In these terms, Hegel's textual edifice is clearly a racially motivated framework used to identify, cancel, and transcend a relentless black subject. Architecture just got in the way.

Recalling the first sentence by Isozaki that started this investigation ("Hegel believed architecture to be the *mother* of all arts"), it now takes on a peculiar significance. If we shift this statement from its intended connotations (mother: the ability to conceive absolutely, as in mother nature) to black figurative language use in the States (mother: a situation signifying an insurmountable predicament, as in "now, ain't that a mother!"), perhaps Isozaki was speaking the trope all along.

References

1   Arata Isozaki, from Kojin Karatani, *Architecture as Metaphor* (Cambridge, MA: MIT Press, 1995), p. x.

2   G.W.F. Hegel, *Aesthetics: Lectures on the Fine Arts* (Oxford: Clarendon Press, 1975), p. 632–3.

3   Martin Bernal, *Black Athena: the Fabrication of Ancient Greece, 1785–1985*, insists that race was significant to nineteenth century scholars. He recognizes two historical models: the Ancient Model and the Aryan Model. David Hume's *Of National Characters* (1748), Thomas Jefferson's *Notes on the State of Virginia* (1801) and Arthur Gobineau's *Essai sur l'inégalité des races Humaines* (1853) are significant texts using aspects of racial theory to legitimize their arguments. This short list of authors, including Hegel, demonstrates the international presence of this subject matter.

4   Anthony Giddens, *Capitalism and Modern Social Theory: an Analysis of the Writings of Marx, Durkheim and Max Weber* (Cambridge: Cambridge University Press, 1971), p. 21.

5   G.W.F. Hegel, *Lectures on the Philosophy of World History* (Cambridge: Cambridge University Press, 1975), p. 12.

6   The reader will notice the curious and obvious omission of architecture as a possible "record" of original history.

7   Hegel, *The Philosophy of History*, p. 14.

8   Hegel, *The Philosophy of History*, pp. 14–15. Hegel also assigns this characteristic to Thucydides, Xenophon and Caesar. They are all given credit for producing masterpieces that are nonetheless naive constructions of history.

9   Hegel describes the terms of this coupling as "indistinguishable."

10 Hegel, *The Philosophy of History*, p. 22.

11 Hegel, *The Philosophy of History*, p. 23.

12 G.W.F. Hegel, *Aesthetics: Lectures on the Fine Arts* (Oxford: Clarendon Press, 1975), p. 9.

13 Hegel, *The Philosophy of History*, p. 24.

14 Hegel, *The Philosophy of History*, p. 27.

15 Herodotus, as translated in Francis Richard Godolphin (ed.), *The Greek Historians: the Complete and Unabridged Historical Works of Herodotus et al.* (New York: Random House, 1942), pp. 92–131. Herodotus also states that a king named Sesostris was "king not only of Egypt, but also of Ethiopia" (p. 132).

16 I am not interested in particular historical underpinnings of Greek or Egyptian culture. My attempt here is to represent to the reader the complexity that arises when these cultural icons are placed against to one another – one representing the cradle of Western civilization, the other an anti-representation of the West.

17 Hegel, *The Philosophy of History*, pp. 172–90. In these examples, Hegel also

demonstrates that he does not have to play by his own rules. For example, his deployment of the consciousness of Negroes onto the Negroes is contrary to his idea that "individuals and nations themselves express their aspirations and their awareness of what their aspirations are." Of course, describing Africa and the Negroes as having no consciousness would resolve this problem in logic. However, the "no consciousness" label is still authored (by Hegel) from outside the individuals and the nation. As such, one could argue that this very description falls in the category of an "obscure record" constructed purely through personal observation – an observation then legitimized by racial determinism. Thus, in terms of Hegel's own standards, these descriptions are not historical.

18   Hegel, *Aesthetics*, p. 75.
19   Hegel, *Aesthetics*, pp. 76–7.
20   Hegel, *Aesthetics*, pp. 77–9.
21   Hegel, *The Philosophy of History*, p. 20.
22   Hegel, *Aesthetics*, p. 79.
23   Hegel, *The Philosophy of History*, p. 24.
24   Hegel, *Aesthetics*, p. 960.
25   Hegel, *Aesthetics*, p. 354.
26   Hegel, *Aesthetics*, p. 615.
27   Hegel, *Aesthetics*, pp. 631–3.

Chapter 4
Space House: the psyche of building
Beatriz Colomina

The block from Lexington to Third avenues on 33rd street is one composed largely of outdated apartment dwellings whose entranceways and facades in general remind one of another day. Walking along the street one's eye may very possibly become enmeshed in the jungle of intricate metalwork composing the fire-escapes that hang overhead. But for a week now a new detail has appeared on the scene that has quickly become a cynosure: a trim, tailored canopy extending to the gutter, whose apron carries in clear, bold type: "Modernage Furniture Co."

     The modern character of the establishment is at once attested by the facade of metal which supports one end of this canopy. It's quite small, this frontage on 33rd street, and so an architectural treatment was needed that was both distinctive and eye-compelling. An asymmetrical treatment in brushed aluminum does the trick.[1]

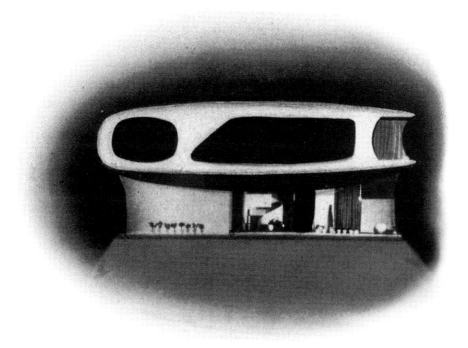

4.1 Space House, New York: front view of model (1933)

Thus begins the coverage of Frederick Kiesler's design for the Modernage Furniture Company in an issue of *Retailing* (1933). First of all, a canopy sticking out of a metal facade on an otherwise old-fashioned street – 162 East 33rd Street. The frontage was small. Something radical was needed to draw attention. Behind the facade, the new headquarters of a company specializing in modern furniture and interior design. The store had been struggling for survival since 1925 but now the showrooms are flooded with visitors. Kiesler has installed a full size model of a family house as the centerpiece. He calls it "Space House" and, according to a newspaper reporter, "many people feel they owe it to themselves to go through it."[2] The house has caused a sensation, appearing in every newspaper and magazine and attracting large crowds.

Modern architecture has been called on, once again, to exercise the role of advertisement, of a lure directing attention to something other than itself, in this case, modern furniture. While the greatest attraction, according to all reporters, is the Space House,[3] its role was just to arouse interest in the 33 furnished rooms in the upper floors of the building. The stairway to the showrooms was also designed by Kiesler in a way that drew the visitor up the steps with sequences of "mushroom lamps" at eye level. These unique metal lamps (in aluminum, copper or chromium) appeared throughout the whole building on walls and ceilings. In fact, Kiesler was responsible for the whole display. The Space House is positioned at the beginning of a long series of lures designed to entice the customers ever further into the building until they are finally seated in the model dining rooms, living rooms, bedrooms, libraries and so on. The sequence, which begins with the canopy sticking out into the street, was understood, as can be seen in the words of one of the reporters, in psychosexual terms:

> Passing through the door – there are no windows at all – one enters a foyer perhaps 20 feet long, executed in dark brown with light gray at the far end, exerting a psycho-function – a "come hither" appeal. This detail, just as hundreds of others do, testify to the meticulous care with which the architect Frederick Kiesler gave to every phase of the store planning.
>
> Passing through the foyer, which has a comparatively low ceiling, one turns at right angles to enter a large open area whose spaciousness and light come almost as a shock. Measuring approximately 30 by 45 feet, it serves to set off the Space house squatting in the distance clear across the floor except for a stairway leading upstairs or to the basement.[4]

Kiesler himself had introduced the concept of "psycho-function" in his 1930 book *Contemporary Art Applied to the Store and Its Display*:

The "psycho-functional" influence is exhibited not only in lines, planes and form, but also in materials and colors. Glass has a different psychological effect from leather, wood from metal. The same applies, of course, to color schemes. Function and efficiency alone cannot create art works. "Psycho-function" is that "surplus" above efficiency which may turn a functional solution into art.[5]

Kiesler continues the argument in the later essay "Pseudo-Functionalism in Modern Architecture," where he writes: "we must strive from the outset *to satisfy the psyche of the dweller*."[6] The house, he says, is a human body, "a living organism with the reactivity of a full-blooded creature," with organs (the stairs are the feet, the ventilation system is the nose, and so on), a nervous system, and a digestive system that can "suffer from constipation."[7] But more than that, he insists, the house, like humans, lives "in emotions and dreams through the medium of his physique." The *psyche* cannot be separated from the body. Indeed, the house is the product of "the erotic and creative instinct" and its experience is erotic. With the concept of "psycho-function," the material condition of the building and its mechanical operations give way to a form of sensuality understood as psychological pleasure.

The passage from the material and mechanical to the psycho-sexual is acted out in the responses to the Space House. All the reporters admire the mechanical operations:

This Space House is a kind of laboratory in modern living. Doors, for instance. Look at this. He pointed to a kind of shutter at the top of an ordinary doorway . . . "Push a button and it rolls down from the top, right down to the floor. What could be better than that?"[8]

But more than that, they are fascinated with the materials: rubber, sponge, straw, rayon, oiled silk:

The rubber sponge in a brownish shade, a half inch thick, is used for a curtain in the main living room, since it is sound proof and at the same time permits ventilation. In the bathroom a blue shade of rubber sponge affords an unusual floor covering. The pearl gray drapes in the dining room are made of a combination of rayon and straw. Endurette, a new transparent water repellent silk, is used for the bedroom drapes to diffuse the light.[9]

The materials are seen as strange. Reporters loved them. They experienced them sensually. The reviews go on and on about the texture, the color, the feel. The erotic charge is everywhere evident. We hear of "an alluring space" in the house, the "compelling attraction" of the house,[10] and so on. Even Martin H. Feinman, head of the Modernage Galleries and sponsor of the house, says to a reporter:

4.2 Space House, New York: rubber sponge floor covering (1933)

In the Space House everything is open ... From the entrance you can see all over the house. You blush. Your imagination is at work. Very well; I push a button here – there will be a button there when it is finished – and that curtain rolls around. At once you have privacy.[11]

The push-button space-age modernity, which exposes the body of the house, revealing every opening, every orifice, produces an unmistakable sexual blush. Kiesler designed that blush. This was his lifelong project. It is in the attempt to produce that blush, to embarrass institutions, that he repeatedly established himself as an avant-garde figure, perhaps the only avant-garde figure in architecture that one can speak of in the United States.

So what is the significance of the Space House, a project that is usually marginalized, if mentioned at all, in accounts of Kiesler's work? In fact, it is the only house that Kiesler will ever get built. It was based on research into "Time-Space-Architecture" going back to the early 1920s in Europe, research that will keep developing right through the 1960s. The term "endless" that Kiesler attached to his well known house project of the 1950s and 1960s had already been used to describe his earliest works. For Kiesler, the Space House was a unique moment in this trajectory. Indeed, he acts as if this was his first realized project since arriving in the United States in 1926. Despite having built the well publicized Film Guild Theater in 1928, he describes the Modernage commission as his first chance to materialize the ongoing research:

> Seven years have passed. Seven years of waiting. Seven years of search and research ... The furniture exposition at Modernage gave me chance to enforce continued presentation of Time-Space-Architecture; this time through a house. The actualization of my plan for a Space-House at the Modernage company represents an approximation of my conception, within given limitations. Adaptation to such limitations permit only a demonstration of the principle, not its full manifestation. Principle: Time-Space-Architecture. Medium: a house. Category: shelter.[12]

The omission of the Film Guild Theater is symptomatic. Kiesler made a clear cut distinction between cinema and theater. In the *New York Evening Post* of February 1929, he insisted that they require "two types of building, as distinct in form and function as a butcher shop and an office building," because one was organized around a two-dimensional surface, while the other was three dimensional: "The film is a play on surface, the theatre a play on space."[13] He understood the house as theater. The model house is an exhibition space and theatrical space. The visitors are the actors. Indeed, as Kiesler often said, his first version of the Endless House was built as a theater in Vienna in 1924 for the Music and Theater Festival of the City. Like all the successive versions of the Endless House, this theater "presented itself as a flattened sphere."[14] The eccentric shape of the Space House, which all the visitors commented on, is part of a sustained polemic. It is the product of a very singular obsession.

4.3 Space House, New York: facade (1933)

As Kiesler would later say: "The three years 1922, 1923, 1924 were the most fruitful years of my life. What I am doing today are follow-ups of these ideas, and I'm still looking, as I was 40 years ago, for a chance to build them."[15] All his life, he says, he had pursued "one basic idea." Sometimes he calls it "Space-in-architecture," or "Time-Space-Architecture" and other times "continuity" or "the endless." The word "space" assumes a key role. The early work is entitled "space-theatre," "space-stage," "space-scenery," "space-sculpture" and so on.[16] He used the word so often that Viennese journalists used to call him "*Doktor Raum*."[17] Everywhere, Kiesler uses the word to mark the breaking out from some kind of confinement. For him, a room, a floor, a wall, the frame of a painting, the proscenium of a theater, in other words, "the finite", are confining. He says, for example, that "the ordinary wall or floor is a concentration camp,"[18] and that his "galaxies," which he traces back to his First World War activities, are some of the ways in which he has "tried to break through the borders of the finite, the prison of the frame."[19]

In the Space House, this liberation involves breaking the walls. Already in 1925, in the "Manifesto of Tensionism," he had written: "We will have NO MORE WALLS, these armoires for body and soul . . . No walls, no foundations."[20] The Space House finds an expression for both these moves. The shell of the house is intended for die-cast unit construction, which does away with foundations. The "eggshell," Kiesler says, "is the perfect example of a structure in which walls, floors and ceiling are self-supporting in an architectural sense."[21] The shell is in continuous tension, a construction principle developed to reduce deadload and to eliminate column support. The column seen in some photographs belongs to the exhibition floor, not the house.[22] Likewise, the house dispenses with walls. "Walls" in the Space House have become something which may no longer qualify for their old terminology. A noise-deafening rubber curtain activated by a push button, for example, constitutes the vertical separation between two spaces (two "segments") at a certain point in time. Kiesler's principle of Time-Space in the house is based on the idea that the same space can be used for different activities at different times:

> The time element converts itself into space if one considers the use of a certain area for the exact amount of time required by that function. Except for the kitchen, garage, and storage area, all segments of the whole sphere are convertible in as many different functions as might be required living in a house. Such as: Recreation, work, sleep, et cetera . . . The whole sphere of the house might be divided or opened into smaller and larger segments. Segments not rooms; segments being indicative as part of an entity while "room" is a final unit in itself.[23]

Rubber curtains aside, space in Kiesler's house is, for the most part, divided horizontally by a system of small differences in levels, setting segments off from other segments. Vision continues but the individual spaces are delimited.

The same principle is applied to the design of doors. The push-button roll down doors in the Space House allow spaces to flow into each other without obstacles. As Kiesler says in the context of his discussion of shop-windows:

Doors, in general are not good. They may be necessities which we must tolerate, but if we can do without them so much the better. Their purpose is to keep out drafts, dust and noise, which can now be eliminated from inside by scientific devices. Sometimes they act as barriers.[24]

Doors are a threat to continuity. Even when open, traditional doors are obstacles that invade space. Roll down doors can be made to disappear. Visual obstacles are the most confining of all. In "Pseudo-Functionalism in Modern Architecture" Kiesler insists:

Form does not follow function
Function follows vision
Vision follows reality[25]

Vision is the sense that is capable of travelling the furthest away from the body, aside from "conscience," which Kiesler describes as a sixth sense. In notes kept in his file on the Space House, he writes:

Our senses are not given us to enlarge our knowledge of the universe but *to limit* our capacity of *understanding*. In that respect we could clarify the degree of limitation of our senses, like:

1   touch – shortest
2   taste – next
3   smell – next
4   ear – next
5   eye – next
6   conscience (?) longest
        (time-space)

The sensuality of Kiesler's house extends from touch into the visual freedom the design affords and beyond into the psyche. A series of sketches illustrates this point. In one, the interaction of the nervous system with a chair becomes part of a multi-sensual engagement with the world. In another, the chair becomes part of an interior and the human is described as "a terrestrial spectra," the environment as a "stellar spectra (with the objects taking the place of stars)." Space for Kiesler is always outer space. No wonder everything in his architecture floats. The floors go up and down, the structure hangs, and even the furniture, the cabinets, the tables, the lighting fixtures, are suspended. Time-Space is a surrealist project.

4.4 Sketch of the interrelations between the human (earthly spirit) and the environment (stellar spirit)

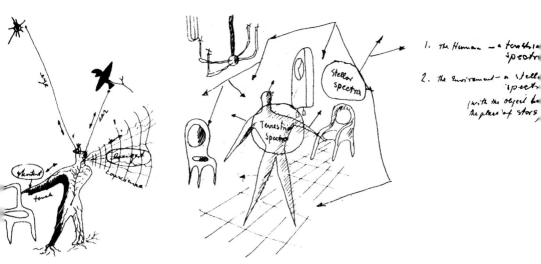

While Kiesler believed that his work on Time-Space had been very influential on architects like Le Corbusier and Mies van der Rohe, his manuscript on the Space House notes that the early space projects were received ambivalently. He goes back to the "City in Space" that was exhibited at the invitation of Josef Hoffmann in the Austrian pavilion at the Grand Palais in the *Exposition des Arts Decoratifs* in Paris 1925. Its attempt to "illustrate" the "Time-Space-Architecture" principles was "ridiculed as to their purpose and theoretical coherence." Le Corbusier is supposed to have asked Kiesler if he intended "to hang the houses from Zeppelins" and Mies dismissed his "Time-Space-Concept." Only Theo van Doesburg and Adolf Loos supported his theories. Van Doesburg published the "Manifesto of Tensionism," which was first printed as a leaflet to be distributed in the exhibition, in *De Stijl*, and Loos, with whom Kiesler had worked in Vienna, came to his defence when the City in Space was under attack.[26]

Kiesler learned a lot from Loos. The idea of the house as theatrical space in which the visitor is some kind of actor may be Kiesler's biggest debt to Adolf Loos. But not just in the sense, often referred to, of his Raumplan, in which each space opens into the next. Loos is taken one step further. Continuity for Kiesler is also linked to new forms of communication. Push-button is everywhere in his architecture. Already in 1923, in his stage design for RUR in Berlin, Kiesler had introduced in the theater a system of other media (film, proto-TV) activated by push button:

This R.U.R play was my occasion to use for the first time in a theater a motion picture instead of a painted backdrop, and also a television in the sense that I had a big, square panel window in the middle of the stage drop which could be opened by remote control. When the director of the human factory in the play pushed a button at his desk, the panel opened and the audience saw two human beings reflected from a mirror arrangement backstage. The actors appeared in this window as a foot-and-a-half tall, casually moving and talking, heard through a hidden loud-speaker. It was quite an illusion, because a minute later you saw the same actors appear on stage in full size. There was, inevitably, a burst of applause at this moment.[27]

This would be a constant in Kiesler's architecture. He pushes a new medium into an old one in order to update it, to literally expand its horizon (film into the theater; television into the shop window, the museum, the house). He often does so even before the new media are established. A 1932 article in the *New York Times*, on the mass-produced house of the future, "Everyman's House" (for those whose income is less than $1,400 a year), reports on Kiesler's idea of the small dwelling as presented in the "Small House Forum" conducted by the American Institute of Steel Construction: "Rooms will be fewer and larger, so that space may be more fully utilized and so that adequate walls may be provided for the inevitable television scenes and motion pictures of the future."[28] Technologies are seen as breaking the limits of a space. As Kiesler points out, when film is introduced in the RUR settings, the spectator is given the illusion of walking into another space, in that case, the space of the factory. The limits of the space of the theater are opened up. The setting itself moved continuously through the performance.[29] The Space House as the Space Theater re-enacted this kind of movement.

Kiesler saw his work in opposition to that of Le Corbusier, Mies and Oud. That is, in opposition to the architects represented in the International Style exhibition organized by Philip Johnson and Henry-Russell Hitchcock in the Museum of Modern Art in 1932. He had reasons for this. The exhibition included Kiesler only in a marginal role, with a photograph of his Film Guild Cinema in a section entitled "The Extent of Modern Architecture." The section, which was organized by country and represented each project by a single photograph, included Kiesler under "USA." In an interview with *Progressive Architecture* he describes the discomfort of the curators with his work:

Philip Johnson came with Henry-Russell Hitchcock to see plans of my work. Among our friends of the De Stijl group it was known that I have deviated from the "quadrat," but van Doesburg stood by enthusiastically, as did Mondrian. The others were doubtful; Mies was neutral and reserved . . . Here were the plans for a building that looked like an egg, not like the customary box. It wasn't square, it wasn't in steel, it wasn't in glass, it wasn't in aluminum, it was absolutely outside the mode of the International Style.[30]

Two years after the exhibition, Kiesler responds in an article on the Space House for *Hound and Horn*, the journal in which Hitchcock's first essays had appeared. Indeed, the Space House itself can be understood as the response. Kiesler insists that what makes his design different is that his house is but one result of an ongoing theoretical enquiry rather than a one-off attempt to build an aesthetic object. The fact that it could be realized was the least significant aspect of it:

> Architecture was always threefold: social, tectonic, structural. But Corbusier, Mies, Oud and others have started *with* the concept of a House . . . They started with the *Idea of a House*: not with a *Unified architectural dogma*. Not from Architecture as a Science, Not from Architecture as Biotechnique . . . The work of these men deals with Houses: aesthetic or semi-functional semi-solutions, from which an architectural principle might be deducted, if the spectator is creatively inclined . . .
>
> Opposing such "designs" I always advocated the principle of a new *unified* theory first – from which new Houses, Factories or whatever structure it might result; not vice versa. That was and still is the difference. I was never eager to build; nothing at the moment can satisfy.[31]

It is as if Kiesler's lack of interest in building for building's sake gives his building more integrity. Others may have seen it that way too. Philip Johnson will later say: "There are about five architects in America who are interested in architecture and not in money, and Kiesler is one of them."[32] Or, in Johnson's famous remark about Kiesler: "He is the greatest non-building architect of our time,"[33] an opinion that made its way into Abrams's *Encyclopedia of Modern Architecture* without attribution, as if it was simply a fact. While the Space House was the only house Kiesler ever built, it was not in a traditional site. Kiesler's dream of mass-production remained a dream.[34] The Space House was never more than an advertisement for modern furniture.

This was not unprecedented in the history of modern architecture in the United States. Already in 1929, the Marshall Field department store in Chicago, which had imported a big collection of modern furniture from France and wanted to attract attention to it, commissioned Buckminster Fuller to set up and demonstrate a model of a house he had recently designed for mass production. It was the first public presentation of the Dymaxion House. Similarly, Robert McLaughlin, a graduate from Princeton University and founder of American Houses, a company dedicated to the mass production of houses, introduced the "Motohome," a prefabricated house, at Wanamaker's department store in New York in 1935, all wrapped in cellophane and tied up with a huge red ribbon. Kiesler himself had designed with Sears Roebuck a project for prefabricated houses that also came to nothing.

In the USA modern architecture is linked inextricably to the department store. Even the International Style exhibition toured the country through department stores, such as Sears Roebuck in Chicago and Bullock's in Los Angeles. But the stores were not trying to sell architecture, they were pushing furniture and industrial design, consumer objects that could modernize space. This confusion between modern architecture and modern furniture is evident in the book published by Modernage and available for free at the Space House, *ABC of Modern Furniture*: "Modern furniture represents the rebellion of this age against stuffy, dark interiors: overdraped windows, dust-collecting curlicues and styles of decoration that are foreign in mood and manner to the spirit of present day living."

The alliance in the USA between modern architecture and commerce, via the department store or the Museum of Modern Art (MoMA), attests to the publicity value of architecture, or more precisely, of the house. The model house is an American institution. From the houses in the Prairie of Frank Lloyd Wright, first published in the *Ladies Home Journal*, to the prefabricated houses for the war worker, to the post-war houses built in the courtyard of MoMA, Americans have always been fascinated with the house. Model houses throughout the twentieth century have stolen the show at every exhibition or fair. In fact, reporters did not compare the Space

House to the International Style houses that were then touring the country but to the popular model houses in the Century of Progress Exhibition in Chicago. The Space House is presented by journalists as the "novelty," "knocking down" its immediate predecessors, the houses in Chicago that were still on display.[35]

The fate of the Endless House is in this respect also symptomatic. Despite his disparaging remarks about building, Kiesler seemed desperate to build it. But nothing seemed to work out. The MoMA was expanding, making impossible the project of building it in the courtyard and the client in Montreal

4.5 Space House, New York: detail of a curtain woven with thread (1933)

had backed off. When finally a developer from Florida showed up and was serious to build it in some swamps near Cape Canaveral in Florida, it turned out that she too wanted the house only for its publicity value. She had 3,000 acres of swamps to sell as lots and thought the Endless House would attract customers. Kiesler, who needed the money, declined the commission:

> The decision must be either to quit or accept the challenge to be just an architect-developer of terrains, a state of mind I never knew or have been in, but which most, if not all, of my colleagues are squandered in . . . It had dawned on me, through my agonizing dilemma — to build or not to build — that: thou shalt not build.[36]

Is it Kiesler himself who boycotts the realization of his own projects? Philip Johnson guessed that he really did not want to see the house built anyway: "That, in a way would be an ending. Kiesler could not bear endings."[37] The Endless House could remain endless only by never being finished. Or, as Kiesler will write: "Strange; it seems I shun an ultimate solution as a cat postpones the killing of a mouse. There is lust in postponement."[38] The resistance to building heightens the very desire he was attempting to design. Even the concept of Endless that underpins the Space House is sexualized. Kiesler said of his Endless House that "there is no beginning and no end to it, like the human body . . . The 'Endless' is rather sensuous, more like the female body in contrast to sharp-angled male architecture."[39] Architecture for him is always erotic. In the press release of the exhibition of his "Galaxies" in the Howard Wise Gallery in New York, 1969, he claimed to have "discovered architecture" when at the age of three he crept under the "voluminous peasant skirts of his Ukrainian nanny and struck a match."

Kiesler cannot separate himself from his architecture. Not by chance are his memoirs entitled *Inside the Endless House*. Psyche and architecture are inseparable. The architect cannot let go of his projects. The great enemy of confinement remains confined within his unrealized, endless projects, the "one basic idea" he worked on all his life. Kiesler was confined in the very idea of escaping confinement, a "pressure chamber" that he describes to a psychoanalyst:

> I visit you haphazardly, now is a chance to dig into this cave. I wonder if today we can't discuss this automatic reluctance of mine to remain alone with my ideas, secluded and shut off from any possibility of making them concrete, that is, three dimensional, to walk in and out of. At such moments my unrealized ideas crowd me in, almost choke me. I feel helpless. It has by now become so intense that I am fearful if there is even a stretch of an hour between two appointments in which I'm left alone. I've become a nuisance to myself. Can't we excavate the roots of this conflict?[40]

The answer was no.

ACKNOWLEDGEMENTS

I would like to thank Lillian Kiesler for providing valuable materials from her archives, Matilda McQuaid for assisting me in the Museum of Modern Art archives and Judy Throm in the Archives of American Art in Washington.

References

1   Alfred Auerbach, "The Completely Stream-Lined Store Appears," *Retailing* (6 November 1933).

2   "Modernage Furniture Co. opened an enormous factory-showroom to a frankly skeptical public eight years ago. Today this showroom, with its famous 'Space-House,' is a modern institution. Many people feel they owe it to themselves to go through it." Fleur Fenton, "New Trend in Furniture Explained," *N.Y. World-Telegram* (4 December 1933).

3   "Kiesler's One-Story Dwelling Proves Big Attraction at Modernage Opening," says Alice Hughes under the headlines of her article "Space House Gives a Peep Into Future," in the newspaper *New York American* (17 October 1933). The house is also acclaimed in: "And Now It's the Space House: Latest Thing in Dwelling Likely to leave You Gasping With Surprise," *New York Sun* (18 October 1933); Lillian E. Prussing, "The Practical Home Made Beautiful" *Midweek Pictorial* (11 November 1933); "Kiesler Model Uses Egg Form as His Ideal in Perfect Home," newspaper and date unknown; "Frederick Kiesler Designs 'Space House,'" New York Times (17 October 1933); etc. But newspapers and the popular press are not the only ones taking notice. The house is also represented in professional journals such as *Architectural Record* and *Architectural Forum.*

4   Auerbach, "The Completely Stream-Line Store Appears."

5   Frederick Kiesler, *Contemporary Art Applied to the Store and Its Display* (New York: Brentano's, 1930), p. 87.

6   Frederick Kiesler, "Pseudo-Functionalism in Modern Architecture," *Partisan Review* (July 1949), p. 735 (emphasis in the original).

7   "A house must be practical. To be practical means to serve. To be serviceable in every respect. In any direction. If any directions are closed, the house suffers from constipation." "Pseudo-Functionalism in Modern Architecture," p. 739.

8   "And Now It's the Space House." The reporter is quoting Martin H. Feinman, head of the Modernage Galleries and sponsor of the Space House.

9   "Kiesler Model Uses Egg Form as His Ideal in Perfect Home."

10   Prussing, "The Practical Home Made Beautiful."

11   "And Now It's the Space House."

12   "The Space House," manuscript in Kiesler Archives, p. 3. Courtesy of Lillian Kiesler.

13   "Architecturally, there is an enormous difference between the theatre and the cinema. The cinema has all interests concentrated on a single point of two dimensions, while the theatre must have the interest dispersed in three dimensions. This means that the theatre and the cinema require two types of buildings, as distinct in form and function as a butcher shop and an office building." Frederick Kiesler, "Building a Cinema Theatre," *New York Evening Post* (February 1929). But it should be noted that even in the cinema Kiesler still looks for an endless space: "The spectator must be able to lose himself in an imaginary, endless space even though the screen implies the opposite." Kiesler, "Building a Cinema Theatre."

14   "When I conceived and finally designed the first 'Endless' and exhibited in Vienna in 1924 at the Music and Theater Festival of the City, it presented itself as a flattened sphere." Frederick Kiesler, "Notes on Architecture and Sculpture," *Art in America* (May 1966).

15   T.H. Creighton, "Kiesler's Pursuit of an Idea," *Progressive Architecture* (July 1961), p. 110.

16   "For most of his 50 years, Vienna-born Architect Frederick Kiesler has been obsessed with his concepts of space and has designed what he calls space-theaters, space-scenery, space-cities, space-houses . . . space-sculptures." *Life* v. 32 (26 May 1952).

17   Elaine de Kooning, "Dickinson and Kiesler," *Art News* (April 1952), p. 20.

18   "Design's Bad Boy."

19   Frederick Kiesler, "Art in Orbit," *The Nation* (11 May 1964), p. 487.

20   Frederick Kiesler, "Manifesto of Tensionism," first published in *De Stijl* (April 1925) and in English in Kiesler, *Contemporary Art Applied to the Store and its Display*, p. 48.

21   "Kiesler Model Uses Egg Form as His Ideal in Perfect Home."

22   See "Space House by Frederick Kiesler," *Architectural Record*, January 1934, p. 45.

23   Frederick Kiesler, "Notes on Architecture: the Space House," *Hound and Horn* (January–March 1934), p. 294.

24   Kiesler, *Contemporary Art Applied to the Store and its Display*, p. 80.

25   Frederick Kiesler, "Pseudo-Functionalism," p.738.

26   "Loos, brilliant pacemaker, came to my rescue in defending Josef Hoffmann, his life long adversary who, after commissioning me to demonstrate a City-in-Space as part of the official Austrian exhibition, was attacked by petit-bourgeois Austrian parliament members for having spent tax money on suspended houses." "The Space House," manuscript.

27   "Kiesler's Pursuit of an Idea," p. 109.

28   "Everyman's House," *New York Times* (29 May 29 1932).

29   "Everyman's House." See also, R.L. Held, *Endless Innovations: Frederick Kiesler's Theory and Scenic Design* (Ann Arbor, MI: UMI Research Press, 1977), pp. 11–17.

30   "Kiesler's Pursuit of an Idea," pp. 113–14. Twenty years later, Johnson would support

Kiesler's work. In 1950 he acquired, for the Museum of Modern Art, the model of the Endless House that had been exhibited in the Kootz gallery. He also facilitated Kiesler's subsequent exhibitions of the Endless House in the Museum of Modern Art: "Two Houses, New Ways of Building," (1952), with Buckminster Fuller; and "Visionary Architecture" 1960, with Bruno Taut, Frank Lloyd Wright, Buckminster Fuller and Le Corbusier.

31   Kiesler, "Notes on Architecture: the Space House," p. 292.

32   *Architectural Forum* (February 1947), p. 140.

33   Philip Johnson, "Three Architects," *Art in America*, n. 1 (1960), p. 70.

34   "When the Space House is ready for manufacture on a serial basis – when mass production of its units begins – a complete house fully adequate for a family of five can be built for $5.000, he said. It is capable of taking an unlimited variety of styles, and the interior as well as the exterior, can be transformed at will to suit the convenience of its occupants." "And Now It's the Space House."

35   "And Now It's the Space House."

36   Frederick Kiesler, *Inside the Endless House* (New York, 1966), p. 444.

37   Helen Borsik, "Fame is Endless," review of *Inside the Endless House*, newspaper and date unknown, Cleveland, Ohio.

38   Kiesler, *Inside the Endless House*.

39   Kiesler, *Inside the Endless House*, p. 566.

40   Kiesler, *Inside the Endless House*, pp. 41–2.

Chapter 5
The fragility of structure, the weight of interpretation:
some anomalies in the life and opinions of Eisenman and Derrida
Clive R. Knights

> When my father had danced his white bear backwards and forwards through half a
> dozen pages, he closed the book for good an'all, – and in a kind of triumph redelivered it
> into Trim's hand, with a nod to lay it upon the 'scrutoire, where he found it. – Tristram,
> said he, shall be made to conjugate every word in the dictionary, backwards and forwards
> the same way; – every word, Yorick, by this means, you see, is converted into a thesis or
> an hypothesis; – every thesis and hypothesis have an offspring of propositions; – and each
> proposition has its own consequences and conclusions; every one of which leads the mind
> on again, into fresh tracks of enquiries and doubtings. – The force of this engine, added
> my father, is incredible in opening a child's head. – 'Tis enough, brother Shandy, cried my
> uncle Toby, to burst it into a thousand splinters.[1]

The residual traces of the early twentieth century developments of "formalism" can
be found lurking to varied extent in a vast majority of architecture produced in the
twentieth century, and to an even greater degree in the continuing predominance of
minimalism and conceptualizing tendencies in sculpture and painting. The crisis of
modernism has often been attributed to a blurring of the distinction between content
and form, meaning and structure, signified and signifier; or maybe even more
pertinently as the inevitable consequence of enforcing the distinction in the first place.
However, perhaps the most allusive recent developments in the instatement of the
priority of form over content have charted a course away from the old utopian avant-
garde rhetoric into more complex and rarefied arguments on the subject of language.

The Saussurian linguistic model and the insistence on its semiological
application across all meaningful cultural domains has been responsible for the
generation of a peculiarly twentieth century understanding of language as first and
foremost a "structure," as a systemized collection of arbitrary terms (signs) whose
power to promote meaning is entirely due to the internal opposition of one term to
another by way of difference. The traditional Greek understanding of language as
"logos," as a primal naming activity, becomes distorted and our perpetration of
meaning and truth through discourse is watered down to a kind of intangible in-
between state where meaning floats tentatively upon the unstable, rippling surface of
differentiality.

It is in a context of "structuralism" that the architect Peter Eisenman and the philosopher Jacques Derrida have utilized this instability for their own problematic creative and discursive ends, the latter proposing a deconstruction of Western metaphysics: a renunciation of the validity of transcendental identity, and an accompanying denigration of discourse into an incessant play of words, an idle juxtaposition of innumerable neutralized terms denied the possibility of a grounding in the world. As virtually all corners of the globe participate voluntarily or involuntarily in the relentless technologizing inertia that is the errant offspring of Western philosophical traditions, we find Eisenman and Derrida abandoning ship, casting off aboard the makeshift raft of Saussurian linguistics, across a treacherous ocean of language in search of its edge: that special domain with no beginning and no end, no history.

SOMEBODY NAMED EISENMAN

In an early essay entitled "Notes on Conceptual Architecture" (1971), Eisenman attempts to establish his position by an allusion to the predominant American conceptual art movement. Briefly, he identifies two modes of intention in art: the "semantic," concerned with meaning, and the "syntactic," concerned with the formal structure of relationships. Both may be present in a work in either a physical/perceptual manifestation or a non-physical/mental construct. The move towards a conceptual art is defined by

> an intention to shift the primary focus from the sensual aspects of objects to the universal aspects of objects. This conceptual aspect to be primary must be made intentional, that is, the result of an a priori design intention, and further it must be accessible through the physical fact.[2]

The "physical fact" thus becomes subordinate to a purely conceptual intention, but not in a manner corresponding to the sign (or signifying structure) in language which, as Saussure would have it, merely directs us to a referential meaning and then disappears. Instead, Eisenman wishes to close the gulf between sign and referent by producing a sign whose characteristics are its referent, not in an onomatopoeic sense, however, but in a sense which removes the antecedence normally enjoyed by the referent over the sign. Here there is a subtle and important distinction with which Eisenman apparently seems to separate himself from the avant-garde formalists by transgressing their obsession with the self-referential "object" (a concrete counterpart to a psychic state) towards the condition of the self-referential "structural relationship." This can be seen as symptomatic of taking on board the whole structuralist ensemble whereby meaning is generated not by objects in themselves but by networks of structural relationships – binary oppositions, differentiations – between objects. Building upon this, armed with the Chomskian definition of surface structures as the outward perceptual manifestation of much more fundamental deep structures, leads Eisenman to conclude that a possibility exists of obtaining a state of originality of structure which can produce its own meaning from within itself and thus "make available a new level of information."[3] The project thus proposed is to open up the possibilities of meaning by exploring the inherent syntactical deep structures; by bringing them to the surface of the architectural work in such a way that they show themselves as primal organizing phenomena, as "a previously less-than-conscious structural order."[4] Its aspirations are to a transcultural predisposition, a structural preconditioning without which meaning just would not show itself, for it would have no form and therefore no existence.[5]

An integral part of Eisenman's standpoint involves the critique of what he calls the continuing "humanist" tradition attributable to a classical, post-fifteenth century sensibility. Such a critique underpins virtually all of his published theoretical essays since the early 1970s but reaches an unreserved peak of perspicuity in "The End of the Classical" (1984), a text which draws together all the loose strands of thought and ties them into a single unitary statement of intent (an expression I imagine Eisenman would find problematic).

In this essay, by way of an unprecedented sweep of vast generalization, Eisenman brackets off what he calls five hundred years of classical "fiction." He then categorizes three fundamental "simulations" which have persistently and unjustifiably preoccupied humanity during this misguided period in world history.

First, "the simulation of meaning"[6] is an attack on "representation;" a disavowal of all architecture which purports to represent a reality beyond itself. His examples include the classical Renaissance, where architecture was intended as a "simulacra of antique buildings,"[7] and the classical Modern, where architecture was intended to resemble its function. Both are deemed classical by way of their "compositional" mode of production, where the former composes according to rules of type laid down by antiquity and allusions to the order of nature, and the latter composes according to rules of type laid down by functional processes – "the message of 'utility' as opposed to the message of 'antiquity.'"[8] For Eisenman, the pretence which architecture has hidden behind for so long must be exposed; architecture *per se* must come out of the closet and into a truly modern condition of non-representation, of looking at itself instead of beyond itself for its justification.

Second, "the simulation of Truth"[9] is an attack on the pre-eminence of "reason" as manifest in post-Enlightenment positivism and the universality of scientific facts. Its detrimental effects on architecture, according to Eisenman, are revealed in the deductive search for logical origins, in the rational determination of *a priori* forms or types with an irrefutable truth value – the work of Durand being a typical case in point. However, there is a sense in which this argument is really a restatement in different terms of the first attack on the so called modern representation of function, where the notion of function is itself an offspring of nineteenth century positivism. Essentially, the concept of representation remains under attack from a slightly different angle; removing the obsession with origins will, Eisenman thinks, remove the attempt to represent them.

Third, "the simulation of the Timeless"[10] is an attack on the rationalization of "history" and in particular the veneration of the absolute relevance of the present embodied by the idealist notion of *Zeitgeist*. Architecture seen as entrusted with the pressing task of embodying the spirit of the age finds itself suppressed by the weight of historical determinacy, a burden which Eisenman sees as misplaced and deformative of what he calls the "inevitability" of architecture.[11]

The essential direction of his argument can actually be foreseen quite early on and it is this: architecture has for centuries been overladen with an abundance of various extraneous, predetermined (and therefore prejudiced) models, beneath which its true nature has been undeservedly disguised and unheard, more or less trampled underfoot. Its bullied existence is to come to an end with Eisenman as the Samaritan/ coach who will resuscitate, coax and encourage its hidden strengths, forcing all other considerations to fall into line. By the removal of the model, architecture is to enter a state of "independent discourse," to become "an architecture as is."[12] It is at this crucial point in Eisenman's essay that a traditional notion of representation is removed and replaced by a condition of supposed non-representation. Where he regards a representation as a product which attempts to negate its relationship to reality, that is, to usurp that reality, Eisenman's non-representation is a humble product which accepts itself as a distinct artificial entity by coming to terms with itself as fiction, thus leaving reality unscathed and unaffected.

There is a paradox looming larger by the minute, and which will continue to loom like an insidious black cloud over the discussion of Derrida to follow. Eisenman, in his confusion over the nature and value of representation, substitutes the condition of the model, which he rejects, with the condition of "no model;" as if somehow by not representing models we miraculously move to the freedom of representing no model, that is, free to represent *per se*, as a pure activity in its own right requiring no external incentive. The inference is that architecture has a legitimate reality of its own beyond its condition as a representative medium, and that its new job is to represent that reality. So, it has to swallow up the paradox; it has to acknowledge its reality as a mere representation but at the same time tell us about its dark side, its hidden reality that allows it to be a mere representation, by merely representing it. "It is a representation of itself, of its own values and internal experience."[13] Architecture as representation is asserted and denied in the same breath. But what can representation possibly mean in this rarefied context?

An architectural project illustrative of one possible answer to this question is Eisenman's 1985 Venice Biennale project for the Romeo and Juliet Castles in Montecchio Maggiore, near Verona, Italy. This project is an exercise in what Eisenman terms "scaling" – where the deliberate superimposition of varied and incompatible scales provides the means to "eschew the anthropocentric organizing principles of presence and origin."[14] Wherever the metaphysical "centrisms" (which Eisenman identifies here as site, program and representation) seem like they might take hold and begin to direct the course of the design towards a sense of wholeness or completeness, Eisenman activates the mutually dependent "destabilizing agents" of scaling, which are discontinuity, recursivity and self-similarity.[15]

Discontinuity asserts the viability of "absence" as a valid organizing principle undermining the privileged status of "presence." By this, Eisenman means that all forms present in perceptual experience contain more than that simple presence – they implicitly carry traces of where they have come from and where they are going to, which dissolve the primacy of where they are at present. Thus the textual entity or sign is conceived in terms of its movement through meaning, from one signification and on to the next, rather than its movement towards meaning where it might suffer the delusion of coming to a halt by its overwhelming pertinence to a particular situation. This aspect of scaling is manifest most blatantly by the description of the general character of the project as "quarry" and "palimpsest," where the site becomes both a pseudo-archaeological excavation and an inscriptional tablet. The site is reduced to a mere enabling functionary, one layer amidst a superimposition of many other planimetric, formal structures such as, for example, the plan of Verona, the plan of the cemetery at Verona, the plan of Juliet's tomb, the plan of the church of Montecchio, the plans of the two castles and so on; in fact, the site remains always a site, for Eisenman never allows it to become a setting or a place.

Recursivity and self-similarity are described respectively as confronting origin and representation. Recursivity, Eisenman says, is a serial elaboration of self-same forms, for instance, the square divided into four squares again and again. Self-similarity involves the analogical comparison of formal structures, not by way of geometric similarity, but by a juxtaposition of "significance." For example, the walls of Romeo's castle are self-similar to the walls of Verona. The significances which underpin the drawing of such analogies arise from Eisenman's structural analysis of the Romeo and Juliet story. In the manner of Claude Lévi-Strauss he singles out the main structural relationships embodied in the literary narrative as "division," "union" and "the dialectical relationship of division and union." Then, he searches for analogous physical structures, structures from other forms of text which are "similar," such as the "wall," with which to create a kind of counterpoint which may be repeated into an "infinite series of infinite superpositions." The manner in which these superpositions are presented takes the form of a series of overlaid and inscribed "glasses" which perpetrate and enhance the surface-level nature of Eisenman's whole operation. None of these glasses carries a definitive representation; each must be taken as just one of many possible, ongoing manifestations. As Eisenman states:

> There is something yet to be written before the reality of the site of Montecchio, and after the fictions of the Verona of Romeo and Juliet. Here architecture does not close or unify, but rather opens and disperses, fragments and destabilizes.[16]

Eisenman incorporates structures from literature, from cartography, and from planimetric drawing, and as structures, where text becomes the common denominator, he can mercilessly and endlessly throw them together in this way or that, that way or this, like a child with its feet in a pond marvelling at the ripples it can create as they diverge and disperse across the surface of the water, bemused by the fact that more and more can be made by a simple reflex of the toes. The primacy that Eisenman ascribes to the rippling surface structures negates both the producer (architect or child) and the receptacle that holds the water (the hollow in the earth). To deny the recognition of these as extra-textual phenomena does not necessarily purify the architectural discourse by removing extraneous influence, as Eisenman imagines; rather, it nullifies architectural discourse by removing its power of reference towards these very things.

The tragedy of Romeo and Juliet is a tragedy for us; the narrative opens us onto a dramatic combination of human events which carry us fully into the tragic scenario. The tragedy of Eisenman's project for the Romeo and Juliet Castles lies in its lack of tragedy, created by its relinquishment of human involvement, its denial of the possibilities of narrative reinterpretation, of retelling the story; and by the conversion of the existing narrative into the linguistic structures that are enclosed within it. For it is not the structural condition of, for example, "division" that carries the full weight of tragic human significance; it is the turn of events, the unexpected consequences of actions, the impossibility of romantic fulfilment and so on, in which "division" may, after the fact, be said to reside.

To adopt and readopt changing positions within the eternal flux of signification evokes, to my mind, a desperate sense of utter futility, a kind of impotence of language operating in a context where all the important questions of humanity seem trivialized, or at least levelled to a common neutralized field where they lie in wait, to be taken up and put down without any sense of genuine concern, in fact where concern is treated with suspicion. Deconstruction, the sign of the conception of language promoted by Derrida and Eisenman, assumes that signification, the agency of communication among humans, predates our taking up of its operations and is, itself, responsible for providing all notions of being, identity, presence, world, now revealed to us as falsely reliable propositions upon which to engender discourse. Delusions of identity are here understood as a symptom of an hereditary disease called signification.

Traditionally, creative activity can be understood as the production of a work, where that work is a representation of reality; not a secondary replication, but a re-presentation which gives us more from that reality than we were initially open to (before the work was made available to our experience). Eisenman is not really very interested in the manifold reality which traditional representation represents; he is more interested in asking representation to look inside itself (in other words, to cast its gaze upon one particular aspect of that manifold reality that is taken up by the phenomenon "representation") and to use its own activity to bring into view a few of its own home truths.

In this sense we can see that traditional representation is never in fact denied (though Eisenman seems to think that it is), rather, its traditional limitless scope of activity in working with reality is reduced by Eisenman to an activity within a limited portion of that reality, that is, the portion which is always already "filled up" with the "act" of representation. The futility of such a reduction of reality by this radical focus of attention, as the all new self-justifying, self-scrutinizing representative activity, is never apparent to him, and yet it seems such a simple oversight. Any representative activity (such as creating art) involves not only the representative medium but also the person who enacts the representative act. To turn the representative act on itself (that is, creating Eisenman's kind of art) in order to uncover its nature must, in order to succeed, encompass in its revelation all of its dimensions – the dimension of the deep organizing structures which might now make themselves visible for scrutiny, and the inseparable dimension of the involved, enacting subject. Eisenman looks for the key to unlocking the self-realization of representation in the product of its action alone, that is, in the structures as they are or as they become visible. But the product is only the product after all! Where does the enacting subject fit in? Is the subject diminished to the status of a mere residual trace beneath the dominance of the structure of her or his product? It is on this question of the anomaly of the subject in the whole idea of the autonomous representative possibilities of architecture that the discussion plunges into deep "deconstructionist" waters, and Derrida's intent to capsize the transcendental identity of the subject once and for all, submerging it beneath the overwhelming priority of language.

SOMEBODY NAMED DERRIDA

The shifting terrain across which Derrida tentatively steps back and forth is perhaps a mere vibration across the more rigid lattices of structuralism which in no way extends the domain of the structuralist position any more than it moves beyond. For Derrida, it seems, takes the same lattices but slides and shimmies them over each other to see what interesting intersections, patterns and gaps might occur which the lattices themselves cannot account for.[17]

As in structuralism, Derrida's feet are in fact firmly rooted to the ground of Saussurian linguistics. Derrida adopts the fundamental propositions of Saussure's systemization of language, that of the arbitrariness and differential character of signs, together with the twofold make-up of the sign itself as concept (signified) and expression (signifier):

> It was Saussure who first of all set forth the arbitrariness of signs and the differential character of signs as principles of general semiology and particularly of linguistics . . . Arbitrariness can occur only because the system of signs is constituted by the differences between the terms, and not by their fullness. The elements of signification function not by virtue of the compact force of their cores but by the network of oppositions that distinguish them and relate them to one another.[18]

Utilizing the logic implicit in this systemization Derrida makes what seems to be a simple deduction: that once the field of differences has been acknowledged as the prerequisite for the production of any kind of meaning (that is, signification) there can be no "first term," no originary sign before all signs, because it simply would not be able to function as a sign on its own. If it is our peculiarly human predicament to be the perpetrators of meaning and that we can come to know ourselves only through its articulation, the logic suggests convincingly that we are in it from the start – in language, in the sign system – and that there can be no conceivable prior condition to our humanity. We are circumscribed by the system from the outset. From here on in, Derrida accepts and enforces the total internalization of our possibilities for generating meaning in a way which does little more than echo the structuralist's closure of language as "an autonomous entity of internal dependencies."[19] Thus, if meaning, and therefore our knowledge of ourselves and the world, is produced wholly by the machinations of a self-sustained sign system, Derrida wishes to delve deeper into its mechanism to discover the nature of its motivation; and he finds it in the so called non-concept of "differance."

> What we note as "differance" will thus be the movement of "play" that produces (and not by something that is simply an activity) these differences, these effects of difference. This

does not mean that the differance which produces differences is before them in a simple and in itself unmodified and indifferent present. Differance is the non-full, non-simple "origin;" it is the structured and differing origin of differences.[20]

Differance, then, overturns any dwindling hopes that we might have clung to that there is a world outside language, and that we have a "being" beyond the linguistic system. For Derrida, differance categorically erases the possibility of such a being. There can be no self-presence. There can be no self-identity which knows itself truly as itself because there must always be the "trace" that institutes difference.

> [The subject] becomes a signifying subject only by entering into the system of differences.
> [D]ifferance is older than the ontological difference or the truth of Being. In this age it can be called the play of traces. It is a trace that no longer belongs to the horizon of Being but one whose sense of Being is borne and bound by this play ... There is no support to be found and no depth to be had for this bottomless chessboard where being is set in play.[21]

The denial of the world and the denial of the identity of the signifying subject undermine the conditions for any authentic ontology.

Derrida's argument in this respect is further fuelled by his observations on the way language in use tends to comprise fundamentally of a "radical absence," conjoined with a notion of ultimate "iterability."[22] Writing, in the conventional sense, exhibits these characteristics rather more blatantly than say, speech, primarily due to its graphic permanence (this is not to say that they are any less present in speech). First, written signs embody the function of signification, which remains present in the graphic inscription even in the absence of a receiver, or indeed of the author. The readability of a piece of writing always remains. In this way, writing inscribes in its very structure the ultimate "death" or "possibility of the death" of the writer or reader and therefore the conclusion of their inessentiality to the nature of the text.[23] It is this capacity which Derrida prescribes to language in general, that is, its iterability, its repeatability for the perpetual absentee, which gives rise to the notion of "arche-writing"[24] as this fundamental function, this interactive operation of all linguistic phenomena. In this sense, writing is always for nobody; that which is written is never exhausted by the moment of its inscription, and as such the written sign takes on a life of its own, it carries with it "a force that breaks with its context, that is, with the collectivity of presences organizing the moment of its inscription."[25] By virtue of the fact that "No context can entirely enclose it"[26] the possibilities for writing (in Derrida's extended sense) can be pursued within a new freedom, a context-free environment where all that matters is the reproduction of meanings in juxtaposition with other meanings: the play of traces and of traces upon traces; sense teasing itself and answerable to no higher, transcendental, repressive authority other than the non-authority of differance. In other words, the world becomes a text (or rather we come to realize that it always had been one), and we relinquish our misguided dealings with worldly things and take up "positions" in the chain of eternal textuality, with no horizon, no beyond – just the interminable whirring of its own internal motivity.

We left Eisenman making representations of the representing activity, or rather, creating an independent discourse in architectural language – independent in terms of referent and by implication independent of author and receiver, and with architecture as an "open-ended tactic" which can stimulate a "pure reading."[27] Of course, the similarity with Derrida's notion of writing as "blind tactics," and as a "strategy without finality"[28] is no mere accident. The parallelism between the later writings of Eisenman and those of Derrida is of sufficient magnitude to justify a critique of their mutual disposition as one. By grafting one to the other, the two-headed monster of Deconstruction can be shown to be fundamentally inadequate without its hermeneutical body.

QUESTIONING THE ANNULMENT OF THE TRANSCENDENTAL SIGNIFIED

> The appearance of a literature which takes its own operations as its theme introduces the illusion that the structural model exhausts the understanding of language.[29]

Having situated deconstruction firmly within the structuralist tradition, the extension of the hermeneutic critique of structuralism can be articulated. It is founded on one primary disagreement, that is, the problem of the distinction between the reality of a world and the reality of a text – a distinction which, as noted above, has been erased by the logic of differance. Where Derrida situates a text within a chain of intra-textual traces, Paul Ricoeur situates it in an extra-textual world. This extra-textual world in no way denies the former its validity but, rather, complements it with a dimension which sustains and enlivens its very necessity. This dimension has been called the "referentiality of discourse."[30] Ricoeur will insist that, following German logician Gottlob Frege, "[t]o understand a text is to follow its movement from sense to reference, from what it says, to what it talks about,"[31] to open up what a language expression literally "says" to what it metaphorically "says it about."

However, Derrida will insist that the movement of a text is in fact solely from sense to another sense, and as such does not talk about anything. For Ricoeur, "to say something" stays with the sheer sense or "ideality" of an utterance; a realm which he believes the structuralist is limited to by the nature and method of her or his enquiry. But discourse, as the general motivation for language, is a genuine and deliberate attempt "to say something about something,"[32] to move the whole signifying apparatus towards a reference, a reality beyond the mere internal contingencies of linguistic structure. Ricoeur sees the relevance and freedom of language in its limitless, active, metaphorical dimension of referentiality, whereas Derrida sees its freedom in a relief from the repression of this transcendence by way of the limitless internal conjugations of sense. In this way Derrida seeks to repossess, on behalf of language, what we have wrongly assumed to be our own, namely, the pursuit of meaning.

In one sense, Derrida's motives can be viewed as a reaction in the midst of the current, late twentieth century crisis in philosophy, as most of the fulfilling aspects of our lives are increasingly modified by an all engulfing technologization. The critique of this predicament generally tends to focus on the misplaced Enlightenment con- viction in the primacy of an all constituting subject over and above an external objective world. Derrida's answer is to attempt to dissolve the primary manifestation of this subject, that is, language (the means by which the human being comes to know itself), into a relational system of differences and oppositions, thus undermining the legitimacy of a subject's self-imposed status. In order to stop us speaking about ourselves with an over-confident air of primacy (the way science still speaks about the world) our means of speaking is to be reappropriated, thanks to Derrida, by the means itself; the assumed, traditional systematic self-sufficiency of language is to be reinstated.

However, such a respect for the integrity of language as a way of cutting the Enlightenment subject down to size endeavours to achieve its aim only by subsuming the subject within its own construct, by putting the subject "literally" into language and denying it an existence outside that language. Of course, the fact that language is a human construct that Derrida will deny, for a human is a "function of language,"[33] but to confound the constituting subject with transcendental identity, as he seems to be doing, and thus to wrap his argument totally around the notion of removing the repressive character of such a subject, is to deny our validity as beings. This is not to collude with the Enlightenment all-constituting subject, far from it. This is to grant, only, that our identity as beings in a world be permitted a hearing.

Ricoeur points out that dispensing with the "subject as a transparent cogito does not mean that we have to dispense with all forms of subjectivity."[34] Hermeneutics insists that the idea of language as the agent of transparency is erroneous given the transcendent condition of human being-in-the-world. The subject is never a discrete entity in a position over and against the world, it is rooted in a relation of reciprocal entwinement finding expression through the creative use of language by means of "the detour of countless mediations – signs, symbols, texts and human praxis itself."[35] It is these existing and persisting cultural mediations that are taken up and transformed by the creative engagement of participants in a culture, and which, by way of the temporal dynamic of continual reinterpretation, constitutes its "traditions." The abolition of any notion of subjective identity whatsoever, suggested by the deconstructive enterprise, negates one player in the dialectic relation of human being and world. The accompanying abolition of any notion of a world-context beyond the circumspective clutches of linguistic phenomena completes the collapse of insurmountable, lived reality towards the introspective, systemized reality of the text.

QUESTIONING THE IDEA OF THE SYSTEMATIC NATURE OF LANGUAGE

That things differ in the world of our experiences is not to be denied. Our world is never perceived in terms of an all-pervading homogeneity, so it would seem reasonable to name the multifarious aspects of our perceptions differently, to allow for distinction.

However, Saussure pounced on this particular aspect, distinction, and with all the logical force of scientific method made it the essential systemizing characteristic of language. But surely, to subjugate the names we give to things to a redefinition as "signs," which indicate by way of combining a mental concept with an arbitrarily related physical signifier, undermines the sheer primacy of our naming activity as an ontological grounding for our situatedness in the world. The subjugation implies that names – now called signs – are more or less disposable after use; we can cast them aside and gather up a few more as required, which in turn will be discarded. In this sense, the name/sign is merely a kind of tool for the job of signification, as if the job itself were a finite process with a preconceivable result, a predeterminable objective, in respect of which we can have full confidence in the complete adequacy of the tool for the execution of the task. The tool's usefulness has been assessed with regard to the job-at-hand. But is this not an impoverished view of the nature of language? Surely, signification, the generation of meaning, cannot be so fully and completely conceived of that its "process" can be exhaustively accounted for. Indeed, can the Saussurian language machine of arbitrariness and differentiality suffice?

Signification through the complex grammatical combination of names, verbs, conjunctives and so on, into the sentences of discourse, seems unfathomable in terms of potential output and yet, as Chomsky wondrously declares, every adult speaker/hearer can comprehend meaning in any of these infinite possible combinations.[36] This suggests to him that although the products of language may be innumerable, the generative principles or rules must be finite since these rules must correspond to the characteristic of commonality between all of us speaker/hearers. Chomsky set himself the task of the accumulation and definition of these generative rules. His belief that such rules could be defined, that the job of signification could be systemized to the degree that we have full control over its every aspect, is merely a late symptomatic development in the general trend of post-Saussurian linguistic theory, a trend which was contemporaneously set up as the exemplary model for so called semiological investigation: the projection of linguistic theory across all culturally meaningful phenomena, and of course, the advent of structuralism.

Derrida has been labelled a poststructuralist, possibly because he appears to be recognizing and dealing with the limitations of structuralism: the stagnancy of its system. However, I would be inclined to see him as more of a fidgety structuralist who refuses to sit still: a structuralism on castors. Lévi-Strauss and others have admirably administered the analytical structuralist apparatus in redefining our cultural awareness in terms of structure, but, as Ricoeur points out, its enterprise is only "legitimate and shielded from all criticism as long as it remains conscious of its conditions of validity and thus of its limits."[37] Derrida seems to react with an awareness of these limits but fails to move beyond them.

Ricoeur has indicated that an understanding of language must take account of what he calls a "surplus of meaning;" that the structures uncovered by structuralist analysis can never exhaust the potentiality for meaning of the segment of language undergoing that analysis, and that a surplus always persists: "a reservoir of meaning ready to be used again in other structures."[38] This reservoir of surplus meaning may be, therefore, without structure but it is certainly not without order, for it is the domain of the "already ordered" – the domain of "structuration" – that which allows the production of structured meaning. This is not to say that the produced structured meaning is the totalized and complete embodiment of "intent," that is, "the wanting to say;" the so structured statement is always destined to be inadequate, but it is our only means of uncovering that prestructured reality, reality on its way to structure. Structures relate to signification, structuring relates to "signifying intention:"

> linguistic laws are not what we attempt to totalize in order to understand ourselves; rather, we are concerned with the meaning of the words, for which linguistic laws serve as the instrumental mediations, forever unconscious. I seek to understand myself by taking up anew the meaning of the words of all men.[39]

What part are we to play in the interdictory manoeuvres of deconstruction? For Eisenman we are contaminators. For five hundred years we have plagued architecture with our presence. The "modern" sensibility demands our exile; purged of our scurrilous activities, the truly modern can arise in the pristine formal purity towards which Le Corbusier strove, but whose degenerate "classical" sensibility could never permit him to attain. And yet, Eisenman tells us, he is not a formalist or a reductionist; he genuinely wants us to "read" his work and to enjoy that reading and the meaning it projects. He is insistent that the pleasure must come from reading alone and that the joy of uncovering the "new" must be wholly associated with our synchronicity with his work through reading; we move with the text as it moves itself, ahead of us all the time. But we are denied interpretation, that is, real hermeneutical interpretation. We are not to appropriate his text, to make it our own. However, as Ricoeur says:

> We can, as readers, remain in the suspense of the text, treating it as a worldless and authorless object; in this case, we explain the text in terms of its internal relations, its structure. On the other hand, we can lift the suspense and fulfil the text . . . restoring it to living communication; in this case, we interpret the text. These two possibilities both belong to reading, and reading is the dialectic of these two attitudes.[40]

It is evident that reading for Ricoeur is not the same as reading for Eisenman. There are two sides to Ricoeur's dialectic of reading: structure and appropriation. There are two sides to Eisenman's dialectic of reading: structure and another structure – it is "a dialectical relationship within the evolution of form itself."[41] Similarly, there are two sides to Derrida's dialectic: the text undergoing deconstruction and the other text undergoing deconstruction. Eisenman leaves no doubt as to what it is he intends when he says:

> The new "object" must have the capacity to reveal itself first of all as a text, as a reading event . . . But further, knowing how to decode is no longer important; simply, language in this context is no longer a code to assign meanings (that this means that). The activity of reading is first and foremost in the recognition of something as a language (that it is). Reading, in this sense, makes available a level of "indication" rather than a level of meaning or expression.[42]

The traditional act of reading is thus drastically restated; we read in order to know that we are reading and absolutely no more. It is simply

> a displacement of man away from the centre of his world. He is no longer viewed as an "originating agent." Objects are seen as ideas independent of man. In this context, man is a discursive function among complex and already-formed systems of language, which he witnesses but does not constitute.[43]

The full contradictory nature of Eisenman's proclamations shines forth in a statement such as this. It seems that language constitutes humanity, that we somehow owe our very existence to the omnipresence of its system.

So where do Derrida and Eisenman situate themselves in language and in the world? It has already been intimated that, for them, the world is a text, so the question of situatedness in the world never arises. Language as text is the full and complete scope of their world, not fixed and immutable but in perpetual flux, a shifting textual quicksand. It is but a gesture in reaction to the constricting positivism and foundationalism stemming from the seventeenth century. A mistrust in the adequacy of our words and concepts in capturing the truth about the world has led the deconstructionist to dispense with the world and therefore with the problem of veritability in language. What has always been the ineluctable background, the world, is parenthesized; its significance in the deconstructionist project is negligible. If anything like "truth" exists it will be a condition and quality of our mode of articulation in language. The truth value of a reality antecedent to our articulations is invalidated and replaced by a search for a truth value simultaneously internal to and yet negated by articulation:

> By way, then, of exposing the deforming power of what we say, of whatever we say, deconstruction enables us to recover what cannot be said, also what makes possible our saying whatever we say, and by doing that, we grasp the nameless wisdom – not the articulate knowledge – of the unavoidability of not saying.[44]

The deconstructionist asks, what does articulation suppress; what does it leave out when it makes a statement? But not, what is it that is left over in the world and therefore left unsaid by this particular statement? Rather, their concern is for what is not allowed to be said during this act of saying, which enables what is said to be articulated. This is what they call the "hidden agenda," the "radically unsayable,"[45] which their pursuit is entirely directed towards. This is a wish to uncover what cannot be said and to leave it unsaid – a kind of perpetually frustrated teleology.

By contrast, the hermeneutician, the interpreter, does not interest her or himself in the unsayable as the essential background to saying, or as the "non-originary origin"[46] of language. For her or him language is simply a matter of saying more, set against the horizon of the sayable, that is, the articulable, in the rich and demanding context of a representable world. Language is useless unless it is given the opportunity to speak about something; its power is not about deforming or deceiving but about representing, without which it falls back into a state of semantic sterility, of inert, self-signifying, formalized constructions leading "know-where."

> The task of hermeneutics is to charter the unexplored resources of the to-be-said on the basis of the already-said. Imagination never resides in the unsaid.[47]

To be able to put oneself in a world, to open up a world to oneself – this is the transcendence that deconstructionists abhor. They deny themselves the pleasure of opening up a world beyond their wildest expectations, they remain afflicted by a kind of linguistic agoraphobia which cancels out the metaphoric possibilities of language for fear of opening onto unexplored terrain, with an accompanying sense of alienation. Through the structures of linguistic commonality, that we all as humans share, they propose to confine us to a monologue of syntactic juxtaposition, an internal haemorrhage of linguistic sense.

It seems that when the structural mechanisms involved in the generation of meaning are given equal status to meaning itself, the very notion of meaningfulness dissolves. Meaningful for whom and in relation to what? This question becomes no longer relevant. Ultimately, the identity of individuals and of cultures will be exposed as nothing but the erroneous aberrations of a misplaced trust in the power of language. A global neutrality will ensue, excited only by the temporary titillation of linguistic pattern-making performed by itinerant jugglers, eventually falling into silence. Why speak if the chatter of words remains just a chatter of words?

References

1   Laurence Sterne, *The Life and Opinions of Tristram Shandy* (Harmondsworth: Penguin, 1967), pp. 397–8.

2   Peter Eisenman, "Notes on Conceptual Architecture – Towards a Definition," *Casabella*, n. 359 (1971), p. 55.

3   Peter Eisenman, "Cardboard Architecture," *Casabella*, n. 374 (1973), p. 24.

4   Eisenman, "Cardboard Architecture," p. 24.

5   Echoes can be heard of early twentieth century Russian avant-garde Futurist poets whose trans-rational tongue, or 'zaum' poetry, dismantled the form and sense of words in order to release the potential for original expression submerged beneath the sedimentation of habitual use.

6   Peter Eisenman, "The End of the Classical," *Perspecta*, n. 21 (1984), p. 156.

7   Eisenman, "End of the Classical," p. 156.

8   Eisenman, "End of the Classical," p. 156.

9   Eisenman, "End of the Classical," p. 156.

10 Eisenman, "End of the Classical," p. 156.

11 Eisenman, "End of the Classical," p. 156.

12 Eisenman, "End of the Classical," p. 156.

13   Eisenman, "End of the Classical," p. 156.

14   Peter Eisenman, *Moving Arrows, Eros and other Errors* (London: Architectural Association, 1986).

15   Eisenman, *Moving Arrows, Eros and other Errors.*

16   Eisenman, *Moving Arrows, Eros and other Errors.*

17   The analogy of the lattice seems particularly appropriate in relation to the work of Bernard Tschumi at parc de La Villette, Paris, and the superimposition of grids as a generating technique for the placement of the so called "folies." The question of the attainability of "arbitrariness" is never adequately answered by this project.

18   Jacques Derrida, "Differance," *Speech and Phenomena* (Evanston, IL: Northwestern University Press, 1973), p. 139.

19   Louis Hjelmslev's definition of structure. Paul Ricoeur, "Structure, Word, Event," *The Conflict of Interpretations* (Evanston, IL: Northwestern University Press, 1974), p. 82.

20   Derrida, "Differance," p. 141.

21   Derrida, "Differance," pp. 146 and 154.

22   Derrida, "Signature Event Context," *Glyph*, n. 1 (1977), p. 180.

23   "To be what it is, all writing must, therefore, be capable of functioning in the radical absence of every empirically determined receiver in general. And this absence is not a continuous modification of presence, it is a rupture in presence, the 'death' or the possibility of the 'death' of the receiver inscribed in the structure of the mark . . . To write is to produce a mark that will constitute a sort of machine which is productive in turn, and which my future disappearance will not, in principle, hinder in its functioning, offering things and itself to be read and to be rewritten." Derrida, "Signature Event Context," p. 180.

24   "This arche-writing, although its concept is invoked by the themes of 'the arbitrariness of the sign' and of difference, cannot and can never be recognized as the 'object of a science'. It is that very thing which cannot let itself be reduced to the form of 'presence.'" Jacques Derrida, *Of Grammatology* (Baltimore, MD: Johns Hopkins University Press, 1974), pp. 56–7.

25   Derrida, "Signature Event Context," p. 182.

26   Derrida, "Signature Event Context," p. 182.

27   Eisenman, "End of the Classical," pp. 170 and 171, n.23.

28   Derrida, "Differance," p. 135

29   Ricoeur, "Structure, Word, Event," p. 85.

30   Paul Ricoeur, "The Hermeneutical Function of Distanciation," *Hermeneutics and the Human Sciences* (Cambridge: Cambridge University Press, 1981), p. 140.

31   Paul Ricoeur, "The Model of the Text: Meaningful Action Considered as Text," *Hermeneutics and the Human Sciences*, p. 218.

32   Ricoeur, "Structure, Word, Event," p. 84.

33 Derrida, "Differance," p. 145. A conflict seems to occur, however, within Derrida's own thoughts on this matter; where he characteristically asserts the indubitable necessity for the notion of the "subject" in order to validate its subsequent submersion into the language system. For example: "I believe that the centre is a function, not a being – a reality, but a function. And this function is absolutely indispensable. The subject is absolutely indispensable. I do not destroy the subject; I situate it. That is to say, I believe that at a certain level both of experience and of philosophical and scientific discourse one cannot get along without the notion of subject. It is a question of knowing where it comes from and how it functions. Therefore I keep the concept of centre, which I explained was indispensable, as well as that of the subject". Jacques Derrida, "Structure, Sign, Play," Richard Macksey and Eugenio Donato, *The Language of Criticism and the Sciences of Man: The Structuralist Controversy* (Baltimore, MD: Johns Hopkins University Press, 1970), pp. 271–2.

34 Paul Ricoeur, "The Creativity of Language," Richard Kearney, *Dialogues with Contemporary Continental Thinkers* (Manchester: Manchester University Press, 1984), p. 32.

35 Ricoeur, "Creativity of Language," p. 32. Maurice Merleau-Ponty makes a similar observation in "Preobjective Being: the Solipsist World," *The Visible and the Invisible* (Evanston, IL: Northwestern University Press, 1968), p. 162: "It is by opposing to the experience of things the spectre of another experience that would not involve things that we force experience to say more than it said. It is by passing through the detour of names, by threatening the things with our non-recognition of them, that we finally accredit objectivity, self-identity, positivity, plenitude, if not as their own principle, at least as the condition of their possibility for us."

36 "Having mastered a language, one is able to understand an indefinite number of expressions that are new to one's experience, that bear no simple physical resemblance and are in no simple way analogous to the expressions that constitute one's linguistic experience; and one is able, with greater or less facility, to produce such expressions on an appropriate occasion, despite their novelty and independently of detectable stimulus configurations, and to be understood by others who share this mysterious ability. The normal use of language is, in this sense, a creative activity. This creative aspect of normal language use is one fundamental factor that distinguishes human language from any known system of animal communication." Noam Chomsky, *Language and Mind* (New York: Harcourt Brace Jovanovich, 1968), p. 100.

37 Paul Ricoeur, "Structure and Hermeneutics," *The Conflict of Interpretations*, pp. 38–9. In a critical review of Eisenman's "Fin d'Ou T Hou S" exhibition (1985), Robin Evans recognises this problem. "[I]t is not difficult to imagine a situation in which the subject of study would be erroneously identified with the reason for studying it. That is to say, there would come a time when, because structure had been dwelt on for so long, a

structure would be assumed to contain all the properties of language if it exhibited a system of relations something like that of language. At which stage of development structuralism could be said to have consumed its own source of inspiration." Robin Evans, "Not to be Used for Wrapping Purposes," *AA Files*, n. 10 (1985), p. 69.

38   Ricoeur, "Structure and Hermeneutics" p. 47.

39   Ricoeur, "Structure and Hermeneutics" pp. 39 and 52.

40   Paul Ricoeur, "What is a Text? Explanation and Understanding," *Hermeneutics and the Human Sciences*, p. 152.

41   Peter Eisenman, "Post-Functionalism," editorial, *Oppositions*, n. 6 (1976).

42   Eisenman, "End of the Classical," p. 172.

43   Eisenman, "Post-Functionalism."

44   Joseph Margolis, "Deconstruction or, The Mystery of the Mystery of the Text," Hugh J. Silverman and Don Ihde, *Hermeneutics and Deconstruction* (New York: State University of New York Press, 1985), p. 141.

45   Gayatry Chakravorty Spivak, interview with John Searle, Channel 4 television (UK, 1988).

46   Nina Hofer, *FIN D'OU T HOU S* (London: Architectural Association, 1985), p. 5.

47   Ricoeur, "Creativity of Language," p. 25.

Tendency 2

Theorised interpretation

Chapter 6
A fitting fetish: the interiors of the Maison de Verre
Sarah Wigglesworth

6.1 Maison de Verre, Paris: front facade from the *court d'honneur* gateway (1963)

The Maison de Verre has become a powerful icon in the history of modern architecture. Built in Paris between the years 1929 and 1931 to the designs of Pierre Chareau at a time when he was in partnership with Bernard Bijvoet, it was intended as the future home for the Dalsaces, a newly-wed couple. It combined a gynaecology practice on the ground floor for Dr Dalsace and the family home above. The building has been acknowledged as an icon of modernism because of its use of prefabricated glass block walling and its open-plan interior furnished with purpose-designed fittings and sophisticated household gadgetry. While it caused a stir at the time of its erection, it was not until Kenneth Frampton's "rediscovery" of the Maison de Verre, made known in his *Perspecta* article of 1969,[1] that its enduring message was consolidated. Frampton's team visited the house when it was still occupied by the original clients and not easily accessible.[2] They made detailed studies, a comprehensive photographic record and a ciné film. The publication of the survey and the detail drawings of its many working parts captured the imagination of a future generation of "hi-tech" architects[3] and secured the place of the building in the history of modern architecture as a literal evocation of Le Corbusier's concept of "a machine for living in." The house interior, especially, has been treated like a cover girl, its image re-presented for consumption in glossy publications throughout the world, and architects today remain seduced by the aura these images convey.[4] Moreover, critics and historians have, by and large, continued to accept this interpretation, which seems to have become a screen veiling other readings and has affirmed its message as an ideology.

It is the Maison de Verre's industrial aesthetic – signifier of the spirit of early modern age – that has made the building an icon of the early modern era. However, it is a connection suggested in the building between the female body and the architecture which this chapter explores, and does so by focusing on the building's interior. I argue that the interior fittings have taken on the characteristic of fetish objects, seducing architects with their forms and surface. However, in keeping with the nature of the fetish, the fitting fetish actually conceals a deeper collective fear – fear of social unrest (in particular the behaviour of woman in a period of female emancipation), and fear of the architect's own ineffectualness. By using the Maison de Verre as a specific example in which a number of issues implicated in modernism are condensed, I show how the ideology of modern architecture represses particular concerns, and in so doing, point the way towards a reappraisal of a neglected aspect of architectural knowledge.

I approach this subject first and foremost as a practising architect, but one who is interested in the dialogue between ideas and designing. I am not an architectural historian and cannot claim that this approach is either comprehensive or fully researched. The ideas contained in this text are the result of ten years of teaching (by myself and others) and they draw on critiques of prevailing architectural ideologies, aiming to reshape an alternative (particularly female) architectural perspective. I am interested in finding out the significance of feminist, psychoanalytic and visual theory (issues which have been somewhat neglected in architectural discourse but which seem central now to cultural discussions at large) for our understanding of architecture. My aim is to help to locate architecture in a broader cultural context which enriches our knowledge of our own art. In raising such issues to consciousness we expand our perceptions as designers and point to new sites of departure in design.

To investigate the fitting fetish, I draw on theories of modernism, exploring in particular references to architecture and buildings as "natural" organisms; in this context, both the city/body and the building/body analogy is made clear. I also draw on feminism and film theory to draw out the parallels between the female body as a site of both desire and fear and the mission of the modern architect to control, through representation and technology, the new interior. The Maison de Verre, with its explicit programme for both housing and curing the female body, provides a specific instance of this project in the history of modernism. In addressing society's social and aesthetic problems, the architect in that era proposed radical "surgical" intervention within the city, but also moved the locus of attention to the wholesale redesign of the interior of the home for the first time. The shift from outside to inside resonates also in myths relating to female sexuality and fear of the mysteries of the interior of the female body. Here, too, the work of the gynaecologist seems relevant. The argument shows how a technical aesthetic is apparently united in a programme to both access and cure internal female maladies and to reinvent the home. However, in achieving the status of fetish objects, the product of this mission – the fittings designed specially for the building – can be read as attesting to the presence of repressed anxieties. I argue that they point to a crucial issue for architects: the futility of desiring control over those who occupy and use their buildings.

THE CITY

In the period when the Maison de Verre was under construction, the city was regarded as in crisis and architects turned their attention to this issue as one of their legitimate concerns.[5] Anxieties about the city's problems were both practical and ideological. They developed the nineteenth century's preoccupation with public health (sanitation, disease, overcrowding) and added a new agenda: mobility. The presence of the motor car intensified the perceived crisis. The automobile offered the potential for speed (associated with futuristic technology, excitement and sexuality), and became an iconic and seductive motif in modernism, largely through the Futurists' legacy.[6] But the reality was that the historical city made speed and mobility impossible, and challenged the spirit of freedom and control to which modernism aspired. Le Corbusier condemned Paris, "with its obsolete centre, impenetrable by cars, completely jammed, surrounded by an immense undisciplined suburb dramatically cut up, or rather inorganic, unorganised."[7]

While Ebenezer Howard had relied on a geometric organisational diagram for his Garden City, later exponents of the urban project drew on an anatomical or biological analogy. Le Corbusier, for instance, described the city as a living organism, illustrating his analogy with a series of sketches of the (male) human body:

> Nature, the eternal lesson.
> Architecture, town planning, determination of functions, classification of functions, hierarchy.
> Architecture, town planning = impeccable biology.[8]

Using words like "organic," "organised" and "organisation," Le Corbusier referred to a natural order which he understood as deliberate, rational and controlled. He believed human beings and natural objects demonstrated this sort of order and logic, which was inherently beautiful. Functional inefficiency, irrationality or excess were to be abjured on the basis that they contradicted nature. The intentional acts of the designer could rectify this ("Architecture, town planning = impeccable biology").

Le Corbusier pathologised the moribund city, describing how it could be revitalised through a process which mirrored the administration of a medical prescription with the architect/town planner playing the role of doctor. In the chapter entitled "Physic or Surgery" in his book *The City of Tomorrow*, Le Corbusier explained two solutions to the problem: radical excision of the offending urban tissue ("surgery") or the treatment of localised problems in a piecemeal fashion ("physic").

> The experience of the past answers: physic and the knife.
> Surgery must be applied at the city's centre.
> Physic must be used elsewhere.[9]

Even more explicitly:

> The conclusion is simple: in city planning "medical" solutions are a delusion; they resolve nothing, they are very expensive. Surgical solutions resolve![10]

The text's message was reinforced by photographs of large scale demolition and continued by listing historical examples of urban destruction and redevelopment to justify similar boldness in the face of contemporary problems. The city was regarded as dirty, worn out, congested and in a state of decay. It was an organism in need of purification and cleansing; Le Corbusier argued for the city's rejuvenation by combining a rational, geometrical organisation which he perceived as "natural" with the poetry of new, simple, forms in open space and sunlight.[11] The existing disorder required rationalising; ancient, dark, filthy buildings must be torn down and cut out and new, light, bright space be allowed to reign in their place. Technology was the key to this operation: the new architecture would be made possible through technology's intervention, since processes and actions which were formerly unpredictable could be brought under control and "disciplined" (that is, made to perform efficiently and reliably).[12]

The building of the Maison de Verre presents an uncanny parallel to this rhetoric, albeit on the scale of an individual building. The original plan was to tear down completely the existing *hotel particulier* which the client had acquired and erect a new edifice in its place. However, unable completely to demolish the building because of a sitting tenant in the top-floor apartment, Chareau cut out the offending tissue of the old, dark house and propped the apartment above, as though he were a surgeon holding open a wound. In the cavity he inserted a completely open-plan, clean, light, fully glazed space which was to become the home and workplace of the Dalsace family. The insertion remakes the old city in the image of rationality, expressed by the mass-produced regular, repetitive panels of the glass block facade. The light-flooded interior, apparently, is a symbol – both aesthetic and scientific – of the health of the modern city, the healthy skin revealing the healthy body. Family life is evidently open to scrutiny, and relations between the parts of this "organism" are laid bare like the internal organs of a patient during a medical examination.

Significantly, the skin of the building is trans-lucent, but not transparent. Its interior is in fact carefully veiled, denying visual inspection even at night when a limited visibility reveals shadows of people and furniture like an X-ray. The act of veiling reaffirms the zone of privacy which is the interior of the house and the gynaecology suite, and conjoins synergetically the body of the woman (patient) with the interior of the house. Not only does the medical metaphor surface again in this context, as Ludmilla Jordanova has pointed out, but so does the tension between surface and substance (exteriority and interiority) which, as Laura Mulvey has explained, focuses on the cinematic appropriation of female identity. In medicine, the act of unveiling is a metaphor for revealing nature, seeking invisible internal structures, clarifying and understand-ing them.[13] The idea of understanding as illumination identifies light as crucial to both the medical encounter and the conceptualisation of it, but this applies equally to cinematic representation, which itself relies on light to project images (along with

6.2 Maison de Verre: front facade at night (1963)

concealed messages). While the translucent glass wall does occasionally act as a back-projected screen producing shadowy images of the family life being enacted behind it, it also effectively masks the internal order of the home, locating it clearly in the realm of the concealed.

> Veiling implies secrecy. Women's bodies, and, by extension, female attributes, cannot be treated as fully public, something dangerous might happen, secrets be let out, if they were open to view. Yet in presenting something as inaccessible and dangerous an invitation to know and to possess is extended. The secrecy associated with female bodies is sexual and linked to the multiple associations between women and privacy.[14]

Mulvey has explained how the female body (exemplified by Pandora) provides a displacement for a number of different ideas and associations.

These associations, one feminine, the other secret, link further to the topography which splits femininity into an inside/outside polarisation. A mask-like surface enhances the concept of feminine beauty as an "outside," as artifice and masquerade, which conceals danger and deception. And lingering alongside is the structure of the fetish which, with its investment in eye-catching surface, distracts the gaze from the hidden wound on the female, or rather the mother's body.[15]

It is in the condensation of issues of the (mother's) body, interiority, surface and image that the interior design of the Maison de Verre becomes interesting. As the site of domesticity, the house is constructed as a feminine domain, and is a metaphor for the female body.[16] The house and its users are re-presented as idealised, glamorised icons of architecture and womanhood. Coincidentally, the Maison de Verre is also the place in which light and technical equipment are used to "cure" the interior. This applies to both the building and the female patient. Yet behind this explicit, visible agenda lie veiled a series of associations which are perhaps less comfortable. It is the mechanism of the veil concealing something fearful which I next explore.

THE MODERNIST PROJECT FOR THE INTERIOR

As part of the propaganda for a new architecture, Le Corbusier recognised the connection between urbanism and the housing problem, articulating his ideas in the chapters "Architecture or Revolution" and "Mass-production Houses" of his manifesto *Vers une Architecture*. His attention focused on the reinvention of the interior, which was one of the first lines of attack in reshaping society in the image of the current *zeitgeist* – the "machine age." The crucial connection between the individual and the social was articulated simply in his phrase: "A man = a dwelling; dwellings = a city."[17] Le Corbusier's collaborator in this mission was Charlotte Perriand; she had been gripped with Le Corbusier's rhetoric about the new interior and had already made personal experiments with a few pieces of furniture echoing similar sentiments. Perriand came to the attention of Le Corbusier, and was hired to design the new furniture which would complete the revolution in domestic design. Just like the historic city centre, the domestic interior was to be cleared of its mass of drab nineteenth century clutter, opened up and reorganised. Furniture was to be streamlined and standardised as an idea and in design. Based on his analysis of *besoin-types* (use-types), the mass of different domestic objects was to be categorised and rationalised ("Furniture is tools. And also servants"),[18] condensed into a set of standard parts: tables for working at and eating; chairs for eating and working; armchairs of different shapes for resting in different ways; and containers (*casiers*) based on filing cabinets for storage.[19] The condensation of *meubles-types* into a standardised set of space-defining and functionally responsive fixtures elevated ordinary furniture to the status of "household equipment."[20]

By making the reinvention of the domestic a modernist project, architecture explicitly extended its remit into the private sphere, uniting the project for a new society with a domestic revolution. This entailed a moral dimension – the avoidance of social turmoil: "the problem of the house is a problem of the epoch. The equilibrium of society today depends on it."[21] Such an idea brought together an aesthetic project with a social project; the control over women's spatial domain was crucial in ensuring its success. As a rule, women were granted a limited creative role in the design of the home but a clear distinction was drawn between the "professional" approach of male designers and the untutored and undisciplined "taste" exercised by women in the role of home-maker.[22] As part of his crusade against an aesthetic which did not conform to his ideology, Le Corbusier equated moral purity with visual purity.[23] The refinement of the domestic interior signified a moral purging; it went hand in hand with a disavowal of a "feminine" aesthetics.

The rendering of furniture and fittings in the image of industrial products or the machine as Le Corbusier envisaged repressed what were regarded as feminine characteristics – the cosy, the ornamental, the untutored, the non-essential – in the architectural interiors of modernism. It reinvented the home as an idealised, clean, rational, functional, essential, orderly open space, part of a grander urban vision. The new "poésie de l'équipage"[24] was apotropaic, since it recast the comfortable interior as a symbol of masculinity, expressing the power to ward off the danger of "undisciplined" aesthetics and unregulated social behaviour (including averting the fear of errant female sexuality)[25] by bringing them under the control of the image of masculine rationality, professionalism and order. This aspect of the house's contents also locates them in the role of fetish, pointing to Marx and the mechanism of the commodity fetish.

According to Marx, the secret of the commodity fetish is that under a surface gloss the eye of the beholder is distracted from the mechanism by which the object is produced.[26] Through the psychic process of disavowal and the literal means of displacement, reference to the social relations which produced the object can be erased and marked. In the Maison de Verre this works in two ways. The fitting draws attention to the fetish of industrial production, even though the objects were actually hand made, disavowing their true method of production. Crucially, the architect's alienation from the site of production ensures that the value of the commodity in which they trade is attained through an autonomous mechanism based on the fetishisation of the commodity. In this process, the commodity gains its value from the stimulus of manufactured associations and representations. In the Maison de Verre it is the association with the products of desire – sexualised images of chromed-steel redolent of cars, the streamlining of autos, ships and aeroplanes, as well as the presence of skin (in the form of leather and fur) – which assures the status of the commodity. Simultaneously, this process also seems to point up the dilemma in the modern architect's own alienation from the building site, and the need to hand down orders from a distant location in an office remote from the building site or factory.

6.3 Maison de Verre: interior of the Dalsaces' bedroom (1963)

Furthermore, in the context of the gynaecology suite, the process of production (the internal, "natural" workings of the female reproductive system) is actually hidden – not only literally, in that it takes place in the hidden sexual organs, but also monitored within the private spaces of the gynaecology suite. The mystery of reproduction is nevertheless represented through the concepts and equipment of science. Likewise, social relations between the doctor and his patient are discretely veiled physically by his tools and the architectural setting, but also because medical ethics demand complex rules of privacy.

HOUSE AS FURNITURE

With its unique programme uniting a domestic situation with a gynaecological practice, the Maison de Verre makes explicit the relationship between science, with its conceptualisation of and control over the (female) body, and architecture, with its own will to power over ordinary people (especially women). Frampton described the building as "a large furnishing element."[27] His phrase calls into question our categorisations concerning what is and is not architecture. One reading of his remark is that the house is a gigantic piece of furniture scaled-up from the size of the body to the dimensions of the city: something both practical and comfortable which inflects and accommodates the body. Another is that the principal innovation of the house was its interior rather than its exterior, for it may be argued that it is fittings and furniture which "domesticate" architecture by transforming its stark spaces into habitable places. This reading is reinforced by the fact that the exterior walls consisted of a simple, homogeneous grid of glass blocks, seemingly demanding almost no design. What is common to both interpretations is a denial of the public role of the architect in favour of an attention to elements of the private interior – an over-attention, perhaps Frampton is suggesting, to the sensual and material comforts of the domestic environment.[28]

Although comfort and practicality certainly characterise some of the furniture and fittings (most notably, those in the salon and Madame Dalsace's day room – the spaces where the feminine touch was at its most evident), the design of many pieces exceeds what might be understood as functionality or efficiency. Rather, familiar domestic items are recategorised as machines and ordinary pieces of furniture are recast in the image of industrial "equipment" or apparatus. In the process, there is an almost obsessive reinvention of the objects used in daily domestic routines based on rationalisation and the use of seductive materials such as glass, chrome, perforated steel and hides. Crucially, the designs call up the *image* of practicality using an aesthetic borrowed from mechanisation, cleanliness and efficiency – yet the result is not necessarily greater practicality. Though it is a powerful ideology in modernism that reinvention by necessity

6.4 Salon, showing the furniture designed by Chareau for the Dalsaces' previous apartment, including low tables with extending leaves and library stairs (1963)

guarantees improvement and represents progress, this is something we want to believe rather than a reality. The heightened ends to which the designs are taken, call up preoccupations beyond the functional, and I look at what these might be in the following sections.

THE INTERIOR OF THE MAISON DE VERRE

Chareau was himself experimenting with interior fittings and furniture in the early 1920s and his first commissions for the Dalsaces were for the designs of furniture for their Paris apartment.[29] Some of this early work demonstrates an interest in furniture with moving parts which expand and contract or perform more than one function, much like the early work of Perriand. In the design for the Maison de Verre, this exercise is taken to the level of excess. No detail of the internal workings of the house is neglected, and we find Chareau considering bookshelves, clothes storage, the cleaner's cupboard, numerous staircases, walls (which are refashioned as screens, shelves and so on), a hatch to Madame Dalsace's day room and even the serving

6.5 Winter garden showing openable windows and their winding mechanism, bookshelves, sliding curtain and movable screens (1963)

arrangements for the dining room – each of which was redesigned to perform specific, clearly defined functions. All are reconceived in an almost over-whelming display of technical prowess using metal, glass and polished wood. Although the use of some of these materials was relatively new in a domestic environment, Charlotte Perriand and Eileen Gray were already experimenting with them as signifiers of the excitement associated with the spirit of the age.[30] Perriand admitted that the use of such materials referred to the romance and stimulation of speed (namely the automobile, an icon of the clarity and streamlining of the modern era).[31] The motor car also gathered around it an aura of sexual excitement and desire, symbolised in its glossy smooth surfaces and mirror chromework.[32]

Within the palette of the new materials, designers approached the invention of modern furniture and fittings in different ways. While Perriand and Le Corbusier tended to reinvent existing approved furniture prototypes in the new materials (which included chromed steel, leather and piebald pony hide), Gray was more interested in a minimalist, almost Japanese economy of means, and architects like Ludwig Mies van der Rohe and Marcel Breuer invented new forms based on the logic of the new materials. Chareau's work at the Maison de Verre seems to have a slightly different motivation. It appears he was interested in inventing new furniture types which were inherently mobile or had moving parts rather like automata, while at the same time playing with the way in which several of these moving parts mediated the view of the user from those who might observe them.

One instance which illustrates this is to be found on the second floor. Here, washing areas are contained within the bedroom spaces and they are divided using movable perforated metal screens which mask the activities behind them. Though ostensibly providing privacy for the bather, the body at its toilette is silhouetted by the light from wall-mounted lamps, and can be seen titillatingly veiled through the porous screen. The bath belonging to the clients' daughter is also screened by perforated metal doors, to each side of which is a bookshelf backed by reinforced glass. Though these devices play with the limits of privacy within the conventions of bourgeois morality, their language situates them in a world where sexuality is apparently recognised, represented and reordered.

In a further example, Chareau designed an ingenious contraption for delivering food to the dining table. A reinvention of the hostess trolley, the device comprised two rails fixed to the ceiling leading from the kitchen, situated in the service part of the house, through a corridor and into the dining room. A hanging device suspended from the rails carried a tray and incorporated a feature which permitted the trolley to negotiate with ease a swing door separating the kitchen from the main house. While highly inventive, the device was eventually removed; it was an attempt to "solve" a problem

6.6 Bathroom showing perforated metal screen around washing area (1963)

which did not exist. The device can be read as an attempt to substitute a mechanism for the (female) servant's body, even though the servant's body is controlled already through a class system which fixes her position as "unnoticed."

In the instances cited, invention overrides necessity, pushing the architecture and its associated fittings far beyond the merely functional and into a completely different order. In these cases the device acts as a mediator, or even a substitute, for the body or the physical presence of architectural elements (e.g. walls) attesting to their absence and acting at the same time as an emblem of their loss. In this sense they affirm and also deny the body and the architecture, behaving in much the same way as a fetish object in Freud's description of the castration complex.[33] Furniture recasts the unpredictable human as a perfected machine, recalling the enduring quest for the perfect automaton (the False Maria in *Metropolis*,[34] Frankenstein,[35] Hadaly).[36] In addition, the image of the living body itself is fetishised because it is re-presented through opaque but translucent screens, walls and windows. Both responses reveal the desire to control – even replace – the body.[37] Technology acts as a mediator by which the body is appraised. It is this connection that returns us to the practice of medicine, and the gynaecology suite on the ground floor of the house.

THE BODY

Women's emancipation was one of the markers of social change during the early part of the twentieth century[38] and was accompanied by external forms of representation such as new fashions and a physique liberated from corsetry.[39] The loosening of female sexual morality remained a potent, if perhaps subliminal, social concern, and accounts to some extent for the reassertion of the home as a cradle of traditional "family values." Reinforced possibly by wartime imagery, the fantasy of domination is signified by the machine aesthetic.[40] Described in these terms, the fittings and furniture of the Maison de Verre take on further the character of fetish objects. Attached to the fetish object is a fear concerning male sexuality and its outward representation (in the phallus) – specifically a fear of loss represented by the female (m)other. As the object of erotic fixation, the fetish averts attention from the fear of male impotency, while simultaneously bringing about a redefining of identity. The desire for mechanisation and control could be regarded as symbolising a repression of female sexuality, and a denial of the "real" female body.

In the Maison de Verre, the setting for curing the maladies of the female's reproductive organs is framed within the order of the architecture of the gynaecology suite and the equipment with which it is furnished. Here, the white walls seem to hint at the purification and cleansing of the sick body. The suite is furnished with the equipment demanded by medicine: couch, trolley, lights and mirrors. The doctor's medical equipment is like a "scientific" version of the furniture of the home, connecting the body, the furniture of the house and the medical equipment in a chain of association. In one direction, the connection points to the domestic counterparts so that the furniture in the home is remodelled in the image of the equipment of science: beds recall couch; bedside table recalls trolley; glass blocks recall medical lenses;

bedside light recalls lamp. In the opposite direction, the equipment is itself anthropomorphic, recalling the body which is mediated using the tools which allow the doctor to access the body. The medical apparatus seems to stand in place of the absent body, just as the anthropomorphism of the empty furniture recalls its occupancy and use. Similarly, the regular gridded backdrop of the glass block facade frames and silhouettes the body of the woman as though signifying the rational measure of science.

Once again there is a relationship between medicine and aesthetics,[41] where curing the body recalls the act of unveiling, revelation, insight and purification. The doctor's work is good since it helps the woman to be healthy. His equipment and techniques are benign: they are good medically and beautiful aesthetically. Their aesthetic "cures" the other pieces of furniture in the house of their domestic connotations, turning them into pieces of "equipment." Meanwhile, the body of the woman submits to the power of the doctor, his gaze and his hands. Using light and the speculum, the doctor is able to view her private "interior," and through his intervention, both tactile and visual, ensure a healthy, orderly, reproductive organism. The patient is manipulated into position by the couch and stirrups, access to her body is mediated by the cold steel of the speculum, the white light of the lamp.[42]

The mechanisms of medicine deal with the body like a passive and inanimate object capable of rational conceptualisation (hence reordering), just as the architect of the early modern era views the built interior and manipulates it in the image and aesthetic of science: rational, metallic, bright and transparent.

In the Maison de Verre the body of the woman and the body of the house are synonymous and their representation is mediated by the intervention of technology. Both the body and the house are veiled as a seductive object and manipulated by mechanisms. Light and cleanliness are essential for this reordering, in which the vagaries of social life and "nature" come under the control of the designer. For the body, the apparatus of the gynaecology suite is the mechanism by which an invisible sickness may be approached. Conceived as a machine under the framework of modern medicine,[43] the parts of the body are functionally fragmented and physically isolated. Likewise, the

6.7 Treatment room in Dr Dalsace's suite (1963)

bourgeois home is fragmented into separate functional zones and its social life is mediated by the apparatus which organises and "cures" the interior. Such props give meaning to the social encounters in the house, granting privacy or servicing the house, for instance; they become substitutes for the body, as in the serving contraption; and, finally, they hold the domestic clutter at bay by organising everything into rationalised categories, then assigning them places. "Free" movement is actually controlled through the intervention of mechanical elements such as the library stairs, the ventilation winding-gear and the telescopic ladder, while the symbolic expression of identity is governed by perforated screens, rippled glass mirrors and glass lenses.

6.8 Sliding screen (one of two) at the base of the staircase leading to the private apartments of the Dalsace family (1963)

Man improves upon nature's art, unable to admit the errant, the abnormal "other" (i.e. non-male).

In the Maison de Verre, these two ideas come together, and their similarities are revealed. The real message – the modern architect's will to power over society in general and women in particular – is masked by the seductive image of the industrial fetish. Yet the mask never fully conceals, as the fetishisation of their image attests. Rather, it refers to what the fetish tries to deny. What is revealed by this image of mastery is the architect's actual impotence over the design of cities and the lives of a building's users. As this inflects in particular upon the female user, the will to power is deeply implicated in patriarchal attitudes inscribed in architecture, so that only recently has this issue begun to be unpacked. In the Maison de Verre the connection between images of science and industrial production and their significance as instruments of control, both professional and socio-sexual, is made explicit. Finally, the architect legitimises his actions by adopting the ethics and practices of the medical profession and the positivist rationale of science.

CONCLUSION

The fittings and furniture in the Maison de Verre seduce us visually with their aura of labour-free freshness, promising a vision of an idealised, sanitised future – the very image of modernity – and asserting the architect's power to mould and shape lives and representations. Transparency and shininess, two symbiotic qualities of glass, seduce the imagination of the viewer, while the mobile nature of many of the props symbolises and supports architects' myth of control: control over movement, social life and material expression. The careful selection of rare and co-ordinated colours and materials offers an image of perfection in a world of bad taste, mass ornament and clutter.

Addressing, therefore, the body, the imagination and the will to power, the elements of the house can be regarded as fetish objects disavowing the reality of architectural production. This reality is that as architects we are thrust out from the comfort of our mother's womb into a cruel and inhospitable world which we cannot control. The attention to surface and the image of control evinced by the fittings transforms them into fetish objects which both reveal, but also conceal, hidden anxieties in the modernist project. In the process, they become fetishes in the architect's imagination, disavowing and displacing attention from the reality of the architect's ineffectualness. Thus the Maison de Verre reveals alternative narratives in the modernist project, ones whose invisible basis lies in patriarchal constructions of our own discipline.

ACKNOWLEDGEMENTS

All photographs were taken by Robert Vickery in 1963. The author would like to express her thanks to Robert Vickery for generously giving permission to use these photographs, and to Valerie Bennett for the loan of the images.

References

1   Kenneth Frampton, "The Maison de Verre," *Perspecta*, n. 12 (1969), pp. 71–129.

2   For a list of collaborators, see Frampton, "Maison de Verre."

3   Richard Rogers, "Paris, 1930," *Domus*, n. 443 (October 1966), pp. 8–19.

4   See, for example, Marc Vellay and Kenneth Frampton, *Pierre Chareau: architecte-meublier, 1883–1950* (Paris: Editions du Regard, 1984); Yukio Futagawa (ed.), *La Maison de Verre [de] Pierre Chareau* (Tokyo: A.D.A. Edita/Global Architecture, 1988).

5   Following those like Parker and Unwin, in the development of the Garden City, architects such as Sant'Elia, Tony Garnier and Le Corbusier made visionary proposals for the city.

6   Kristin Ross, *Fast Cars, Clean Bodies: Decolonization and the Reordering of French Culture* (Cambridge, MA: MIT Press, 1995).

7   Le Corbusier, "The Voisin Plan for Paris," *Précisions* (Cambridge, MA: MIT Press, 1991), p. 193.

8   Le Corbusier and François de Pierrefeu, *The Home of Man* (London: Architectural Press, 1948), p. 124.

9   Le Corbusier, *The City of Tomorrow* (London: Architectural Press, 1947), p. 268.

10   Corbusier, "Voisin Plan for Paris," p. 172.

11   "Architecture is the masterly, correct and magnificent play of masses brought together in light." Le Corbusier, *Towards a New Architecture* (London: Architectural Press, 1927), p. 31.

12   "Everything is possible by calculation and invention, provided that there is at our disposal a sufficiently perfected body of tools, and this does exist." Corbusier, *Towards a New Architecture*, p. 266.

13   Ludmilla Jordanova, *Sexual Visions: Images of Gender in Science and Medicine between the 18th and 20th Centuries* (London: Harvester Wheatsheaf, 1989), p. 99.

14   Jordanova, *Sexual Visions*, pp. 92–3.

15   Laura Mulvey, *Fetishism and Curiosity* (London: British Film Institute, 1996), p. 56.

16   Mark Wigley, "Untitled: the Housing of Gender," Beatriz Colomina (ed.), *Sexuality and Space* (Princeton, NJ: Princeton Architectural Press, 1992). Note also the equivalence in identity between the body and the building suggested by Marx's remark equating the buyer of a product with the objectified labour it represents: "[t]he buyer of labour power is nothing but the personification of objectified labour." Karl Marx, *Capital: a Critique of Political Economy. Volume 1* (Harmondsworth: Penguin, 1990), pp. 1003–4.

17   Corbusier, *Précisions*, p. 141.

18   Corbusier, *Précisions*, p. 108.

19   Corbusier, *Précisions*, p. 108.

20   Corbusier, *Précisions*, p. 121.

21   Corbusier, *Towards a New Architecture*, p. 210.

22   Lisa Tierson, "The Chic Interior and the Feminine Modern: Home Decorating as High Art in Turn of the Century Paris," Christopher Reed (ed.), *Not At Home: the Suppression of Domesticity in Modern Art and Architecture* (London: Thames and Hudson, 1996), pp. 18–33.

23   "If we eliminate from our hearts and minds all dead concepts in regard to the houses and look at the question from a critical point of view, we shall arrive at the 'House-Machine,' the mass-production house, healthy (and morally so too) and beautiful in the same way that the working tools and instruments which accompany our existence are beautiful." Corbusier, *Towards a New Architecture*, p. 210.

24   Literally, "poetry of apparatus." Kenneth Frampton uses this phrase to describe what he perceives as a new aesthetic in the Maison de Verre. Frampton, "Maison de Verre," p. 78.

25   See, for example, Elizabeth Wilson, *The Sphinx in the City: Urban Life, the Control of Disorder, and Women* (London: Virago, 1991).

26 "The objective conditions essential to the realization of labour are alienated from the worker and become manifest as *fetishes* endowed with a will and a soul of their own." Karl Marx, *Capital*, p. 1003. See also Emily Apter and William Pietz (eds), *Fetishism as Cultural Discourse* (Ithaca, NY: Cornell University Press, 1993).

27 Frampton, "Maison de Verre."

28 Frampton's description comes in a passage where he is trying to explain why Chareau never again in his career succeeded in producing a building of such exceptional originality. He wants to assert the building's importance in the history of modern architecture and suggests that it was Bijvoet who was responsible for the "architecture." In this way, he can demote Chareau's role to that of furniture or interior designer.

29 See Brian Brace Taylor, *Pierre Chareau: Designer and Architect* (Cologne: Taschen, 1992); Frampton, "Maison de Verre."

30 See Philippe Garner, *Eileen Gray: Designer and Architect* (Cologne: Taschen, 1992); Charlotte Benton, *Charlotte Perriand: Modernist Pioneer* (London: Design Museum, 1996).

31 Mary McLeod, "Charlotte Perriand: Her First Decade as a Designer," *AA Files*, n. 15 (Summer 1987), pp. 3–13.

32 Laura Mulvey notes that the development of sexualised femininity in the cinema and in the new advertising and promotional industries was the equivalent of the glamour inherent in the bodywork of the motor car. Mulvey, *Fetishism and Curiosity*.

33 In this explanation the boy fixes on an erotic object just before the moment of realisation that his mother fails to possess a penis; the discovery is so disturbing that the boy represses the knowledge of his own potential impotency: this is the castration complex. The object is fetishised as an emblem which both records the moment of realisation but it also stamps the act of repression, effectively revealing the existence of the source of anxiety. Sigmund Freud, "Fetishism," *Standard Edition of the Complete Psychological Works. Vol. 21* (London: Hogarth Press, 1961); Mulvey, *Fetishism and Curiosity*.

34 Fritz Lang's film of 1925.

35 Mary Shelly, *Frankenstein* (Harmondsworth: Penguin, 1988).

36 P.A.M. Villiers de l'Isle-Adam, *L'Eve future* (Paris: Flammarion, 1992).

37 Hal Foster, *Compulsive Beauty* (Cambridge, MA: MIT, 1993).

38 See, for example, Sheila Rowbotham, *A Century of Women* (Harmondsworth: Penguin, 1997).

39 Le Corbusier remarked: "Women have preceded us. They have carried out the reform of their clothing . . . to follow fashion was to give up the advantages of modern techniques, of modern life . . . So women cut their hair and skirts and their sleeves. They went off bareheaded, arms naked, legs free. And get dressed in five minutes. And they are beautiful; they lure us with the charm of their graces of which the designers have accepted taking advantage." Corbusier, *Précisions*, pp. 107–8.

40   In the work of Otto Dix during the First World War, for example, men are frequently depicted as armed soldiers, and in a cruel twist, with machines replacing the limbs they lost in battle, like disfigured, pathetic automata, slaves to their macho weapons. This is antithetical to his representations of the female body which regularly portray women as prostitutes, simultaneously voluptuous but also revolting, providing men with maternal succour but at a price (such as disease).

41   Jordanova, *Sexual Visions*.

42   See, for example, James V. Ricci, *One Hundred Years of Gynaecology, 1800–1900* (Philadelphia, PA: Blakiston Company, 1945).

43   William Ray Arney, *Power and the Profession of Obstetrics* (Chicago: University of Chicago Press, 1982), p. 6.

Chapter 7
Sublimation (el Pedregal)
Helen Thomas

Organising the world around us into complex conceptualisations of phenomena is a way of making sense for ourselves. The construction of mythologies often sustains the magnetic force that holds together these groupings within our imaginations, determining their boundaries both within and on the edges of our lives. By necessity they privilege one knowledge above another, determining the terms on which things exist and are understood, while submerging others. The mythology which I am concerned with here is influential in defining the way that modern Mexican architecture is perceived today, and is generated from the work of the architect Luis Barragán.

Condoned and nurtured by Barragán in his lifetime, and carefully maintained after his death, the tenacity of this myth depends upon the countless descriptions, both textual and visual, of the "poetic" experiences that his architecture lends itself to. Seen as a catalytic turning point in his work, the beginnings of this mythology are usually located in the development of "Los Jardines del Pedregal de San Ángel" (Jardines del Pedregal). This was his first attempt at the land speculation which became his occupation after "retiring" from architecture in 1940. The extraordinarily limited definition of this project as a self-defining subject for discussion isolates it from both Barragán's own previous work and that of his contemporaries. With its meaning both constrained and popularised in this way, Jardines del Pedregal has been left without context; a mute and purely formal image.

It is precisely this lack of context which I am concerned with, and here it is taken literally to mean the site's geography. This is determined principally through its geological conditions, and the extraordinary power that these have within the imagination of Mexico City's inhabitants. These factors contribute to its state as an instance of the sublime, a place of both physical and conceptual intensity. This seemingly incongruous juxtaposition – a place intrinsically of the twentieth century with an eighteenth century aesthetic ideal – is strangely appropriate when recontextualised here, in a modernising Mexico City. The transformation of the possible meaning of the sublime in this context can be readily reinterpreted through physical transformation occurring over time, both in response to, and on the, site of el Pedregal. Now it can begin to exist outside its previous hermetic sphere. The translation of the idea of the sublime into a new context also allows a questioning of the original conditions of its emergence, and their parity with another, different place and time.

This move is influenced, indirectly, by the project begun in the field of literary criticism, which intends to read work made in a postcolonial context by breaking down the commonly accepted universal narratives that define them. This chapter seeks to bypass the literal application of these theoretical ideas, since they derive from a quite different cultural form to the one that I am concerned with here. The essential difference between literature, and even painting, and building is that the former can be transformed only in their literal hermeneutic. Their physical form remains unchanged. The common perception outside Mexico of Jardines del Pedregal is as a timeless place, known only through static images. As a successful property development, however, transformation and literal disintegration over time is an essential characteristic. So time becomes the essential factor here, and it is where I will begin.

TIME

> This is the dead land
> This is cactus land[1]

Like T.S. Eliot's "Waste Land", the vast plain of el Pedregal is a place heavy with time. Although there is a sequence to its history, there is no simple linear narrative to explain its existence. The familiar narrative of what Fernand Braudel calls "traditional history" with "its concern for the short time span, for the individual and the event" is disrupted by the intervention of "history capable of traversing even greater distances . . . to be measured in centuries . . . the history of the long, even of the very long time span, of the *longue durée*."[2] It is this idea of history which connects the site of Jardines del Pedregal to its geological origins. Some regions in the world bear only traces and residues of long ago geological events – the most recent ice ages, or dormant volcanoes. In places like Mexico City, geological activity – the moving of continental plates and the dramatic formation of new ground which causes earthquakes and volcanic activity – is a constant possibility. In these places the time span of the longue durée is impossibly contracted; the remote past penetrates the present and Braudel's normally superimposed time scales coalesce.

This infusion of the longue durée into the present is called *geological time* here, a time both immediate and very distant, connected by the emotions of fear, anxiety and hope. It is vast, incessant, and uncomfortably present – the geological cycle which underlies the rest, implying the infinite. In this sense an awareness of the sublime permeates the familiar rather than remaining at a distance, and it is to a further exploration of this idea to which I now turn as I make a connection between the possibility of extremely destructive natural forces, the landscapes that they produce, and the idea of the sublime.

The sublime is a quality or effect of certain powerful and evocative places, an idea connected to the great landscapes of our past and seemingly lost now in the age of innocence which produced them. Throughout the eighteenth and nineteenth centuries in Europe and parts of America its properties could be found at specific sites of natural greatness and apparent immutability: dark forests, oceans and endless wastelands, vast mountain ranges – all locations rich in the myth and superstition essential to tradition. These places were often accessible to the cultivated traveller, hence the importance of the Alps and the Lake District to the British imagination, the rocks and giant trees of the Black Forest to the Teutonic, and Niagara Falls to those living in the new world.

Encountering such places was to cross the threshold of everyday experience towards a higher state of understanding, a keener sense of beauty and moral worth – evoking God, surpassing death. It was an ordeal that invoked, in Immanuel Kant's words, "a faculty of mind transcending every standard self."[3] The origins of the sublime, as a concept based in eighteenth and nineteenth century aesthetic theory, spring from an impulse to seek these sites. This grew from fundamental changes in the way the world was understood. During this period the concept of infinite space began to replace the God of infinite power, throwing into turmoil the means of locating oneself in time and the universe. Johannes Kepler's discovery of the planets' elliptical trajectories around the sun meant that humans were no longer the centre of the solar system, surrounded and protected by God, but had been thrown into a limitless void.

An ability to appreciate the beauty and grandeur of the potentially terrifying, to seek out places of particular aesthetic and emotional meaning in which the sublime could manifest itself, developed, therefore, as a means to survival. Balancing the grow-ing fascination with that beyond the capacity of the human imagination, in the Western imagination, was a will to overcome it, to rationalise and humanise the uncontrollable, and to sublimate it through denial. What is implicit here, as Eliot articulates, is a transfer of the typical site of the sublime from one of great physical power to an interior world. This fugitive move is inherent in the thoughts of Kant and it is this process as it enveloped the desert of el Pedregal both physically and symbolically during the mid-twentieth century to which I will be returning.

The experience of the sublime was both repulsive and desired. Sublime sites essentially embodied two opposing aspects affecting the psyche: physical conditions inspiring promise, and moral uplift countered by echoes of danger, death, hell and insanity. Like the bare rocks of el Pedregal, they were not locations that people would call home. Unlike the potentially beautiful and picturesque places of the familiar and the inhabited, these were sites beyond the arena for human action; they were deserted waste lands – barren, vast, timeless, where the outcome of geological manoeuvres overshadowed any human-made intervention. The model of nature which this implies is one of a "divided landscape:" improvable nature to be cultivated and lived in, versus sublime nature to be visited, revered and left untouched, essential but beyond the limits of the everyday.

In this sense the concept of the sublime is usually associated with the momentum of Enlightenment thought, connected to the process of industrialisation and the changing means to appropriation of the land that this entailed. A foil to the transient in its immutability, its strength lay in its capacity to reconcile the opposing perceptions of the world that science was making apparent: the terrible and the infinite could exist to inspire an elevated quality of spiritual, intellectual, aesthetic or moral worth beyond the familiar. The sublime mediated between the frightening unknown and the disquietingly strange of the new human-made industrial landscapes.

In the context of twentieth century Mexico, this condition finds parallels with the periods of rapid modernisation and land reform that took place during the nineteenth and twentieth centuries in Mexico's own experience of industrialisation and modernity. These were problematised, however, by the parallel existence of an elite of European origin and the native American classes, dissonances which provoked the revolution of 1911. To the people of these differing times and places, the sublime site was always, however, a representation of the unchanging natural world alongside the ephemeral human one. The difference lay in the type of site that would be considered sublime. In this sense the existence of the sublime is produced through necessity from the imagination, internal to the individual; as Kant believed "it comes that the sublime is not to be looked for in the things of nature, but only in our own ideas."[4] The sublime perception of a physical location is a psychological effect which depends upon particular historical circumstances for its existence – political, social and economic factors, which are as important as the metaphysical and mythical attributes with which it is usually endowed.

If we return to our reflection upon Braudel's definitions of time here, one can start to develop an approach to Jardines del Pedregal through this idea of the sublime. By isolating three types of time – *geological time*, *dream time* and *historical time* – the complex relationship of the project of el Pedregal to its site can be opened up. *Geological time*, as previously suggested, runs concurrently with the other types of time used here to explore the phenomenon of Jardines del Pedregal, and allows the associational aspects of the land itself to come into play. *Historical time*, which takes on the oppositional characteristics of a European elite time and a native American time, inhabits *geological time* with a quicker human pace, concerned with fleeting events. Its power and meaning move in and out of focus, mediated by revolutions, people and their heroes, religions and traditions and enables el Pedregal to be connected to contemporaneous events. By contrast, other senses of time hardly exist at all. *Dream time* is the imaginary time of desires and timeless myths, a challenge to Barragán's intentions and a fracturing of Jardines del Pedregal's static image.

GEOLOGICAL TIME

> breeding
> Lilacs out of the dead land, mixing
> Memory and desire, stirring
> dull roots with spring rain[5]

Stories such as this, set in Mexico, sometimes begin with the tale of Henrán Cortés' sheet of crumpled paper: a succinct articulation of the complexities and challenges of the territory and its land embodied in its irregular and folded surface. The densely populated city of Mexico, centre of the modern-day Republic, lies within a fertile basin inland among these restless peaks. Its site was once a saline lake shored by vast expanses of lava rising up to the volcanic craters which surround the valley. This was a lake which boiled even as Cortés approached inexorably over the mountains in 1519. It was gradually drained, a process hindered by its sinking bed, and now the city floats upon a layer of alluvial deposits and volcanic ash, a jelly-like ground, more water than soil.

Perception on a geological scale is intrinsic to being in Mexico City. This phenomenon is manifest in numerous everyday experiences, from signs advising action after earthquakes, to the sight of tilting, deformed buildings left derelict, empty and lost. These remnants of a vast, inhuman power, unpredictable and destructive, are both familiar and sublime in their meaning. Geological and human time are inextricably linked, condensed when traces of huge changes in the natural world are raw and new. Attempts in the human-made world to counteract the consequences of these prehistoric fragments of time in the present move under an impulse to sublimate their meaning. The result is a city "all of it at an altitude of about one and a half miles, crushed under a layer of frozen air, and surrounded by a jail of circular mountains: garbage imprisoned."[6]

The site we are concerned with here lies at the margins of this city of 20 million people. Once part of the brooding grey and black lava beds (el Pedregal as opposed to Jardines del Pedregal, the latter being Barragán's development) its barren rocky plains extended from the city's edge in huge swathes, as far as the eye could see to the Desert of Lions and the volcanoes beyond. Its fearful presence has dominated the imagination of Mexico City's inhabitants in various different guises since the beginning of its history. Between 1945 and 1953, caught up in the phenomenal urban growth at the moment of the city's most rapid modernisation, it was transformed into a place of iconic status within the history of Mexican architecture.

This place is "Jardines del Pedregal de San Ángel" (Jardines del Pedregal), an affluent residential development situated in the south-western reaches of Mexico City. The origins of its existing condition lie in three gardens at El Cabrio on the edges of el Pedregal (1944, now demolished). These experimental landscapes which tended to the quality of the rock, mediating it with pools of water, pathways, steps, were laid out by Barragán, who often passed the time of day here with friends. Among them were the painters Diego Rivera, Dr Atl and "Chucho" Reyes, and the historian Edmundo O'Gorman, all of whom were involved somehow in drawing out a definition of "mexicanidad" from the complex legacy of Spanish colonisation.

Through a series of architectural interventions, Barragán made this desolate land canonic through an aestheticisation of something once seen to be barren and dangerous, repulsive and fascinating; a wilderness outside and excluded from the city. The site of Jardines del Pedregal, in its original state and within the Mexican imagination, encapsulated many of Edmund Burke's essential qualities of the sublime: a powerful aspect (capable of inflicting pain), obscurity (uncertainty about an object's boundaries), privation, vastness, difficulty and uniformity.

The occurrence of the sublime is not restricted to sites such as these in Mexico City, however, for it is an idea inextricably bound up within its fabric. It surrounds and penetrates it, and is part of everyday life. Unlike its European counterpart, it is not searched for, but always visible in the form of the deserts and volcanoes at the city's periphery; there has always been an ambiguity about its location. The edges of the "divided landscape" that existed in Europe are blurred here, and the domesticated and the wild happen simultaneously in a volatile relationship. The subliminal presence of this danger in the mind of the city dweller is evident in a preoccupation with the powerful landscape, in the ways that it is inhabited and represented: reflected through repeated and compulsive reproduction of the lava wastelands of el Pedregal by painters living through Mexico's periods of modernisation.

The first period of industrialisation was between 1876 and 1910. This was when Mexico would make more economic progress than at any time since Independence, transformed by the modernisation of the export economy. New industries were started and infrastructure laid which marked the land with the effects of progress. This was the time of the Porfiriatio, and its effects on the areas surrounding the city were recorded by one of Mexico's most famous artists, José Maria Velasco (1814–1912).

Velasco painted the valley of Mexico many times. Canvases like *Valley of Mexico* (1875), and *Mexico* (1877), are typical of his conception of the city within its wider context. Viewed from barren, rocky slopes and encompassing a vast expanse, the gaze is stopped short at the edge of a broad plain only by the presence of a wall of volcanoes on the horizon. Upon the valley floor human interventions are represented as a fragile, temporary layer. The mighty city is barely perceptible within the greater scale of the site's geology, unrecognisable as an inhabitable place. Occupants of the painting are invariably dwelling in nature, not the city. Often they are making their way through the barren terrain away from urban centre, tiny inhabitants of its edges.

The barren, scaleless lava formations of places like el Pedregal were often a subject in themselves, reproduced in uninhabited drawings and paintings like *Crags of Atzacoalco* and *The Hill of the Warrior in Guadalupe* (1873). The rocks here have more presence, power and durability, pushing up through the soft land, than the ephemeral products of man. A fascination with these wild and scaleless places remained in the Mexican consciousness, represented well into the twentieth century, up until Barragán's interpretation of their aesthetic and sublime possibilities. Images of el Pedregal contemporary to Barragán indicate a continuing awareness of its power. *Paisaje Metafísico* (1948) by José Clemente Orozco is one example. The presence of the sublime is extracted from the land to become a huge, threatening void, its blackness rigidly rectangular in a vast and brooding sky which looms over the wilderness, diminished in comparison.

It was through the work of the painter Gerardo Murillo, commonly known as Dr Atl, and the photographer Salas Portugal that Barragán particularly came to know el Pedregal. Dr Atl was one of the first people to consciously inhabit el Pedregal, living as a hermit among the reptiles and scorpions for six months of the year. He was a well-known, influential and eccentric figure whose friendship was cultivated by Barragán, a frequent visitor to his retreat. Dr Atl was obsessed with the volcanic landscape around Mexico City and he made many studies of it, including a series of books called *Volcanoes of Mexico*, published in the late 1930s. He drew in rigorous detail the infinite variations of the wrinkled, skin-like surface of the lava, broken and fissured by time and earthquakes. Repeatedly he painted the great snow-capped volcano Popocatépetl, sometimes erupting, which could be seen then from any part of the city but is now surrounded by a yellow veil of pollution.

At around the same time that Barragán was building up his friendship with Dr Atl, another person was researching the lava plains. In 1943 Barragán saw an exhibition of photographs by Armando Salas Portugal of the very same landscapes in their raw state. Captured in an extraordinary white light, the exotic plants and shapes appeared strange and enticing. He bought several of these photographs for his collection and began a collaboration with Salas Portugal which was to prove very productive as the development of Jardines del Pedregal accelerated.

The presence of El Pedregal de San Ángel, formed by the eruption of the volcano Xitle around AD 76, was an emblem of the sublime in the Mexican imagination, its physical existence an outcome of the earthquakes and volcanic eruptions which threatened the city. The cultivation (in an urban sense) of the area is subsequently an allegory for its time, where the natural is devoured and its meaning sublimated in favour of the human-made. The site contained a vast, untapped imaginative potential, therefore, of which Barragán as both aesthete and developer was well aware. His intentions for this wide expanse of lava, this ancient landscape as he called it, anticipated its destruction even as he determined its destiny. "Overwhelmed by the beauty of this landscape I decided to create a series of gardens to humanise, without destroying, its magic . . . melted rock by the onslaught of powerful prehistoric winds,"[7] said Barragán in his Pritzker Prize address in 1980. He was not alone in his reaction to sublime nature. Ansel Adams, a photographer whose work is present in Barragán's personal library, said of his own subject, Yosemite National Park, "there is some deep personal distillation of spirit and concept which moulds these earthly facts into some transcendental emotional and physical experience . . . unfortunately to keep it pure we have to occupy it."[8]

DREAM TIME

> I could not
> Speak, and my eyes failed, I was neither
> Living nor dead, and I knew nothing
> Looking into the heart of light, the silence[9]

Here Eliot connects the eighteenth century to the twentieth, describing fragments of the modern world. He evokes an intellectual desert great in its extent, power, obscurity and uniformity, sublime but no longer natural. According to the Barragán mythology, he shared his contemporary Eliot's view of the modern world, and his desire was to make a retreat from the everyday life of the city. He considered urban life unbearably public, a psychic wasteland devoid of the spiritual and unsuited to the life of solitude and contemplation necessary to feel at home in the world. His dream land was an "antidote against anguish and fear," a place for "developing the personality and avoiding standardisation of the mind."[10]

Along with businessman José Bustamante, Barragán set up a company in 1945 to develop the lava desert into a wealthy residential district. His vision for Jardines del Pedregal cherished the rocky terrain, but in a aestheticised and humanised form. He conceptualised it as "a beautiful garden [where] the majesty of nature is ever present, but it is nature reduced to human proportions and thus transformed into the most efficient haven against the aggressiveness of contemporary life." Despite his obvious attraction to el Pedregal he shared the dread it inspired through what it represented – "the certainty of death is the spring of action and therefore of life, and in the implicit religious element in the work of art, life triumphs over death."[11] His colleague in this and later projects, artist Mathias Goeritz, was critical of this act of sublimation, which he described as "a sea of rocks, a savage land" transformed by "a Faustian type that has confronted the task of converting everything into a human work of art."[12] As Kant said, "[t]here is no science of the beautiful, but only a Critique."[13]

Barragán's concern was with the nature of the ground surface itself – the qualities which made it uninhabitable. Its aridity, unevenness and vast scale were fascinating. He countered this with fountains, steps and lawns, experienced essentially within the huge space of the

7.1 Street, Jardines del Pedregal, Mexico (1997)

lava field, viewed against the volcanoes in the distance. The rocks themselves were very important within the gardens and the small number of houses which he was involved with at Jardines del Pedregal. Sometimes, as in the house at 140 Avenida de los Fuentes which he built with Max Cetto, they would be an integral part of the structure, penetrating the domestic interior.[14] Artificial horizontal surfaces acting both as foils to the rugged surface of the rock and as facilitators to its inhabitation were equally as important as the famous walls, and were composed through various different means – often perfect green lawns flooding the spaces between rocky outcrops, sometimes the lava itself formed into pavers, tamed.

The number of projects which Barragán built in Jardines del Pedregal is very small: the sales office and the show garden, laid early in 1945; two houses on his own and two houses with Max Cetto; the Plaza de los Fuentes and the Fuente de los Patos, at the site's original entrance; and two public gardens which partially remain today. The majority of these were made to attract prospective buyers, and are known through the images of Salas Portugal which were produced originally for the sales brochures and magazine advertisements. Sometimes these images are inhabited by ecstatic individuals looking up to the sky. Usually they are empty, disembodied from the recognisable world: a sheet of rock and a fountain; a mysterious pathway through crevices, marked by steps; a mass of exotic vegetation through which a scaleless wall can be discerned, abstracted from its context.

If Barragán's architectural interventions into the landscape were very few, built in the short time between 1944 and 1953, it is as a developer that he effectively transformed beyond all recognition the lava plains of el Pedregal. The ambiguous status of Barragán's responsibility for its effective destruction is exacerbated by such vague inventions as the purported construction code that he devised to limit the inevitable damage to the site caused by transforming it into a financial proposition.

He was not, however, the only one speculating on its latent possibilities as an empty place to be inhabited. Rivera wrote a fairly comprehensive document in 1945 analysing and reflecting upon its potential for development, which is possibly the catalyst for the myth of Barragán's code.[15] He describes the ideal "maritime" climate of el Pedregal, due to the heat retaining capacity of the rocks, and the ease of making foundations in the solid ground of the rocks, quite unlike the shifting sands of the old lake bed where the existing city lies. He is concerned that the area maintain its essential geographical characteristics, and outlines several measures to ensure this. These include strict rules about the amount of stone that can be quarried, restricting it to that required for construction while promoting the use of local stone. He also describes ideal plot sizes of at least 10,000 square metres, a sixth of which should be developed.

Whatever the means to control them, however, the effects of the development were not slow to accumulate. In 1950 about 50 houses occupied the site, by 1960 there were more than 900. One of the supposed requirements in Barragán's code was that prospective inhabitants of Jardines del Pedregal had to hire an architect to plan their house and garden, the design of which has been reported to have been a choice between "Pedregal style" or French. One allowed the presence of the rocks, the other eradicated them. Apparently, designers were restricted by a rule allowing only "modern" constructions. The "California Style," a curious hybrid imported from California where it developed as a translation of the Spanish Colonial and ubiquitous in affluent areas throughout the city, was publicly derided by Barragán. Emilio Ambasz, who supplemented Barragán's growing fame in a MoMA exhibition in 1976, describes this as an attempt to make a place in which to develop an architecture to "express longings in the context of Mexico's natural and cultural conditions."[16]

By 1953 Barragán had lost control of the development, which had gained a fantastic momentum, and he resigned from his position in the business. The dream of Jardines del Pedregal had proved fleeting and impossible to maintain, merely an event, a "utopian moment [to] be potentially prized open, revalued and used."[17] Immortalised in the photographs of Salas Portugal, it was disseminated first throughout Mexico City, and then the world in the MoMA show of 1976, becoming an archetypal image of modern Mexican architecture. As Antonio Toca Fernandez points out, this, as one of Barragán's later works, has received the same treatment as Mies van der Rohe's Barcelona Pavilion (1929): almost totally unknown in its time, it was later canonised as "the most important building of the twentieth century."[18] This is questionable, since images of Jardines del Pedregal were widely disseminated at the time of its construction, both as advertisements in Mexican newspapers and magazines such as *Hoy*, and in architecture and design journals like *Espacios* and *Arquitectura*

Mexico as part of the bid to attract investors, and also occasionally appearing abroad in magazines like *Madame*, *Interiors*, *Harper's Bazaar* and *Arts and Architecture*.

Colonising the wasteland of el Pedregal has been a continuing process of constant transformation of the physical landscape up until the present day. The only remaining evidence of Barragán's dream are the memories of its possibilities captured in photographs. Connecting the two vastly different perceptions of el Pedregal de San Ángel that have been discussed so far – the sublime natural desert and the modern waste land – is the history of human intervention, begun by Dr Atl and Eng. Barragán. The dreams of sublimation which rendered impotent the spectre of the volcanic field were not unusual for their time. Concurrent with the development of Jardines del Pedregal, on an adjacent site, was the construction of the huge new University City. Initiated in 1947, it was only part of the explosive growth of the city contemporary with the establishment of Jardines del Pedregal.

> You find explanations
> To satisfy the rational and enlightened mind.
> Second, you neglect and belittle the desert.
> The desert is not remote in southern tropics,
> The desert is not only round the corner,
> The desert is squeezed in the tube-train next to you.[19]

HISTORICAL TIME

> They brought her by Mercedes to a new house surrounded by walls in the Pedregal district, a house for forgetting she told herself, because she recognised nothing there, wanted nothing there, and everything she touched she forgot.[20]

This is the immediate time surrounding the development of Jardines del Pedregal – its direct context, political, sociological and economic time at a human scale. Between the years of 1946 and 1952, the dream years of Jardines del Pedregal, Miguel Alemán was the ruler of the Republic. He was the first non-military president of Mexico, and the first to receive a US president on Mexican soil.

Industrialisation was given great emphasis during Alemán's administration, and there were many inducements for the investment of both native and foreign capital. His rule was to become known as the period of the most intense modernisation of the Mexican economy, fundamentally transforming on a huge scale the landscapes of nation. Massive dam and irrigation projects, technical agricultural improvements, the construction of thousands of miles of road ways and electrical cables, and the development of the mines marked the rural districts. The emphasis on land distribution was replaced by growth in other, more profitable, aspects of agricultural production, and the "Democracy of the Workers" was tellingly replaced by the increasingly abstract "Democracy and Social Justice."

It was in Mexico City, however, that the most radical physical changes were to occur, in a process impelled by a will to be equal to world-wide trading partners, sometimes described as import-substituting industrialisation. "Suburban land booms in price" was the headline in an *Architectural Forum* of July 1946. "Trying to leap the whole span of the Industrial Revolution within the space of a few years, Mexico is also going through an explosive urbanisation . . . like the entire nineteenth century of an American city building compressed within a single decade."[21] Real estate on the city's periphery became a prime investment as the new urban population put increasing pressure on the surrounding land. The colonisation of el Pedregal was inevitable.

> This is better than paradise. Better than reality. A "something" that you can see, touch and buy.[22]

At the time when the image of Jardines del Pedregal was the property of Barragán, it was a frontier on the threshold of the old, a place of resistance to the life of the city. More importantly for the up and coming, though, it was a place to buy. The origins of ownership of the latter day waste land are unclear. One source says it was acquired by the illegal exchange of communal land, called el Pedregal de San Ángel;[23] for land elsewhere, a process called *permuta* operated and was feasible only for elite landowners. Common property hence became privately owned, its emptiness doomed.

Although constructed on the site adjacent to Jardines del Pedregal, upon an identical ground of congealed lava, the University City owned by the state is very different from its contemporary, the privately owned Jardines del Pedregal de Ángel, where many of the politicians and business people closest to Alemán came to live. The University City is the architectural epitome of the Alemán era, a self-conscious monument to his administration, and a huge and ambitious project. Designed for 20,000 students, its purpose was to educate the technicians and bureaucrats necessary for the new and independent world which Mexico was rushing to become. Again the *Architectural Forum* has a commentary to make, in which three influences are cited: Le Corbusier, the volcanoes and pyramids, and the "Functionalist" style. "It is on an unprecedented 'regional site,'" continues the report, "a wild lava bed whose sublime possibilities had only just been discovered since World War II by architect-genius, Luis Barragán."[24]

One of the factors influencing the choice of site was its essentially "Mexican" character, linked to the extraordinary relationship that the Institution of the Revolution (embodied in the sole political party) maintained with Mexico's pre-conquest past.

This reliance on an imagined bygone era created a tendency for history to permeate the present within Mexican architecture, causing it always to belie its essentially modernist intentions. This was explicit in many of the new university buildings, and especially evident in Rivera's relief murals in lava rock on the University Stadium, and O'Gorman's mosaic mural of the Mexican History of Ideas which covers twelve storeys of the Library.

The renewed mythological status of the sites for Jardines del Pedregal and the University City was due in no small part to the excavation by Manuel Gamio in 1917 of the site of Copilco, a village settlement of 1300–800 BC, now just north of the University City on the edges of the lava field. A few years later, in 1922, Gamio and Byron Cummings started to examine a mysterious lava hill, subject of many local myths, situated to the south of this site and deep within el Pedregal, formed when Xitle erupted around AD 76.[25] This emerged as the Cuicuilco Pyramid (*c.* 500 BC), the earliest stone structure in Mesoamerica, constructed during the "archaic" period of Mexico's past and long before the lake city of Aztec Tenochtitlán. It very quickly became an invaluable part of the new nationalist cultural understanding, a place of legend which authenticated the new regime with the history of many centuries, inextricably connected to this particular piece of volcanic land.

The "use of ancient materials to construct invented traditions"[26] was a fundamental and much described factor in Barragán's plan to reclaim the modern for Mexico. Many references are made in describing his work, by both him and his historians, to the Mexican, or more specifically Jaliscan and "vernacular" Moorish architecture (of the Alhambra and also of Morocco), the influence of which was to be found in pre-conquest Spanish architecture, as well as references to the equestrian tradition of his privileged childhood, among various others. In this they were following an important means of validating any cultural activity in Mexico at the time. Eric Hobsbawm's astute observation quoted here is aimed at nineteenth century Britain, a time and location altogether different, but one which bears some parallels with this other place in its impulse to create a national identity.

The subsequent development of the two sites, University City and Jardines del Pedregal, could not have been more different. Much of the university land endures as it was in 1947, with some additions like the new Cultural Centre built during the 1970s. The only remains of the original landscape of el Pedregal are protected by an extensive ecological zone within the university territory which prevents them from being built upon. The new Cultural Centre housed various sculptural projects, such as the Paseo Escultorico (1979), a collaborative effort by six artists including Barragán's one time colleague, Goeritz. The fascination with the lava rocks is celebrated in this a striking place which lays the lava entirely bare, fetishising the rocks by razing them of all vegetation. Surrounding a large circular area of el Pedregal, a high wall creates

7.2 Paseo Escultorico, Mexico (1979); artists Mathias Goertiz and others

a space that is theatrical in implication, like a bull ring but devoid of life. Like the site of Cuicuilco, it is a place where the individual becomes isolated within a physically powerful situation, a self-conscious trace of the sublime. Both remain places for contemplation, much as Barragán's original dreams for Jardines del Pedregal. Arriving at the site, the visitor looks over a lava field covered by wild, abundant vegetation towards the city. Barely visible in the distance is a wall of tall buildings along Reforma, which mark the centre of the city.

The grounds of the university exist in remarkable contrast to the present state of Jardines del Pedregal, under which the lava still lies dormant. The development is almost completely unrecognisable now from the images of it produced in the advertisements of the late 1940s and 1950s, in the photographs in glossy books, or even to the original inhabitants. The famous Plaza de los Patos, the iconic entrance to the site, has been enveloped by politicians' gardens, one side bounded by a multi-storeyed reflective glass facade. All that remains is a strange reptilian figure by Goeritz, stranded and struggling to get free of the ground. The once transparent views across the landscape, mediated by carefully placed abstract forms, are now barred by high walls paced by private police. The perimeters of Jardines del Pedregal are carefully guarded from the world outside.

7.3 Entrance to Jardines del Pedregal (1997)

References

1   T.S. Eliot, "The Hollow Men," *Selected Poems* (London: Faber and Faber, 1961), p. 78.

2   Fernand Braudel, *On History* (London: Weidenfeld and Nicolson, 1980), p. 27.

3   Immanuel Kant, "The Analytic of the Sublime," *Critique of Judgement* (Oxford: Clarendon Press, 1952), p. 98.

4   Kant, "Analytic of the Sublime," p. 97.

5   T.S. Eliot, "The Waste Land," *Selected Poems*, p. 51.

6   Carlos Fuentes, *Christopher Unborn* (London: Picador, 1990), p. 82.

7   Luis Barragán, "Official Address, Pritzker Architecture Prize," Raúl Rispa (ed.), *Barragán: the Complete Works* (London: Thames and Hudson, 1996), p. 206.

8   Ansel Adams, quoted in Simon Schama, *Landscape and Memory* (London: Fontana, 1995), p. 9.

9   Eliot, "The Waste Land," p. 52.

10 Luis Barragán, "Address before the California Council for Architects and the Sierra Nevada Regional Conference," *AIA Journal* (April 1952), p. 167.

11 Barragán, "Official Address, Pritzker Architecture Prize," p. 205.

12 Mathias Goeritz quoted in "El Arte en El Pedregal," *El Occidental* (19 February 1950), p. 66.

13 Kant, *Critique of Judgement*, p. 165.

14 The influence of Frank Lloyd Wright in Mexico at this time is well documented, and his idea of "organic architecture" was certainly known. The most direct parallel here is between "Falling Water" of 1936–9 and the Pedregal house of 1950.

15 This is reproduced in full in Keith Eggener, "Luis Barragán's 'El Pedregal' and the Making of Mexican Modernism," (unpublished dissertation, Stanford University, 1995), pp. 204–7.

16 Emilio Ambasz, *The Architecture of Luis Barragán* (New York: MoMA, 1976), p. 106.

17 Hal Foster, *Recodings* (Port Townsend, WA: Bay Press, 1985), p. 95.

18 Antonio Toca Fernandez, "Looking and Seeing," Rispa (ed.), *Barragán*, p. 14.

19 T.S. Eliot, "The Rock," *Selected Poems*, p. 109.

20 Fuentes, *Christopher Unborn*, p.30.

21 *Architectural Forum* (July 1946), p. 10.

22 *Construcción Moderna* (November/December 1951), p. 59.

23 Peter Ward, *Mexico City* (Boston, MA: GK Hall, 1990), p. 148. This is contradicted in Eggener's more reliably sourced "Luis Barragán's "El Pedregal' and the Making of Mexican Modernism," p. 52, where the land is reported to have belonged to the Rancho Contongo and exchanged through a legal sale.

24 *Architectural Forum* (September 1952), p. 102.

25 There are many dates given for the eruption, the most precise is in César Carrillo Trueba, *El Pedregal de San Ángel* (Mexico: UNAM, 1995), p. 19.

26 Eric Hobsbawm, *The Invention of Tradition* (Cambridge: Cambridge University Press, 1989), p. 6.

Chapter 8
Beyond the empire of the signs
Murray Fraser and Joe Kerr

> Baudrillard seems to enjoy himself. He loves to observe the liquidation of culture to experience the delivery from depth . . . He goes home to France and finds it a quaint, nineteenth-century country. He returns to Los Angeles and feels perverse exhilaration.[1]

The fragility of architecture as an intellectual subject has been a distinguishing characteristic of the last few decades. What was missing was a wider conceptual framework for architecture; an approach that could embrace activities from patronage through to construction and use, and could locate these within the entire spectrum of economics, politics and social practices. This is precisely where cultural theory now fits in. Cultural theory proposes, without reservation, that existing conceptions of architecture need to be replaced by broader and more inclusive types of readings which address issues such as race, gender, space, image and the unequal distribution of resources and opportunities.

We agree completely with the premise of cultural theory, but what we want to do here is to highlight an intellectual problem that lies behind many current texts and projects. For, despite a stated desire to be as open and discursive as possible, too much cultural theory seems to hold at its heart the belief that the purity and primacy of the theoretical proposition or concept is what ultimately matters. Echoes of this can be seen in the approach of Bernard Tschumi, who desires architecture to "be considered as a form of knowledge comparable to mathematics or philosophy,"[2] or in that of Beatriz Colomina, by whom we are assured that the mass media is "the true site within which modern architecture is produced."[3] The unfortunate product of these and other overriding theoretical dictates is the creation of an illusory critical space, a tendency that is best exemplified in the writings of European theorists on contemporary American cities and architecture. What we will suggest instead is that a more positive contribution is offered by the notion of hybridisation developed in postcolonialist studies. In turn, we will try to show that a hybridised reading can provide a richer analysis of two key cultural projects of the moment: Richard Meier's scheme for the new Getty Center in Los Angeles, and the widely touted Guggenheim Museum in Bilbao by Frank Gehry.

8.1 Approaching the Getty Center, Los Angeles (1997); architect Richard Meier

How, then, might a cultural interpretation of architecture avoid the twin dangers of theoretical reductivism and the falsification of critical distance? We believe that the first move has to be an explicit rejection of any notion of conceptual purity in architecture. Contrary to what Tschumi or others might suggest, no hopes should ever be entertained that architecture might be considered as a form of knowledge comparable to mathematics or philosophy; nor can it ever be annexed as a branch of media studies. Instead, we see far more potential in the concept of hybridisation as a complex, inclusivist approach. Insights into cultural hybridisation have been articulated most fully by the literary theorist and critic Edward Said, and it is his ability to pursue these ideas through a detailed textual analysis that has made him the leading postcolonialist interpreter. In his earlier texts, Said drew heavily on post-structuralist writers such as Michel Foucault to argue that the intellectual constructions formulated by dominant colonial powers, in which colonised countries were conceived as the exotic and less civilised "other," were essential elements in the ideology and practice of imperial control.[4] The problem of Said's initial position was that it was partial in its nature. The concept of the "other," however critical it was in intention, tended to sustain the notion of cultural hierarchies and disparities, and led to no prospect of modification or reconciliation.

8.2 Approaching the Guggenheim Museum, Bilbao (1999);
architect Frank O. Gehry

A typical problem created by the concept of "other," and one which particularly fascinates us, is the inverted interpretations of American buildings and cities advanced by European intellectuals this century. The collective view of European writers has tended to suggest not just that the USA can be understood only in terms of its supposed "otherness" to Europe, but also that this understanding can be perceived only from the standpoint of the Old World. Thus, while the USA might manifestly represent a global destiny, it yet lacks some vital ingredient that might bestow on it a true cultural value; its relative newness will always deny it the necessary historical understanding of authentic culture. Such a position has developed as a means to deal with the ascendancy of the USA over the past one hundred years, which has been of a much different order to that of any previously dominant nation. In the context of the globalisation of modern economics and communications, the United States not only became the economic and military superpower of the twentieth century, but crucially also emerged as the supreme imperialist of culture. In doing so, it first threatened and then destroyed the cultural authority that Europe had collectively imposed on the world for centuries; European writers felt compelled to respond.

In the 1920s, the notion that Europe had become irredeemably effete, and must inevitably bow to the strength and vigour of a younger nation, formed a highly visible strand of Modernist thinking after the cataclysmic First World War, whose conduct and outcome were themselves compelling evidence for this belief. The USA forcefully promoted itself as the visual paradigm of the new era of mass culture, and its gigantic landscapes of deserts and cities were collectively consumed as the common horizons of the Modernist imagination. To the theorists of the European avant-garde the raw and primitive power of mighty America represented few intellectual problems; it did not as yet threaten their conceptual citadel. For although on one hand it might provide a necessary corrective to the exhaustion of the Old World, it still required the Enlightenment disciplines of order and discernment for it to flourish, which only a European sensibility could provide. "If in America they feel and produce, here we think!" wrote Le Corbusier. He went on:

The discovery of the New World. It has been made a subject for the poet, inspiring enthusiasm and admiration. As for beauty, there is none at all. There is only confusion, chaos, and upheaval. The unexpected reversal of all our ideas excites us, but beauty is concerned with quite different things; in the first place, it has order for its basis.[5]

By the late 1930s it had become clear that, as Europe once more prepared itself for mutual destruction, American culture was developing higher aspirations than merely articulating the new communication languages of mass consumption. Strengthened by the diaspora of the Modernist vanguard, the privileged elites in the United States were laying siege to the bastion of "high culture." After the Second World War, they had emerged as its victorious occupants. While opposition to American cultural imperialism during the Cold War era was widespread in "occupied" Europe, the inevitability of the shift of power across the Atlantic was also reconciled intellectually through movements such as the Nouvelle Vague, Pop Art and New Brutalism, a knowing celebration of (American) consumer kitsch transformed by its incorporation into "high art" practices. Indeed, the Modernist tradition of praising the United States as ethically and culturally superior to Europe was not only sustained, but possibly reached its zenith in the work of a number of post-modern European theorists. Semiotics, in particular, with its cultural dissection of the visual and linguistic codes of film, advertising, fashion, has enthusiastically presented late twentieth century USA as the ultimate glittering spectacle of consumption. This, however, has not been based on an acceptance of American values or propositions, but rather on a barely veiled intellectual hostility which sought to reduce and label the USA as the "Empire of the Signs."

Once again the intent of European intellectuals has been to construct a notion of American "otherness" to reinforce fixed ideas about cultural difference. This has paradoxically been achieved by portraying the United States as a terrain simply to be passed through and experienced instantaneously. A mode of writing has been constructed which consists of a literal "progress" through the American landscape; a modern version of the traditional European Grand Tour, but now transported to the new cultural terrain of the twentieth century. Such journeys of "discovery" by intellectual colonists like Reyner Banham, Umberto Eco and Jean Baudrillard have had an enormous impact on post-modern interpretations of the USA, and are profoundly ingrained in the accepted understandings of such iconic American environments as Las Vegas and its surrounding deserts. What they have in common is the apparent acceptance of the vitality and centrality of American culture in specific contrast to Europe; a celebration of an environment that is perpetually in the present, which is modern in its totality, in ways that older countries cannot ever be. A whole new development of semiotic analysis, the philosophy of hyperreality, has been elaborated exclusively to reinterpret the mythic qualities of the American landscape, and especially the conceptual expanses provided by the city and the desert. In what was described as "traveller's tales from the land of hyperreality," Eco journeyed in search of what he termed the "absolute fake." Not surprisingly, he found what he wanted to find:

> If America is the country of the Guggenheim Museum or the new skyscrapers of Manhattan, then Disneyland is a curious exception and American intellectuals are quite right to refuse to go there. But if America is what we have seen in the course of our trip, then Disneyland is its Sistine Chapel, and the hyperrealists of the art galleries are only the timid voyeurs of an immense and continuous "found object."[6]

Sometime later, Jean Baudrillard wrote a collection of "postcards" from what he labelled "the only remaining primitive society," as a self-affirming confirmation of his own phantasmic creations of simulations and simulacra:

> For me there is no truth of America. I ask of the Americans only that they be Americans. I do not ask them to be intelligent, sensible, original. I ask them only to populate a space incommensurate with my own, to be for me the highest astral point, the finest orbital space. Why should I go and decentralize myself in France, in the ethnic and local, which are merely the shreds and vestiges of centrality ? I want to excentre myself, to become eccentric, but I want to do so in a place that is the centre of the world. And, in this sense, the latest fast-food outlet, the most banal suburb, the blandest of giant American cars or the most insignificant cartoon-strip majorette is more at the centre of the world than any of the cultural manifestations of old Europe.[7]

In the texts of Baudrillard, there is no concern at all with celebrating the values of the United States, much less with their analysis. Instead we are offered the latest European intellectual defence of their traditional monopoly ownership of culture, as a bravado attempt to fly in the face of the overweening influence of globalised mass culture and the American inheritance of global power from the French and British empires. A typical post-structuralist conceit is that the notion of American supremacy is predicated on concepts not that far removed from the old discredited colonial concept of primitiveness. For example, Baudrillard claims on behalf of all Europeans that for us the whole of the USA is a desert: culture exists there only in a wild state which sacrifices all intellect and all aesthetics in a process of literal transcription into the real. Baudrillard's discussion of the United States presents a microcosm of the concerns about theoretical reductivism, and yet amazingly has been used as the springboard for even more fantastical post-structuralist speculations purportedly about the USA: a literary tendency which Mike Davis has shrewdly criticised as offering nothing more than "guidepost clichés for Postmodernism's Club Med."[8]

Said has also during the 1990s grown more concerned with the limitations of post-structuralism, especially as it has manifested itself in the academic departments of American universities. Said began to look for a more politically engaged and inclusivist conception appropriate to a "postcolonialist" age. Hence, in *Culture and Imperialism* there is the view that all countries in the world – whether they were wealthy and powerful colonisers, or subjected nations – have been drawn together by the workings of imperialism over the past few centuries. Indeed, Said argues that colonialism, and the national resistances that it spawned, must be seen as an essential part of the modernisation process which has transformed the world. The consequence is that he sees all cultures now as interlinked, complex, diffuse, even if they all also manage to retain their own specific characteristics. Imperialism through its most blatant manifestations created an entire network of political and economic disparities between different racial and ethnic groups across the world, but it also affected relations among the more privileged and dominant countries which promoted the supranational expansionism of capitalism. This has crucial implications today for the whole study and practice of architecture; indeed if we can paraphrase one of Said's key sentences:

> Partly because of empire, all architectural projects [our insertion] are involved with one another; none is single and pure, all are hybrid, heterogeneous, extraordinarily differentiated, and unmonolithic.[9]

Such a postcolonialist proposition is important not just because it allows for the specific and often practical issues of contingency and cultural interaction, but also because it allows a framework for a genuinely broad synthesis of theory, practice and politics of architecture. By accepting and indeed thriving on the particular conditions of architecture, there is no need left to try to emulate other intellectual disciplines, nor to attempt to theoretically purify the subject.

The concept of architecture as a central process of cultural hybridisation seems particularly useful to reinterpret buildings which are being designed and built today within the differential power relations between Europe and the United States. It is also a useful tool to scrutinise architects whose oeuvre is typically discussed in relation to notions of "high culture." Richard Meier's project for the new Getty Center in Los Angeles, opened in December 1997, is an intriguing example, not least because Meier is so often lazily described as an architect who pursues purity, clarity and order through the use of neo-Corbusian motifs. The architect himself helps to foster an image of being totally obsessed with formal geometry, the modulation of light, and an almost unbearable whiteness of being.[10] But it takes little to see the limits of this interpretation. Even a glance at Meier's other artistic output, which takes the form of collages and sculptures, reveals someone not just self-consciously mimicking the artist-architect hero of 1920s modernism, but also trying to express a myriad of conflicting feelings about contemporary existence.[11] His "scrapbook" collages conflate, rather mechanically, the multilingual newspaper articles, restaurant bills, ticket stubs and general ephemera that are accumulated by a global professional. Many of his sculptures start with stainless steel casts taken from architectural models produced by his office, and then, in a bizarre process of artistic cannibalisation, are enmeshed along with metal found-objects trawled from scrap-yards. It is as if the false purity desired by his designs was consciously being thrown as a sacrifice to the junk-culture of modern America. The cultural tension revealed in these artworks is also present, if more hidden, in Meier's buildings. It is the effort to suppress or even deny the presence of tension that speaks volumes. To walk around the far-too-generous circulation ramps in the High Museum in Atlanta (1980–3), or in the Museum of Contemporary Art in Barcelona (1987–95), is to be presented with a troubling sequence in which images of artworks, passing spectators, and the city outside are superimposed endlessly upon each other, with no explanation of why this should be.

In the project for the Getty Center all pretence at purity is immediately blown out of the water.[12] For a start, the buildings are predominantly beige; white now appears only as a relatively privileged highlight. Although this design decision arose as the result of local planning restrictions, which were deployed to stifle his trademark all-white architecture, the way in which Meier takes on board the need to introduce colour and texture shows a different type of intention. It is in the layout and planning of the Getty Center that cultural hybridisation makes greatest impact. The Getty Collection acts as a lonely outpost of European artistic culture on the West Coast, and the first Getty Museum in nearby Malibu is famously housed in a reconstruction of a Roman villa. For the expansion of the Getty Center, a much higher profile site was acquired in the expensive but fashionable suburb of Brentwood, symbolising a desire to form more clearly a part of the cultural constellation of Los Angeles (though this in itself creates problems: Getty staff were apparently instructed not to refer to the new location as Brentwood after the sleazy associations that the suburb gained in the wake of the O.J. Simpson trial). Yet for all its apparent car-based accessibility, the new building closes itself off from its closest neighbour in the valley below, the busy San Diego Freeway. Pulling off the freeway slip-road, the visitor is invited to park in an under-capacity, submerged car park: a hostile reception sequence if there

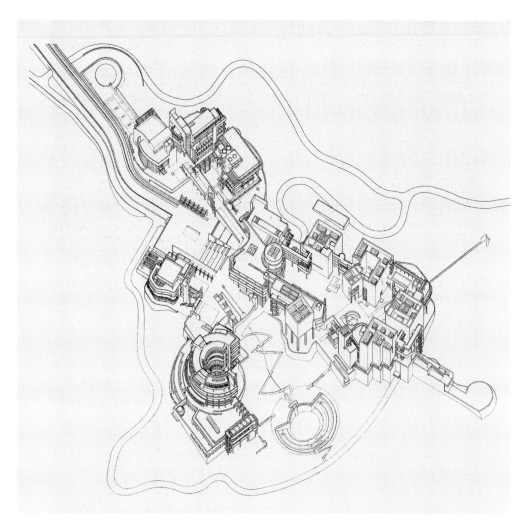

8.3 Axonometric of the Getty Center; drawing by Richard Meier and Partners

ever was one. Then in a bizarre transposition of urban park-and-ride schemes – ironic given that the car versus public transport dialectic of most Western cities barely troubles LA – a monorail tram takes you up to a hilltop plaza which is intended to act as a focal point for the various Center buildings which are distributed around it (the Getty is administratively split up into seven different functions to maximise tax benefits).

The generating idea for the composition and spatial sequence is taken explicitly from Italian notions of urbanism. As one member of the architectural committee appointed to draw up the design brief declared:

8.4 Empty plaza at heart of the Getty Center

> Ultimately, Italian examples provided both a historical context and a point of departure for developing answers that fit Los Angeles. The gardens and hill towns of Italy engendered a variety of inspirational experiences in settings similar to our own. The specifics were not the point.[13]

Not so much the Getty Center, more the Spa-Getty Center. Meier, an East Coast architect who has had relatively little contact with Los Angeles, claims that he indeed did start from Italianate archetypes. But in a typical Italian city, when you get off at the train station, the No. 1 tram will take you straight to the cathedral square, where there is little doubt about which are the significant buildings and what are their social relations. At the Getty Center, the pseudo-tram delivers you to what appears to be a main square (ominously termed Arrival Plaza), where the visitor is instead presented with an urban void: a central emptiness which derives from the fact that all the buildings turn their back on the square. The reason for this is that the blocks have been orientated in the other direction in order to enjoy the many iconic views of LA that are offered by the site. The research building looks across to the Baywatch coastline; the cluster of museum pavilions has views across sprawling suburbs towards the office needles of Downtown; the trust administrators gaze directly into the hissing lawns of the Hollywood Hills. It is the paradox of an intended urban cluster behaving like a series of private suburban mansions that creates an unsettling and peculiarly hybridised effect. It is as

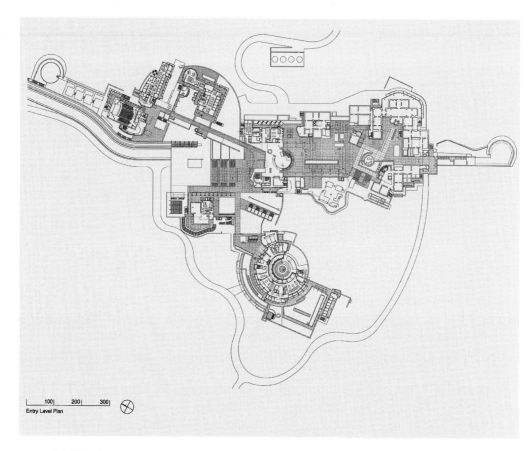

100 | 200 | 300 |
Entry Level Plan

8.5 Plan of entry level at the Getty Center; drawing by Richard Meier and Partners

if Assisi was remodelled by Richard Neutra in the manner of the Lovell House, or Siena transformed into a Case Study enclave in the Pacific Palisades. Part of the social pathology of Los Angeles is for the city to disguise its lack of urban coherence or connectivity by continually inventing itself as a sequence of panoramic views. True to form, Meier defends the new location for the Getty Center – visible but deliberately remote – in terms of a condition of urbanism based on spectacle:

> I think that when you go up there, the site is more related to Los Angeles than any other location could be, because of the way you experience the city from the site, and the ways you see the site from different points of the city. The fact that it's visible, the fact that it's prominent, and that you can see it in different ways, is very positive.[14]

8.6 View out from the Getty Center over the Hollywood Hills

Elsewhere, in an example of visual one-upmanship that also accurately reflects the insecurities inherent in the city's form, he has written:

> Many are likely to come to the Getty Center just for the views. From the hilltop terraces and gardens, one can see and understand Los Angeles more clearly than from any other location.[15]

However, even Meier's portrayal of the design as a cluster of buildings laid out along the contours to maximise the panoramic views, and mediate with the diffuse urban layout of Los Angeles, tells only part of the story. Most of the estimated $1 billion budget for the project was spent on sumptuous landscapes, water features and high-quality architectural finishes above ground level. Below grade level are three enormous floor-plates which silently link together the various structures above, and where the quality of finishes and the working conditions contrast brutally with those above. Thus the careful, individualised design of the separate pavilions that appears above the hilltop – a preciousness that is most marked in the complex configurations of the architectural fragments in the zone for museum display – is contradicted directly by the highly integrated, functional systems that make the Getty Center work from below. Much has been written about a similar spatial bifurcation in the Disney Corporation's theme-parks. Here it is a functional sleight-of-hand that also serves the more rarefied aspirations of the Getty Center, with its need to present a specific image of European culture. It is the split between operational systems that are open in nature, but hidden from sight, and the careful promotion of a visible image of permanence that – far more than the architect's self-conscious and predictable references to Hadrian's Villa or Baroque palaces – speaks of a cultural mediation between American and European values. As Meier has summarised the Getty Center project:

> Besides this American attitude of openness, warmth, flexibility, and invention, my vision of the building also has to do with a more European-derived ideal of permanence, specificity and history. The materials used should reaffirm this image of solidity, of permanent presence in the landscape.[16]

8.7 Interior of the main museum pavilion in the Getty Center

8.8 Detail of open-jointed stone cladding used in the Getty Center

True to his word, Meier continued the process of cultural infusion through the building materials deployed in the Getty Center. Stone was chosen to surface the numerous retaining walls needed to construct such a large institution on a hilltop site, and once again the manner of the design reflects hybrid intentions. Meier imported a cleft travertine from Italy in which deep fissures and fossils are left exposed to create an appearance of rough, untreated nature. But then the raw travertine is guillotined into ruthlessly square cladding panels, measuring 30 inches across and 6 inches thick. In their smallish scale and repetitive precision, the stones echo the highly machined porcelain-enamelled steel cladding panels (Meier's trademark material) which face the buildings above. Furthermore, the method chosen to finish off the stonework was consciously intended to intermingle different cultural conditions. As Meier has explained:

> The design of the travertine exterior wall is based upon an open-joint panel system, which we had developed in our European work, in contrast to the American technique of sealing the joints with mortar. By allowing water to drain behind the outer skin, the European method protects the surface from streaking and ensures that the buildings will look as good tomorrow as they do today.[17]

Here is but one physical manifestation of the cultural hybridisation that lies at the heart of the Getty Center's mission. Richard Meier has become perhaps the best representative of a new, increasingly globalised form of American architecture that can adapt relatively easily to working either at home or in Europe. The outcome in terms of the Getty Center is a remarkable fusion of notions of European elitism and cultural longevity, cross-blended with the more American values of programmatic efficiency and a deep psychological fear of ageing. The building complex reveals its nature somewhat reluctantly, but in essence it is an exemplar of an increasing tendency towards heterogeneity in architecture.

> Perhaps more than any other art institution in the world, the Guggenheim understands the power of a single building to define its image.[18]

On first sight, the new Guggenheim Museum in Bilbao offers a more straightforward instance of hybridised architectural design. As a state-of-the-art example of American building located deep in the old territory of Europe, it brings together a number of intriguing cultural factors only too obvious to commentators:

> If you want to look into the heart of American Art today, you are going to need a passport. You will have to pack your bags, leave the USA, and find your way to Bilbao.[19]

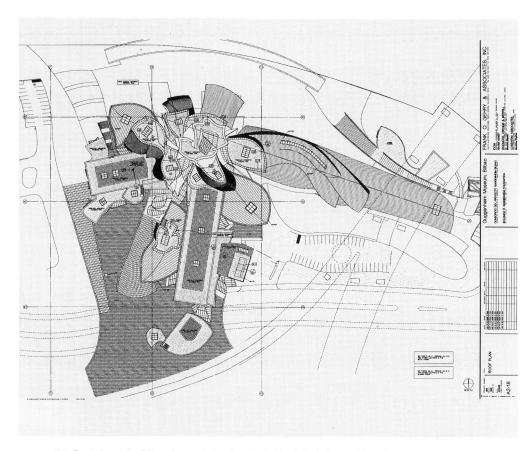

8.9 Roof plan of the Bilbao Guggenheim; drawing by Frank O. Gehry and Associates

The international media coverage, fuelled by the genuine public interest which preceded the opening of the Bilbao Guggenheim in October 1997, was perhaps without precedent for a single work of public architecture. It has launched its architect, Frank O. Gehry, from the status of being a star within architectural circles to that of a genuine international celebrity. It has also clearly met the ambitions of its regional paymasters, whose aim was to locate Bilbao on the map of international economic investment by first placing the town prominently on the European cultural map. "Bilbao has lately become a pilgrimage town," the *New York Times* has dutifully noted, and indeed the museum has been compared in its impact on the city's identity to landmarks such as the Sydney Opera House.

By and large, the initial critical reception for this eye-catching building was favourable, perhaps surprisingly so, given the conservative nature of its patron and the idiosyncrasies of the design. What seems to have caused the greatest conceptual

8.10 Bilbao Guggenheim from the adjacent river bridge

problems has been a general uncertainty about the cultural provenance of the design, the architect and even of the institution which commissioned it. Here is a building designed by a Canadian-American architect, whose practice has been based in the Los Angeles area for twenty years, created for a New York cultural institution which has traditionally displayed a Eurocentric tendency in its patronage of contemporary art, and then built in a Spanish city which itself is a prominent centre of Basque culture. It would be hard to conceive of a building project which so clearly exemplifies the workings of cultural imperialism, or the effects of global capitalism in this unholy alliance between an expansionist American institution and the regional government of a decayed heavy industrial area of Spain. On the one hand the Guggenheim was seeking to establish a new European base as part of its policy of "franchised expansion," and on the other hand the Basque Administration desired to establish a major cultural facility as part of an ambitious programme of urban renewal. But, as the Guggenheim Foundation explained in a candid expression of the unequal cultural relationship between the two bodies (and one which totally reverses the accepted notion of European superiority), "the Basques did not have an internationally renowned collection to put on view in the new museum, nor did they have the expertise to run it. There the Guggenheim could fulfil a vital role."[20]

This it did. It has been estimated that the cost of the Bilbao Guggenheim exceeded the total expenditure on all new art galleries in Spain over the previous decade. In a forthright expression of the Guggenheim's new identity as a global purveyor of trade-marked culture, its Director, Thomas Krens, praised his own building thus:

> With Frank Gehry's Guggenheim Museum Bilbao, a new star shines brightly in the Guggenheim constellation . . . A museum for the twenty-first century, it perfectly complements our New York City base.[21]

In terms of analysing the building itself, as with any large work of contemporary architecture, the process of hybridity is not merely manifested within the visual and formal concerns of design, but permeates every level of the highly complex and differentiated processes entailed in its construction. Most critics have commented on the formal dualism between the strict orthogonality of the stone base, and the aesthetic freedom of the curving titanium-clad walls above. In fact the hybridisation of the design extends much further. As one example, the computer software used to facilitate the

8.11 Detail of stone-clad elements used in the Bilbao Guggenheim

8.12 Detail of titanium cladding used in the Bilbao Guggenheim

fabrication of the skin of the building was adapted from that developed by a French manufacturer of military aircraft, rather than coming from perhaps a more obvious source in California's Silicon Valley. Furthermore, the titanium cladding, which has been suggested as providing some kind of visual association with such former local industrial activities as ship-building, is in fact the least contextual use of a building material imaginable. For, as the Spanish architect and critic Luis Fernández-Galiano has pointed out, the titanium was "mined in Australia, smelted in France, laminated in Pittsburgh, stripped in Great Britain, and folded in Milan before delivery in Bilbao." The same writer elaborates on the inherent contradictions in an institution such as the Guggenheim providing a Gehry-designed building as the new cultural symbol of the city: "Identity is paradoxically obtained through a global trademark and signature, and uniqueness depends on planetary design tools and work processes."[22]

To give some notion of the confusion of critics attempting to characterise the cultural identity of the architecture, the building has been variously presented in the USA as a real American cultural achievement at a time of a prevailing trend towards anonymous kitsch, whereas the less astute reviewers in Britain have resorted to the usual clichés about the Disneyfication of modern life. In an effort to break out of this ontological uncertainty regarding the architecture, one English writer has instead highlighted the complex lineage of the parent institution and its new European project:

> To the European mind, the original Guggenheim collection on East 88th Street in New York City is quintessentially American, housed in a quintessentially American building, designed by a quintessentially American architect, Frank Lloyd Wright, in an uptown neighbourhood of New York, a great American city. Manhattan's Guggenheim, however, thinks of itself as European, and with some justification.
>
> The modern art in its collection is largely European, ranging from Picasso to de Kooning . . . What's more, Thomas Krens, the fourth director in the museum's 60-year history, is the first American to have held the post. His predecessors included an Irishman and a Czech. None has been as eager as Krens to establish a European base for the museum, to reconnect it, so to speak, to its artistic roots.[23]

It is useful to be reminded that this is a cultural institution whose primary purpose is the display of modern art. The first curated show at the Bilbao Guggenheim will be an accumulation of works by artists who collectively represent what Krens describes as "a transistorised history of twentieth-century art." Significantly, this list of familiar names is not confined to a single country or even continent. We have long become familiar with the notion of this particular cultural sphere being absolutely global in its influence and practice, and we do not have conceptual problems with witnessing this disparate practice being assembled and viewed together (although encountering paintings familiar from their previous Manhattan milieu in Bilbao is in itself culturally dislocating). Of course we ought to recognise that architectural culture is equally dispersed, but yet older ideological constructs such as "affinity to place" or "attachment to local culture" still seem to trouble critics when confronted with such a trans-cultural object as the new Guggenheim. It seems especially that an architect whose home is in Santa Monica cannot build in Europe without being accused of acting as a latter-day stooge for Walt Disney.

When confronted by a project of such evidently complex and conflicting meanings and values, it should be the role of cultural theory to come to the rescue of critics and historians still trapped in the habit of thinking of buildings as simple objects of ideology, endowed with clear and unitary meanings. An acceptance of hybrid cultural ideas would seem to accord most closely with the actual design approach of Gehry. As he has remarked in relation to another of his European buildings:

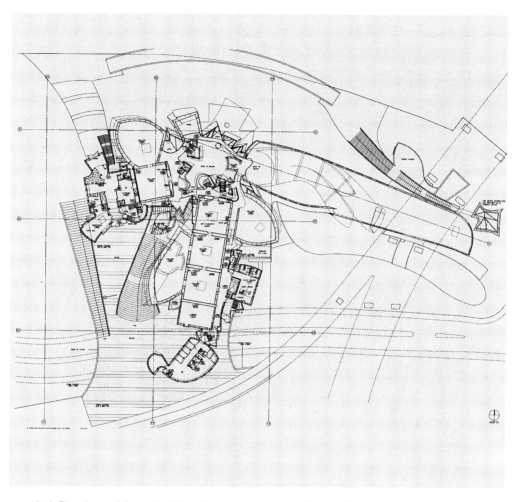

8.13 Plan of second floor of the Bilbao Guggenheim; drawing by Frank O. Gehry and Associates

> I think pluralism is wonderful. That is the American way. Individual expression. It hasn't hurt us in painting and sculpture. It hasn't hurt us in literature. And it won't hurt us in architecture.[24]

However, rather than enter an inquiry into the nature of architectural pluralism, critics have preferred to try to force Gehry's designs into sets of theorisations that are manifestly inappropriate for the Bilbao Guggenheim. Most commonly this has involved the formulation of a highly speculative relationship between his idiosyncratic architectural forms and the Derridean literary theory of deconstruction, or else it has produced attempts to read the building as an essay in psychoanalytic "free

8.14 Detail showing elevational complexity of the Bilbao Guggenheim

association" (which at least has permitted commentators the therapeutic exercise of listing as many different associative metaphors as possible to represent the building's extraordinary formal and spatial vocabulary).

We believe that such reductive views are part of an in-built tendency towards formalism in architectural analysis, and that this problem is best overcome by studying late twentieth century architecture as a product of a fragmented, supranational, hybridised urban culture. Hence the Bilbao Guggenheim must be understood in terms of overlapping and often conflicting determinants. For this building equally represents the considered response of an important contemporary architect to the specific problems of displaying contemporary art, and the ambitions of a multinational organisation engaged in transforming our notions of the art museum (this accounts for the deliberate contrast between the confined display spaces and the enormous sinuous galleries that are provided for large-scale or dynamic works). The Guggenheim displays the evidence of a globalised system of cultural production, yet manages to represent the interests of its local sponsors. It utilises the very latest digital technology to facilitate its design and execution, and yet makes a substantial impact on the specificity of its location: something which has largely been overlooked. The widely published images which show the swooping titanium roof-line gleaming out at the end of tight side-streets suggest a building that wishes to have the same dramatic impact on urban scale and experience as, for instance, the Duomo in Florence.

In conclusion, it is worth considering why these two examples of complex architectural hybridisation have been built at this juncture. Our view is that a closer intermingling between the United States and Europe, which in effect reverses the condition of underlying cultural hostility that drenched the era of the Cold War, forms part of a response to a wider shift in global economics and cultural values. With the collapse of Communism, and the attendant impact of the burgeoning economies of the Asian Pacific Rim, a profound challenge has been issued to the residual colonial mentalities that underpin European culture along with the dominant cultural producers in the USA. For those in the cultural elites in North Europe and America, the worry is that control of the visual language of Western culture might be slipping from their grasp. In fact, even the very search for new visions of the art museum suggests that control and display of cultural values has passed beyond the capacities of any one nation or continent. Thus the reinforcement of the link between European and American practices in the Getty Center and the Bilbao Guggenheim helps to shore up the image of a Western cultural hegemony that is increasingly perceived as being under threat. In this sense the designs of both Meier and Gehry are innovatory and reactionary at the same time. It is perhaps no accident that two such important buildings should be sited along problematic "fault lines" within the global economic system, rather than in more traditional centres of high culture. Architecture certainly provides a vivid manifestation of the complex workings of hybridity in the places where such forces are most extreme.

Architectural hybridisation can hence be seen as a response to new forms of cultural and power displacement which are being produced by, and in reaction to, widespread forces of globalisation. Cultural theory needs to be more open in taking such factors into account, while also continuing to stress the importance of local differentiations. Rem Koolhaas has pointed out the racist implications of a Western dominance in modern architectural thought, which has tended to divide the world up into that part where architecture was deemed possible and the other part where it was not.[25] If we are to be able to broaden the conceptual and literal horizons of architectural discourse, to embrace the cities of Asia and elsewhere, then we need also to open up the cultural analysis of buildings produced by those in the USA and Europe who have hitherto tended to condition our contemporary visions of architecture. The consequences of globalisation involve not just an opening up to other cultural spheres, but also a critical re-examination of ourselves.

What implications might all this have for a broader understanding of architecture? In terms of postcolonialist theory in general, it would suggest that the design and construction of buildings and spaces forms one of the key spheres in which rival cultural interpretations are played out. Buildings are far too often regarded as singular objects with fixed meanings that are meant, however implausibly, to "reflect" or "embody" certain ideals. The notion of hybridisation runs counter to this, and suggests that the possible meanings and experiences of architecture remain as diffuse as are our reactions to other forms of cultural production. Thus architecture is not just the physical endgame of patterns of economic accumulation and politicised activity, but is more a mechanism for the infusion of differing values and aspirations.

The specific implications for a cultural interpretation of architecture are also important. Aside from pointing out the retrogressive futility of trying to identify fixed "national" or "regional" characteristics (such as Nikolaus Pevsner's notion of "Englishness" rooted in a picturesque sensibility, or Kenneth Frampton's suggestion of a role for "critical regionalism"), it would also suggest a stance for modern architecture that is far more provocative. If architects are released from the prison of trying to maintain a national or regional approach to design, and are spared the usual inquisition as to why certain ideas or approaches might have been taken from other countries, then the deployment of architecture as a cultural mediator becomes far more potent. Much has been written about the processes of globalisation that are transforming the contemporary world in a series of highly differentiated and unequal patterns. Manuel Castells has suggested that the purpose of architecture and planning might be to assert the value of places of experience in opposition to the increasingly powerful "spaces of flow" that are dominated by systems of information technology and international capital. Castells' personal view is refreshing:

> My proposal is to start using experimentation in architecture in public spaces all over the world, as a way to trigger a debate that allows for a diverse architecture that follows the diversity of society. In other words, I think that current architectural trends have to be able to go beyond nostalgia and market forces; they must introduce a new tension between individual creation and collective cultural expression in order to reconstruct meaning in our environment.[26]

It is curious that the best argument for radical and innovative architecture (which would also mercifully mean the eradication of polite modernism and its equally boring postmodern variant), should come from someone who is not an architect. Of the contemporary architects who are trying to make a splash, Koolhaas comes closest to a persuasive approach, and this is because his ideological framework is the most postcolonialised, open and speculative in its range. We believe that it is no accident that there is a link with the dangers of fetishising theory within cultural studies, which we mentioned earlier. Analysis through the use of theoretical proposition is an important device, but it is also demonstrably limited in the face of diffuse and rapidly changing empirical and experiential conditions. Our contention, as befits a postcolonialist insight, is not based just on some abstract reading of the inherent flaw of theoretical systems. It is also a constituent aspect of contemporary experience. It has been said that we live in an age of simulation, but this is, at best, only partly accurate. Rather, we now live in an age of projection in which the mixture of observation and participation, of real and virtual worlds, and the desire to weld together disparate cultural values has become the norm. The defining cultural icon of our times is not the CNN satellite news, but the Sony PlayStation. Hybridisation is accepted as the currency in our other cultural experiences, and it is time that we more openly acknowledged its effects within architecture.

References

1   *LA Weekly* (1989), quoted in Mike Davis, *City of Quartz: Excavating the Future in Los Angeles* (London: Verso, 1990), p. 54.

2   Bernard Tschumi, *Architecture and Disjunction* (Cambridge, MA: MIT Press, 1994), p. 18

3   Beatriz Colomina, *Privacy and Publicity: Modern Architecture as Mass Media* (Cambridge, MA: MIT Press, 1994), p. 14.

4   Edward Said, *Orientalism* (New York: Vintage Books, 1979).

5   Le Corbusier, *The City of Tomorrow* (London: Architectural Press, 1927).

6   Umberto Eco, *Travels in Hyperreality* (New York: Harcourt Brace Jovanovich, 1986).

7   Jean Baudrillard, *America* (London: Verso, 1986), pp. 27–8.

8   Davis, *City of Quartz*, p. 54.

9   Paraphrased from Edward Said, *Culture and Imperialism* (London: Chatto and Windus, 1993), p. xxix. The other key text on hybridisation is written by one of Said's followers: Homi Bhabha, *The Location of Culture* (London: Routledge, 1994).

10   See, for example, Philip Jodidio, *Richard Meier* (Cologne: Taschen, 1995); *Richard Meier* (Lugano: Victory Interactive Media, 1996).

11   Richard Meier, *Collages* (London: Academy Editions/St Martin's Press, 1990); *Richard Meier: Sculpture* (New York: Rizzoli, 1994).

12   Harold M. Williams, Bill Lacy, Stephen D. Rountree and Richard Meier, *The Getty Center Design Process* (Los Angeles: John Paul Getty Trust, 1991); Harold M. Williams, Ada Louise Huxtable, Stephen D. Rountree and Richard Meier, *Making Architecture: the Getty Center* (London: Thames and Hudson, 1997); Richard Meier, *Building the Getty* (New York: Alfred A. Knopf, 1997); *A + U* (November 1992), special issue on "Richard Meier: the Getty Center," Yukio Futagawa (ed.), *GA Document Extra 08: Richard Meier* (Tokyo: ADA Edita, 1997), pp. 162–91.

13   Stephen D. Rountree, "The Architectural Program," Williams *et al.*, *The Getty Center Design Process*, p. 16.

14   Quoted in Jodidio, Richard Meier, p. 44.

15   Richard Meier, "A Vision for Permanence," Williams *et al.*, *The Getty Center Design Process*, p. 40.

16   Richard Meier, "The Design Process," Williams *et al.*, *The Getty Center Design Process*, p. 20.

17   Meier, "A Vision for Permanence," p. 35.

18   Thomas Krens, "Preface," Coosje van Bruggen, *Frank O. Gehry: Guggenheim Museum Bilbao* (New York: Guggenheim Foundation, 1997), p. 9. See also Francesco Dal Co and Kurt W. Forster, *Frank O. Gehry: the Complete Works* (New York: Monacelli Press, 1998).

19   Herbert Muschamp, *New York Times* (7 September 1997).

20   Bruggen, *Frank O. Gehry: Guggenheim Museum Bilbao*, p. 18.

21   Krens, "Preface," p. 9.

22   Luis Fernández-Galiano, "Bilbao Song," *ANY 21: How the Critic Sees* (New York: Anyone Corporation, 1997), p. 18.

23   Robert McCrum, "Where to Go to See a Masterpiece," *Observer*, "Life" section (12 October 1997), p. 17.

24   "On the American Centre, Paris. An Interview," *GA Architect 10* (Tokyo: Ada Edita, 1993), p. 178, quoted in Charles Jencks and Karl Knopf (eds), *Theories and Manifestos of Contemporary Architecture* (London: Academy Editions, 1997), p. 120.

25   Rem Koolhaas, "Architecture and Globalization," William S. Saunders (ed.), *Reflections on Architectural Practice in the Nineties* (New York: Princeton Architectural Press, 1996), p. 233.

26   Manuel Castells, "Globalization, Flows, and Identity: the New Challenges of Design," in Saunders (ed.), *Reflections on Architectural Practice in the Nineties*, p. 204.

Chapter 9
Dark lights, contagious space
Henry Urbach

At the beginning of the 1880s in Paris, the decade that would close with the construction of the Eiffel Tower, another proposal was put forth for a tower more than 1,000 feet high, Jules Bourdais' Tour Soleil. Bourdais envisioned a tower capped with floodlights sufficiently strong to illuminate all of Paris from a single point. The public rejected Bourdais' idea, however, for fear that such powerful light would disturb or even blind the eyes of Parisians below.

Since at least 1870, electric light had been described in France as *lumière éblouissante*, dazzling light, and seen to threaten the eye's capacity for sight. In 1870, Louis Figuier wrote about visiting a construction site that was lit by electricity to speed the workers' progress. There, he recalls, "I was stopped, dazzled (*ébloui*) by the sudden clarity . . . My eyes overwhelmed and exhausted from the dangerous contemplation of this dazzling spectacle, I continued on my way."[1]

Figuier was speaking of the early arc lamps which preceded the incandescent light bulb generally attributed to Thomas Edison. After the invention of the Edison bulb, it was possible, in 1882, for Henri de Parville to write in the past tense of electric light that was "sparkling, hard on the eye, obnoxious, constantly changing in intensity, varying in tone, and pallid." Now, he claimed, France had an improved form of light that was, in his words, "civilized."[2]

Electric light was soon marshalled for advertising purposes and, in 1899, the first electrically illuminated advertising sign in Paris appeared on a balcony above the Place de l'Opéra. The luminous letter K, for Kodak, had already been installed above New York's Times Square and London's Piccadilly Circus; now it announced a new spectacle of advertising light for the Ville Lumière.[3] Illuminated signs mounted on building facades and rooftops projected, as formed light, commercial names and logos. They not only extended the hours, but also expanded the terms by which exchange could take place, introducing a nocturnal circulation of images to accelerate the diurnal circulation of goods.

In 1910, Georges Claude launched Claude Lumière and the industrial production of bendable glass tubes filled with neon, argon and other rare gasses. When electrified, the sealed gas would emit colored light that could be seen clearly in daylight, fog and rain. Red and blue were the earliest colors available, but it was not long before technical refinements, basically having to do with the combinations of gas and tinted glass, yielded a palette of approximately 40 different colors.

Working with signmakers Paz et Silva, in 1912, Claude Lumière installed above a hair salon on the Boulevard Montmartre the world's first neon advertising sign. This same year, an observer of the Parisian street wrote:

> Near the Madeleine, calm still reigns. But, passing through the place de l'Opéra around dusk, you enter into a sort of furnace: the facades are ablaze. It seems that a strange and enormous fire . . . licks them with its flames . . . The windows blink, the balconies throb, the rooftops stutter.[4]

By the mid-1920s, the fire, and the fantasies it sparked, had spread considerably. The "civilized" light of early electric illumination had now become, with the proliferation of neon, decidedly more charged. Scrawled across the facades of Paris, luminous advertising signs were becoming a significant point of reference – a lightning rod, a mirror, a closet – for the articulation, desublimation and resublimation of other, more troublesome anxieties.

Because of the way that electrical energy was administered and financed in the various world capital cities, Paris was not – and would not be – as aflame as New York, Chicago or Berlin. In fact, during the period around 1930, a considerable national rivalry animated the Parisian debate about luminous advertising, a debate about whether the City of Light had to keep up with other rapidly illuminating world capitals. Nonetheless, along the major boulevards and at important intersections, in districts of concentrated shopping and entertainment, bit by bit, neon signs spread to efface the facades of the Ville Lumière, continuing to proliferate until the black-outs of the Second World War.

It was at the Eiffel Tower, in 1925, that neon was first presented to Parisians as a public spectacle. In preparation for the Exposition International des Arts Décoratifs, Fernand Jacopozzi installed a luminous advertising sign, 600 feet high, along the tower's shaft, where it was elaborated over the course of several years. The empty tower – which Roland Barthes would later describe as performing both sexes of sight, always seen and always seeing – now stood in full drag, its own tumescent filigree laced with the advertisement's cursive and arabesque markings.

Man Ray incorporated Jacopozzi's sign into his rayograph "La Ville," published, along with nine other images of electricity in daily life, in a limited edition promotional brochure of 1931 for the electrical distribution company of Paris. In his introduction to the brochure, Pierre Bost described the rayographs as "completely naked [and] completely true because they are completely false."[5] Recapitulating a widespread association of electricity with an alluring but duplicitous femininity, Bost claimed that the images show electricity to be "a dangerous goddess" – harmful to those who fear her, but benevolent to those who grant her honor.

In Man Ray's image, phrases of light taken from actual signs around Paris hover weightlessly like garments that have been cast off. Freed from their architectural scaffolding, the lights of advertising are presented here as mobile and independent apparitions, masks that reveal nothing behind. Through this image and other contemporary representations, advertising light is depicted as a kind of overflowing hyper-sprawl, a great graffiti-gob spreading along – and mutilating – the surfaces of the nocturnal city. Splattered across the city, the signs were collectively imagined to orbit in what Georges Bataille called, in "La nécessité d'éblouir," an "excremental constellation" of fire, specters, light, color, cadavers, diamonds and the sun.[6]

From Montparnasse to the carrefour Richelieu-Drouout, from the Opéra past the Madeleine along the Champs-Elysées, in Montmartre and Pigalle: by 1927, there were over 6,000 luminous signs in Paris. They advertised many things: the names of establishments, luxury goods, liquor, tobacco, automobiles, travel destinations, perfume, and so on. To visualize the new metropolitan consumer culture, they repositioned the names of things, and signs of their allure, in what Walter Benjamin called, in "One-Way Street," the "dictatorial perpendicular."[7]

Among other significant responses to the new signs, ordinances were enacted to moderate the spread of advertising light. In 1921, for example, a law was passed that prohibited the daytime illumination of freestanding signs advertising goods sold off-premises, except on Sundays and holidays. In 1929, another ordinance required the removal of all lit signs advertising goods sold off-premises. The later law served to limit the visible presence of signs, illuminated or not. By favoring advertisements for things sold in the buildings to which signs were attached, the law also served to control the degree to which the signs, as signifiers, could float free from the surfaces that propped them up.

All this was, of course, occurring alongside the lively and tumultuous social transformations of the late 1920s and early 1930s, the period that would later become known as the Années Folles. "Since the last war," André Warnod wrote in *Visages de Paris* of 1931, "we are less certain of our beloved Paris."[8] It was that war, with its spectacles of explosion, that might have given considerable psychic charge to the luminous campaigns of advertising, recapitulating a kind of post-traumatic visual disorder into a form of civic light that was itself structured by the repetition of bursts and flashes. (It is interesting to note that the other major use of neon light during the period was for aviation runway lights.) The interwar years witnessed the transformation of anxiety about political, social and economic dislocations into a kind of exuberant, metropolitan madness. The emergence and spread of neon lights figures prominently in historical accounts of the period – their brashness, their phatic intensity often symbolizing the fervor with which pleasures were pursued and anxiety discharged.

Among the many important social transformations of interwar Paris, it is the renegotiation of feminine identity that I want to consider in relation to the architecture of advertising. Across a wide range of discourses, essential categories of gender were beginning to loosen as more fluid and performative notions of identification emerged. A vision of a newly empowered femininity was announced by Victor Margueritte in *La Garçonne* of 1922, one of the great literary successes of the interwar period. Still other feminine identities were constructed and elaborated among gay men and lesbians, played out across a range of popular and newly visible institutions. Men dressed up for drag balls, calling themselves by such pet names as the Duchesse de Bouillon, la Brioche, Nana and so on. According to one account of a 1931 masquerade ball,

> the startling make-up, the multi-colored gems, the golden finery, the feather boas and the glittering tiaras . . . lift the walls and the ceiling with a thousand glittering sparkles. Here everything is lit up, over-emphasized, laid bare. Tonight, everything is possible, anything goes.[9]

Sparkle and exposure, disguise and dazzle: these tropes described not only the look of the new nocturnal pleasures, but also, across many texts of the period, the look of the newly illuminated street and its dressed-up facades.

Viewed as fragments of a broad cultural discourse, descriptions of lit signs from the period chart a certain oscillation between wonder and disgust. Fiction, journalism, criticism, technical writing – as these and other documents reveal how significance was attributed to advertising light, they demonstrate widespread enthusiasm for the new light. At the same time, they show how this light was rendered abject – reviled and cast out, but weakly and repeatedly so in order to sustain other, comparatively pure identities.[10]

Many Parisian writers welcomed advertising light as an exciting sign of metropolitan modernity. They regarded it as the most modern form of light and therefore indispensable to the Ville Lumière. For Louis Chéronnet, writing in 1927, "only luminous signs can embellish our nights, lend poetry to our evening walks, enchant our eyes and uplift the City, radiant under a dazzling sky."[11] A few years later, a lighting designer for the Compagnie des Lampes, Jacques Chappat, warned that Paris could not remain a significant world capital without sufficient *publicités lumineuses*: "Paris, the city of lights, has been surpassed with respect to light," he wrote in 1933.

> We are trying to attract foreign tourists. To entice them to come – and entice them to stay – it is necessary that they discover the sense of happiness and intensity they are looking for. Instead of condemning the "invasion" of lit advertising, it would be better to welcome it.[12]

Advertising light could "entice" and "attract" because, from the start, it was feminized. Not only was electricity figured as a benevolent or powerful goddess (as in Raoul Dufy's "La Fée Electricité," or Pierre Bost's introduction to Man Ray's rayographs), and not only was advertising often figured as a kind of feminine wiliness, but in fact, again and again, advertising light was explicitly represented as a seductive and beguiling woman.

The notion that advertising light is, like a woman, enchanting and artificial appears in another statement by Chéronnet:

> It is particularly for the long winter nights that the street loves to dress herself up. Like a pretty woman, she puts on her diamond and all her luminous gems, and shines with a thousand commercial flames. Thanks to the dressed-up street, the night no longer surprises us, and we no longer live in a harmful, provincial darkness. Instead, we rejoice in a nonstop nocturnal celebration.[13]

Likewise, in a 1933 issue of *Figaro Illustré*, Marius Boisson wrote:

> As soon as night falls . . . the lights bring a certain artificial tone that is one of the charms of nocturnal Paris. The buildings are like aging actresses that recover a certain sparkle under the right light.[14]

The women-lights of Paris were alluring, to be sure, but their allure was also imagined to be artificial and duplicitous.

Idealizing and abjecting tropes of femininity converged as, together, bodily and architectural masquerade became suspect. Recapitulating traditional associations of femininity with contagion and danger, the discourse of advertising light reiterated and sustained a traditional conjunction of heterosexual male desire with the woman who simultaneously excites and threatens. Internal dangers were, in this way, abjected and deposited just over *there*, on the faces of buildings across the metropolis, where they were tentatively contained but far from absent.

I cannot be altogether certain that it was the new Parisienne or the new, masquerading gay man who were phobically conceived and returned, as spatial apparition, to haunt nocturnal Paris. But I do want to speculate that, whatever complex anxieties were displaced into a discourse about luminous signs, the architecturalization of anxiety would serve not only to sublimate but also to *attenuate* these concerns. Architecture and its associated representations could keep the lights of advertising visible to sustain a fear that was somehow reassuring.

At the same time, and sometimes by the same people, other, more fearful fantasies were voiced. In 1924, essayist and novelist Pierre MacOrlan wrote:

> The somber veil of night only falls on districts where people sleep at night . . . A building which, until recently, used to vanish into shadow now displays itself at night with a tiara of golden beads. The contagion spreads from building to building. Tiny lights, quick and mischievous as a mouse, jump from one balcony to the next.[15]

A few years later, designer Pierre Patout described the contagion of advertising light – however playful for MacOrlan – as a kind of unstoppable invasion.

> Every night, electric light, in its many guises, conquers new territory . . . Luminous advertising, having already entirely transformed the appearance of . . . the boulevards and Montmartre, has overtaken the Champs-Elysées, decorated the facades of music halls, invaded the waiting rooms of rail stations and taken hold of pedestrians, even in districts where darkness once seemed absolutely basic.[16]

Even Chéronnet, who gleefully proclaimed "a drunkenness has overtaken the signs . . . [and] the eye is delighted to see this happy confusion," would nonetheless say that the city had "fallen prey to a fire that can never be extinguished."[17]

The Parisian discourse of *publicités lumineuses* imagined and constructed, as an articulation of public fear, a new urban sublime: an absolute illumination, a total light that both terrorized and invigorated. The signs' discursive allure, their erotic and reassuring promise of *éblouissement* or bedazzlement, became ever more palpable as the signs themselves went through a period of rapid technical development, quickly gaining new colors, forms and even animation techniques. Blinking, pulsating, flashing, grabbing again and again for viewers' attention – advertising light was constantly reproduced to reiterate an unavoidable immediacy of shock. Ultimately, it would be imagined to have a kind of independence and even subjectivity. According to Patout, "Light now writes whatever it wishes . . . going blurry and vanishing amid the confusion of its metamorphosis."[18]

At once a new architectural object and a new metropolitan subject, advertising light was invested with sadistic impulses that are rather remarkable. Consider a generally enthusiastic statement from 1926 by the editor of *Cahiers d'Art*, Christian Zervos:

> No matter how we resist . . . our life will have to unfold at a shrill pitch . . . In the speed and continuity of change, there is delirium, passion, excitement and a kind of greatness. Towers that rise, lights that grab and splatter us . . . this is the new rhythm.[19]

Or a long but extraordinary passage from Warnod's *Visages de Paris*:

> The Champs-Elysées offers a magical spectacle with the multicolored flames of its luminous signs and the feverish determination of their colors to devour themselves, to

destroy themselves only to return ever more lively, a silent, tumultuous, impassioned battle that fills the sky with signs of exasperation.

This battle between darkness and light is even more feverish along the boulevards and place de l'Opéra, more stubborn, more chaotic. Here, everything is all mixed up. Luminous signs spring up and disappear, blossoms of light spread open and shut again. A serpent slithers, writhes and contorts in order to trace fiery red letters into the night; but its tail is devoured instantly by another serpent, this one green, following the traces of the one it devours so the same letters can pop up again.

Everywhere there is fire and light, vibrant colors surging forth then disappearing again, while forceful and dazzling lines of fire, letters and words – orange, blue, yellow, green – stand up to the uncoordinated assaults of this chaotic spectacle.[20]

In a sort of post-Edenic apocalypse, a place where serpents roam and the sky is exasperated, the pulse of advertising light carries traces of psychosexual trauma. One could probably dedicate a lot of time to Warnod and his fantasies. But, more to the point, observe how his traumatic scene – and the trauma of the discourse at large – has been radically depopulated, void of human bodies, and repopulated instead by an obscene and animal architecture.

If advertising threatened to "contort" the face of the Parisian street, its threat to a particular part of the viewer's face proved, in this exchange of projections, particularly alarming. The lights of advertising looked back at those who would look at them, giving architectural presence to the metropolitan gaze. For Warnod, the look of advertising was brutal. "With posters like brass knuckles," he wrote, "the street has become a sparkling display that hits the passerby, stopping him for a second so he can see everything in the blink of an eye."[21] Another observer reminds us that it is the task of luminous signs to "hit the eye in a certain and clean manner and maintain a steady power of attraction."[22] To hit the eye *and* maintain steady attraction! Here the discourse of advertising light presents us with the contradictions of a curious male eye trying to defend itself from the danger of light while, nonetheless, indulging its own insistence on sight.

I want to speculate that the fuss about advertising was a displacement or projection of anxiety about the aggressive and erotic aspects of vision. The viewer's own scopophilia and voyeuristic impulses were projected onto the architectural facade, only to be reflected back as spatial anxiety. The threat represented by the lights would, in this reading, have been an anticipated punishment for greedy vision: castration, blindness, or (most lenient of all) *éblouissement*. Advertising light was not the cause of this fear, but its displaced target.

Fearful of the aggressive look of luminous facades, this interwar discourse displays, along with considerable fascination and wonder, symptoms of *photophobia*, an irrational and persistent fear of light. This form of spatial phobia, which often involves an extreme avoidance of sunlight, has not been studied widely . It is thought, however, that photophobia is a disorder having to do with anxiety about voyeurism and its consequences. The photophobe avoids light because it threatens to expose his or her greedy glance. With respect to the Parisian discourse of advertising light, it is important to recognize the particular qualities of this photophobia: fear of artificial light, or more specifically, neon light or, more precisely still, the light of advertising signs. With each of these qualifications, the threat of light becomes, as it did in Paris around 1930, increasingly entangled with the fantasies of beguiling feminine danger it articulates.

Parisian anxieties about advertising light demonstrate how the architectural elevation can serve to express moments of collective cultural defence. The facade (and its interior equivalent) can accept and hold displaced feelings: wishes that have to be disavowed, worries that are projected outward but not excluded altogether. However "dictatorial" this perpendicular plane may be, the architectural elevation can, in any case, act as a powerful and compelling mirror. Psycho-facades, such as the luminous advertising walls of interwar Paris, confront us with idealized and distorted images of the social body. They hold waste for us, along with the feelings of dissolution, disgust and delight that traces of waste provoke. Architecture makes them bearable and captivating, even as it props up and sustains their danger.

There were many architectural projects connected with advertising light during the 1920s and 1930s, including Michel Roux-Spitz's Immeuble Ford, Adrienne Gorska's Cineac and Robert Mallet-Stevens' Garage Alfa Romeo, to name a few. I want to focus, if briefly, on a single project, the Maison de la Publicité by Oscar Nitzchke, because it was so successful at interpreting the discursive condition to which it belongs.

Planned for the Champs-Elysées, the Maison de la Publicité was designed between 1934 and 1936, but never built because the client, an entrepreneur named Martial, fled Paris during design development. The project achieved a tentative, edgy accord between advertising and architecture through the simultaneous dissociation and reconciliation of interior and exterior space along the facade. A six-storey advertising screen pulls away from the building like a veil, separated from the (hermetically sealed, fully air-conditioned) interior by a system of catwalks and ladders. Workers descend from the upper level advertising workshop to install, within the facade, a changing display of signs. The facade presents a dissimulating screen of logos, words, and both moving and still imagery, a dematerialized and floating plane that hints at nothing behind its densely coded surface.

Yet, despite all its hovering, the advertising facade was inextricably linked to the building through the transposition of interior elements into a compressed and coded surface inscription. At least three major elements are represented both on the facade and inside the building. Systems of mobile, temporary display were arranged on the exterior surface as well as the lobby interior, where moveable glass cases (similar to those found on German city sidewalks of the period) were positioned. Nitzchke's description of the cases suggests that they function like the advertising signs of the facade:

> The spatial freedom afforded by mobile elements makes it possible to imagine all kinds of advertising possibilities in the entry hall; the important thing is to have a big space in which the director of advertising will be able to test his creative whims, as though it were a backdrop on a theatrical stage.[23]

Second, the below-ground newsreel cinema was reiterated on the facade as a rear-projection cinema screen. Finally, the free plan of the interior returned, on the facade, as a freely organized elevation that was structured so loosely that any part of the facade could be rented out to individual advertisers.

Although Nitzchke's project is an extraordinary historical artefact, and remarkable for the theoretical and formal contemporaneity of its concerns, it has nonetheless been abjected or, at least, left out of the history of modern architecture. Its absence may have to do with the general photophobia of modern architectural historiography. With few exceptions, architectural historians have demonstrated an overarching, irrational and persistent fear of advertising light. The silence of writers such as Henry-Russell Hitchcock, Nikolaus Pevsner and others may be an effect of the historical discourses that feminized artificial light; in other words, the past abjection of a historical subject may delimit or blind its historical retelling. But it may also reflect, as Mark Wigley has argued, more specific disciplinary concerns.[24] The photophobia of architectural history may, in this sense, have participated in the consolidation of an identity for modern architecture based on the disavowal of advertising, fashion, and other, more overt forms of display and styling.

Sometimes the silence has been broken as, occasionally, photophobic historians of modern architecture have made direct and telling statements about the relation of architecture and advertising. In some cases, this has involved an explicit denial of their entanglement. Sigfried Giedion, for instance, has said that

> Artificial light seldom affects the appearance of architecture. But when it does, architecture is turned into an object of advertising.[25]

Giedion must have been looking away if he failed to see that artificial light frequently and significantly affects the appearance of architecture. In fact, the significance of illumination for the development of modern architecture and urbanism is nothing less than altogether obvious.

A pair of statements by Bruno Zevi likewise reveals a kind of photophobia, while also suggesting that the disavowal of advertising light expresses anxiety about feminine masquerade. Zevi once claimed the superiority of modernism over classicism by equating symmetry with "fear of living . . . schizophrenia . . . [and] passivity, or, in Freudian terms, homosexuality."[26] Later, in "Light as Architectural Form," Zevi made the jump from the abjection of femininity to the abjection of light. He stated, in no uncertain terms, that the expressive use of artificial light is "offensive and antithetical to architectural values."[27]

References

1   Louis Figuier, *Merveilles de la science ou description populaire des inventions modernes* (Paris: Furne, Jouvet, 1870); Patrice Carré, *"Claire, nette, mais dangereuse?" La France des Electriciens 1880–1980* (Paris: PUF, 1986), p. 401.

    All quotations from primary sources have been translated by the author.

2   Henri de Parville, *L'électricité et ses applications* (Paris: Masson, 1882); Carré, *"Claire, nette, mais dangereuse?,"* p. 402.

3   Paris has been known as the City of Light since at least the seventeenth century because of the widespread use of lanterns and bonfires to mark civic events and religious festivities.

4   C. Fischer, "Le boulevard en feu," *L'Opinion*, n. 3 (February 1912); Bruno Ulmer, *Ecritures de la nuit* (Paris: Syros–Alternatives, 1987), p. 20.

5   Man Ray, *Electricité: dix rayogrammes de Man Ray et un texte de Pierre Bost* (Paris: Compagnie Parisienne de distribution d'électricité, 1931).

6   Georges Bataille, "La nécessité d'éblouir," *Œuvres Complètes* (Paris: Gallimard, 1970), p. 140.

7   Walter Benjamin, *Reflections* (New York: Schocken, 1978), p. 78.

8   André Warnod, *Visages de Paris* (Paris: Firmin–Didot, 1930), p. 323.

9   Jean Laurent, *La Rampe*, n. 1 (April 1931); Gilles Barbedette and Michel Carassou, *Paris Gay 1925* (Paris: Presses de la Renaissance, 1981), p. 17.

10 See Julia Kristeva, *Pouvoirs de l'horreur* (Paris: Editions du Seuil, 1980) translated as *Powers of Horror* (New York: Columbia University Press, 1982).

11 Louis Chéronnet, "Paris la Nuit," *L'Art Vivant* (1927), p. 27.

12 Jacques Chappat, "Les Enseignes Lumineuses," *L'Architecture d'Aujourd'hui*, 3 (April 1933), p. 66.

13   Chéronnet, "Paris la Nuit," p. 27.

14   Marius Boisson, "Paris, La Nuit," *Figaro Illustré* (December 1933), p. 604.

15   Pierre MacOrlan, *Aux Lumières de Paris* (Paris: Georges Crès, 1925); *Œuvres Complètes* (Paris: Gallimard, 1971), p. 26.

16   Pierre Patout, "Publicité Lumineuses," *Arts et mètiers graphiques*, n. 4 (1928), p. 252.

17   Chéronnet, "Paris la Nuit," p. 27.

18   Patout, "Publicité Lumineuses," pp. 250–1.

19   Christian Zervos, "Amérique, *Cahiers d'Art*, n. 1 (1926), p. 60.

20   Warnod, *Visages de Paris*, pp. 349–50.

21   Warnod, *Visages de Paris*, p. 333.

22   Colonel Doizon, "Les Enseignes Lumineuses (Paris la Nuit)," *Figaro Artistique Illustré* (March 1931), p. 33.

23   Oscar Nitzchke, quoted in Christian Zervos, "Architecture et Publicité," *Cahiers d'Art*, ns. 6–7 (1936), p. 208.

24   See Mark Wigley, *White Walls, Designer Dresses* (Cambridge, MA: MIT Press, 1995).

25   Sigfried Giedion, quoted in Sokratis Georgiaidis, "Giedion and the 'Third Factor,'" *Daidalos*, n. 27, p. 61.

26   Bruno Zevi, *The Modern Language of Architecture* (Seattle, WA: University of Washington Press, 1978), p. 17.

27   Bruno Zevi, "Light as Architectural Form," *World Architecture*, n. 14 (1991), pp. 56–9. He distinguishes between a (bad) "architecture of light" and (good) "light as architectural form." Artificial light, he claims, should be used only to enliven interior space.

Chapter 10
Colonialism, Orientalism and the canon
Zeynep Çelik

The recent inquiry in art and architectural history that centers on "rethinking the canon" is linked closely with the current focus on sociocultural intersections of the "Western" and "non-Western" worlds. This is clearly manifested, for example, in the growing inclusion of non-Western art and architecture in survey courses.[1] Considering art and architecture within the broadened parameters of intricate power relations has resulted in a reframing of the canon and new readings of it. On the whole, this does not mean that the traditional perspective has been replaced, but that additional ways of seeing and understanding works of art and architecture have been introduced. Although at times the repositioning seems to render the conventional interpretations obsolete, in its essence it only exposes meanings hitherto excluded from the discourse. Perhaps this process can best be explained by a technical term borrowed from engineering and adapted by sociology as a research tool: triangulation. Triangulation, used in land surveying to determine a position, offers the possibility of multiple readings in history. In Janet Abu-Lughod's words, triangulation is based on the understanding that "there is no archimedian point outside the system from which to view historic reality."[2]

Undoubtedly, Edward Said's *Orientalism* (1979) marked a turning point in the awareness we have of viewing cultural products through a lens that highlights the underlining politics of domination. Art and architectural history have responded to Said's challenge, albeit on a more subdued scale than some other academic fields. Not surprisingly, much of this recent scholarship follows the model established by Orientalism and engages in a series of analyses focusing on works of art and architecture that contribute to the construction of an "Orient." As Said himself stated, Orientalism was a study of the "West" alone. It was not intended as a cross-cultural examination and did not claim to give voice to the "other" side – an issue Said addressed in his later writings.[3] Art historians have followed him and offered innovative and critical readings of Orientalism, but always focusing on the "West."[4]

To introduce new viewing positions on the map by listening to historically repressed voices complicates any neat framing of the canon, engages it in an unfamiliar and uncomfortable dialogue, and resituates it. Yet the fruits are worth the effort. Here are two case studies: an 1830s urban design intervention in a colonial setting, the city of Algiers; and the thematic repertory of a turn-of-the-century "Orientalist" Ottoman artist, Osman Hamdi. Colonialism and Orientalism are newcomers to the discourse. While their inclusion displays the broadening in the definition of the canon, "rethinking the canon" is also about breaking through conventional interpretations.

Algiers was the capital of France's most important and most problematic territorial possession *outre-mer*. The colonial city *par excellence*, its "modernization" was particularly charged with political overtones. The first episode of French planning that followed the conquest of Algeria in 1830 germinated the conflicts that would surface sporadically until the end of French rule in 1962. The French began their urban renewal of the city by opening an immense area, a Place Royale or Place d'Armes (later, Place du Gouvernement) in the heart of the city and easily accessible from the harbor – in order to assemble the troops. The initial clearing was random and resulted

10.1 Old Algiers, partial air view (1935): above, the Casbah; bottom centre, Place du Gouvernement, with surrounding area restructured between the 1830s and 1850s

in an irregular plaza with haphazard boundaries, soon deemed unworthy of representing the glory of France. A series of projects in the 1830s and 1840s that attempted to regularize this space into a neat geometric form, surrounded by buildings of uniform height with classical details and arcades on the ground level, responded to the call by the French administrators for an appropriate monumentality. The resulting Place du Gouvernement, with its grand image and efficiency, was accompanied by the enlargement of three existing streets, all converging on the new square: rue Bab el-Oued, rue Bab Azzoun and rue de la Marine, now lined with "French-style" buildings with uniform arcades. These designs carried the premise that the "style of the conqueror" would carve the image of France onto the Algerian scene, and, with its aesthetic and scalar difference (which formed a dramatic contrast to the urban and architectural forms of precolonial Algiers), establish a visual order that symbolized colonial power relations.[5]

Historians have commonly presented the French interventions in al-Jaza'ir (as the city is called in Arabic) solely as examples of military and practical planning that imprinted the French victory onto the city's form and image.[6] Critics of colonial urbanism, too, have emphasized the military prowess behind the interventions, while pointing, albeit very briefly, to the "protests of indigenous populations,"[7] or blaming the schemes for their "expression of an imperialist colonization, [with its] contempt and ignorance of the subservient culture."[8] The few scholars who have discussed the scale and content of the demolition undertaken in Algiers during the early years of the occupation have approached the topic again from the French side only, alluding to the insensitivity of the colonizer to the culture of the colonized.[9] The cumulative discourse has thus reduced Algerians to an ultimate status of inertia, even when it took a critical look at colonial policies.

Demolition was a particularly sensitive issue in the dense fabric of al-Jaza'ir, and its practice clearly distinguished French planning in the colony from French planning at home. In terms of regularization of the urban fabric and the creation of monumental squares and streets, the operations in Algiers do not appear at first sight different from the practices in French towns since the seventeenth century. Yet, from Henri IV's great squares in Paris to the Place de la Concorde, and to Nancy's spectacular system of squares (Place Royale, Place de la Carrière and the Hemicycle), demolition in French towns was minimal and the new designs were applied to vacant sites. If the compulsory acquisition law of the Napoleonic Code facilitated expropriation and demolition, it was not applied on a large scale in France until the rebuilding of Paris under Napoleon III and Baron Haussmann. The construction of the rue de Rivoli itself under Napoleon I had called for the demolition of some structures, but no monuments, and certainly no religious or sociocultural icons, were destroyed.

The situation was different in Algiers. French interventions were not only formally oppositional to the architecture and urbanism in place, but they diced and sliced the city, appropriating and demolishing indiscriminately. In addition to a large number of commercial and residential structures, public and religious buildings of varying sizes and degrees of importance were torn down.[10] In the colony it was acceptable to practice what was not allowed at home. The abrupt violence of the first interventions made the city and its architecture contested terrains in the confrontation between the colonizer and the colonized, as revealed in the oral literature from the time of the conquest. Consider the following song that lamented the invasion and appropriation of the city and highlighted the violation of its most revered icons:

> O regrets for Algiers, for its houses
> And for its so well-kept apartments!
> O regrets for the town of cleanliness
> Whose marble and porphyry dazzled the eyes!
> The Christians inhabit them, their state has changed!
> They have degraded everything, spoiled all, the impure ones!
> They have broken down the walls of the *janissaries*' barracks,
> They have taken away the marble, the balustrades and the benches;
> And the iron grills which adorned the windows
> Have been torn away to add insult to our misfortunes.
>
> Al-Qaisariya had been named Plaza
> And to think that holy books were sold and bound there.
> They have rummaged through the tombs of our fathers,
> And they have scattered their bones
> To allow their wagons to go over them.
> O believers, the world has seen with its own eyes.
> Their horses tied in our mosques.[11]

The demarcation of the French from the Algerian in the city played a central role in the creation of the notion of *espace contre* or "counter space," a term coined by the Algerian sociologist Djaffar Lesbet to indicate the antagonistic nature of the two areas.[12] The residents of the Casbah, the heights of al-Jaza'ir left untouched by the colonizers, spoke back by turning in upon themselves, consolidating their unity, tightening and redefining their own mechanisms of maintenance and control over the public and private spaces of their neighborhoods. As interpreted by Frantz Fanon, the diametrically opposed stances of the Casbah and French Algiers abolished any possibility of overall harmony: "The two zones are opposed, but not in the service of a higher unity. Obedient to the rules of pure Aristotelian logic, they both follow the principle of reciprocal exclusivity. No conciliation is possible."[13] This opposition persisted to the end of the French rule and made the Casbah not only the symbol, but also the actual locus of resistance.

Whether presented within the history of nineteenth century French planning or, more critically, as an example of oppressive practice, interventions in the urban fabric of Algiers have been viewed conventionally only from one side. By highlighting the colonizer as the main actor on the scene, the discourse helped to reiterate his empowerment. Yet the colonizer and the colonized existed and confronted each other within a complex interactive web, in which each exercise of power was counteracted by some form of resistance that redefined the shape and the balance of the relationship. Bringing the latter part of the equation into the discourse disrupts the frozen status of both the colonizer's unilateral power and the disquietening powerlessness of the colonized.

Cities of the Near East and North Africa were often collapsed into an imaginary "Orient" by nineteenth century European literary and artistic discourse; nevertheless, the political and sociocultural setting of Istanbul was very different from that of Algiers. The nineteenth century was the time of intensive Westernizing reforms in the Ottoman Empire. European forms and norms, however, were not imposed by external colonization; they were initiated and implemented from within by the ruling elite, with imported expertise from the "advanced" world. As the capital of the empire, Istanbul was the prime site of new experiments, which ranged from governmental reorganization to all aspects of cultural production.

Osman Hamdi (1842–1910), a prominent artist, was born into this scene. The son of Ethem Hamdi, the Grand Vezir who was particularly committed to cultural issues, Osman Hamdi enjoyed a privileged education, which included several years in Paris. There, he was drawn to the atelier of Gustave Boulanger and possibly also to that of Jean-Léon Gérôme, and his own work matured under the technical and thematic influence of the French Orientalist school. Nevertheless, his "scenes from the Orient" provide acute and persistent critiques of mainstream Orientalist paintings. They represent a resistant voice, whose power derives from the painter's position as an Ottoman intellectual, as well as his intimate acquaintance with the school's mental framework, techniques and conventions. Osman Hamdi's men and women – dressed in colorful garments in the Orientalist fashion and placed in "authentic" settings – are thinking, questioning and acting human beings who display none of the passivity and submissiveness attributed to them by European painters.

Osman Hamdi addressed the major themes of Orientalist painters from his critical stance as an insider within the outside. He presented Islam as a religion that encouraged intellectual curiosity, discussion, debate, even doubt. In painting after painting, his men of religion, reading and discussing books, maintain their upright posture as an expression of their human dignity, against a background of meticulously articulated architectural details.[14] Osman Hamdi's home scenes form a striking alternative to the myriad familiar and titillating views of harem and bath by French painters. Several of his works depict a couple in a tranquil domestic environment, the seated man being served coffee by the woman.[15] While the hierarchical family structure is unquestioned, the man of the house is not the omnipotent, amoral, sensual tyrant of European representations, enjoying his dominion over scores of women at his mercy and pleasure. Instead, a dialogue is offered that redefines the gender relationships of Orientalist paintings.

Osman Hamdi's point becomes even more acute when he focuses on a single woman. His response to Orientalism's innumerable reclining odalisques is *Girl Reading* (c. 1893). The painting shows a young woman stretched out on a sofa, totally immersed in a book. Her relaxed and casual pose implies that she is not reading a religious text, but perhaps a work of literature. The composition has the familiar collage

10.2 *Girl Reading* (c. 1893); artist Osman Hamdi

of Orientalist details, but the shelves behind her are filled with books, making the statement that reading occupies an important part of her life. The "girl" is hence given back her thinking mind and intellectual life, which had been erased by Orientalist painters.

Despite several exhibitions in Paris salons and at the world's fairs, Osman Hamdi's attempts to correct the epistemological status of Orientalist representations remained overlooked in France and were not incorporated into art history's discourse on Orientalism until very recently. Yet this episode of repressed history was not an isolated case, but part of a broader debate among Ottoman intellectuals at the time. Ahmed Mithad, an Ottoman writer, described sarcastically the formulaic odalisque of European fantasy in his 1889 *Avrupa'da Bir Cevelan* (A Tour in Europe):[16]

[This] lovable person lies negligently on a sofa. One of her slippers, embroidered with pearls, is on the floor, while the other is on the tip of her toes. Since her garments are intended to ornament rather than to conceal, her legs dangling from the sofa are half-naked and her belly and breasts are covered by fabrics as thin and transparent as a dream . . . In her mouth is the black end of the pipe of a narghile, curving like a snake . . . A black servant fans her.[17]

Like Osman Hamdi, Ahmed Mithad offered a corrective to the falsification:

This is the Eastern woman that Europe depicted until now . . . It is assumed that this body is not the mistress of her house, the wife of her husband, and the mother of her children, but only a servant to the pleasures of the man who owns the house. What a misconception![18]

While the limitations of this type of response, with its drive to substitute one received truth or representation for another, must be acknowledged, its entry into the repertory of art history expands the worldliness of the canon. The voice of certain alterities, kept silent by the valorized culture, begins to enter the dialogue, thereby complicating the meanings and contextual fabrics of the art objects and disrupting inherited historiographic legacies. This, in turn, helps to contest the familiar reductive formulas that explicate sociopolitical relationships and re-establish them in their social density.[19] Furthermore, as Gayatri Spivak observes, when the "hegemonic discourse" repositions itself so that it can "occupy the position of the other," it, too, becomes subject to a major transformation, to its own decolonization.[20]

ACKNOWLEDGEMENTS

This chapter originally appeared in *Art Bulletin*, v. 78 n. 2 (June 1996), pp. 202–5. It is reprinted here by permission of the College Art Association. I would like to thank Diane Favro, Eve Sinaiko and Perry Winston for their comments and suggestions.

References

1   Survey textbooks also reflect this trend. A remarkable example is Spiro Kostof, *A History of Architecture* (Oxford: Oxford University Press, 1985), which goes beyond mere "inclusion" and pulls the non-Western material into the heart of the argument. Kostof pairs, for example, Cairo with Florence in the late Middle Ages and Venice with Istanbul in the sixteenth century.

2   Janet Abu-Lughod, "On the Remaking of History: How To Reinvent the Past," Barbara Kruger and Phil Mariani (eds), *Remaking History* (Seattle, WA: Bay Press, 1989), p. 112.

3   Among his numerous writings dealing with this issue, see, for example, Edward Said, "Intellectuals in the Post-Colonial World," *Salmagundi*, ns 70–1 (Spring–Summer 1986), pp. 44–64; Edward Said, "Third World Intellectuals and Metropolitan Culture," *Raritan*, v. 9 n. 3 (1990), pp. 27–50; Edward Said, *Culture and Imperialism* (New York: Knopf, 1993).

4   For the first article to deal with the significance of Said's work in the interpretation of nineteenth-century painting, see Linda Nochlin, "The Imaginary Orient," *Art in America*, v. 71 n. 5 (1983), pp. 118–31 and 187–91.

5   I analyze French interventions in the urban fabric of Algiers in Zeynep Çelik, *Urban Forms and Colonial Confrontations: Algiers under French Rule* (Berkeley, CA: University of California Press, 1997).

6   Among more recent literature, see, for example, François Béguin, *Arabisances* (Paris: Dunod, 1983), p. 103; Xavier Malvert, "Alger: Méditerranée, soleil et modernité," *Architecture française outre-mer* (Liège: Mardaga, 1992), p. 31.

7   René Lespès, *Alger* (Paris: Librairie Félix Alcan, 1930), p. 201.

8   J.-J. Deluz, *L'Urbanisme et l'architecture d'Alger* (Algiers/Liège: Pierre Mardaga and Office des Publication Universitaires, 1988), p. 11.

9   See Lespès, *Alger*, passim. An excellent reconstruction of the center of Algiers prior to the French conquest has been done by André Raymond, "Le Centre d'Alger en 1830," *Revue de l'occident musulmane et de la Méditerranée*, v. 31 n. 1 (1981), pp. 73–81.

10   For example, the eighteenth-century mosque of al-Sayyida, qualified by Raymond as "one

of the most elegant religious monuments of Algiers," was demolished to make room for the Place du Gouvernement.

11   Quoted in A.A. Heggoy, *The French Conquest of Algiers, 1830: an Algerian Oral Tradition* (Athens, OH: Ohio University Press, 1986), pp. 22–3.

12   Djaffar Lesbet, *La Casbah d'Alger* (Algiers: Office des Publications Universitaires, c. 1985), pp. 39–48.

13   Frantz Fanon, *The Wretched of the Earth* (New York: Grove Press, 1968), pp. 38–9.

14   *Discussion in Front of the Mosque*, for example, depicts three "teachers," one reading aloud (commenting on?) a book, while the others listen with great attention, holding onto their own books. *The Theologist* (1901, private collection, Istanbul) focuses on one man, reading in a mosque; on the floor and on a shelf behind him are other books. For an astute analysis of Osman Hamdi's paintings, see Ipek Aksügür Duben, "Osman Hamdi ve Orientalism," *Tarih ve Toplum*, n. 41 (May 1987), pp. 283–90.

15   For example, *The Coffee Corner* (1879, private collection, Istanbul) and *After the Iftar* (1886, Türkiye Is Bankasi Gallery).

16   For the tendency to "correct" misrepresentations, see Zeynep Çelik and Leila Kinney, "Ethnography and Exhibitionism at the *Expositions Universelles*," *Assemblage*, n. 13 (December 1990), pp. 40–1.

17   Ahmed Mithat, *Avrupa'da Bir Cevelan* (Istanbul: Tercüman-I Hakikat, 1890), pp. 164–5.

18   Mithat, *Avrupa'da Bir Cevelan*.

19   Edward Said, *The World, the Text, the Critic* (Cambridge, MA: Harvard University Press, 1983), p. 23.

20   Gayatri Chakravorty Spivak, *The Post-Colonial Critic* (London: Routledge, 1989), p. 121.

Chapter 11
Women and space in a Renaissance Italian city
Diane Ghirardo

The fresco cycle known as the "Sala dei Mesi," painted during 1467–9 by Francesco del Cossa for Duke Borso d'Este in the Palazzo di Schifanoia, Ferrara, depicts the socio-spatial principles of this Renaissance city. Its tripartite division locates Ferrara in relation to the cosmos, where on the upper levels idealized images of each month of the year center on an Olympian deity flanked by symbols indicative of that deity's attributes. For the month of April panel, Venus in her chariot is surrounded by images of springtime and its related activities, such as fertility, signaled by rabbits and festively dressed young people coyly embracing one another.

Below the idealized celestial images and a middle section of astrological and other figures associated with the zodiac, the lower section presents an equally idealized rendering of day-to-day agricultural and civic activities. Duke Borso is depicted as a wise and noble ruler, on the one hand administering the city and on the other fully inserted into the life of the community, hunting, riding, meeting with the city's wise men and visitors against a backdrop of residents collaborating to nurture the town by provident planting, harvesting, building construction and festive celebrations.

Within this section of the fresco I want to direct attention to a small strip on the upper left. Also tripartite, it depicts horses, asses, men and women running on the street level; above them on the middle level various nobles on foot, seated or on horseback are framed by the most refined and contemporary fifteenth century architecture; on yet a higher level, noble women stand on their balconies observing the events below. The spatial division of this fresco both illustrates and reinforces the spatial reality for women in Renaissance Ferrara, and forms the basis for a larger inquiry into the relation between gender and the built environment in Italian Renaissance cities.

This segment of the April panel depicts the Palio, a race held several times annually on important feast days, most significantly on the 23 April feast of St George, Ferrara's patron saint. By contrast with the Palio traditionally held in Siena, which is a popular contest between the various *contradas*, or sections of the city, Ferrara's Palio was both popular festival and aristocratic display, drawing noble participants from great distances. Called Palios because the first prize was a *palio*, or length of valuable cloth such as brocade or velvet, similar races were held in other Italian cities, including Asti, Florence, Mantua and Rome.

11.1 "Sala dei Mesi" fresco, Ferrara, detail of "April" (1467–9); artist Franceso del Cossa

Francesco del Cossa's fresco collapsed several different races into one frame. Beginning from the right and working back to the left, he started with the most prestigious race for thoroughbred horses, where relatives and nobles from other cities came to Ferrara to measure the merits of their most valuable and prized steeds. Following this race was a comic version with mules; then one for young men on foot, followed by another comic version, either with Jews or *ribaldi*, and finally another with women.[1] As their dishevelled clothing and the exposed genitals of the first woman indicates, some of the women are prostitutes. Engaging prostitutes in such urban spectacles has a long history in Italy, dating at least to the early Middle Ages.[2] A good, if not entirely reliable, report of one such race comes from Johann Burchard in the first years of the sixteenth century. In recounting the festivities in Rome for the marriage of Alfonso d'Este of Ferrara to Alexander's daughter Lucrezia Borgia in 1502, Burchard writes about races of wild boars from Campo dei Fiori to Piazza S. Pietro, followed by "a contest between a great number of prostitutes, and they also ran from the pyramid in the Borgo into the piazza di S. Pietro."[3]

11.2 "Palio in Florence;" artist Giovanni Butteri

In del Cossa's fresco, the prostitutes represent the complete reverse of the respectable women overlooking the scene from the balconies of their family palaces. To the prostitutes with their loose clothing and exposed bodies and wild, dishevelled hair are counterposed the noble women confined tightly within their stiff gowns and head-dresses.[4] Shielded from full view by the expensive oriental tapestries that signal the high status and wealth of their families, the noble women stand above and at a distance from the spectacle on the street, protected symbolically and actually by the architectural and domestic structures of home and family. A second painting by Giovanni Butteri of a Palio held in Florence reveals the same relationship among respectable women, lower-class women, and men in the public sphere. If respectable women could not so freely inhabit the city's thoroughfares, the men of the city, the *giudici dei savi* and the other noble individuals, held the public sphere between these two contrasting modes of female presence; only they were able to move freely between the two spheres. Indeed, the men's figures are larger than those of either the women above or those below, emphasizing their "larger-than-life" status in relation to the women.

The fresco emphasizes the contrast between the types of sexual activities embodied by the two groups of women: the state- and church-condoned sexuality of respectable women, family oriented and contained within the bounds of social laws and the domestic setting; and the transgressive, uncontrolled behavior of prostitutes, that eluded male supervision. Put another way, the respectable women represented erotic work, childbearing, satisfying spousal needs and chaste control within the domestic environment and off the public streets of the city, while the prostitutes represented dangerous but fascinating erotic play visible in the public thoroughfares of Ferrara.[5] The spatial relationship between the women and their representation in del Cossa's fresco illustrate the status of Ferrarese women with striking clarity, not only because of what the fresco shows, but what it conceals. In fact, the spatial locations of respectable women (house) and unrespectable women (street) schematize the presence and role of women in part by omitting large groups of women, as I examine further on.

A considerable body of scholarship has been devoted to women and the family in medieval and Renaissance Florence, Venice and Rome, but only rarely have questions about space, geography and architecture figured in the discussion.[6] Likewise, cities outside of the three major centers have been largely ignored by scholars. My research involves the study of women and space in Ferrara, one of the leading and most powerful Renaissance courts of the fifteenth and sixteenth centuries. The research spans a period of nearly two hundred years, from 1400 to 1597, when the Este court moved to Modena and the city came under the direct administration of the papacy.

My intention is to produce a woman's topography of Renaissance Ferrara as a specific challenge to traditional historical studies of architecture and cities. My operating assumption is that space is gendered, even though the way historians and architects commonly analyze the meanings of Renaissance space and spaces leaves the impression that spaces are gender neutral, that is, that the values that they embody are shared even though shaped by white Western males.[7] Instead, philosophers and some historians are now understanding that spaces embody relations of power and, in most instances, conflict and contradiction, since power structures have rarely been uncontested.[8] French sociologist Pierre Bourdieu argued that the organization of space is governed by the same contrasts found in the practical and lived experience and knowledge of individuals.[9] In his analysis of the Berber House, Bourdieu therefore contended that spatial meaning derives not only from the way objects are placed, but also from the activities of individuals and the social and economic conditions that inform them. Spaces, then, acquire meaning through practice, and practice in turn is shaped by conceptual schemes, assumptions about the world, people, gender and how they interact. In other words, the way a particular group or culture understands divisions based on sex, age, class and race is reproduced in the way its members order space, and at the same time, this spatial ordering reproduces those power relations again and again, so much so that over time they come to seem absolutely natural, given, rather than arbitrary.

Studying women and space as a direct challenge to the current practices of architectural history constitutes an effort to illustrate how architectural historians reproduce, in both the objects of study and the standards of evaluation, the practices of a social system in the profession of architecture that has been and continues to be sexist and patriarchal. Famous buildings by famous architects treated as the objects of genius: this has typically been the content of architectural history courses, certainly those which take the Renaissance as the object of analysis. Absent from architectural history as taught to both undergraduates and graduates is an understanding of how the built environment was produced, what values these processes endorsed and gave shape to, and how the patriarchal system of building excluded women from direct roles, occluded the ways in which gender defined places and spaces, and concealed the tensions and conflicts that animated the gendering of spaces.

With this in mind, among the questions I am asking about Ferrara is how spaces embodied relations of power, how meanings came to be attached to places in Renaissance cities, and how social practices maintained those meanings over time. I specifically wish to look at women in the public sphere, and not only noble women, but women of all classes: what were their relations to the public spaces of the city? One of the most challenging aspects of my research is finding evidence about the lives of women who were not from the upper classes: for the most part, they do not present themselves to history through letters, poetry or other forms of literature, but rather were represented by men in a variety of ways: in municipal statutes, in censuses, occasionally in communal diaries or travel logs, in various types of legal records, from wills to criminal proceedings but also to some degree by themselves.[10] Although it has not been possible to hear their voices, information about the spatial practices in which they were enmeshed has emerged. Because my project entails archival research in documents that have not been studied from the perspective of what they reveal about gender and space, the material raises more questions than I can answer. This is very much a work in progress, and the present chapter is only a preliminary presentation of findings.

WOMEN IN THE CITY

In the most general terms, houses and spaces in Renaissance Italian cities were differentiated according to gender, expressing the basic idea that men worked, women maintained the house and children. Men occupied ranks in the community according to occupation, property ownership, social status based primarily on birth, and participation in civic administration. But as the statutes of Polesine, a commune under Este control near Ferrara, and those of Ferrara itself demonstrate, women were measured according to their marital state (virginity, motherhood, widowhood) and the money they brought with them into marriage (dowry).[11] Men held the power to impose spatial orders that reflected values that favored them, making their power and authority and the comparably inferior status of women appear natural, obvious, unquestionable.

The lower the class status of these women, the less we know about them in any detail. Most scholars do not believe that women had a "Renaissance" the way men did; in fact, the relative openness of guilds to widows who kept up their husband's trade or to women in general working in the trades, often independent of a man, began to decline in the fourteenth and fifteenth centuries, so that they became more and more bound to the home, and to the care of house, husband and children, either their own or as domestic servants to upper class families.[12]

The possibilities for women inside and outside the patrician classes were limited: marriage, religious life or prostitution.[13] When a woman married, she brought with her two precious commodities: her virginity and a dowry, or bridewealth. In Renaissance Ferrara and its possessions, the regulation of sexual relations and of dowries was considered a civic concern, a matter of public order the larger community was obligated to oversee.[14] Women emerged in the statutes, into the public sphere, then, insofar as they were involved in various types of illicit sexual encounters, as bodies who brought wealth with them into marriage, and as heirs of their birth families or of their spouses. In Chapter 3 of *The Book of the Family*, Leon Battista Alberti outlined the underlying principles of Italian civic statutes such as those of Ferrara: women, not as strong of character as men, are timid by nature, soft, slow, and most useful when they sit still, stay home and watch over the things belonging to men: men bring things home, women guard them.[15]

What was the relationship between married or single women and space in Ferrara? The higher a woman's social class, the less visible she was in the public realm. A married woman typically spent her day in the house, garden and the immediate vicinity, attending mass and acquiring supplies.[16] While city statutes protected the honor of *donne honeste* (decent women) from dishonorable behavior by men, a woman forfeited this protection if an assault occurred in a street known to be frequented by prostitutes, a street, in other words, where an honest woman should not have been found. Constraints on movement for *donne honeste*, then, aimed not only to preserve their honor but also to distinguish them from women who were potential prey for men. Everywhere beyond the home presented a serious threat especially to unmarried patrician and cittadino women. As Bishop Agostino Valier of Verona wrote in 1577, "The Devil schemes to find his way into virgins' hearts through their eyes, and by inviting them to . . . public places and public spectacles."[17]

Working as domestics, as agricultural laborers or in their family shops meant that lower-class women who traversed the city's streets and piazzas became visible to men, vulnerable to the male gaze in places such as laundries and fountains.[18] Structures such as laundries have largely disappeared over time, consumed by the growth and transformation of cities; rarely preserved as such, they were not valued precisely because they were associated with women and domestic activities. Laundries were understood as female public spaces even in the seventeenth century: a papal scribe recorded how women met in the "laundry piazza" of San Silvestro in Rome and conducted their own governance and variations on male civic activities – but he denigrated their concerns as having only to do with trivial matters such as fashion, carriages and clothes. Laundries and licentious behavior, including prostitution, enjoyed a long-standing link; female camp followers, for example, often doubled as laundresses.[19] Because women doing laundry rolled up their sleeves and pinned up their skirts in public, thereby becoming unusually visible to men, laundry facilities, whether fountains or on river banks, were repeatedly denounced as dangerous by the clergy.

Although dedicated laundry facilities during the Renaissance in Ferrara are long gone, later prints and drawings of the seventeenth and eighteenth centuries locate them along the Giovecca, the canal leading from the Castello Estense to the eastern gate of the city. Women hefting baskets of laundry, washing and hanging out clothes for drying, and rows of clothing festooning the approaches to the former ducal palace proved an irresistible scene for countless travellers who recorded their views of the city: in fact, during the eighteenth and nineteenth centuries, Ferrara was typically represented in travel books almost exclusively by views of the cathedral and of women doing laundry adjacent to the Castello Estense. Women who washed clothes in public usually lacked access to fresh water in their homes; since most Ferrarese homes had wells, the women in the public laundries would have been wives or daughters from the poorest families.

Other than their appearance in such drawings, lower-class women emerge in wills or other notarial records. Even though statutes specified that they could not inherit from husbands if children or any other eligible male relatives existed on the husband's side within the third degree of kinship, women inherited from their natal families and regularly drew up wills to ensure that their property was disposed of as they wanted after they died. Because of the formulaic language of notaries, these documents are often provocatively mysterious. When Chiara Ambrosi, widow of Giovanni Agodi, drew up her will in the early fifteenth century and left her property to one Giacomo Carri, a

11.3 Laundry in Piazza Castello, Ferrara (nineteenth century); anonymous artist

strazzarolo (clothing merchant), for example, we have no way of knowing what relationship lay behind her bequest.[20] The pact drawn up between Teodora Lenti and her son-in-law Ippolito Beltrami in a contract of 1559 is more transparent: in exchange for board and room, Teodora agreed "for reciprocal convenience" to bequeath to him and her daughter Ludovica the house in which they all lived. Old age for widows was full of uncertainties, and this arrangement ensured that Teodora would live in her home in modest comfort for her remaining years.[21] Nearly forty years later, Ippolito still lived there.[22]

Theodora's story raises the question of the fate of widows in a sociey where women's value lay chiefly in their function of childbearers. Once a woman fulfilled this function, and especially after her husband died and his property passed on to his heirs, widows often faced difficulties, including losing a secure place to live. Communal records indicate that a row of *chiusi* (single room apartments) was erected for widows on via Mortara in 1402 with a bequest from Francesco Bendedei, but it may have already been established in the late thirteenth century.[23] Sandri in 1826 reported that the small apartments were "given for charity" to widows and other poor women by

11.4 Widows' housing, Ferrara (c. 1402)

ministers and officials of the so-called Scala confraternity as early as 1281. In addition to shared one-room apartments, the complex contained a common kitchen and meeting area, kitchen gardens in the rear and small structures to store firewood. The simple brick facades reflected the typical residential construction of fourteenth century Ferrara, but their salient characteristic was location: originally outside the walls on a road leading to the church of the Consolation, spatial marginalization reflected the women's economic and social relation to the life of the city. Already marginalized by virtue of age, marital status and poverty, the widows who lived in the row houses found their position reinforced every time they left the *chiusi* and had to pass through the symbolically significant gates to enter the city.

Given the statutory constraints regarding property transmission, it is therefore surprising to find that, by the end of the sixteenth century, an inventory taken to exact a road-cleaning tax identified women as owners of nearly 400 of the approximately 4,400 houses inventoried in Ferrara, or over 9 per cent of the housing stock. While the inventory does not enumerate 20 streets and thus cannot be definitive, it nonetheless offers suggestive evidence about property ownership and the number of women who lived as heads of households, perhaps alone. Many were identified as widows, only four as having a profession: a profumier, a woman who owned a weaving shop, a female innkeeper and Caterina Stovara who owned a *stufa*, or stew (public bath), often a thinly disguised site of prostitution. Property ownership by women was

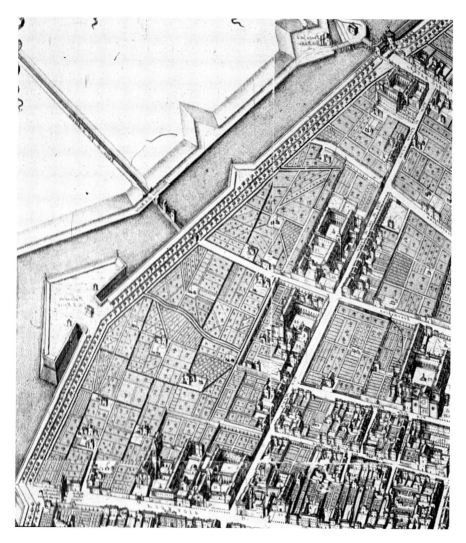

11.5 Andrea Bolzoni's Map of Ferrara (1782): detail showing row of housing for widows at intersection of via di cal di Pozzo (now via Mortana) and via Stortichina

clustered in the smallest houses: women owned 18 per cent of the 572 smallest, one storey houses, and a descending percentage of the other five categories of houses. Although women owned property throughout the city, because of house size they tended to be clustered in the oldest, more marginal streets. On the other hand, almost 12 per cent of the 271 shops listed in the inventory belonged to women, although unfortunately no details on the types of shops or who operated them were included. Only when women's property ownership is connected to wills and sales contracts will it be possible to answer these questions. In any case, the inventory demonstrates that some women from the lower classes owned their houses, lived as widows or single women and, in some cases, owned more than one house.

RELIGIOUS FACILITIES

Two other structures associated with women, the convent and the brothel, round out the living opportunities available to most women. Families did not welcome the birth of daughters, and Duke Ercole I of Ferrara was no exception; he was so disappointed when a second daughter was born in 1475 that he omitted the usual public celebrations following a royal birth; chroniclers tell us that "he wanted a son."[24] Too many female children presented a problem for upper class families as well as those of lower status. Poor families in Italy practised female infanticide, and female infants were often abandoned in convents to the care of the church.[25] Because families wanted to conserve dowry funds for the marriages of one or two daughters, leaving intact most of the estate for sons to inherit, the convent became a convenient alternative to paying too many dowries.[26] Any real estate women brought with them

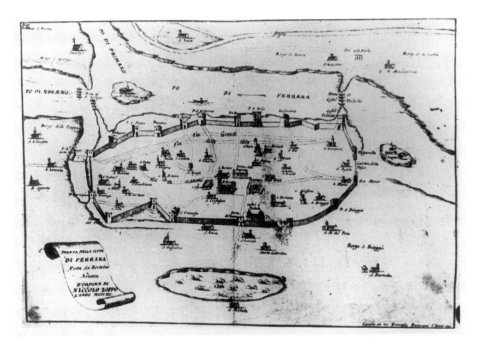

11.6 View of Ferrara (1390): visible outside the pre-1500 walls are the convents of S. Guglielmo and S. Caterina, with the hospitals of S. Anna and parish churches in the city's *borghi*; artist Fra Bartolomeo Novara

became the property of the convent, which usually rented it for a regular income. Although upon taking final vows a nun renounced her claim to any interest in the family estate, in Ferrara there are nonetheless several instances in which a nun retained ownership of a house or shop (as many priests did), for example, Sister Clementia Montecucoli, who owned a small house in the Contrada delle Vecchie.[27]

Despite living in groups of two dozen to over one hundred women and governed by a set of explicit rules administered on a day-to-day basis by an Abbess, the women remained under the control of one or another order of priests, the local bishop, and through them, the Pope. By the end of the sixteenth century, Ferrara boasted nearly two dozen convents, often connected to hospitals.[28] Although several antedated 1400, an unusually large number were founded during the fifteenth and sixteenth centuries. Communities of women in prayer served as bulwarks against evil entering a city, defences against infestations from plague and war to poor harvests.[29] Their importance magnified by the power of prayer, numerous convents testified to a city's piety, not to mention the abundance of girls destined to remain unmarried.[30]

The practice of consigning excess daughters to the convent extended from the patriciate to the richest families of the *popolo*, but the class system persisted even in convents. Augustinians were drawn largely from the *cittadini*, or urban middle classes,

11.7 Santa Caterina da Siena (*c.* 1826)
Antonio Sandri, *Origine delle chiese di Ferrara e luoghi delta provincia*, manuscript, BCA 10/1985, Archivio Fotografico del Comune di Ferrara

while patricians joined the Poor Clares.[31] The results of such class associations were visible more in the decoration of churches than in their locations: the higher the class of the women, the more richly endowed the convent. Some were cloistered, such as the Carmelites; others engaged in urban good works, managing hospitals for the aged and infirm, taking in abandoned infants, caring for girls at risk of becoming prostitutes, or helping "convert" former prostitutes.

Throughout the fifteenth and sixteenth centuries, new convents were located on the periphery of inhabited areas; Duke Ercole I's extension of the city walls at the turn of the fifteenth century more than doubling the city and bringing within the walls convents that formerly lay outside, such as S. Guglielmo, as well as the housing for poor women and widows near the church of the Consolation. The *addizione erculea*, consisting largely of fields and a few sanctuaries, became the site for many of the convents founded during the sixteenth century. Although often located near the city's gates and walls during earlier periods as bulwarks against evil, newly founded convents evidenced no particular spatial pattern.[32] Usually the city, the Este family or a benefactor donated the land, often because a daughter was a member of the order. Santa Caterina of Siena, for example, was founded by Duke Ercole I in 1499.[33] Not only did he underwrite the construction of the church and convent, he spent two years wrangling for a nun from Viterbo, Suor Lucia Broccoleti, and a group of followers, to be its first inhabitants. His gift of property guaranteed the 66 nuns a good income "in perpetuity."[34]

Suor Dorotea and seven companions of the order of the Blessed Virgin of Carmine, who transferred to Ferrara from Reggio, were the first to staff the hospital at S. Gabriele founded by Eleanora of Aragon, Duchess of Ferrara, in 1480. Two patrician women, Vittoria Pasqualetti and Bianca Sardi, left their cloister at S. Agostino in 1537 to found a new convent dedicated to Santa Lucia near Castel Tedaldo, subsequently transformed into a cloistered Carmelite convent in 1581.[35] The earliest version of what we now call shelters for battered women were operated by nuns and connected with conservatories or oratories, such as Santa Maria de Bocche. Women generically known as *malmaritate*, or badly married, received shelter in exchange for performing domestic tasks, often joined by former prostitutes who had decided to change their lives.[36] For the latter, this often became the first step toward joining a religious order of *convertiti*, or former prostitutes.

During the fifteenth century, women in most of Ferrara's convents seemed able to move about with relative freedom, maintaining close relations with their families and at times travelling outside, sometimes participating in public processions, but usually they even attended mass within the confines of the convent and its church. This freedom lasted until the Council of Trent in 1560, when widespread complaints from clergy that convents had become centers of licentiousness and vice led to significantly greater controls.[37] The convent of San Guglielmo in Ferrara garnered such a reputation for licentiousness that a papal bull demanded that it be cleaned up prior to an ecumenical council to be held in Ferrara in 1438–9.[38] The deep misogyny of the clergy makes the veracity of their reports suspect.[39] The ugly reality of this system, however, was that women from the patrician and *cittadino* class especially were forced into convents against their will. As Stanley Chojnacki puts it, "a sexually mature unmarried daughter was regarded as a menace to family honor, [so] it was better to consign her to a convent where at least the fiction of chastity would shield her family from sexual disgrace."[40] Enclosed in a convent and officially out of public view, a woman became unavailable for seduction, nor did she risk being confounded with a prostitute or courtesan and imperilling her family's honor: this was determined by visibility in public, even from the confines of the family palace, and therefore that of the family.

Nonetheless, the vehemence with which the clergy protested the presence of women – nuns included – in the public realm, in the streets and piazzas of Italian cities, is striking. Unattached women not available for marriage were not supposed to appear in public or be seen by unrelated men – hence the horror of clergymen if nuns stepped out of the convent, even if dressed in religious garb. Once housed in a conservatory or orphanage, girls rarely left them except to marry. The nubile wards of *ospedali* such as S. Spirito in Rome emerged from the private realm in which they had been raised out of sight of men to be paraded as adolescents in the city's streets precisely to make them available to the male gaze, but only for the purpose of being chosen for marriage.

Civic and religious authorities were convinced that women, whether married, widowed or enclosed within the walls of a convent, were weak and needed to be protected from their own weaknesses as well as from the attentions of men.[41] Spatial controls reflected this conviction, as did the mere presence of numerous convents in Italian cities. Not all women entered a convent because of religious conviction, nor were all women with sincere religious convictions willing to enter convents. The case of the lay community founded by Bernardina Sedazzari exemplifies the struggle waged by a group of women to live together in a lay community.[42] With the full support of her parents, Bernardina left the convent at S. Silvestro and established her own pious lay community, a type known as *pinzochere*, with a small group of middle class women in 1406 on a site known as Il Praissolo outside the walls in the *contrada* of San Salvatore. Before her death in 1425, she left her closest assistant Lucia Mascheroni in charge, with a promise to maintain the group's autonomy. Within a few years Lucia's desire to respect Bernardina's wishes and maintain the lay community came into conflict with the desire of a patrician woman, Verde Pio da Carpi, to transform it into a Poor Clare community. They waged a fierce struggle for several years, but the greater power of Verde Pio and the fiscal realities of religious communities prevailed ultimately. Quite simply, a convent established under the rule of a religious order counted upon subsidies from the church as well as the dowries of daughters from upper-class families to preserve the convent's fiscal stability over time, not to mention additional bequests from families to continue supporting the convents where their daughters lived. Lay communities, on the other hand, precisely because they were not institutionalized as religious orders, were less attractive to wealthy families anxious to ensure the futures of their unmarried daughters or as beneficiaries of pious bequests. After being subjected to enormous pressure, Lucia finally acquiesced, and in 1452 the 99 women of Corpus Domini were officially recognized as Poor Clares.

The chief difference between a lay community and a convent was that the women living in the latter fell under a particular rule, or religious order, meaning that they were under the supervision of a male cleric from a nearby monastery or parish. Although women living in a lay community could not escape the thoroughly patriarchal control of Italian cities, they could escape direct male supervision of their community simply by virtue of not being institutionalized. While in this instance patrician women pressed for institutionalizing the group within a religious order, the story of Corpus Domini is nonetheless indicative of the difficulties women faced in attempting to live outside of institutional structures and direct male control. Institutionalization at Corpus Domini meant that the Este family began to send its daughters there, including Eleonora d'Este, whose father Alfonso I Duke d'Este lavished perennial bequests on the community. Another Ferrarese noble, Count Giovanni Romei, left his family palace to the convent in 1483, whereupon the windows were bricked up to join it to what was now a cloistered community.[43] The express purpose of blocking or limiting windows was to prevent the nuns from seeing outside, but also from being seen.[44] Other architectural barriers within convents included the room in which nuns met with outsiders but were prevented from seeing or being seen by means of a wheel (*roda*), a screened, revolving turntable such as the one still visible at Corpus Domini, and the separation of nuns from others within convent churches by means of grilles.[45]

Bernardina established her lay community in a normal house outside normal institutional structures. When the community came under the rule of the Poor Clares, it also received a new convent near the hospital of Santa Maria Novella. A convent appropriately under the supervision of male clerics and city fathers, protected by high walls and without windows on the street, stood at the center of a series of co-ordinates of institutional controls which reaffirmed the social practices of spatial control and patriarchal domination, reinscribing them into the city's built fabric.

Although convents gathered the unmarried daughters of noble and upper-class families, they also fulfilled other roles. The limited legitimate options available for women meant that orphans, impoverished young women in families where the male head of household had died or disappeared, or infants abandoned at birth by their mothers risked death or a life of prostitution. Conservatories cared for such girls in most Italian cities, and Ferrara was no exception. The Conservatory of Santa Maria della Rosa housed young girls who received instruction in domestic arts and eventually a dowry in anticipation of marriage.[46] In the wake of Ferrara's devastating earthquake of 15 November 1570, Barbara of Austria, wife of Duke Alfonso II d'Este, established the church and convent of Santa Barbara on Ferrara's main street, via Giovecca, as a refuge for girls left homeless or orphans.[47] Historian Guarini, writing only 40 years later, noted that Ferrara suffered acutely the poverty and misery afflicting Italy as a whole in the last decade of the sixteenth century, with many starving spinsters wandering the city aimlessly, alone and vulnerable, often ending up being raped.[48] Margherita Gonzaga established the conservatory of Santa Margarita for such girls in 1590 near the church of Sant'Agata, under the administration of Bernarda Maneci Viniziana, where they stayed until they moved to new quarters across from the parish of Sant'Agnese. Within less than two decades, 155 women and girls, in addition to 40 nuns, lived at Santa Margarita.[49] Although Bernarda operated the conservatory on a day-to-day basis, like other conservatories and convents, a group of noble male overseers helped fund it, supervise its finances and deal with problems they believed she could not handle. Girls in these conservatories benefited from the pious bequests of wealthy Ferrarese men, who often left sums of money in perpetuity to provide dowries for "honest" girls designated by the respective conservatories. With such funds a girl could leave the cloistered world of the conservatory, but only to go directly into matrimony: there were no intermediate stops for impoverished young women.[50] Perhaps more to the point, the generosity of donors often concealed the intense labor these girls engaged in, particularly their needlework and weaving for elaborate gowns and decorations for patrician families. Nuns performed similar labors, such as at the convent of S. Antonio in Polesine, where nuns helped embroider bed hangings in 1457 for Borso d'Este.[51]

Beyond being repositories for surplus females, convents also helped control the spatial movement of women in cities. As Guarini remarked, the mere fact that young women roamed the city alone made them vulnerable to attacks by men. Efforts to exert spatial control of women of all classes and occupations in Renaissance Italian cities were pervasive; there is even evidence that upper-class women were sequestered within their homes – much as the paintings by del Cossa and Butteri suggest.[52] In general, the higher a woman's social class the less freely she could move about the city, and certainly never on her own. No laws proscribed such movement, but custom frowned so deeply upon it that it was palpably dangerous. Fear that she might be corrupted by a passing male or, more importantly, that she might become pregnant by a man other than her husband and hence risk the purity of the paternal line and the orderly transmission of property and other wealth lay behind such social controls.[53] However, the records of Italian cities bulge with the evidence that married women and nuns managed to evade even the most stringent controls and engage in illicit affairs.[54]

PROSTITUTION

Anxiety over sexual behavior was particularly acute regarding prostitutes.[55] Fornication was sinful, according to medieval theologians, and women were believed to be the source of the problem ever since Eve. Despite these widely held convictions, prostitution flourished in medieval and Renaissance cities. Late medieval cities established a *modus vivendi* with prostitution first by excluding the prostitutes from inside city walls, and then by establishing public brothels, where prostitution could be regulated and taxed. In line with these practices, Italian cities enacted spatial controls of various kinds on prostitutes. In Ferrara, for example, the city statutes of 1287 explicitly excluded prostitutes from living and working in the center, in the area bounded by via dei Sabbioni to the north and the Po river to the south.[56] Additional areas closed to prostitutes lay outside of the city walls, in Borgo San Benedetto near the Benedictine monastery north of the city, and in Borgo San Leonardo, or dei Leoni, where Poor Clare nuns lived in the convent of San Guglielmo.[57] Nearly one hundred years later, Marquis Nicolò II ordered the expulsion of all prostitutes from the confines of the city, and at the same time, prostitutes were required to wear a white neck cloth and a bell, both of which were typical of other Italian and European cities.[58] Marginalized along with Jews and lepers, prostitutes joined drunks and gamblers as regular targets of clerical wrath.

Despite proclamations against prostitution by the church and the state, not only did it flourish, but also it was augmented by public brothels in many cities. The *postribuli*, or public brothels, were envisioned as separate and distinct locations where prostitutes could practice their trade under civic supervision, and to which they were restricted except by special dispensation. Statutes reserved the most severe penalties for female procurers, or *ruffiane*, which may previously have been the most typical form of prostitution, largely because it was clandestine, hence spatially dispersed within the city and much more difficult to tax. The statutory objective of confining prostitution to regulated settings aimed to remove it from public view to a confined location to be controlled and taxed. For Gamba, the proscriptions against prostitutes living within the walls of Ferrara in 1287 referred to the clandestine prostitute, or *ganea*, rather than the public prostitute, or *meretrix publica*.[59] The latter lived in the public brothels supervised by an appropriate communal office. In Florence, the *Ufficio dell'Onestà* fulfilled this function, while in Ferrara in the late fourteenth and fifteenth centuries, the task fell to the *Ufficiali della Gabella grande o di piazza* (tax officials), and later to the *Superiori delle Bollette.*[60]

Within the city, the brothel was then at once a private setting, its inhabitants supposedly invisible to the general public, and a manifestly public one, in that the location was clearly specified and officially recognized. In this respect the brothel was uncannily similar in concept to the convent, and indeed women in both cases were to be cloistered from public view – except that the effort appears to have been even less successful with prostitutes. As the fifteenth century drew to a close, the greater tolerance for prostitution in Italian cities was linked to an increasing concern about sodomy.[61] The records available do not permit a similar conclusion for Ferrara; even though four men were put to death for sodomy in 1468, 1497 and 1552, the century

11.8 Prostitute
Cesare Vecellio, *Habiti antichi et moderni di tutto il mondo* (Venice, 1598)

11.9 Prostitute and two gentlemen
"Mores Italiae"

that separates them and the absence of other data make it difficult to verify a comparable degree of anxiety, even if the statutes and proclamations make it clear that prostitution was seen as the lesser of two evils with respect to the risks for *donne honeste*.[62]

Anxiety about sodomy makes cross-dressing, one of the typical strategies adopted by prostitutes to evade spatial controls, especially intriguing. As Cesare Vecellio described them, "most [prostitutes] wear a somewhat masculine outfit: silk or cloth waistcoats adorned with conspicuous fringes and padded like young men's vests . . . they wear a man's shirt . . . many wear men's breeches."[63] Dressing as men allowed women to change quickly and, more importantly, to move freely precisely where they were not supposed to go alone – city streets, hostelries, taverns. Many northern and central Italian towns prohibited cross-dressing because of the freedom of movement men's clothing allowed women and because of the dangerous gender confusion that could result.[64] Forbidden and scandalously different, cross-dressing was also no doubt exciting for potential clients.

Despite efforts to contain it, prostitution spread out from the public brothels to different parts of Ferrara, causing renewed anxiety at the potential risks of *donne honeste* coming into contact with it.[65] Repeated proclamations throughout the fifteenth and sixteenth centuries suggested the problems associated with the diffusion of prostitution: not only did it offend and endanger other women and risk evading taxation, but also it encouraged riotous behavior. The *postribuli* usually were connected to an *osteria* (hostelry) where clients could obtain refreshment; but as prostitutes moved out of brothels, they haunted the rest of the city's inns and occasionally became embroiled in mêlées and altercations.[66] It was no accident that a lengthy and angry addition to Ferrara's statutes prohibiting bad behavior by prostitutes and others was promulgated on 25 April 1496, immediately after the running of the Palio for the feast of S. Giorgio, which must have been rife with ribald behavior, much as del Cossa's fresco suggested.[67] In 1476, also three weeks after the Palio, another statute enjoined prostitutes against stealing from, insulting, or otherwise committing dishonest acts against citizens.[68] The two acts specifically mentioned by the statute were dragging men into the bordello against their will or knocking off their hats. As Sharon Strocchia has shown, grabbing or knocking off a man's hat was one of the typical physical insults in central and northern Italian codes of honor during the Renaissance, highly charged gestures carried out in public that challenged gender codes of behavior.[69] The atmosphere surrounding inns and hostelries was anything but tranquil, and even when the prostitutes themselves were not involved in the tumult, they were seen, along with foreigners in general, as one source of the problem.

In the fifteenth century, the official brothels stood at the periphery of Ferrara's inhabited center, the locations mirroring their inhabitants' origins and social position.

Although no census of prostitutes has survived, other sources suggest that both prostitutes and pimps often originated from other Italian and European cities.[70] In 1438, for example, fourteen pimps were recognized in Ferrara, of whom only two were from Italy; three others were German, but nine were from the Low Countries.[71] Among the recorded names of prostitutes, for example, are Ursolina da Udine, Lucia di Bologna and Margherita di Marco, called "Schiavolina," meaning from Dalmatia.[72]

Two *postribuli* dated from the fourteenth century: one in the *contrada* of San Romano, directly behind the cathedral in what is today Piazza Trento Trieste, the second nearby in the *contrada* of San Paolo, on the street today called via Porta Reno.[73] In the fifteenth century, the public brothel known as "del Gambero" in San Romano was situated to the north just outside the city's walls, across the canal that became via Giovecca; another bordello backed up against the city walls between the *contrade* of Rotta and Mutina on via di Malborghetto near San Biagio in the northwest part of the city; and another in the *contrada* of Santa Croce on today's via Croce Bianca.[74] Associated with the brothel on via del Gambero was an *osteria* and a *stufa*, public baths traditionally linked to prostitution, much as massage parlors are today.[75]

In the sixteenth century, at least two additional locations were associated with prostitution, both near *osteria* owned by Cesare d'Este. On the via di Santa Maria de Bocche adjacent to the Palazzo del Paradiso stood his *osteria* along with several apartment blocks; his second *osteria*, Osteria dell'Angelo, was situated at the corner of via Ripa Grande and via di San Paolo and had been Este property for well over a century. Located near the city gate of San Paolo and adjacent to one of the city's two major streets of shops, with its two dozen commodious rooms the Osteria dell'Angelo was ideally located to collect travellers, along with two others in via delle Volte, the Osteria dal Sole and the Osteria dal Moro.[76] Around the corner from d'Este's *osteria* on via dell'Inferno was a *stufa* operated by Caterina Stovara.[77] Ercole I's decision in 1494 to confine prostitutes to the area around Sant'Agnese probably increased his income, but also contributed to making the area a flourishing center of the flesh trade – as did the transfer in 1561 of Ferrara's university and its abundant male student population from the Piazza del Mercato to Palazzo del Paradiso, which sat precisely between the stew and the *osteria* of Cesare d'Este.[78]

The association of prostitution with Ferrara's streets, from at least the fourteenth century forward, lives on in their names: via del Gambero, for example, derived from the name of the brothel located there.[79] Many records referred to the street in the fifteenth and sixteenth centuries as via dei Bastardini, for the large number of abandoned infants (presumably illegitimate ones) left for the convent of San Cristoforo to raise.[80] Via Malborghetto, meaning bad or evil district, was associated with the brothel connected to the Osteria Montealbano and its successors.[81] Via dell' Inferno

11.10 Conservatory of S. Agnese (c. 1826)
Antonio Sandri, *Origine delle chiese di Ferrara e luoqhi delta provincia*, manuscript, BCA 10/1985

(Hell), although initially connected to heretics who lived there, linked the street with sin because of its constellation of hostelry, stew and brothel; it was later more explicitly called via del Bordelletto, or little brothel. The persistent association of particular streets with prostitution in Ferrara is remarkable; via Malborghetto has retained its name, and while via del Gambero became Bersaglieri del Po during the twentieth century, the name survives in a small alley leading off of it, vicolo del Gambero. Via delle Volte, on the other hand, where two major *osteria* were located, remained a center of prostitution through the middle of the twentieth century, preserving its characteristic activity and reputation for over five hundred years.[82]

Space and spatial practices coincided with gender ideologies, then, and the limitations on movement for prostitutes through the sixteenth century reinforced the gendered spatial hierarchy of Ferrara. The control of *meretrici* included three components: temporal, spatial and dress. In 1450, for example, prostitutes were confined to their brothels except for Saturday, when they were allowed to go to market in the town center.[83] Always off limits were places such as *osteria* and taverns, and Ferrarese residents were likewise forbidden to house them or their pimps.[84] The bell and/or the identifying cloth at the neck continued to be required dress whenever they left the brothels. Just how seriously officials took these regulations will never be known because of the absence of judicial records. Two types of evidence suggest that enforcement was not rigid: first, the repeated proclamations enjoining prostitutes who were not living in brothels to move there promptly, sometimes two in one year, indicate a high rate of evasion. Second, at various times Este family members owned some of the major inns in the city, and the operation of brothels was awarded to the highest bidder, suggesting that the income from alcohol and prostitution discouraged repressive treatment of offenders.[85]

Two letters from Ercole I d'Este to his wife, Eleonora of Aragon, demonstrate the relationship between income, prostitution and the struggle over space.[86] Giangiorgio of Milan, proprietor of Osteria La Nave, rented a house across from the oratory of S. Sebastian at the church and monastery of S. Francesco, from one Don Giovanni.[87] The monks claimed that Giangiorgio maintained a house of prostitution at his *osteria* and that he planned to extend the activity to the house. Evidently, Eleonora allowed the monks to evict him so he in turn appealed to Ercole, noting that the house had first

11.11 Decree against prostitutes, pimps, procurers, sodomites and others, Statua ferrariae (1476)

been offered to the monks, but when they turned it down, Don Giovanni had rented it to him, and Giangiorgio insisted that he planned to live there with his wife because the adjacent inn was too crowded. Giangiorgio was also prepared to offer the Duke a significant increase in the tax he paid for the inn, going from about 100–120 to 200 *libre* per year. Although the Duchess tried to intercede on behalf of the monks, Ercole insisted on returning the house to Giangiorgio, pointing out to her that such women had always frequented the inn without ever generating concern from the monks. Ercole made it clear that the additional taxes Giangiorgio was willing to pay more than offset any potential inconvenience connected with women of ill-repute.

Ercole's actions fully embodied the conflicts that shot through gender relations in the fifteenth and sixteenth centuries. On the one hand he spent lavish sums to induce a woman of reputed sanctity, Lucia di Narni, to establish a convent in Ferrara; on the other he pragmatically encouraged prostitution and even strategically located it close to his *osteria*. Ferrarese citizens, nonetheless, spontaneously enacted their own methods to keep prostitution from their neighborhoods, such as sale contracts that specified that the house would never be rented to prostitutes, as was the case for a piece of land sold in the *contrada* of Sesto San Romano by Sigismondo da

Consandolo.[88] Nonetheless, despite ducal injunctions and threats of penalties, rooms and houses continued to be rented for brothels. The rental contracts depict such quarters as spare, minimally furnished one room units let out for prostitution. The brothel rented by two brothers from Milan on via di Malborghetto in 1469 consisted of twenty-three *chiusi*, probably of one room each, along with the Montealbano hostelry, a stew, courtyard and well.[89] Significantly smaller, the brothel on via del Gambero consisted of four rooms rented furnished with beds, covers, tables and chests, plus kitchen utensils in the room to be used to serve wine.[90] Later in the sixteenth century the hostelry on via di Malborghetto, then known as La Casa della Barbiera (the barber's house), was operated by a woman, as were the stew on via dell'Inferno and the Osteria della Giusta on via S. Paolo.[91]

Topographic location was one method for distinguishing a *meretrice* from a *donna honesta*, but it was not the only one. A second device for determining if a woman was *dishonesta* was her *fama publica*, or public reputation. Whether she earned money for sexual favors or not, a reputation for promiscuity as attested to by neighbors, properly confirmed and adjudicated by city officials, was sufficient to force a women into a brothel.[92] Any woman not registered as a prostitute, but adjudicated promiscuous by civic courts, risked a punishment known as the *scopa* or broom, as she was paraded partially nude through the streets to suffer insults, ridicule and rotten food thrown by the crowds.[93] The public streets that were available only in a limited way to an "honest" married or single woman became the stage for her punishment if she breached the code of sexual behavior according to public opinion, as expressed in the city's streets and squares.[94] In the first instance, exposure on city streets rendered her "public," an openly fallen woman just like a prostitute, therefore removed from the protection of the private domain and vulnerable to ridicule and humiliation such as no respectable woman would ever have to face. Being physically and socially exposed in this shaming ritual was but a logical corollary of becoming "public."[95]

Space and public reputation converged, then, not only with women accused of promiscuity, but also with those declared by *fama publica* to be saints.[96] In the titanic struggle between good and evil, just as nuns in convents supposedly helped erect an invisible shield around the city to protect it from evil, so prostitutes were conduits of evil, among those first blamed when good was defeated and evil invaded the city. And the struggle in Ferrara was engaged between convents and brothels jostling next to one another for space and souls on the city's streets. A group of poor women established the convent and hospital of San Lazzaro in 1579 on via Santa Croce, precisely in the midst of a flourishing trade in prostitution.[97] Bernardina Sedazzari founded her lay community initially in S. Salvatore, a historic center of prostitution; twelve prostitutes who decided to give up their profession and take

11.12 View of Ferrara (*c.* 1500); anonymous artist

religious orders established S. Maria Maddalena on via delle Porte Serrate, again near a major zone of prostitution, and infants presumably abandoned by via del Gambero's prostitutes were collected at the church of San Cristoforo ai Bastardini on the same street.[98]

The spatial relationship among women, men and specific buildings in the city became epic symbols of the best and worst in cities and individuals, of the struggle between good and evil, honest and dishonest, order and disorder. Containing women within the various categories of buildings – convents, brothels, private homes – was understood as a means of maintaining public order, an order defined by and supervised by the men.[99] But the spatial definition of this order was anything but tranquil; on the contrary, it was tense and conflicted, a battle waged daily on the streets and in the institutions within which women were contained. Ferrarese women were anything but docile victims of patriarchy. While many supported the existing codes of gendered spaces, others clearly did not. Teodora Lenti's contract with her son-in-law requiring that she receive board and room for the rest of her life and Lucia Mascheroni's resistance to being forced to turn a lay community into a religious order are but two examples of women challenging the gendered space in Ferrara. The prostitutes who insulted the honor codes of honest men by knocking off their hats, or who insisted on living or working in areas of the city that were off limits to them, likewise asserted their resistance to contemporary codes regarding gender and space.

Perhaps the most fitting conclusion to this discussion of gendered spaces in Ferrara are the emblematic fates of two Ferrarese women, Lucia and Laura. When she died in 1544, Suor Lucia Broccoleti (Lucia di Narni) was buried in the convent of S. Caterina da Siena, her body conserved in a glass case and showered with honors, until a papal decree ordered that it be returned to her home town of Narni to an equally splendid display in a sumptuous chapel in the Cathedral.[100] The former prostitute Laura, on the other hand, sought to repent by being closed in a small room in the tribune of the Cathedral of San Giorgio in Ferrara, where she died in 1507, out of view and without celebration.[101] In their own ways, both of these women embodied the gendered spatial practices confronted by large groups of women – nuns and former prostitutes – and, like working class women who engaged in domestic and other types of labor, were occluded in del Cossa's scheme of women and space in Renaissance Ferrara.

ACKNOWLEDGEMENTS

A grant from the Graham Foundation in 1996 allowed me to continue archival research in Ferrara which I began in 1993. I have been helped by a number of people at different times, all of whom have given generously of time and knowledge to help me complete this project. Ana Betancourt, Sibel Bozdogan, Serenella Di Palma, Valezra Earl, David Friedman, Angelica Gamba, Eunice Howe, Mark Jarzombek and Nasser Rabbat offered help, advice, friendship, debate and warm hospitality at key points. Deanna Shemek shared an early version of her article on gender in Ferrara with me, enormously assisting my development of this chapter. Ilaria Savino and Luigi Ficacci of the Gabinetto Nazionale delle Stampe and Laura Bigoni of the Archivio Fotografico del Comune di Ferrara helped in locating images, while Loretta of the Archivio di Stato, Ferrara, helped locate documents. I was able to complete the chapter during the summer of 1998 as a Visiting Professor at the University of Technology, Sydney, Australia, where the generous encouragement and support of Dean Geoffrey Caban and Associate Dean for Research Steven Harfield made it possible to work in tranquility. Anne Wenham and Lyndall Silbey were more than generous with their time and assistance; to all of them I am grateful for the wonderful opportunity to learn about their university and their city. I also presented versions of this chapter in talks at the Massachusetts Institute of Technology, University of New Mexico, University of Illinois, Chicago, and the Graduate School of Design at Harvard University, where I benefited from the comments of the audiences.

References

1   Deanna Shemek, "Circular Definitions," *Renaissance Quarterly*, v. 48 n. 1 (Spring 1995), pp. 1–40; Diane Ghirardo, "Surveillance and Spectacle in Fascist Ferrara," Martha Pollak (ed.), *The Education of the Architect* (Cambridge, MA: MIT Press, 1997), pp. 325–62; Alan Dundes and Alessandro Falassi, *La Terra in Piazza* (Berkeley, CA: University of California Press, 1975); Luciano Artusi and Silvano Gabbrielli, *Le feste di Firenze dalla Candeloro a Berlingaccio* (Rome: Newton Compton, 1991), pp. 184–9; Nino Franco Visentini, *Il Palio di Ferrara* (Rovigo: Istituto pagano di arti grafiche, 1968); Dino Tebaldi *et al.*, *Ferrara e il Palio* (Ferrara, 1982).

2   Maria Serena Mazzi, *Prostitute e lenoni nella Firenze del Quattrocento* (Milan: Il Saggiatore, 1991), p. 186.

3   Johann Burchard, *At the court of the Borgia, being an account of the reign of Pope Alexander VI written by his Master of Ceremonies, Johann Burchard* (London: Folio Society, 1963), pp. 194–5.

4   Francesco Barbaro, "De re uxoria," Eugenio Garin (ed.), *Prosatori latini del Quattrocento. La Letteratura italiana, storia e testi* (Milan: R. Ricciardi, 1952), pp. 121–5.

5   Shemek, "Circular Definitions," pp. 33–8.

6   Dennis Romano, "Gender and the Urban Geogaphy of Renaissance Venice," *Journal of Social History*, v. 23 (1989), pp. 339–53; Robert C. Davis, "The Geography of Gender in the Renaissance," Judith C. Brown and Robert C. Davis (eds) *Gender and Society in Renaissance Italy* (London: Longman, 1998), pp. 19–38; Samuel Cohn, *Women in the Streets* (Baltimore, MD: Johns Hopkins University Press, 1996); Karen Scott, "Urban Spaces, Women's Networks, and the Lay Apostolate in the Siena of Catherine Benincasa," E. Ann Matter and John Coakley (eds) *Creative Women in Medieval and Early Modern Italy* (Philadelphia: University of Pennsylvania Press, 1994), pp. 105–19; and Diane Ghirardo, "Cherchez La Femme?" Katerina Rüedi, Sarah Wigglesworth and Duncan McCorquodale (eds), *Desiring Practices* (London: Black Dog, 1996), pp. 156–73.

7   Ludwig H. Heydenreich and Wolfgang Lotz, *Architecture in Italy, 1400 to 1600* (Harmondsworth: Penguin, 1974); Peter Murray, *The Architecture of the Italian Renaissance* (London: Thames and Hudson, 1986).

8   Nancy Frasier, "Rethinking the Public Sphere," Bruce Robbins (ed.), *The Phantom Public Sphere* (Minneapolis: University of Minnesota Press, 1992), pp. 1–32; Henrietta Moore, *Space, Text and Gender* (Cambridge: Cambridge University Press, 1985), p. 74.

9   Pierre Bourdieu, "The Berber House," Mary Douglas (ed.), *Rules and Meanings* (Harmondsworth: Penguin, 1973).

10 Margaret Rosenthal, *The Honest Courtesan* (Chicago: University of Chicago Press, 1992).

11 *Statuta civitatis Ferrariae 1456*, Biblioteca Comunale Ariostea, Ferrara (henceforth BCA); Luciano Maragna (ed.), *Gli statuti del Polesine di Rovigo durante il dominio Estense* (Ferrara: Copy Express, 1996).

12 Joan Kelly-Gadol, "Did Women Have a Renaissance?," Renate Bridenthal, Claudia Koonz and Susan Stuard (eds), *Becoming Visible* (Boston, MA: Houghton Mifflin, 1987), pp. 175–201.

13 Christiane Klapisch-Zuber, *Women, Family and Ritual in Renaissance Italy* (Chicago: University of Chicago Press, 1985); Judith Brown, "A Woman's Place Was in the Home," Margaret Ferguson, Maureen Quilligan and Nancy Vickers (eds), *Rewriting the Renaissance* (Chicago: University of Chicago Press,1986), pp. 206–24.

14 Stanley Chojnacki, "Daughters and Oligarchs," Brown and Davis (eds), *Gender and Society*, pp. 63–86.

15 Leon Battista Alberti, *Della famiglia* (Columbia, SC: University of South Carolina Press, 1969).

16 Thomas V. Cohen and Elizabeth S. Cohen, *Words and Deeds in Renaissance Rome* (Toronto: University of Toronto Press, 1993).

17 Agostino Valier, *Modo di vivere proposto alle vergine che si chiamano dimesse* (Venice, 1577), cited in Virginia Cox, "The Single Self," *Renaissance Quarterly* v. 48 n. 3 (Autumn 1995), pp. 513–56 n. 32.

18 Dennis Romano, *Housecraft and Statecraft* (Baltimore, MD: Johns Hopkins University Press, 1996).

19 Otis, *Prostitution in Medieval Society*; Trexler, "La prostitution florentine;" and "Editto che non si va notare o lavarsi al fiume senza mutande," (4 August 1612), Camera Apostolica, Archivio di Stato, Roma.

20 Archivio Storico Comunale, Ferrara (henceforth ASCF), Fondo Deputazione di Storia Patria, Testamenti 1448–1873 (henceforth Testamenti), b. 35, I. 4, 925 (18 April 1448). "Testamento di Chiara filias quondam Domenico Ambrosi, vedova di Giovanni Agodi."

21 ASCF, Testamenti, b. 36, VI 2.b. 2541/2 (22 August 1559). "Testamento di Teodora filias quondam Guidonio Lenti, moglie di Giulio Laziosi."

22 Archivio di Stato, Ferrara (henceforth ASF), Serie Patrimoniale, B. 30, f. 11, Fondo Montecatini, "Compendio di tutte le strade case palazzi e conventi," (henceforth "Compendio"), p. 27v.

23 Antonio Sandri, *Origine delle chiese di Ferrara e luoghi della provincia*, manuscript, BCA, 10/1985, p. 87r.

24 *Diario ferrarese dal 1409 sino al 1502 di autori incerti*, Giuseppe Pardi (ed.), *Rerum Italicum Scriptores*, Tomo XXIV/7 (Bologna: Nicola Zanichelli, 1937); Thomas Tuohy, *Herculean Ferrara* (Cambridge: Cambridge University Press, 1996).

25 BCA, *Libro dei Giustiziati 1441–1577*.

26 Chojnacki, "Daughters and Oligarchs," pp. 75–84; see also Cox, "The Single Self," pp. 513–56.

27 ASF, "Compendio," p. 49r.

28 Sandri, *Origine delle chiese*; Marc'Antonio Guarini, *Compendio Historico dell'origine, accrescimento e Prerogative delle chiese, e Luoghi Pii della città, e diocesi di Ferrara* (Ferrara: Vittorio Baldini MCD XXL [1630]); G. A. Scalabrini, *Memorie storiche delle chiese di Ferrara e dei suoi borghi* (Ferrara: C. Coatti 1773).

29 Gabriella Zarri, "Monache e sante alla corte estense XV–XVI secolo," Francesco Bocchi (ed.), *Storia illustrata di Ferrara*, v. II (Repubblica di San Marino: AIEP, 1997), p. 418.

30 Zarri, "Monache e sante," pp. 417–26.

31 Zarri, "Monache e sante," p. 25.

32 Angelica Gamba, "La prostituzione a Ferrara nel tardo medioevo," (unpublished thesis, University of Ferrara, 1997).

33 Sandri, *Origine delle chiese*, p. 65r.

34 Gabriella Zarri, "Pieta e profezia alle corti padane," *Le sante vive* (Turin, 1990), pp. 54–5.

35 Guarini, *Compendio Historico*, p. 143.

36 Guarini, *Compendio Historico*, p. 276; Samuel K. Cohen, "Convertite e malmaritate," *Memoria* 5 (1982), pp. 46–63.

37 Guido Dall'Olio, "La disciplina dei religiosi all'epoca del Concilio di Trento," *Annali dell'Istituto storico italo-germanico in Trento*, 21 (1995); Gabriella Zarri, "Gender, Religious Institutions and Social Discipline," Brown and Davis (eds), *Gender and Society*, pp. 193–212; Gabriella Zarri, "Monasteri femminili e città (secoli XV–XVIII)," Giorgio Chittolini and Giovanni Micoli (eds), *Storia d'Italia. Annali 9* (Turin: Einaudi, 1986), pp. 357–439.

38 A. Lazzari, "Il signore di Ferrara ai tempi del concilio del 1438–39 Nicolò III d'Este," *Attraverso la storia di Ferrara, Atti e Memorie*, n. s., X (Rovigo, 1954), cited in Gamba, "La prostituzione a Ferrara," Part I, ch. 2.

39 Zarri, "Gender, Religious Institutions," pp. 193–212.

40 Chojnacki, "Daughters and Oligarchs," p. 70.

41 Paolo da Certaldo, "Libro di buoni costumi," Vittore Branca (ed.), *Mercanti Scrittori* (Milan: Rusconi, 1986), pp. 25–6.

42 Mary Martin McLaughlin, "Creating and Recreating Communities of Women," *Signs* (Winter 1989), pp. 293–321. See Guarini, *Compendio Historico*, pp. 283–5.

43 Sandri, *Origine delle chiese*, p. 62v.

44 Archivio Estense, Archivio di Stato, Modena, Offitio delle Monitione e Fabbriche, 1501, b. 37, 69; Tuohy, *Herculean Ferrara*, p. 180.

45 Tuohy, *Herculean Ferrara*, p. 181.

46 Sandri, *Origine delle chiese*, p. 111r.

47 Sandri, *Origine delle chiese*, pp. 72v and 73r.

48 Guarini, *Compendio Historico*, pp. 208–9.

49 ASF, Archivio Storico Patrimoniale, Serie Patrimoniale, b. 9, fasc. 64 (1608). "Attestazioni delle donzelle di S. Margarita."

50 ASCF, Testamenti, b. 35, I. 9n40 (1432). "Testamento Dott. Fabio Antimacco;" b. 35, III. (10 July 1591), "Testamento Alfonso Cattaneo."

51 Archivio Estense, Archivio di Stato, Modena, Libri dell'Amministrazione della Casa, "Tapezerie," 2, 1457, "Ricami de apparamenti da seda," cited in Tuohy, *Herculean Ferrara*, p. 39.

52 "Camilla the Go-between," Cohen and Cohen, *Words and Deeds in Renaissance Rome*, pp. 159–87.

53 Baldessare Castiglione, *The Book of the Courtier* (Baltimore, MD: Penguin, 1967).

54 Mazzi, *Prostitute e lenoni*, pp. 132–7.

55 Leah H. Otis, *Prostitution in Medieval Society* (Chicago: University of Chicago Press, 1985); Jacques Rossiaud, *Medieval Prostitution* (Oxford: Blackwell, 1988); Rinaldo Comba, "'Apetitus libidinis cohercaetur. Strutture demografiche, reati sessuali e disciplina dei comportamenti nel Piemonte tardomedievale," *Studi Storici*, v. 27 n. 3 (1986), pp. 529–76; Gamba, "La prostituzione a Ferrara;" Mazzi, *Prostitute e lenoni*; Richard Trexler, "La prostitution florentine au XV siècle," *Annales E.S.C.*, 36 (1981), pp. 983–1015.

56 BCA, *Statuta Ferrariae anno MCCLXXXVII*, W. Montorsi (ed.) (Ferrara, 1955), IV, p. 275, rubrica LXXI.

57 BCA, *Statuta Ferrariae*, IV, p. 275, rubrica LXXII.

58 Luigi Cittadella, *Notizie amministrative, storiche, artistiche relative a Ferrara*, v. I (Ferrara: Domenico Taddei 1868, reprinted Bologna: Forni, 1969), v. I, p. 290.

59 Gamba, "La prostituzione a Ferrara," Parte I, ch. II.

60 BCA. *Statuta et provisiones gabellarum platae civitatis Ferraria*, in *Statuta provisiones et decreta gabellarum civitatis Ferrariae 1602*, pp. 67–8, rubrica CCLVIII, "Pacta postribuli."

61 Mazzi, *Prostitute e lenoni*, pp. 71 and passim.

62 *Libro dei giustiaziati*; Mazzi, *Prostitute e lenoni*, pp. 187–9.

63 Cesare Vecellio, *Habiti antichi et moderni di tutto il mondo* (Venice, 1598).

64 Valerie R. Hotchkiss, *Clothes Make the Man* (New York: Garland, 1996).

65 ASF, *Statuti*, ch. 45v, 46r, rubr. 131 (25 April 1496).

66 Gamba, "La prostituzione a Ferrara," Parte II, ch. V.

67 ASF, *Statuti*, ch. 45v, 46r, rubr. 131 (25 April 1496); Cittadella, *Notizie*, pp. 291–7.

68 ACF, *Statuti*, ch. 40v, rubrica 114 (17 May 1476).

69 Sharon T. Strocchia, "Gender and the Rites of Honour in Italian Renaissance Cities," Brown and Davis (eds), *Gender and Society*, pp. 39–60.

70 Mazzi, *Prostitute e lenoni*, pp. 293–301.

71 ASF, Archivio Storico Comunale, Serie Patrimoniale, *Statuti dell'Ufficio delle Bollette*, b. 9, fasc. 17 (henceforth *Statuti*), ch. 18v, rubrica 48 (20 June 1447). "De iurisdictione officialium contra lenones."

72 Gamba, "La prostituzione a Ferrara," Part II, ch. 2; SF, Archivio Storico Comunale, *Libro delle commissioni ducale e proclami dall'anno 1462 all'anno 1475*, ch. 111 (8 November 1471).

73 Gamba, "La prostituzione a Ferrara," Part II, ch. 1.

74 ASF, *Statuti*, ch. 40v, rubrica 114 (17 May 1476); Gerolamo Melchiorri, *Nomenclatura ed etimologia delle piazze e strade di Ferrara*, E. Mari (ed.) (Ferrara: Industrie Grafiche, 1988), pp. 19–20.

75 ASF, Archivio Notarile Antico, Notaio Vitale Lucenti, matr. 201, b. I, c. 24r, 13 January 1473, and Gamba, "La prostituzione a Ferrara," appendix 22.

76 ASF, "Compendio," pp. 4v, 5r, 32r; Archivio di Stato, Modena, *Cancelleria Ducale*, carteggio fattorale, b. 22/1, fascicolo 25, letter from Giacomo Prisciani to Duke Ercole (4 May 1491); and Gamba, "La prostituzione a Ferrara," appendix 18.

77 ASF, "Inventario," p. 57v.

78 *Diario ferrarese dal 1409 sino al 1502*, p. 268, lines 15–20.

79 Gamba, "La prostituzione a Ferrara," Part I, ch. 1.

80 Sandri, *Origine delle chiese* pp. 112r, 113v.

81 Gamba, "La prostituzione a Ferrara," Part II, ch. 1.

82 ASF, *Statuti*, ch. 37, rubrica 105.

83 ASF, *Statuti*, ch. 23, rubrica 68 (23 April 1450), "Contra meretrices et hospites."

84 ASF, *Statuti*; including ch. 23, rubrica 68 (23 April 1450); ch. 26, rubrica 80 (28 December 1461); ch. 30, rubrica 90 (23 August 1464); ch. 34, rubrica 125 (21 July 1489).

85 ASF, "Compendio," pp. 4v and 57v; and ASCF, Testamenti, b. 36, II.3, 1060/8, "Testamento dell'Illustrissimo et Eccellentissimo Alfonso Duca di Ferrara (28 agosto 1533), codicillo fatto l'anno 1534, 28 agosto."

86 Archivio di Stato, Modena, *Cancelleria Ducale, Leggi e decreti*, C.V. p. 200, Letter of Ercole I to his wife, Duchess Eleonora (26 October 1478); C.V. p. 211, Letter from Ercole to the Duchess on the Giangiorgio case (12 November 1478); and Gamba, "La prostituzione a Ferrara," appendices 8 and 9.

87 Sandri, *Origine delle chiese*," c. 93v.

88 A. Franceschini, *Artisti a Ferrara in età umanistica e rinascimentale. Testimonianze archivistiche*, Part II, Tome I, *Dal 1472 al 1492* (Ferrara: Corbo 1993), p. 221.

89 ASF, Archivio Notarile Antico, Notary G. Castelli, matr. 128, b. 3, pp. 13rv, 14rv (25 November 1469), "Affictus Santini de mediolano e fratris a Simone e fratre de Mediolano," cited in Gamba, "La prostituzione a Ferrara," Part II, ch. 1.

90 ASF, Archivio Notarile Antico, Notary L. Portelli, matr. 217, b. I, pp. 37rv, 38rv (6 August 1476), "Affictus Federici de Flandria et Petri de Salandria magistro Zanini de Picardia," cited in Gamba, "La prostituzione a Ferrara," Part II, Chap. 1.

91 ASF, "Inventario," pp. 14r, 33r, 57v.

92 ASF, *Statuti*, ch. 10v, rubrica 8, 1438; ch. 94 (December 1468).

93 ASF, *Statuti*, ch. 28r–29r, rubrica 83 (29 April 1462).

94 ASF, *Statuti*, ch. 28r–29r, rubrica 83 (29 April 1462).

95 ASF, *Statuti*, ch. 16v, rubr. 40 (24 July 1438).

96 Sandri, *Origine delle chiese*, 52r, 63r, 65r.

97 Sandri, *Origine delle chiese*, p. 75r.

98 Sandri, *Origine delle chiese*, pp. 89r–v.

99 Daniella Frigo, "Dal Caos all'ordine," Marina Zancan (ed.), *Nel cerchio della louna* (Venice: Marsilio 1983), pp. 57–93.

100 Sandri, *Origine delle chiese*, p. 65r.

101 Guarini, *Compendio Historico*.

Tendency 3

Theorising historical methodology

Chapter 12
Heterotopia deserta: Las Vegas and other spaces
Sarah Chaplin

In this chapter I wish to trace the historiography of two separate phenomena: the heterotopia and Las Vegas. Both Michel Foucault's work on the heterotopia and contemporaneous studies of Las Vegas have become imbricated in architectural discourse, each eliciting provocative insights and new critiques since the late 1960s, as different theorists have responded to and developed these ideas. Foucault first referred to the heterotopia in *The Order of Things*, published in 1966, and then developed the notion into a set of principles with spatial and typological examples in a lecture entitled "Of Other Spaces," which he gave to a group of French architecture students in 1967. During the same period of the mid-1960s, Las Vegas was also capturing the attention of a generation of architecture students: in 1965 Tom Wolfe published an enigmatic essay on the subject, a piece which Reyner Banham claims gave rise to *Learning from Las Vegas*, the outcome of a studio at Yale taught by Denise Scott Brown, Steve Izenour and Robert Venturi. By bringing the heterotopia and Las Vegas together in the context of this discussion, I hope to offer a critical intersection from which to consider the issue of *otherness* in relation to space, and its representation and mediation within contemporary culture.

Otherness is regarded by feminist architectural historian Mary McLeod as "one of the primary preoccupations of contemporary architecture theory,"[1] but she claims that the nature of this desire for otherness on the part of architects and architectural theorists alike is "largely unexplored in recent architectural debate."[2] She sees this concern with otherness as a superficial form of postmodern avant-gardism on the part of certain architectural practitioners, for whom anything that might be deemed "other" is singularly desirable in a culture which prizes newness and celebrates difference. In her view, however, architects seek and identify otherness in the wrong places and for the wrong reasons, and that, like Foucault, their definition of otherness relies on exclusive and elitist categorisations of space. McLeod's primary contention is that until architects and architectural theoreticians engage with a broader notion of what constitutes the other in spatial terms, this quest is flawed.

I will address a broader notion of spatial otherness by extending the debate beyond the production and design of space, which is the emphasis architectural history has traditionally favoured, to consider otherness from the point of view of the consumption of space, that is to say by treating otherness as a factor of consumption, as witnessed in Las Vegas. In particular, I want to show how otherness becomes a constructed spatial condition which undergoes a process of commodification in Western culture, leading ultimately to its desertification as a concept, an outcome which may be seen to have both positive and negative connotations.

Apart from Foucault, McLeod, Wolfe, Venturi/Scott Brown/Izenour et al., I will also draw upon the work of Gianni Vattimo and Arthur Kroker whose theories are of historiographical significance to the present discussion. In addition, I will refer to Banham's *Scenes in America Deserta*,[3] and Jean Baudrillard's *America*,[4] as two key texts on the American desert, and which offer insights where Las Vegas is concerned. In some senses, I am positioning Las Vegas as the "other" with respect to Los Angeles. Quite apart from Banham's own study of Los Angeles,[5] and Mike Davis' influential account of the city,[6] much of the work by urban geographers on the heterotopia has made LA the dominant urban case study: in particular, Edward Soja,[7] Edward Relph,[8] Derek Gregory,[9] and even architectural historian Charles Jencks[10] have argued that the heterotopia is a key concept in postmodern geography, important for understanding a post-metropolis such as Los Angeles. This chapter aims to complement, albeit in a very brief way, work on Los Angeles, but in so doing I hope to show that Las Vegas is in fact a more powerful exemplar in discussions concerning other spaces and the heterotopia.

There is one characteristic which, above all, links the historiographies of Las Vegas and the heterotopia, namely ambivalence. Both have been represented as ambivalent phenomena *per se*, so too have their respective theorisations proved ambivalent in their treatment of them as phenomena.

12.1 Las Vegas as heterotopia (1998)

12.2 Casino as heterotopia (1998)

There is clearly a discursive ambivalence in the way the heterotopia is thematised in Foucault's own work – a cause for concern among some theorists who have probed his writings to account for his ever-drifting emphasis. Benjamin Genocchio has critiqued Foucault's writings on the heterotopia for failing to explain how a spatial separation is effected between heterotopias and their surroundings:

> Foucault's argument is reliant upon a means of establishing some invisible but visibly operational difference which, disposed against the background of an elusive spatial continuum, provides a clear conception of spatially discontinuous ground. Crucially, what is lacking from Foucault's argument is exactly this.[11]

However, far from rendering the heterotopia conceptually unstable and hence unreliable, as Genocchio has hinted, it is Foucault's ambivalent arguments that are so important in gaining an understanding of the way in which other spaces are established culturally. In fact, the positioning of heterotopia both semantically and physically cannot be stable and fixed, since its very purpose is to effect contingency and disrupt continuity.

Henri Lefebvre also accused Foucault of ambivalence on another front, namely for failing to distinguish between two kinds of spatiality:

> Foucault never explains what space it is that he is referring to, nor how it bridges the gap between the theoretical (epistemological) realm and the practical one, between mental and social, between the space of philosophers and the space of people who deal with material things.[12]

12.3 Nevada desert (1998)

12.4 Las Vegas as everyday other (1998)

I am, however, working with this conflation, since I believe that Foucault's lack of explanation was intentional: the spatial ambivalence in his work drew attention to the interdependency between spatial theory and spatial practice. Rather than a gap requiring to be bridged, I would argue that this represents a productive fuzzy field in Foucault's references to different kinds of space. Furthermore, the fact that Foucault's ideas are left so open to interpretation makes his glossing of the heterotopia not necessarily definitive: the reworking of Foucault's ideas in subsequent texts simply take the concept on their own terms and develop it in new ways, discovering new relevance for the heterotopia within other contexts.

So let me give a brief overview of what Foucault in "Of Other Spaces" called "a sort of systematic description or heterotopology,"[13] in which he elaborated six principles of the heterotopia, citing particular architectural typologies for each principle:

1   There is no culture in the world which is not made up of heterotopias, and in every human group there will be counter-sites. Foucault identified two main types, heterotopias of crisis and of deviance, spaces such as prisons, sanatoria and boarding schools which are set aside, placed in parentheses, with sharply demarcated boundaries and rules.

2   Heterotopias invariably undergo transformations over time, as in the cemetery's relationship to a city or a mausoleum's relationship to a house, whereby "a society may take an existing heterotopia, which has never vanished, and make it function in a different way."[14]

3   Heterotopias which have the power of juxtaposing in a single real place different spaces and locations that are incompatible with each other. Foucault cited theatres, cinemas and gardens.

4   In heterotopias of juxtaposition there is a perpetual accumulation of items or experiences over time, such as with museums, libraries, holiday camps and travelling fairs, where these spaces function as "heterochronisms" which can be either permanent or ephemeral.

5   Heterotopias have their own systems of opening and closing "that isolates them and makes them penetrable at the same time."[15] Foucault stated that barracks and Turkish baths operate in this way, as well as American motels.

6   The heterotopia exists between the two poles of illusion and compensation. At one extreme lies the brothel, and at the other, the colony. The final manifestation of the heterotopia which Foucault put forward is the ship, which he says is "the heterotopia par excellence."[16] The ship is both illusion and compensation: it transports its passengers to other worlds, depositing them on foreign shores to discover as yet unknown other spaces, and it also recreates in its own

architecture of decks and bridges, saloons and cargo holds, cabins and cocktail lounges, an ordered arrangement which parallels lived reality on *terra firma*.

It is but a small step from the illusory yet compensatory quality of the cruise ship to the saloons and cocktail lounges of a Las Vegas casino. At the level of Foucault's symptomatic principles, Las Vegas would seem a yet more perfect example of the heterotopia, combining the attributes of theatre, cinema, garden, museum, holiday camp, honeymoon motel, brothel and colony, as well as that of the ship. In Las Vegas, heterochronism exists in the form of a multitude of themed resorts which borrow from other places and other times and are then juxtaposed along the Strip without any logical historical or geographical ordering. However, there is more to be derived than this superficial interpretation from a historiographical consideration of the heterotopia in relation to Las Vegas, and vice versa.

Beyond Foucault's six principles, there is a strategic similarity between the staging of Las Vegas' historiography and that of the heterotopia, and in the way that they have become absorbed into architectural discourse. First, there is the discovery of an "other" space, one which operates or displays qualities which were previously unknown, unacknowledged, or whose mere existence or whereabouts was unknown. Second, this space is then identified, mapped or marked in some way (the desert). This has the effect initially of calling attention to its otherness, and then of bringing its otherness under control (Las Vegas, the meadows). Gradually any trace of otherness is reduced or making it disappear by rendering its otherness similar to what is already known (Las Vegas, the frontier town). This process happens in the construction of discourse as much as in the construction of the built environment: new concepts are identified, theoretical neologisms coined, which are then gradually tamed by research, to the point where they become accepted and incorporated within discourse. Lastly, to compensate for the inevitable assimilation and disappearance of the otherness of the other, there is an attempt to reproduce or manufacture otherness with reified images or appropriated and recontextualised examples, as a form of textual, visual or spatial gaming which masks reality (Las Vegas, the spectacle). This follows the precept which Wlad Godzich outlines in his foreword to Michel de Certeau's *Heterologies*: "Western thought has always thematised the other as a threat to be reduced, as a potential same-to-be, a yet-not-same."[17]

The whole historiographical sequence can thus be summarised as a shift down through the gears: name-tame-same-game. It is a colonial progression, which establishes on the one hand the colonisation of the desert/Wild West as a frontier in the case of Las Vegas, and on the other hand characterises the intellectual colonisation of Michel Foucault's notion of the heterotopia. By using what might seem an overly linear and mechanistic model to structure this chapter, resting lightly on these headings in order to navigate through the parallel historiographies of the heterotopia and Las Vegas, this is also intended to reflect the capacity for architectural discourse to enter its own "game" stage.

NAME

In response to Foucault's six principles and their attendant examples, Steve Connor observes that "once a heterotopia has been named, and more especially, once it has been cited and recited, it is no longer the conceptual monstrosity which it once was, for its incommensurability has been in some sense bound, controlled and predictively interpreted, given a centre and illustrative function."[18] Naming thus serves to remove power deriving from otherness, an inevitable consequence of claiming the land or theorising an idea or impression: the other is only truly powerful when it remains unnamed, more so if it proves unnameable. For the other space of the desert to be conquered by civilisation, it first had to be named as a spatial condition; likewise the heterotopia had to be named as an idea in order for it to become discursively apparent and available. This Foucault achieved mainly by differentiating the heterotopia from other ideas to which it relates, in particular the utopia.

Foucault states that the heterotopia is

> a sort of counter-arrangement, or effectively realised utopia, in which all the real arrangements that can be found within society are at one and the same time represented, challenged and overturned: a sort of place that lies outside all places, and yet is actually localisable. In contrast to the utopias, these places are absolutely *other* with respect to all the arrangements that they reflect.[19]

A common reading of Las Vegas is that of an effectively realised utopia, a bizarre other world which exists in the middle of the desert, distant from "normal" American cities, a place in which traditional American values are inverted, where other rules apply, and where the natural logic of night and day is abandoned, a city which rearranges the normal relationship between consumption and production. Each individual casino attempts to create an ostensibly utopian environment, designed to appeal to a particular sector of society through its theming and decor, and thereby luring people into the warm embrace of gambling. Nowadays, Las Vegas' main preoccupation is how to sustain its mass appeal and maintain the American public's desire to gamble and be entertained.

Jean Baudrillard, in his ruminations on the United States, identifies this scenario with sweeping Eurocentric chauvinism:

> The US is utopia achieved. We should not judge their crisis as we judge our own, the
> crisis of old European countries. Ours is a crisis of historical ideals, facing up to the impos-
> sibility of their realisation. Theirs is the crisis of an achieved utopia, confronted with the
> problem of its duration and permanence.[20]

This places a city like Las Vegas in a paradoxical historical situation: as an achieved utopia, it is the ultimate development of civilisation under capitalist society, and at the same time a manifestation of what Baudrillard famously calls "the *only remaining primitive society*."[21] By implication, Baudrillard attributes a degree of conceptual ambivalence to Las Vegas while at the same time depicting the perpetuation of a utopian condition as a doomed prospect: "*Utopia has been achieved here and anti-utopia is being achieved*: the anti-utopia of unreason, of deterritorialisation, of the indeterminacy of language and the subject, of the neutralisation of all values, of the death of culture."[22] Baudrillard's assertions show that utopia inevitably gives way to a new state, one which corresponds to Foucault's depictions of the heterotopia, while at the same time heralding the impending desertification of American culture. Baudrillard is typically moralistic in his attitude towards the USA, and clearly regards the inevitable move towards anti-utopia as an apocalyptic slide. This can be detected in his perception of the desert:

> American culture is heir to the deserts, but the deserts here are not part of a Nature
> defined by contrast with the town . . . the natural deserts teach me what I need to know
> about the deserts of the sign. They induce in me an exalting vision of the desertification
> of signs and men. They form the mental frontier where the projects of civilisation run into
> the ground.[23]

In a particular passage in *The Order of Things*, Foucault articulates the utopia/ heterotopia distinction somewhat differently as a form of mental frontier, arguing that:

> Utopias afford consolation: although they have no real locality, there is nevertheless a
> fantastic, untroubled region in which they are able to unfold; they open up cities with vast
> avenues, superbly planted gardens, countries where life is easy even though the road to
> them is chimerical. Heterotopias are disturbing, probably because they secretly undermine
> language, because they make it impossible to name this *and* that, because they shatter
> or tangle common names, because they destroy "syntax" in advance, and not only the
> syntax with which we construct sentences, but also that less apparent syntax that causes
> words and things (next to and also opposite one another) "to hold together." This is why
> utopias permit fables and discourse: they run with the very grain of language and are part

of the fundamental dimension of the *fabula*; heterotopias desiccate speech, stop words in their tracks, contest the very possibility of grammar at its source; they dissolve our myths and sterilise the lyricism of our sentences.[24]

It is clear that Foucault regards the ability to resist naming as a fundamental characteristic of the heterotopia: its evasiveness provides a powerful sense of agency with which to challenge the easy complacency of utopia.

Italian theorist Gianni Vattimo takes up the challenge which the heterotopia represents with respect to utopia, postulating that there has been a paradigm shift from utopia to heterotopia since the 1960s, a change which he regards as "the most radical transformation in the relation between art and everyday life."[25] Vattimo argues that this shift has brought about a change in the dominant aesthetic sensibility, making contemporary Western society more predisposed towards images and sites of imperfection, compromise, hybridity and incompletion. His interpretation of heterotopia aligns it neatly with the discourse of postmodernity which favours inclusivity, and reproduces it as the post-revolutionary other which single-handedly usurped the previous modernist regime. Vattimo treats the heterotopia as both the impetus that produces this shift and also as a *zeitgeist* or prevailing hegemony in its own right, responsible for legitimating the collapse of any distinction between high and low culture, between elitist and popular taste, and facilitating a denial of the autonomous function of art. Likewise, *Learning from Las Vegas* also treats the city as a site of incompletion, issuing a challenge to the architectural establishment to abandon modernist rhetoric in favour of a more popular, ordinary aesthetic.

TAME

Vattimo's own historiographic staging of the heterotopia takes an unexpected turn, however, when he predicts that

> the wager on heterotopia, so to speak, will escape being merely frivolous, if it can link the transformed aesthetic experience of mass society with Heidegger's call to an experience of being that is (at last) non-metaphysical . . . only [then] can we find a way amidst the explosion of the ornamental and heterotopian character of today's aesthetic.[26]

In his final analysis, the heterotopian paradigm is recast as one of mindless decoration lacking emotional depth and intellectual direction, a manoeuvre which invokes elitist class distinctions that reproduce the heterotopia not as a post-revolutionary other, but as a lightweight other to the seriousness of lived experience, and to a proper understanding of meaning. Las Vegas is present indirectly in these statements, not least because of Vattimo's gambling metaphor, but also in linking the heterotopia to an aesthetic which revolves around mass culture, ornamentation and excess. His naming of the current status of contemporary culture as a heterotopia and his subsequent positioning of the heterotopia as no more than an aesthetic has the effect of taming the concept, shifting it from the status of transitive verb to a vaguely derogatory adjective. Like Baudrillard, Vattimo's reaction to mass culture is Eurocentric and hierarchical, in which his own high-brow taste, to use Pierre Bourdieu's terms,[27] is inescapable.

If the shift from utopia to heterotopia is to do with the bringing together of art and everyday life and a revolution of taste values, then at its heart lies Pop Art. According to Reyner Banham, by the end of the 1950s Las Vegas was "a classic Pop artefact . . . an expendable dream that money could just about buy, designed for immediate point-of-sale impact, outside the canons of Fine Art."[28] At this stage, the image of Las Vegas was untamed by architectural discourse, in that it was largely unmediated by critical commentaries. It was, however, mediated within popular culture: in his book *Viva Las Vegas* Alan Hess shows the extent of mediation evident even in the pre-war period, by highlighting the caption to a 1939 map: "Las Vegas: still a Frontier Town."[29] This indicates that already Las Vegas had been not only named but also tamed, and that it had become necessary to self-consciously invoke its wilder past as a means of self-promotion. The lawlessness of frontier towns had by the 1930s already been romanticised and mythologised, and the image of Las Vegas' legislative ambivalence was perpetuated through a number of cinematic representations during the 1940s and 1950s, such as *Las Vegas Shakedown* and *The Las Vegas Story*. Then in 1965 Tom Wolfe published his influential essay "Las Vegas (What?) Las Vegas (Can't Hear You! Too Noisy) Las Vegas!!!!" in *Esquire* magazine. Banham admits that after reading the Wolfe essay, he was persuaded that Las Vegas was a necessary stop on his desert itinerary planned for December of that year. By 1966 he claimed that it was on the itinerary of most architectural students,[30] and these factors combined to legitimise Las Vegas as an official object of study for architecture: the Venturi/Scott Brown/Izenour team arrived on the scene to record their observations of banal Strip-side architecture like good Beaux Arts scholars a year later, but with the intention of upsetting the architectural apple cart, or at the every least redirecting it towards a consideration of consumption.

It was a populist concern with banal everydayness that brought Venturi, Scott Brown and Izenour to Las Vegas, and led their students to call the Strip "The Great Proletarian Cultural Locomotive." Until this pioneering study (for it was here that architecture found its own metaphorical frontier) Hess remarks, "the rapid growth of this commercial roadside landscape had attracted little attention in the professional press. It was not generally considered architecture."[31] In that sense, Las Vegas stood outside the prevailing architectural discourse in the 1960s, and offered a real, ordinary, banal space which functioned as a counter site with respect to "serious" avant-garde architecture of the time. But Las Vegas was not only "other" to the architectural establishment. Paradoxically, it also maintained its position in a populist context as other when compared to the real, banal spaces of American suburbia. This makes Las Vegas evade an absolute classification, an ambivalent space, and also makes the relativism of the heterotopia self evident. For one social group (what Wolfe called the "culturati"), Las Vegas was vulgar and stood apart from their endeavour. For another, much larger social group, the consumers of the neon spectacle of Las Vegas, it represented something extraordinary, beyond their everyday lives. It was thus simultaneously ordinary and extraordinary, real and unreal. In other words, depending on which perspective is chosen, Las Vegas is heterotopian either by virtue of its everyday qualities, or by virtue of its ability to exist outside the everyday. It is tamed simultaneously by two different discourses, emerging with two different cultural identities relative to two different audiences, one academic, the other consumerist.

SAME

Guy Debord in *The Society of the Spectacle* observed dryly that

> tourism, human circulation considered as consumption, a by-product of the circulation of commodities, is fundamentally nothing more than the leisure of going to see what has become banal. The economic organisation of visits to different places is already in itself the guarantee of their equivalence.[32]

The proliferation of spaces of equivalence or sameness produces a situation which Kroker has called panic culture. In his estimation, "panic culture is where we live on the edge of ecstasy and dread."[33] In the 1990s, panic is both a product of and the producer of the banal, reworking difference and otherness into sameness, so as to provide safe, predictable experiences for consumers, while still generating desire for the thrill of the other. Kroker sees Foucault as key to an understanding of this culture of panic, maintaining that "in Foucault alone there are to be found all the key panic sites at the fin de millennium."[34] This makes Foucault a "sliding signifier" for Kroker, producing "an ironic meditation on the fate of the relational, sidereal, and topographical postmodern scene."[35]

This notion of panic illuminates a moment in the historiography of both heterotopia and Las Vegas. To return to the issue of the spatially discontinuous ground ambivalently implied in Foucault's heterotopology, a significant change may be seen to be operating in Las Vegas, whereby the spatial discreteness of the casinos as counter-sites gives way to the spatial continuity of Las Vegas as a total leisure environment. Previously, casinos modelled themselves as miniature citadels, each promoting voluntary incarceration with a myriad of ploys: externally advertising competitive deals, rates and odds, and internally operating a ground plan which was designed specifically to make it difficult to find the exit. However, recent ambitious resort developments have begun to reproduce Las Vegas as a collective spectacle or series of spectacles, in which the Strip functions as a flow of spaces between which pedestrians can move from one fantasy to the next at timed intervals: from a Caesar's Forum shopping mall where the sun sets every hour and the statues come to life, to an erupting volcano at The Mirage, then on to a full-scale pirate battle at Treasure Island, before experiencing the computerised extravaganza of Fremont Street.

Arthur Pope in his study *Ladders*, which details the historiography of urban form in the USA, characterises this shift as part of a general urban trend:

> with the post-war decline of the open urban centre, the possibility of a heterotopia or countersite that may once have existed in the exclusive suburban enclave or fated asylum has diminished. In the absence of open cities, closed developments no longer function as countersites which are both a reflection of and a retreat from the greater urban world. Rather they are now themselves obliged to be the greater world that was heretofore represented by the city and the metropolis.[36]

Pope presents the problem of incipient urban sameness as a demise of heterotopian space. For Pope, this is a primary site of panic in late twentieth century urbanism, and he argues that it also invalidates the depictions of casinos in *Learning from Las Vegas*, in which "gambling rooms are established as an antithesis to the street."[37] In his view, the closed casino developments which Venturi, Scott Brown and Izenour studied now operate as one continuous mass, such that "what was, in 1968, a chaotic poly-nuclear field has been unified around a single armature of corporate development. The recent appearance of atriums, skybridges and the massive 'theme park casinos' make the case apparent."[38] Movement along this armature, however, cannot be solely pedestrian, since the distances are immense. In order to transport the (mostly elderly) visitors from one casino event to the next, or from pavement to casino, there are now moving pavements and monorail systems linking them all together.

Thus at the level of individual casinos, Las Vegas is no longer a collection of different counter-sites but a continuous leisure-orientated mono-culture. Similarly, on a larger scale, Las Vegas no longer functions as a singular urban counter-site with respect to other western cities, since its *modus operandi* is now the same as that adopted by every city in the USA. The virtually pedestrianised Strip is now not much different from strategies adopted by, for example, downtown San Diego or Minneapolis, which have remodelled themselves on leisure environments, and are now intended to be experienced as malls or theme parks in their own right. This reflects, in part, the expectations of the average consumer, for whom the produced space of the theme park represents an ideal environment: safe, clean, predictable yet diverting.

GAME

In Pope's analysis of Las Vegas, Banham's 1975 predictions regarding the effect of Las Vegas in terms of *laissez-faire* urban planning and aesthetic control would seem to have been realised. Banham claimed that architects and planners were concerned that Las Vegas pointed the way for all architecture in the future, and that it had become a counter-image representing "the total surrender of all social and moral standards to the false glamour of naked commercial competition."[39] For a time, Las Vegas wielded a heterotopian-style agency, with the effect of questioning the normal syntax of city planning, and dissolving the certainties on which such principles of planning had depended. The result is that city centres throughout Europe and North America have become "urban entertainment centres," much like the Las Vegas Strip, where consumption is the new production, and where "culture industries" replace manufacturing, in a bid to attract the global tourism market.

As such, beyond the literal gaming which takes place in the casinos, Las Vegas has entered its own game stage, capable of prompting a series of reconsiderations of its own aesthetic *raison d'être* along with that of other spaces. Kroker once again

12.5 Caesar's Forum shops, Las Vegas (1998)

12.6 Travelators make casinos into one continuum (1998)

sees Foucault as an insightful thinker where the issue of aesthetic impact is concerned, proposing that "Foucault was one who refused history as a game of truth, only to install in its place the game of effective history, a "history which descends.'"[40] This game of history is present in the way in which Las Vegas manages its own image of otherness today. Since the publication in 1975 of Banham's essay "Mediated Environments or: You Can't Build That Here," Las Vegas has reinvented itself yet again by means of more and more theatrical architectural forms, and its image has been subject to further cinematic representations; in recent years there has been a plethora of films which use Las Vegas as the main location: Martin Scorsese's *Casino* (1995), Mike Figgis' *Leaving Las Vegas* (1995), Adrian Lyne's *Indecent Proposal* (1993) and Andrew Bergman's *Honeymoon in Vegas* (1992), to name but a few, while Will Smith's pop video for *Gettin Jiggy Wi' It* was shot using a succession of the major resort casinos as backdrops.

Recently, as if to compete with Los Angeles' profiteering from Las Vegas as a film location, the city has taken to staging its own mediation, self-consciously marking moments in the city's unfolding history: 31 December 1996 witnessed the televised demolition of the old Hacienda casino to make way for a more lavish resort. Further evidence of a "game of effective history" lies in the famous Boneyard, where old neon signs are stored. This is now being repackaged to form the "Neon Museum" where Las Vegas icons from the past are preserved and re-presented. In this way, Las Vegas has successfully created its own collective memory, one which is deliberately mythologised in the interests of marketing. The game plays with the image of Las Vegas as place of constant change, in which the main agent at work is theming. Theming is employed as a means to get beyond the basic problem of sameness, and

12.7 Boneyard, Las vegas (1998)

12.8 Theming: New York New York, Las Vegas (1998)

to disguise and prolong the gaming among the various casino developers by making an artificial differentiation between adjacent environments which are otherwise identical in purpose: to maximise profits through gambling and other receipts. This is not to say that theming produces a genuine effect of difference or otherness, since it steers a path close to recognisable familiarity: Mark Gottdiener argues that "themed environments display a surprisingly limited range of symbolic motifs because they need to appeal to the widest possible consumer markets."[41]

The Las Vegas skyline has changed over recent years not only because the developer stakes have been raised (neon is now seen by many casino owners as passé), and the clientele has changed somewhat, but also because there has been a historiographical shift in the choice of the themes themselves. As mediated environments, casino resorts and other attractions have moved away from referencing the desert, Hispanic, frontier-town otherness of Las Vegas (the Sands, the Dunes, Desert Inn, El Rancho, Barbary Coast, Golden Nugget, the Frontier) or images associates with gambling itself (The Mint, Lady Luck, Horseshoe), towards themes which seek to create the image of otherness for Las Vegas by means of imported and re-presented other places, producing an exotic mix and a masked reality. The new range of referents can be divided into: historical European (Riviera, Monte Carlo, St. Tropez, Caesar's, Continental, San Remo and the newest clutch: The Venetian, Paris, Bellagio); those based on other cities in the United States (New York New York, Orleans, Bourbon Street); those which conjure up exotic or mythical locations (Mirage, Aladdin, Luxor, Treasure Island, Imperial Palace, Excalibur, Tropicana, Rio); media or music-derived themes (MGM, Debbie Reynolds, Liberace, All Star, Hard Rock); and those which draw on outer space or the future (Stardust, Stratosphere). These are, in many ways, no more than face-lifts, an inevitable consequence of what Baudrillard calls "astral America:" "As for American reality, even the face-lifted variety retains its vast scope, its tremendous scale, and, at the same time, an unspoilt rawness. All societies end up wearing masks."[42] Even Baudrillard, however, ultimately admits his own ambivalence towards Las Vegas, when he evokes a seductive and totalising image of "astral America:" "The direct star-blast, as against the fevered distance of the cultural gaze . . . Starblasted . . . transpolitically by the power game, the power museum that America has become for the whole world."[43]

Las Vegas can be regarded as perhaps the most prominent example of this power museum, a hyped-up heterotopia of perpetual accumulation, which survives the numbing onset of sameness by constantly adding to its collection of re-presented architectural trophies which it holds in its cultural gaze: New York, Paris and Venice are shrunk down, remixed and repackaged for the consumer of mediated otherness in a space of convenience. Increasingly, what makes the theming of casinos work is not the architectural facades they present to the street, however, but the selective importation of merchandise and cuisine from these other places available inside, such that a visit to the resort becomes a reified sampler. As Gilles Deleuze has remarked, "the real is not impossible; it is simply more and more artificial."[44]

After excessive gaming is there only cultural exhaustion? What can Las Vegas tell us about the meaning of cultural desertification or the future of the heterotopia? Baudrillard asks the question "how far can we go in the extermination of meaning, how far can we go in the non-referential desert form without cracking up and, of course, keep alive the esoteric charm of disappearance?"[45] In *America*, he establishes a link between gambling and the desert, which harks back to the early themes of the casinos:

> there is a mysterious affinity between the sterility of wide open spaces and that of gambling, between the sterility of speed and that of expenditure . . . it would be wrong-headed to counterpose Death Valley, the sublime natural phenomenon, to Las Vegas, the abject cultural phenomenon. For the one is the hidden face of the other and they mirror each other across the desert.[46]

In making Las Vegas synonymous with the desert, Baudrillard assumes that desertification is culturally disastrous. However, it need not be the case. Iain Chambers has suggested:

> If, as Jean Baudrillard is fond of reminding us, the desert is the place of the empty repetition of dead meanings and abandoned signs, it is also the site of infinity: a surplus, as Emmanuel Levinas argues, that permits others to exist apart and irreducible to ourselves. So the occidental metaphor of emptiness and exhaustion – the desert – perhaps also holds the key to the irruption of other possibilities: that continual deferring and ambiguity of sense involved in the travelling of sounds and people who come from elsewhere, but who are now moving across a landscape that we recognise and inhabit.[47]

By implication, this viewpoint allows for a more positive stage in the historiography of Las Vegas, and at the same time salvages the banalised notion of the heterotopia with a new shift, one which takes into account the temporal and social dynamics of an other space. It also points to the hidden side of Las Vegas, its own resident others: as one of the fastest growing cities in the United States, Las Vegas is home to diverse multi-ethnic groups who have migrated from elsewhere, bringing with them their own cultures and spatial practices. In Las Vegas, there are two kinds of constant deferral in operation: one is highly visible and relates to the deterritorialisations and reterritorialisations of the casinos as they are demolished, rebuilt and renamed (such as El Rancho, whose naming changed twice before any work was done to remodel the casino itself: in January 1996 its sign declared it was to reopen as the Starship Orion, then a year later it had changed to announcing "The Future Home of Countryland"); the other deferral relates to the communities in flux which arrive, establish themselves, and move on.

12.9 El Rancho: "future home of Starship Orion", Las vegas (1997)

12.10 El Rancho: "future home of Countryland", Las Vegas (1998)

The notions of infinity and surplus also serve to re-establish some of the primitive, raw energy to Las Vegas, preserving it from the apocalyptic image that Baudrillard associates ultimately with the desert, and hence precluding an absolute desertification of Las Vegas and the heterotopia as productive cultural forces. For while Baudrillard's reading of Las Vegas would deny the reconstitutive power of the heterotopia, and hence also deny the future as a productive next stage, a more Deleuzian reading preserves something of its positive mobilising force: instead of exhaustion, the desert is a smooth space in which desires may be freely exercised, within which identity can be renegotiated.

Heterotopia deserta, far from existing as a space of abandoned signs, like the Boneyard, is more likely to be found in the irruption of other possibilities: Las Vegas might now be conscious of its past, and seek to profit from it, but it is still dealing in the one commodity which in any society remains perpetually other: the future. Levinas conceives of our relationship to the future in spatial terms: "The exteriority of the future is totally different from spatial exteriority precisely through the fact that the future is absolutely surprising . . . The future is what is not grasped, what befalls us and lays hold of us. The other is the future. The very relationship with the other is the relationship with the future."[48]

References

1   Mary McLeod, "Everyday and 'Other' Spaces," Debra Coleman, Elizabeth Danze and Carol Henderson (eds), *Architecture and Feminism* (New York: Princeton Architectural Press, 1996), p. 1.

2   McLeod, "Everyday and 'Other' Spaces," p. 2.

3   Reyner Banham, *Scenes in America Deserta* (London: Thames and Hudson, 1982).

4   Jean Baudrillard, *America* (London: Verso, 1988).

5   Reyner Banham, *Los Angeles: Architecture of the Four Ecologies* (London: Pelican, 1973).

6   Mike Davis, *City of Quartz* (London: Verso, 1990).

7   Edward W. Soja, *Postmodern Geographies: the Reassertion of Space in Critical Social Theory* (London: Verso, 1989).

8   Edward Relph, "Postmodern Geographies," *Canadian Geographer*, n. 35 (1991), pp. 98–105.

9   Derek Gregory, *Geographical Imaginations* (London: Blackwell, 1994).

10   Charles Jencks, *Heteropolis* (London: Academy Editions, 1993).

11   Benjamin Genocchio, "Discourse, Discontinuity, Difference: the Question of Other Spaces," Sophie Watson and Katherine Gibson (eds), *Postmodern Cities and Spaces* (Oxford: Blackwell, 1995), pp. 38–9.

12   Henri Lefebvre, *The Production of Space* (Oxford: Blackwell, 1991), p. 4.

13   Michel Foucault, "Of Other Spaces," Joan Ockman (ed.), *Architecture Culture, 1943–1968* (New York: Rizzoli, 1993), p. 422.

14   Foucault, "Of Other Spaces," p. 423.

15   Foucault, "Of Other Spaces," p. 425.

16   Foucault, "Of Other Spaces," p. 425.

17   Wlad Godzich, "Foreword: the Further Possibility of Knowledge," Michel de Certeau, *Heterologies* (Minneapolis: University of Minnesota Press, 1986), p. xiii.

18   Steve Connor, *Postmodern Culture* (London: Blackwell, 1989), p. 9.

19   Foucault, "Of Other Spaces," p. 422.

20   Baudrillard, *America*, p. 77.

21   Baudrillard, *America*, p. 7 (emphasis in the original).

22   Baudrillard, *America*, p. 97 (emphasis in the original).

23   Baudrillard, *America*, p. 63.

24   Michel Foucault, *The Order of Things* (London: Routledge, 1989), p. xviii.

25   Gianni Vattimo, *The Transparent Society* (Cambridge: Polity Press, 1992), p. 62.

26   Vattimo, *The Transparent Society*, p. 74.

27   Pierre Bourdieu, *Distinction: a Social Critique of Judgement* (London: Routledge, 1994).

28   Reyner Banham, "Mediated Environments or: You Can't Build That Here," C.W.E. Bigsby (ed.), *Superculture: American Popular Culture in Europe* (London: Paul Elek, 1975), p. 78.

29   Alan Hess, *Viva Las Vegas* (New York: Chronicle Books, 1993).

30   Banham, "Mediated Environments," p. 79.

31   Hess, *Viva Las Vegas*, p. 18.

32   Guy Debord, *The Society of the Spectacle* (London: Wheaton, 1977), para. 168.

33   Arthur Kroker, *The Possessed Individual* (Toronto: Culture Texts, 1992), p. 159.

34   Kroker, *The Possessed Individual*, p. 159.

35   Kroker, *The Possessed Individual* p. 159.

36   Arthur Pope, *Ladders* (New York: Princeton Architectural Press, 1996), p. 179.

37   Pope, *Ladders*, p. 195.

38   Pope, *Ladders*, p. 198.

39   Banham, "Mediated Environments," p. 80.

40   Kroker, *The Possessed Individual*, p. 159.

41   Mark Gottdiener, *The Theming of America* (Oxford: Westview Press, 1997), p. 156.

42   Baudrillard, *America*, p. 118.

43   Baudrillard, *America*, p. 27.

44   Gilles Deleuze and Felix Guattari, *Anti-Oedipus, Capitalism and Schizophrenia* (Minneapolis: University of Minnesota Press, 1983), p. 34.

45   Baudrillard, *America*, p. 10.

46   Baudrillard, *America*, p. 67.

47   Iain Chambers, *Migrancy, Culture, Identity* (London: Routledge, 1994), p. 84.

48   Emmanuel Levinas, *Time and the Other* (Pittsburgh, PA: Duquesne University Press, 1987), p. 77.

Chapter 13
Thick edge: architectural boundaries in the postmodern metropolis
Iain Borden

Boundaries present themselves to us as the edge of things, as the spatial and temporal limit between the here and there, in and out, present and future. The boundary in all its manifest forms – wall, facade, gate, fence, river, shore, window – appears as a discrete separation between alternate sides of its magical divide; things are dispersed and ordered in space.[1] Yet for postmodern urban space, in which architects assay the wrapping and layering of space, and urban managers increasingly review its representation and control, nothing could be farther than the truth; boundaries are not finite, but zones of negotiation.

The more thoughtful theoreticians of architecture have always understood buildings as possessing this kind of boundary-negotiation when considering the mechancial and servicing elements:

> the array of different reservoirs in buildings is defined by a multitude of *boundaries*. These boundaries may be the metal pipes and ducts of servicing systems; they may perhaps be the different material boundaries to damp air passages in lofts; they may also be the faces of masonry walls, where the solid material acts as reservoir for heat energy; and they may be defined by material content: timber has to have a moisture content (MC) above 20% to support fungi, so that the MC level in effect becomes a boundary to fungal action. There are also grain boundaries.[2]

They are also aware of the differential nature of boundary effects.

> Some boundaries are opaque to one entity, but transparent or permeable to another (i.e. semi-permeable): dry rot or radon can pass through brickwork, whereas pet budgerigars cannot.[3]

Yet this is not always evident in the treatment of social boundaries, where we must remember that, as Henri Lefebvre points out, the segregation of classes, ethnic groups and peoples of all kinds does not come from a clear set of rules and precisely demarcated boundaries, nor from a uniform strategy of enforcements, but from a variety of tactics and procedures, at once voluntary, spontaneous and fully programmed.[4]

Power never allows itself to be confined within a single logic. Power has only strategies – and their complexity is in proportion to power's resources.[5]

It is impossible to say how often one pauses uncomfortably for a moment on some threshold – the entrance of a church, office or "public" building, or the point of access to a "foreign" place – while passively, and usually "unconsciously," accepting a prohibition of some kind. Gates and railings, ditches and other material barriers are merely the most extreme instances of this kind of separation.[6]

Thus while dominant boundaries between social groups may now be disappearing, they are also being replaced by new scarcely visible limits demarcating centres of power.[7]

CLEAR BLUE WATER

On London's Kingsway in Holborn sits the church of Holy Trinity. A theatrical inwardly curved facade grandly enfolds a smaller semicircular portico, but beyond splendorous Edwardian aesthetics,[8] Belcher and Joass' baroque design also provides a kind of public micro-retreat from the couriers, buses and taxis on Kingsway. As a church, Holy Trinity offered an embracing welcome to its visitors, drawing them off Kingsway first onto the ambiguous stage defined by its facade, then into the codified doorway of its portico, and onwards to the interior within. Forsaken by 1991 as a place of worship,[9] the church rapidly became a focus for the many homeless and street-people of Holborn, a semi-permanent place for sitting and sleeping away from the more exposed doorways around the corner in the Strand. It was now a stage set of a different kind, an appropriated piece of urban space, at once open to the public domain and private to those seeking shelter, defensible space and their own form of "illegal real estate."[10] Clusters of homeless recomposed a niche space from many layers of clothes, cardboard and classical architecture.

Except that a line has been drawn: a plane of wood, painted a striking resonant blue and 3 metres high. It spans the full length of the Holy Trinity front, so that the semi-public stage set becomes, like the interior, shut off from the street and divorced from passers-by. Yet, of course, it is not really the building that is being shut off from people: people – and particularly the homeless – are being shut off from it. To the more artistic cognoscenti, the screen may suggest a Christo-esque device, or even allusions to Derek Jarman's reductive film screen *Blue* (1993), and certainly it does insert a startling colourist disjunction to the grainy grey of Holborn. But for the new owners of the church, the Post Office, this is a far more considered attempt to keep architecture as things, and space as the distance between objects. For in protecting their new purchase, the new owners have created a boundary of exclusion, a brutally frontal relation which physically repels the unwanted and the unwashed from the site. It is the architecture of separation, of clear blue water between spaces and peoples.

13.1 Boundary of exclusion and blankness: blue screen, Holy Trinity Church, Kingsway, London (1996)

13.2 Bob, Kingsway, London (1996)

I learned much of this from a man called Bob, a small Geordie with a flat cap and weathered lines from decades of life on the streets of London.[11] To him and the other former residents of the Holy Trinity portico, this is indeed a pure boundary of separation, demarcating the now uncrossable chasm between ownership and use, public and private, recent history and immediate future. Architectural boundaries like this have finite social effects on the ground which cannot be denied.

But what is the socio-spatial nature of this boundary? Architecture has too often been conceived as the product of design intention, from which social effects simply follow. The "second nature"[12] of capitalism and its architecture is thought to be simply the artificial replacement for the old Nature, and so to operate in the same way. Space, as both first and second natures, is the pregiven space or condition to which people come, and which they respond to without being active in its reproduction. But this view of space ultimately offers little more than what Edward Soja has termed the "illusion of opacity:"

> spatiality is reduced to physical objects and forms, and naturalized back to a first nature so as to become susceptible to prevailing scientific explanation in the form of orderly, reproduceable description and the discovery of empirical regularities . . .

geographical description is substituted for explanation of the social production of space and the spatial organization of society.[13]

Since the 1970s, a socially and politically minded approach to architecture emerged in some areas of architectural history, and space here certainly began by implication to take on more of the character of the social. These discussions still, however, tended to focus on alternatively one of two things: either the notion of function, in which the building remains primarily a designed object, and the social activities of users are seen as simply being signed in the design and particularly in the plan of the building; or, the notion of social history, whereby the building is conceived of as a pregiven space, an architectural backdrop to the drama of everyday life. In either case, the essential interrelation of buildings, spaces, culture and people is reduced to a false dualism between designed object and social use.[14]

In contradistinction to this dualism, a strain of architectural thought conceives of architecture and space as active constituents of social relations, rather than as pregiven entities or produced objects. Taking their cue from sources as diverse as the anthropologist Marc Augé, urban geographers Edward Soja and David Harvey, historian Michel Foucault and, in particular, the philosopher Henri Lefebvre, architectural historians and theorists are reconceptualising architecture as a space of flows – not as an object in space, but as the product of, and interrelation between, things, spaces, individuals and ideas.[15] Bernard Tschumi is the most persistent architectural theorist in this movement.

> Can one attempt to make a contribution to architectural discourse by relentlessly stating that there is no space without event, no architecture without programme? . . . Our work argued that architecture – its social relevance and formal invention – could not be dissociated from the events that "happened" in it.[16]

As Adrian Forty remarks of the "Strangely Familiar" project,

> the moment in history when the building was finished . . . is the very point at which the historian's work should begin . . . architecture, like all other cultural objects, is not made just once, but is made and remade over and over again each time it is represented through another medium, each time its surroundings change, each time different people experience it.[17]

Architecture is both produced and reproduced, designed and experienced, and is at once social, spatial and temporal. Architecture is a medium and not a message, a system of power relations and not a force, a flow and not a line.

So how can we can conceive of the boundary? Nearly 70 years before Lefebvre's most spatialised writings, Georg Simmel noted that social and urban boundaries make social orders more concrete, more intensely experienced and clarify conflictual relations.[18] They stand in contrast to the purely physical and arbitrary boundaries of nature in that they are indeterminate in themselves, their significance being the interaction on either side of the line. For Simmel, the "boundary is not a spatial fact with sociological consequences, but a sociological fact that forms itself spatially."[19] Boundaries do not cause sociological effects in themselves, but are themselves formed by and in between sociological elements.

The blue screen of the Holy Trinity shows this sharply. While the immediate, physical effect of the boundary on those who experience it is very real, we must consider not only that its social effect changes the historical nature of that boundary, dislocating its significance away from the object itself, but also that this effect is simultaneously an attempt by an institution to control the relation between people and property. In particular, while the ownership of property is ultimately a social relation between people, the Post Office is seeking to render that relation into one of objects and things, and negotiating the relationship between itself and the homeless by erecting a physical screen which both hides – metaphorically and literally – its own concerns; in experiencing the screen we should then remember with Debord that such things are also spectacles, and thus "not a collection of images, but a social relation among people, mediated by images."[20]

The experience of the blue screen purely as object is, then, a false one, both in terms of its social effects and its social grounds. But there is also another way in which the boundary is a socio-spatial one, and that is through the materiality of its implementation. The obvious function of the blue screen is to keep the undesirable off the stage-space beyond, and the height and smooth texture of the surface provide a strong deterrent to this end. This much accords with its role as a hindrance to the movement of the human body, preventing the vertical and, in particular, horizontal transition from one space to another. Apart from this, the blue screen offers another, more pervasive control over the space and time of the would-be-invasive body. In front of the stage-set space is a low wall, of the right depth and height to sit upon and, potentially, to sleep upon. For this reason, the vertical sweep of the screen makes a sudden 45° deflection, so that instead of resting just behind the low wall it rests half-way across its depth, leaving only 150 mm of wall clear in front. The condition produced is both subtle and important; through the precise control of the screen and wall in relation to the thickness of the human body, the low wall is no longer deep enough or sheltered enough for a person to sleep upon, nor comfortable enough for anyone to sit upon for any length of time. Many similar edge-hardenings have also begun to sprout up around London, where spiked window-sills, 45° "decorative"

railings, concrete wedges, studded flower-planters and automatic sprinkler systems which come on in the middle of the night to "clean" shop and office doorways are being used to repel the public from the edge of the street.[21]

In the case of the Holy Trinity screen, even the "respectable" pedestrian is discouraged from stopping. Besides erasing temporary resting space, the clear blue surface of the screen is a smooth space devoid of exactly that detail interest and tactility that Merleau-Ponty sought to reassert against the domination of vision.[22] It deflects attention away, presenting a blank no-thing to the interrogative eye. There is no occasion to linger, to observe or to inspect.

What appears to be a simple, planar boundary, is, therefore, quite different; the blue screen discloses the boundary as a zone of negotiation, in which vision is just one of a series of body-centric architectural devices and cultural signs. The space of the body is used to control its interrelation with the screen and, by extension, the socio-spatial

13.3 Boundary of bodily depth: blue screen, Holy Trinity Church, Kingsway, London (1996)

influence of the screen is projected beyond its surface to the pavement in front. Passers-by continue to pass by, discouraged from stopping to rest by the screen's materiality. The boundary is not a surface but a thick edge, a 5 metre deep in-between zone in which social relations are challenged, controlled and formed through architectural materiality.

RIGHTS OF PASSAGE

If the blue screen of the Holy Trinity offers frontal control over property and social relations through its physicality, what of the boundaries that control space and property in a more ambiguous manner? What of those new urban spaces – the shopping mall, the forecourt and the rail concourse – those "creative paradoxes"[23] at once public and the private?[24]

One of the most famous of these new privatised-public spaces is the Broadgate office development, constructed for the post "Big Bang" (October 1986) deregulated financial centre in the City area of London.[25] Developed by Rosehaugh Stanhope in conjunction with British Rail over the lines and concourses of Liverpool Street

and the old Broad Street train station, the 29-acre Broadgate site offers 4 million sq
ft of high quality office space and three internalised urban squares to the City. Large
floor plates of over 30,000 sq ft, generous atria, multiple vertical cores and a high
technical servicing capacity meet the demands of modern office and trading
activities.[26]

13.4 Bishopsgate offices and Exchange Square, Broadgate, London (1994); architects Skidmore,
Owings and Merrill

But Broadgate is also an area which works very hard to define its social
character, and the dominant presence of well-salaried and be-suited office workers
is reinforced by a number of different measures, including high salaries, frequent pay
rises and bonuses beyond the comprehension of most other kinds of urban workers.[27]
This particular aesthetic enclave within the fragmented postmodern city contains
Americanised "fashion effect" architecture designed by Arup Associates (Stage 1,
1984–8) and Skidmore, Owings and Merrill (Stage 2, 1988–91), yielding a general
ambience prestige and wealth.[28] This is what Lefebvre calls the model of the "New
Athens," where new centres of decision-making incorporate the managerial "new
Masters" who enact control over all those who work there.

> Coercion and persuasion converge with the power of decision-making and the capacity to consume. Strongly occupied and inhabited by these new Masters, this centre is held by them. Without necessarily owning it all, they possess this privileged space, axis of a strict spatial policy . . . Around them, distributed in space according to formalized principles, there are human groups which can longer bear the name of slaves, serfs, vassals or even proletarians . . . Subjugated, they provide a multiplicity of services for the Masters of this State solidly established on the city.[29]

Lefebvre's comments here were made about the role of the state in the 1960s. Broadgate, of course, like other development projects of its era, was constructed in the context of diminishing state power, or perhaps more properly of an increasing reluctance on the part of the state to intervene in matters of space, and hence Broadgate had to assume the role of the state itself, managing not just built structures but also social structures and relations, behavioural patterns and conflicts, interiors and boundaries. Correspondingly, there are no "fringe," "festival," "marginal" or "liminal" spaces at Broadgate,[30] and none of the crowded conflicts of pedestrians and pavement cafés to be found in Soho to the West.[31] "They have eliminated all participation . . . The centralized site is going to take charge of the forces that reject it and, in essence, contest it."[32] Carefully demarcated shops, golfing emporia, health clubs, Japanese restaurants and champagne bars cater for senior-executive tastes and business-account pockets, while displaying signs barring entry to those not in "smart" dress. The *Broadgate Broadsheet* business community newspaper provides a booster guide to news and events, such as the much-publicised "Broomball" contests on the Broadgate Arena ice rink – a hideously stage-managed version of ice hockey. During the summer the ice rink is converted to a performance space: events in 1994, for example, funded by office service charges and private sponsorship, included displays of Sumo wrestling, Spanish horses, rollerblading and a dog show.[33] There is, then, an apparent diversity here, but it is a diversity based only on image and appearance, where the logic of vision is used to stand for historical truth.

> The predominance of visualization . . . serves to conceal repetitiveness. People *look*, and take sight, take seeing, for life itself. We build on the basis of papers and plans. We buy on the basis of images. Sight and seeing, which in the Western tradition once epitomized intelligibility, have turned into a trap: the means whereby, in social space, diversity may be stimulated and a travesty of enlightenment and intelligibility ensconced under the sign of transparency.[34]

Following this logic of visualisation, and in contrast to the Broomball and other activities that take place in the radiant bath of arc-lights, service workers like the many office cleaners and maintenance staff are kept out of sight, hidden beneath the surface in dark, subterranean undercroft of access roads and maintenance circuits.[35] In a similarly Disneyfied scopic regime, undesirables are rapidly escorted off the scheme, litter is instantly removed, and in a bizarre extreme fight against dirt, hawks are brought in weekly to scare away pigeons.[36] Social difference within the 20,000 working population is accommodated, but only within a class, gender and race framework based on the middle-class Oxbridge-educated businessman.[37]

13.5 City workers, Exchange Square, Broadgate, London (1994)

13.6 Service road and undercroft, Broadgate, London (1998)

There is also a logic of time at work here, for, as Lefebvre notes, the "New Masters" have the especial privilege to possess and control time.[38] In particular, where time in nature is inscribed in space as season, diurnal change and generation, in capitalism time comes to be measured only by clocks, lived only as carefully demarcated periods of work and leisure.[39] Space, and economic space most evidently, now comes to subordinate time, treating it as a political threat and hence as something to be evacuated.

> The primacy of the economic and above all of the political implies the supremacy of space over time ... Our time, then, this most essential part of lived experience, this greatest good of all goods, is no longer visible to us, no longer intelligible. It cannot be constructed. It is consumed, exhausted, and that is all. It leaves no traces. It is concealed in space, hidden under a pile of debris to be disposed of as soon as possible; after all, rubbish is a pollutant.[40]

At Broadgate, time, hence, is highly circumscribed, ranging from the economic time of property development instilled into highly complex lease arrangements, the ultimately private ownership of the land protected by one-day-per-year complete closures of the site (under British law long periods of uninterrupted access would lead to the establishment of public rights of thoroughfare, so Broadgate is normally closed on Christmas Day), to, perhaps most telling of all, the "public" toilets at Exchange Square being open only for a few hours of the day – at the lunch-time period to cater for the sandwich-eating office workers out to enjoy a few moments of fresh air. Pervading through all this is an attitude of efficiency that is at once functional (quick service dry-cleaning booths, espresso vendors, newspaper stands and sushi bars) and symbolic (clocks in coffee bars showing different global time zones, escalators that transport the neck-tied worker direct from train to office foyer). Time is money, time is for investment, time is for work not play. Time is, like space, to be controlled, allowing minimal confrontation of the Other, and hence minimal distraction from the business at hand.

Various kinds of subterranean flow therefore exist here – some literally underground, some socially and temporally hidden – but which are left undisclosed by the resolutely positivist architecture. In turn, as Lefebvre notes, we render our own bodies and lived experience into fetishised abstractions, and have no critical thoughts.[41] Because the space is classified, we tend to accept it at face value.[42] We play Broomball, at the allotted time and in the allotted space, instead.

There have, of course, been some kinds of threat which even the City of London has been unable to ignore: the IRA bombs of 1992 and 1993, both within 400 metres of Broadgate, and the later attack on the Docklands and Canary Wharf in 1996, causing serious injuries, a number of deaths, widespread devastation and, perhaps most importantly, an absolutely heart-gripping shock to the confidence of the financial sector. Even here, however, Broadgate itself was able to maintain its smug assertion of "no problem"; indeed, in the post-bomb aftermath its letting agents had the busiest weekend on record, rapidly off-loading large tranches of remaining office space that was suddenly and dramatically in urgent demand. Nonetheless, given the scale of bomb damage, it might have been expected that the scheme would follow the financial centre as a whole in adopting a series of measures to toughen the outer walls of its enclave – and certainly some buildings such as 1 Appold Street have strengthened their telecommunications rooms and used perforated metal blinds to reduce personal injury from flying glass. Individual buildings have also adopted a range of measures to control access both from outside and internally between departmental "Chinese Walls:" techniques like identity cards, electronic audit trails of internal movements, closed-circuit television (CCTV), turnstiles and biometric finger recognition are complemented by qualification and reference checks on workers, ever intrusive surveillance of working patterns and performance,[43] and immigration and passport checks on foreign workers. Yet, because of these internalised building-boundaries, and because the "Ring of Steel" armed road-checks and the 24-hour "Camerawatch" CCTV networks organised by the City of London police have successfully (for the City) redirected both terrorism and armed robbery to other parts of London, in terms of the project's overall boundaries Broadgate's managers are content to rely on their own extensive system of private security guards and surveillance cameras.[44]

The extant Broadgate boundaries are therefore free to be configured toward more social ends, creating a further but more subtle and social ring of defence within the City's militaristic frontier, and in this they are close to the concerns identified by Mike Davis in his account of middle class fear and spatial apartheid in Los Angeles.[45] Restrained yet distinctive signs mark this inner social cordon. Brass rails let into the pavement signify the edge of the property line. Richard Serra's massive 45-tonne public art sculpture "Fulcrum" signals the southernmost entrance to the scheme, while other public works perform similar boundary-marking and culture-reinforcing roles: pieces include Jacques Lipchitz, "Bellerophon Taming Pegasus;" George Segal, "Rush Hour;" Stephen Cox, "Ganapathi & Davi;" Barry Flanagan, "Leaping Hare on Crescent & Bell;" Fernando Botero, "Broadgate Venus;" Xavier Corbero, "Broad Family;" Artigas, "Tile Fountain;" and Jim Dine, "Venus." Various gates denote the

13.7 "Broadgate Venus," Broadgate, London (1993); artist Fernando Botero

transition from public to private realms, while armorial devices record the borough thresholds, and the significance of these latter signs should not be underestimated: the north-west area of the Broadgate scheme originally lay within the London Borough of Hackney, and on 1 April 1994 was transferred into the City of London jurisdiction in a deal whereby Hackney's loss of future income from business rates was offset by massive one-off compensation payments.[46]

Foremost among these various kinds of boundary-signifiers is a very curious device north of the Broadgate Arena, marking the northern edge of the first phases of the scheme near to 1 Appold Street. Designed by the artist Alan Evans,[47] the "Go-Between Screens" seemingly offer the usual boundary control, being open during the day and closing at night to prevent unwanted access. Except that these are not normal gates, in that even when "closed" it is possible to walk around their sides, a 2-metre gap being left for this purpose. The boundary here is in fact not closed to the moving body, and operates in a manner other than physical exclusion or control. This feeling is reinforced by the artful materiality of the "Go-Between Screens" which, in contrast to the highly machined hard granite surfaces of the surrounding buildings, are made of 24 forged mild steel panels, with line forging used to create a "soft" visibly hammered surface.[48] The monolithic granite elements of Cox's "Ganapathi & Davi," just a few metres to the north, further aid in the construction of this artistic turnstile.

13.8 Boundary as interrogation and mirror: "Go-Between Screens," Broadgate, London (1993); artist Alan Evans

What the Broadgate gates do is less prevent the horizontal movement of the body and more challenge the self-perception of visitors, at the moment they pass through the gate, as to whether they are allowed on to the site. As privatised urban space under corporate control, Broadgate in effect has no resident-owners, and everyone who enters the scheme is either a worker, visitor or trespasser. As Foucault notes of heterotopias, "Anyone can enter one of these heterotopian locations, but, in reality, they are nothing more than an illusion: one thinks one has entered and, by the sole fact of entering, one is excluded."[49] To control this ambiguity, the combination of hard architecture, soft gates and other boundaries, unlike the blue screen of the Holy Trinity, works not so much to physically exclude the unwanted, but to provoke in their own mind, as they momentarily pass through the thickness of the edge, the questions, "Should I be here, and now? Do I have the right of passage?"

Since the nineteenth century there has been an intensification of self-regulation through social themes – sex, morality, work, the family:

> everyone was his own mentor, responsible for the repression of his own desires, the control of his instincts; the result was asceticism without an ascetic dogma, without anyone enforcing asceticism; the whipping boy and scapegoat being sexuality.[50]

Here, then, is part of the increasing *spatial* concomitant to that process of self-regulation, wherein architecture asks us to regulate ourselves.

In this context, the temporality of the passage through the gates is also important, as it provides the momentary yet urgent actuality of this questioning process. The gates are not just the space but also the lived time through which the visitors check themselves in relation to Broadgate. As a result, space, temporality, body and identity are mutually confronted and constructed, in a version of Marc Augé's "non-place as a turning back on the self" and a checking of the contractual relation between the individual and that non-place.[51] More material and mental suggestion than brute physicality, this is the ultimate extension of the Benthamite project of surveillance, in which each and every citizen surveys and disciplines themselves.[52]

What, we might ask, is the architectural mechanism by which this process occurs? The answer lies in seeing the building surface as mirror, for if architectural monumentality previously allowed each member of society an image of that membership, a "recognition effect"[53] produced by an "experience a total being in a total space,"[54] and permitting "a continual back-and-forth between the private speech of ordinary conversations and the public speech of discourses, lectures, sermons, rallying-cries, and all theatrical forms of utterance,"[55] then in abstract space such social processes have all but disappeared. Today, just as walking in the city affirms or interrogates the places of the city, making spaces go away and reappear,[56] the city simultaneously interrogates the walker in a manner analogous to Rachel Whiteread's conception of the "wall looking back."[57] Its architecture is a reduction of the "real" to "the flatness of a mirror, of an image, of pure spectacle under an absolutely cold gaze."[58] Foucault notes of the mirror, that, as the space between the utopia and the heterotopia, it acts both to create the unreal space of the reflection, and to project an effect back on to the place of occupation, causing the viewer to turn back on themselves, "beginning to turn my eyes on myself and reconstitute myself where I am in reality."[59] The "Go-Between Screens" are thus a form of mirror, by which the visitors are ultimately returned not a view of Broadgate as object but a view of themselves playing a role within it.

> What he is confronted with, finally, is an image of himself, but in truth it is a pretty strange image . . . The passenger through non-places retrieves his identity only at Customs, at the toll-booth, at the check-out counter. Meanwhile, he obeys the same code as others, receives the same messages, responds to the same entreaties. The space of non-place creates neither singular identity nor relations; only solitude, and similitude.[60]

The visitors reconfigure themselves in the normative character of Broadgate, such that, in a resonance with Disneyland's staff, everyone becomes a "cast-member."[61] Just as people today are no longer expected to be individuals, but are expected to play a role,[62] so here they check if they are on the right stage, whether the scenery fits their face, and vice versa.

We might even consider that if Broadgate's architecture, as mirror, acts as a kind of Sartrean "other's look," conferring spatiality on the viewer, then it too is looked back upon, the gaze being returned.[63] This architecture is then absorbed within the self, dissolving the organic space of the body and the social space in which it lives, and entering that "betweenness of place" beyond objectivity and subjectivity.[64] As such, the boundary is validated by the anthropological ritual of passing through[65] – its presence does not act upon the visitor, but is a projection outward by that visitor considering themselves in relation to the architecture.

But of course there is also a power relation at work here; visitors cannot, with any accurate political regard to their material positioning, project *any* presence that they might wish onto the boundary-architecture. Rather, the visitor understands and concedes to the face of abstract space of Broadgate, that face which, just as surely as if an armed sentinel stood guard at its entrance, reduces difference and enforces homogeneity through a configuration of its geometric formants (its reduction of three-dimensional space to two-dimensional surfaces), its optical formants (its dominant logic of visualisation) and its phallic formants (emphasising male power and latent violence).[66] Thus where the geometric and the optical tend to reduce architecture to the void of the plan and to the flatness of the mirror, the phallic enters into that space, filling it with "a plenitude of destructive force."[67]

The visitor's body is hence rendered passive, subjects being forced to consider only through their eyes (against the "mirror" of the Broadgate buildings) and through carefully measured walking (via the space-time depth of the "Go-Between Screens"). In those few metres and seconds, the visitor's body is slowed down at the very point of entrance into the citadel, seeing not just architecture but the self and architecture together, entering into an unholy consensual agreement about this asymmetrical relation. Finally, the viewer/experiencer incorporates the architecture and, in doing so, yields to its impregnation, allowing it to grow inside and take control.

> The "object-world" – the world of automobiles and highways, industrial and household goods – invades body and thought with the result that its alienated existence absorbs the alienated "subject." What becomes of the dimension proper to the mind – that of criticism, refusal, negation? It withers and disappears.[68]

This is not a space that is "read" via Barthian semiology, but which is experienced through the vision and the body in a highly circumscribed manner – a process of interiorisation and exteriorisation rather than of decoding.

> Space commands bodies, prescribing or proscribing gestures, routes and distances to be covered. It is produced with this purpose in mind: this is its *raison d'être*. The "reading" of space is thus merely a secondary and practically irrelevant upshot, a rather superfluous reward to the individual for blind, spontaneous and *lived* obedience.[69]

Thus while abstract space may be characterised as the space of commodities, state, vast networks of banks, business centres, airports, motorways and information lattices,[70] ultimately, abstract space and places like Broadgate are not defined by certain architectural configurations, by the absence of trees, by commercial centres and plazas, but by its negation of the perceptions of human subjects and, above all, its negation of the differential space-time which they have the potential, as human subjects, to produce.[71] It is a space of confused power rather than of a single message.[72] It is space where very little is said, and creative life is stifled, and where the subject becomes rendered into a sign.

THROUGH THE GOLDEN ARCH

Boundaries are doubly useful to capitalism. First, boundaries become part of those extensive systems of power delineated by Foucault which enable capitalism to both control social relations and to render them more productively efficient.[73] The two boundaries of the blue screen and the gates operate within this logic.

Second, boundaries aid in the accumulation of capital. History is full of architecture where the old frontal attitude of the boundary toward inside and outside allows this to happen directly – medieval walled cities, toll-gates, customs houses, train stations and so on. The postmodern boundary has a more indirect task to perform, contributing to that insidious process identified by Adorno, Debord, Marcuse and Lefebvre: the further intensification of capitalism into everyday lives through ever more subtle and penetrative techniques.[74] Public spaces are increasingly being seen simply as opportunities for consumerism, with shops, boutiques and other retail outlets filling up all available space. Rail stations, for example, like airports before them, are now becoming more like shopping malls than places of transport. Through such processes, it always costs more and more to simply exist out of the home.

There are also other, more indirect forms of taxation on our lives. Advertisements are one of the most common forms of this process, lining the routes and edges of our journeys. The blue screen, for example, quickly became covered with bill posters and other advertisements, while in a reassertion of the control of the surface the Post Office screened the screen, adding a trellis matrix over the blue in order to prevent even the body of the advertisement from settling on its property. This boundary, once a dividing line betwixt public and private, is now a piece of contested real estate all of its own.

13.9 Blue screen with advertisements, Holy Trinity Church, Kingsway, London (1997)

13.10 Blue screen as contested surface, Holy Trinity Church, Kingsway, London (1998)

Such events serve to highlight the continual search by advertisers to find new sites, new spaces and times in which to shout their message; consequently, we are now well accustomed to advertisements inserting caesuras in our reading and television viewing, settling on our bodies through Benetton clothes, Nike shoes and Giorgio Armani spectacles, and even turning the sporting body into a pornographically mediated image of itself.[75] The British athlete Linford Christie took this to a new extreme in the 1996 Olympics held in Atlanta, USA, wearing contact lenses with the logo of his main sponsor – Puma, the sports shoe company – during media appearances. Instead of the athlete's eyes, viewers saw two small Puma cats – the commodification of the eye. The idea here was obviously to cash in on the media sensation these things produced – the sensation of the technological marvel – as much as on their direct effect as advertisements, as the Puma-eyes were not particularly legible except during close-ups. Nonetheless, they point towards an increasing tendency in clothing that now threatens to invade the body itself. All these things are indirect taxations on our experience of everyday life.

As the task for capitalism is to find ever new activities and needs to commodify, and ever more sites on which to promote them, commuters in London have in recent years become accustomed to exactly this on their daily underground journeys, with advertisements having spread from platform walls, elevator sides and train interiors (and even whole train exteriors) onto the backs of tickets and ticket barriers.

These new micro-hoardings have now been supplemented by an even greater heightening of the capitalist project of intensifying commodification. Appearing first at Liverpool Street and Tottenham Court Road stations in central London, this phenomenon has rapidly spread to any tube station with a nearby McDonald's. As travellers leave the station they are confronted with the commodified staircase, a set of steps on which the risers have been transposed into a wall of advertisements, indicating both the presence and direction of the nearby fast-food burger restaurant. Unlike conventional advertisements, these are only unavoidable, as they must be looked at in order to judge and negotiate the steps safely. As Lefebvre points out in *Eléments de rythmanalyse*, the rhythm of the body, largely unconscious and unknown to the negotiator of urban space among other rhythms of sound and rumour, becomes briefly explicit whenever acts like crossing a street are undertaken and when "a calculation must be made of the number of steps to be taken."[76] Here, the body has to pass up and over the advertisement, the paced calculation now necessarily involving consideration of McDonald's signs. The crucial components here are distance and its negotiation through movement, for it is here that we confront architecture as human creation rather than cold, crystallised form.[77] The commodified steps recognise this movement, and exploit its open dialogue with architecture. At this level, they insert themselves directly into the line of sight, working through the eye/body co-ordination of travellers as they move around the city. These micro-hoardings are also directly instructive – the golden arches being accompanied by a wall of arrows telling travellers where to go as soon as they leave the station – and repetitive – telling you over and over again, riser after riser, golden arch after golden arch, that the great American hamburger is but a few metres away.

Moreover, like the Broadgate gates, they also work through the mind of the traveller and in a particularly subtle manner, as "ambient advertising."[78] Advertising messages have already been developed into a sophisticated form whereby they seek to avoid being either opaque or boring to the viewer; instead, advertising is explicitly cryptic, in order to provoke a thought in the mind of the viewer.[79] In these McDonald's advertisements, this technique finds it spatial and temporal equivalent, as the exact moment of intrusion is precisely judged in time as well as space, invading the psychology of the traveller at the very moment of decision-making, and in a manner

13.11 Boundary as interrogation and commodification: McDonald's advertisements, Tottenham Court Road station, London (1995)

that recalls Foucault's identification of the "materiality of power operating on the very bodies of individuals."[80] Just as they leave the semi-somnambulant passivity of the tube station and escalator journey and make the transition to the decisive activity of the busy urban street, the advert recognises this move, selecting this space and this moment of awakening awareness into which to inject its message. As one manager of Transportation Display Incorporated, responsible for London Underground advertising space, explains, "The intrusive element is a plus point . . . Ambient media effectively means ambush media. People have to walk around a corner and be startled to see it."[81]

Nor is this kind of ambient advertising confined to the boundaries of stations. Other moments of the changing state of body and mind are also being identified and exploited by advertisers. One such campaign for Vaseline underarm deodorant, orchestrated by the Initiative Media group, places its advertisements inside tube carriages during summer months.

> We are hitting consumers in exactly the right environment, and at exactly the right time. Tubes are sticky, especially in the summer, and we are catching people just as they reach up for a strap — just the time they will be thinking about body odour.[82]

Other examples have included bus stops that spray "Impulse" perfume at passers-by, advertisements on shop floors and ceilings, advertisements at eye level over men's urinals, and others on petrol pump handles, supermarket trolleys, eggs, car park barriers and even inside golf holes. The boundary is a moment as well as a space of commodification, a thought as well as a material presence, a body as well as an object.

Significantly, the nature of the boundary also changes in this condition, mutating from the modernist conception of crossroads as meeting place to the postmodern interchange where nobody intersects.[83] The crossroads offers a carefully mannered sequence of stops and starts, of movements and waitings, of looking and listening – what Lefebvre calls a "strict harmony" of alternating rhythms.[84] The train station as intersection offers similar rhythms, but they are not coalesced into a single harmonic pattern; instead there is a continual exchange of bodies from one part of the concourse to another, creating a swarm of multi-movements, multi-settlings seemingly devoid of any greater coherence. As such, the advertisement has to exploit this change of rhythm, on the one hand using old techniques aimed at predictable movements and sight-lines (the billboard advertisement near the indicator board) but on the other hand using new techniques to intercept the less predictable, more diverse patterns of the interchange (micro-hoardings of all kinds). Furthermore, because the movements are so diverse, this is also to some extent a remarking, even a creation of a threshold where previously none had existed. This is a commodification of a boundary as an *enactment* of that boundary *qua* commodity.

If capitalism brings the boundary into being through the act of commodification then it also, in turn, transposes the human subject from passenger to "customer," the person defined less because of what they are *doing* and more because they are a *purchaser* with money to spend. This is that centrality of the capitalist city where exchange takes over from use, and where spatial practices, ideas and experiences are subordinate to economic logic.

> What is said and written, comes before everything else: it is the world of commodities, of the language of commodities, of the glory and extension of exchange value. It tends to absorb use value in exchange and exchange value.[85]

Indeed, the abstraction of the purchasing-subject into "customer" further suggests that they are merely an element, a passive human body as mechanism for symbolic exchange, the body-space concomitant of the "McDonaldization" of society which renders everyday life into a form of flexible standardisation,[86] and so part of Baudrillard's "genetic code, an unchanging radiating disk of which we are no more than interpretive cells."[87] If "money goes through circuits"[88] there is also a spatiality and corporeality to this circulation: each person becomes simply a flow of money, a

13.12 Prostitutes' advertisement, British Telecom phone box, Hyde Park, London (1995)

return of wages into the circuit of capital; and architecture as boundary becomes a channel of communication along which money surges. In this context, it is unsurprising that equally forceful and unavoidable micro-hoardings have also sprung up in another kind of urban site: the plethora of cards advertising prostitutes' services that now plaster the interior of every phone booth in central London. Sex reduced to sign, desire next to telephone, bodily need arranged via communication cable – each such boundary-body encounter is a pinprick into the body of blood money, each message/ needle releasing a tiny amount of flow.

Such things are the true postmodern boundary, both controlling and commodifying the urban domain. It is not then, as Paul Virilio mistakenly claims, that "telematics replaces the doorway,"[89] but that the doorway is being ever developed in new physical forms and socio-spatial configurations. This architecture is that of the everyday, operating at the most quotidian of sites and through the subconscious and conscious spatial decisions of the urban dweller. "A boundary," stated Martin Heidegger, "is not that at which something stops, but . . . that from which something *begins its essential unfolding*."[90] The boundary emerges as not a plane but a zone, not physical but socio-spatial, not a division of things but a negotiation of flows. The boundary is a thick edge. So is architecture.

References

1   See, for example, Kevin Lynch, *The Image of the City* (Cambridge, MA: MIT Press, 1960).

2   Stephen Groák, *The Idea of Building: Thought and Action in the Design and Production of Buildings* (London: Spon, 1992), p. 28.

3   Groák, *Idea of Building*, p. 28.

4   Henri Lefebvre, "Right to the City," Eleonore Kofman and Elizabeth Lebas (eds), *Writings on Cities* (Oxford: Blackwell, 1996), p. 139.

5   Henri Lefebvre, *The Production of Space* (Oxford: Blackwell, 1991), p. 162.

6   Lefebvre, *Production of Space*, p. 319.

7   Henri Lefebvre, *The Explosion: Marxism and the French Revolution* (New York: Monthly Review, 1969), p. 94.

8   Edward Jones and Christopher Woodward, *A Guide to the Architecture of London* (London: Weidenfeld and Nicolson, 2nd edition, 1992), p. 245.

9   Ben Weinreb and Christopher Hibbert (eds), *The London Encyclopedia* (London: Papermac, revised edition, 1993), p. 401.

10   Papo Colo, quoted in Neil Smith, "Homeless/Global: Scaling Places," Jon Bird *et al.* (eds), *Mapping the Futures: Local Cultures, Global Change* (London: Routledge, 1993), p. 89. See also *October*, n. 47 (1988).

11   Conversation, Kingsway, London, January 1996.

12   Lefebvre, *Production of Space*, p. 109; Henri Lefebvre, *The Survival of Capitalism* (London: Allison and Busby, 1974), pp. 14–15.

13   Edward W. Soja, *Postmodern Geographies: the Reassertion of Space in Critical Social Theory* (London: Verso, 1989), p. 123.

14   See, for example, Iain Borden and David Dunster (eds), *Architecture and the Sites of History: Interpretations of Buildings and Cities* (Oxford: Butterworth Architecture, 1995); Mark Girouard, *Life in the English Country House: a Social and Architectural History* (New Haven, CT: Yale University Press, 1978); Gwendolyn Wright, *Building the Dream: a Social History of Housing in America* (Cambridge, MA: MIT Press, 1983).

15   Iain Borden, Jane Rendell and Helen Thomas, "Knowing Different Cities: Reflections on Recent European City History and Planning," Leonie Sandercock (ed.), *Making the Invisible Visible: Insurgent Planning Histories* (Berkeley, CA: University of California Press, 1998), pp. 135–49.

16   Bernard Tschumi, "Spaces and Events," *Questions of Space: Lectures on Architecture* (London: Architectural Association, 1990), p. 88.

17   Adrian Forty, "Foreword" to Iain Borden, Joe Kerr, Alicia Pivaro and Jane Rendell (eds), *Strangely Familiar: Narratives of Architecture in the City* (London: Routledge, 1996), p. 5.

18   Georg Simmel, "The Sociology of Space," David Frisby and Mike Featherstone (eds), *Simmel on Culture* (London: Sage, 1997), pp. 137–70. See also Frank J. Lechner, "Simmel on Social Space," *Theory, Culture and Society*, v. 8 n. 3 (August 1991), pp. 195–202; David Frisby, "Social Space, the City and the Metropolis," *Simmel and Since: Essays on Georg Simmel's Social Theory* (London: Routledge, 1992), pp. 98–117; Benno Werlen, *Society, Action and Space: an Alternative Human Geography* (London: Routledge, 1993). pp. 168–78.

19   Simmel, "Sociology of Space," p. 143.

20   Guy Debord, *Society of the Spectacle* (Detroit, MI: Black and Red, 1983), para. 4.

21   Mark Cole, "Making a Point with Spikes and Studs," *Independent* (Wednesday 12

October 1994), p. 26. See also Mike Davis, *City of Quartz: Excavating the Future of Los Angeles* (London: Verso, 1990), pp. 223–63.

22   Maurice Merleau-Ponty, *Phenomenology of Perception* (London: Routledge and Kegan Paul, 1962), pp. 207–42. See also Martin Jay, *Downcast Eyes: the Denigration of Vision in Twentieth-Century French Thought* (Berkeley, CA: University of California Press, 1994), pp. 263–328.

23   Edward W. Soja, "The Stimulus of a Little Confusion: On Spuistraat, Amsterdam," Borden, Kerr, Pivaro and Rendell (eds), *Strangely Familiar*, p. 30.

24   This section of the chapter has benefited from work carried out by students at the School of Architecture and Interior Design, University of North London, and at The Bartlett, University College London. I am particularly grateful to A. Keightley-Moore, N. Murray, S. Warren and Warren Whyte.

25   "Centrefolio: City of London," *Property Week* (5 May 1994), pp. 35–59; DEGW, "Accommodating the Growing City," (London: DEGW Report for Rosehaugh Stanhope, 1985); Jane M. Jacobs, *Edge of Empire: Postcolonialism and the City* (London: Routledge, 1996), pp. 38–69; Anthony King, *Global Cities: Post-Imperialism and the Internationalization of London* (London: Routledge, 1990), pp. 87–100; Michael Pryke, "An International City Going 'Global': Spatial Change and Office Provision in the City of London," *Environment and Planning D: Society and Space*, v. 9 (1991), pp. 197–222; Saskia Sassen, *The Global City: New York, London, Tokyo* (Princeton, NJ: Princeton University Press, 1991.

26   Patrick Hannay, "Squaring Up to Broadgate," *The Architect's Journal* (25 September 1985), pp. 28–31; Patrick Hannay, "Squaring Dance," *The Architect's Journal* (6 January 1988), pp. 22–5; Network SouthEast, "Facts and Figures: Liverpool Street Station, Broadgate and Liverpool Street," (fact sheet, no date); Andrew Rabenek, "Broadgate and the Beaux Arts," *The Architect's Journal* (24 October 1990), pp. 37–51; Mark Swenarton, "Full Circle at Broadgate," *Building Design* (4 March 1988), pp. 14–16.

27   Nigel Thrift, "On the Social and Cultural Determinants of International Financial Centres: the Case of the City of London," in Stuart Corbridge, Ron Martin and Nigel Thrift (eds), *Money, Power and Space* (Oxford: Blackwell, 1994), pp. 327–55.

28   David Harvey, *The Condition of Postmodernity: an Enquiry into the Origins of Cultural Change* (Oxford: Blackwell, 1989), p. 66; Graham Ive, "Commercial Architecture," Borden and Dunster (eds), *Architecture and the Sites of History*, pp. 372–86; Andrew Rabenek, "Broadgate and the Beaux Arts," *The Architect's Journal* (24 October 1990), pp. 37–51.

29   Lefebvre, "Right to the City," p. 161.

30   Rob Shields, *Places on the Margin: Alternative Geographies of Modernity* (London: Routledge, 1991); Bruce Willems-Braun, "Situating Cultural Politics: Fringe Festivals and the Production of Spaces of Intersubjectivity," *Environment and Planning D: Society and Space*, v. 12 (1994), pp. 75–104.

31   Will Bennett, "Snatch Squads Strike in Council's War on Al Fresco Eating," *Independent* (Saturday 8 July 1995), p. 6.

32   Lefebvre, *Explosion*, p. 52.

33   *Broadgate Broadsheet*, n. 6 (April/May 1994), p. 4.

34   Lefebvre, *Production of Space*, pp. 75–6.

35   John Allen and Michael Pryke, "The Production of Service Space," *Environment and Planning D: Society and Space*, v. 12 (1994), pp. 453–75; Steve Pile, "Going Underground," Iain Borden, Joe Kerr, Jane Rendell with Alicia Pivaro (eds), *The Unknown City: Contesting Architecture and Social Space* (Cambridge, MA: MIT Press, forthcoming); Trevor Boddy, "Underground and Overhead: Building the Analogous City" in Michael Sorkin (ed.), *Variations of a Theme Park: the New American City and the End of Public Space* (New York: Noonday Press, 1992), pp. 123–53; Michael Sorkin, "See You in Disneyland," Sorkin (ed.), *Variations of a Theme Park*, p. 230; Dennis R. Judd, "The Rise of the New Walled Cities," Helen Liggett and David C. Perry (eds), *Spatial Practices: Critical Explorations in Social/Spatial Theory* (London: Sage, 1995), pp. 144–66.

36   Callum Murray, "The Art of Development," *The Architect's Journal* (24 October 1990), pp. 29–31.

37   *Broadgate Broadsheet*, n. 6 (April/May 1994), p. 1; Jacobs, *Edge of Empire*, p. 54, after M. Lisle-Williams, "Merchant Banking Dynasties in the English Class Structure: Ownership, Solidarity and Kinship in the City of London," *British Journal of Sociology*, v. 35 (1984), pp. 333–62; Y. Cassis, "Merchant Bankers and City Aristocracy," *British Journal of Sociology*, v. 39 (1988), pp. 114–20.

38   Lefebvre, "Right to the City," p. 161.

39   Lefebvre, *Production of Space*, p. 95.

40   Lefebvre, *Production of Space*, pp. 95–6.

41   Lefebvre, *Production of Space*, p. 93.

42   Lefebvre, *Production of Space*, p. 281.

43   Seumas Milne, "Call to Regulate Growth in Workplace 'Spying,'" *Guardian* (Thursday 18 February 1999), p. 9; Michael Ford, *Surveillance and Privacy at Work* (London: Institute of Employment Rights, 1999).

44   City of London Police, *Camerawatch. Closed Circuit Television Scheme: Code of Practice* (London: City of London Police, 1994); Corporation of London, *Security Camera, Planning Advice Note 1* (London: Department of Planning and Building Security, 1993); *Evening Standard* (Monday 11 March 1996), pp. 1–2; *Guardian* (Monday 26 April 1993), pp. 1–3 and 21; *Independent* (Tuesday 27 April 1993), p. 3; *Independent on Sunday* (Sunday 25 April 1993), pp. 1–3; *Sunday Times* (Sunday 25 April 1993), pp. 1 and 24; *The Times* (Wednesday 9 June 1993), p. 6; Oliver Bennett, "Here's Looking at You," *Independent on Sunday*, "Real Life" section (Sunday 3

December 1995), p. 3; Ben Brown, *CCTV in Town Centres: Three Case Studies* (London: Home Office Police Department, Police Research Group, Crime Detection and Prevention Series Paper no. 68, 1995); Louise O'Brien, "Watch the Camera," *Living Marxism*, n. 89 (April 1996).

45   Davis, *City of Quartz*, pp. 223–322; Mike Davis, "Fortress Los Angeles: the Militarization of Urban Space," Sorkin (ed.), *Variations on a Theme Park*, pp. 154–80; Mike Davis, "The Infinite Game: Redeveloping Downtown L.A.," Diane Ghirardo (ed.), *Out of Site: a Social Criticism of Architecture* (Seattle, WA: Bay Press, 1991), pp. 77–113.

46   *Broadgate Broadsheet*, n. 6 (April/May 1994), p. 1; and briefing by Patrick Robinson of Herbert Smith to University College London Graduate School "Social Space" group, Exchange House, Broadgate (4 December 1994).

47   *Broadgate Visitor's Guide* (Wordsearch for Rosehaugh Stanhope, no date); David Lister, "Private Deals that Spawn Public Art," *Independent* (Monday 26 June 1996); Sara Selwood, *The Benefits of Public Art: the Polemics of Permanent Art in Public Places* (London: Policy Studies Institute, 1995); Malcolm Miles, *Art, Space and the City* (London: Routledge, 1997).

48   *Broadgate Visitor's Guide* (Wordsearch for Rosehaugh Stanhope, no date).

49   Michel Foucault, "Of Other Spaces: Utopias and Heterotopias," Joan Ockman (ed.), *Architecture Culture 1943–1968: a Documentary Anthology* (New York: Rizzoli, 1993), p. 425. See also Sarah Chaplin's chapter in this volume.

50   Henri Lefebvre, *Everyday Life in the Modern World* (New Brunswick, NJ: Transaction Books, 1984), pp. 146.

51   Marc Augé, *Non-Places: Introduction to an Anthropology of Supermodernity* (London: Verso, 1995), pp. 92 and 101–2.

52   Michel Foucault, "Panopticism," in *Discipline and Punish: the Birth of the Prison* (Harmondsworth: Penguin, 1979), pp. 195–228.

53   Lefebvre, *Production of Space*, p. 220.

54   Lefebvre, *Production of Space*, p. 221.

55   Lefebvre, *Production of Space*, p. 224.

56   Michel de Certeau, *The Practice of Everyday Life* (Berkeley, CA: University of California Press, 1984), pp. 91–110.

57   Rachel Whiteread, public lecture, School of Architecture and Interior Design, University of North London (20 March 1995).

58   Lefebvre, *Production of Space*, p. 287.

59   Foucault, "Of Other Spaces," pp. 420–6. See also John Rajchman, "Foucault's Art of Seeing," *October*, n. 44 (Spring 1988), pp. 89–117.

60   Augé, *Non-Places*, p. 103.

61   Sorkin, "See You in Disneyland," p. 228.

62   Erich Fromm, *Man for Himself* (New York: Rinehart, 1947), pp. 81–2; Henri Lefebvre,

Critique of Everyday Life. Volume 1: Introduction (London: Verso, 1991), pp. 15–16 and 136.

63 Jean-Paul Sartre, *Being and Nothingness: an Essay on Phenomenological Ontology* (1943), pp. 252–302, and quoted in Jay, *Downcast Eyes*, p. 289.

64 J. Nicholas Entrikin, *The Betweenness of Place: Towards a Geography of Modernity* (London: Macmillan, 1991); Anthony Vidler, *The Architectural Uncanny: Essays in the Modern Unhomely* (Cambridge, MA: MIT Press, 1992), pp. 168 and 172.

65 Shirley Ardener, "Ground Rules and Social Maps of Women: an Introduction," in Shirley Ardener (ed.), *Women and Space: Ground Rules and Social Maps* (Oxford: Berg, revised edition, 1993), p. 13.

66 Lefebvre, *Production of Space*, pp. 285–7.

67 Lefebvre, *Production of Space*, p. 287.

68 Lefebvre, *Explosion*, p. 27. Lefebvre is here following Herbert Marcuse.

69 Lefebvre, *Production of Space*, p. 143.

70 Lefebvre, *Production of Space*, p. 53.

71 Lefebvre, *Production of Space*, pp. 50–1.

72 Lefebvre, *Production of Space*, p. 142.

73 Michel Foucault, "Two Lectures," Colin Gordon (ed.), *Power/Knowledge: Selected Interviews and Other Writings 1972–1977* (New York: Harvester Press, 1980), pp. 78–108; Paul Hirst, "Foucault and Architecture," *AA Files*, n. 26 (1993), pp. 52–60.

74 Theodor Adorno and Max Horkheimer, *Dialectic of Enlightenment* (New York: Herder and Herder, 1972); Debord, *Society of the Spectacle*; Lefebvre, *Everyday Life in the Modern World*; Lefebvre, *Critique of Everyday Life*; Herbert Marcuse, *One-Dimensional Man: Studies in the Ideology of Advanced Industrial Society* (Boston, MA: Beacon Press, 1964); Jonathan Charley, "Industrialization and the City: Work, Speed-Up and Urbanisation," Borden and Dunster (eds), *Architecture and the Sites of History*, pp. 344–57; and Jacob J. Goldberg, "Corporate Capital and the Techniques of Modernity: Problems in the Mass Production of Space, Image and Experience," *Journal of Architectural Education*, v. 48 n. 4 (May 1995), pp. 227–39.

75 Malcolm Bradbury, "Physicality," *Independent on Sunday Magazine* (Sunday 22 May 1993), pp. 16–17.

76 Henri Lefebvre, *Eléments de rythmanalyse. Introduction à la connaissance des rythmes* (Paris: Syllepse-Périscope, 1992). Chapter 3, "Vue de la fenêtre," translated as "Seen From the Window," in Lefebvre, *Writings on Cities*, p. 220.

77 August Schmarsow, "The Essence of Architectural Creation," Harry Francis Mallgrave and Eleftherios Ikonomou (eds), *Empathy, Form and Space: Problems in German Aesthetics, 1873–1893* (Santa Monica, CA: Getty Center for the History of Art and Humanities, 1994), pp. 281–97.

78 Richard Thomas, "Ambushed by the Advertisers," *Guardian* (Saturday 9 August 1997), p. 26.

79 Belinda Moore, "Advertising Fulfils a Function Within Society that Written and Spoken Language Cannot Achieve," (unpublished BA dissertation, Central St. Martin's, London, 1994), p. 56.

80 Michel Foucault, "Body/Power," Gordon (ed.), *Power/Knowledge*, p. 55.

81 Mike Barker, quoted in Thomas, "Ambushed by the Advertisers," p. 26.

82 Helen Shannon, quoted in Thomas, "Ambushed by the Advertisers," p. 26.

83 Augé, *Non-Places*, p. 107.

84 Lefebvre, "Seen From the Window," p. 220.

85 Lefebvre, "Right to the City," p. 170.

86 George Ritzer, *The McDonaldization of Society: an Investigation Into the Changing Character of Contemporary Social Life* (London: Sage, 1995); George Ritzer, *The McDonaldization Thesis: Explorations and Extensions* (London: Sage, 1997); Barry Smart (ed.), *Resisting McDonaldization* (London: Sage, 1999).

87 Jean Baudrillard, "Symbolic Exchange and Death," Mark Poster (ed.), *Jean Baudrillard: Selected Writings* (Cambridge: Polity Press, 1988), p. 140.

88 Lefebvre, "Seen From the Window," p. 225.

89 Paul Virilio, "The Overexposed City," Neil Leach (ed.), *Rethinking Architecture: a Reader in Cultural Theory* (London: Routledge, 1997), p. 383.

90 Martin Heidegger, "Building, Dwelling, Thinking," in *Basic Writings* (London: Routledge, revised edition, 1993), p. 356.

Chapter 14
"Serpentine allurements:" disorderly bodies/disorderly spaces
Jane Rendell

This chapter looks at the bodies and spaces of prostitution in early nineteenth century London, represented through rambling texts, specifically Pierce Egan's *Life in London* of 1821 and the sequel *Finish to Life in London* of 1828. Both theoretical and historical, this chapter interprets the spatiality of prostitution in relation to the work of Luce Irigaray, in particular her notion of the "exchange of women."[1] The argument is divided into three sections. The first looks at the theoretical reasoning behind choosing the "ramble" as an object of study for feminist architectural history. Subsequent sections examine in more detail the disorderly bodies and spaces represented in the rambling texts in relation to "mobility" and "visuality."

Despite disciplinary differences, feminist analysis of gender and space has tended to focus on critiquing the paradigm of the separate spheres (the binary system which describes gendered space as an oppositional and hierarchical with two mutually exclusive categories – the dominant male public realm of the city and the subordinate female private realm of the home). This paradigm is problematic because, as a patriarchal and capitalist ideological device, it perpetuates certain assumptions regarding sex, gender and space, and prioritises the relation of men to the city.

I argue here that the binary parameters of the separate spheres represent a patriarchal appropriation of the public sphere, and instead follow feminist critiques or "deconstructions" of this binary. I suggest that the gendering of space can be reconceptualised through feminist theory, specifically through the work of Irigaray. By looking at rambling, an urban movement which represents early nineteenth century London as a series of gendered spaces, I argue that the gendering of space can be understood as a form of choreography, a series of performed movements between men and women, both real and ideal, material and metaphoric, which are constructed and represented through social relations of looking and moving – exchanging, consuming and displaying.

My decision to focus on the early nineteenth century ramble demonstrates a number of criteria. First, this is an important historical period for contemporary feminists investigating gender and space: it precedes the patriarchal "fixing" of the separate spheres as the most pervasive ideology of gender and space in the mid nineteenth century. But although I consider an examination of the early stages of articulation of an ideology important in order to grasp its workings, it is not my intention here to explain why the separate spheres came into being; rather, I am interested in looking at how issues of gender were raised in connection with the public spaces of the city.

Second, the ramble represents a spatial configuration which describes the interpenetration of private and public: defined in terms of ownership, the rambler visits both public and private spaces in the city; defined in terms of spatial morphology, the rambler visits both inside and outside spaces; and defined in terms of activity, the ramble is involved in both formal and intimate pastimes. In crude terms, I argue that through movement the ramble represents the city as a blurring of public and private.

Third and finally, the spaces visited by the rambler are places of leisure and consumption – the important notion here is that as a socio-economic activity consumption is neither reproduction nor production and does not fit into the separate spheres ideology. For women in their capacity as workers and consumers, consumption takes place simultaneously both in the home and in the city. Further, following Irigaray, in patriarchal society women are treated as commodities – objects or signs of exchange circulated among men. Women are the objects, as well as the subjects, of consumption. It serves to highlight women's role as commodities that in the early nineteenth century the word commodity was used to refer to a woman's sex: a private commodity was a modest woman, and a public commodity was a prostitute.

In the early nineteenth century, increasing urbanisation and the expansion of capitalism resulted in the rising cultural importance of certain social spaces of leisure, consumption, display and exchange. These were the site of conflicting concerns, those of public patriarchs seeking to control female occupation of the city, worried that their female property – mothers, wives, daughters – would be visually and sexually available to other men, and those of consumer capitalists aiming to extend the roles of women as cheap workers and consumers in the city. In order to examine the gendering of space in early nineteenth century London, this chapter looks at rambling as a mode of movement which celebrates the public spaces of the city and the excitement of urban life from a masculine perspective.

The rambler visits sites of leisure, pleasure, consumption, exchange and display in early nineteenth century London: the theatre, opera house, pleasure garden, park, club, sporting venue and bazaar. By traversing the city, looking in its open and interior spaces for adventure and entertainment, the rambler creates a conceptual and physical map of the city. Rambling rethinks London as a series of spaces of flows of movement rather than a series of discrete architectural elements. I argue that the ramble represents such spaces as gendered in a number of ways: through the exclusion of women, in taverns, sporting venues and clubs; and through the establishment of male dominance in spaces occupied by men and women. The perpetual movement of the ramble places urban locations in sequential relation, framing social events, activities and rituals in time and space. Gender differences are articulated spatially, through relations of movement and vision: moving and being-moved, viewing and being-viewed, consuming and being-consumed, exchanging and being-exchanged, displaying and being-on-display.

RAMBLING

> We have already taken a promiscuous ramble from the West towards the East, and it has afforded some amusement; but our stock is abundant, and many objects of curiosity are still in view.[2]

> The gaze of the flâneur articulates and produces a masculine sexuality which in the modern sexual economy enjoys the freedom to look, appraise and possess.[3]

The verb "to ramble" describes incoherent movement, "to wander in discourse (spoken or written), to write or talk incoherently or without natural sequence of ideas." As a mode of movement, rambling is unrestrained, random and distracted: "a walk (formerly

14.1 George and Robert Cruikshank, "The Corinthian Capital," from Pierce Egan, *Life in London; or, the day and night scenes of Jerry Hawthorne, Esq. and his elegant friend Corinthian Tom, accompanied by Bob Logic, the Oxonian, in their Rambles and Sprees through the Metropolis* (1820–1)

14.2 Abstract

any excursion or journey) without any definite route or pleasure."[4] In the early nineteenth century, the verb specifically described the exploration of urban space: "This day has been wholly devoted to a ramble about London, to look at curiosities."[5] Rambling was concerned with the physical and conceptual pursuit of pleasure, specifically sexual pleasure – "to go about in search of sex."[6] Closely related activities were "ranging" or "rangling" or "intriguing with a variety of women."[7]

The rambling genre has its origins in texts published from the sixteenth century onwards, which delved further into the London underworld, pretending to be authentic and using sensational tales as their framework, but revealing no more than graphic detail. These texts, partly moralising, partly titillating, were aimed at "Johnny Raws" from the country, and not only tempted the reader with the excitement of urban life, but also warned against the corrupting influence and sophisticated criminals of the city. Such texts may be distinguished by their structure and take the form of "spy" tales – journeys through the city.[8] Spy tales tell of various country gentlemen's initiations to the adventures of city life under the guidance of a street-wise urban relative – wise, that is, to the delights and entertainments, as well as to the tricks and frauds, of the urban realm. The tradition continued into the eighteenth century, focusing on the seamy side of metropolitan life, with stories and pictures of crime, robbery and prostitution.[9]

The term ramble appeared alongside that of spy in the eighteenth century, and, although they were often used in an interchangeable way, their emphases differed slightly. Spy texts were fascinated with the darker aspects of urban life, while rambles were involved with excitement in the form of fun and pleasure. By the first decades of the nineteenth century, some publications continued to follow earlier models and focus on the detection and exposure of criminal codes, but a number of publications – including *Real Life in London*,[10] Egan's *Life in London*,[11] William Heath's *Fashion and Folly*,[12] and Bernard Blackmantle's *The English Spy*[13] – differed from the earlier texts in a number of ways.

Unlike the earlier primarily scripted descriptions which included only a few black and white woodcuts, the new rambles were highly visual documents, with coloured lithographs, engravings and etchings. Instead of addressing themselves to the country visitor, these new rambles provided a place for urban dwellers to look at themselves. The "look" of the urban explorer changed, from the secretive spy looking but not wanting to be looked at, to the fashionable rambler of the 1820s, a self-conscious man demanding to be visually appreciated. In the shift from the spy to the rambler, the importance of urban exploration and knowledge was retained, but the emphasis on the excitement of revealing secret activities was replaced by a new attention to fashion, display and spectacle. In the decade following the Napoleonic Wars, this attention to display coincided historically with the return of military men from Europe, especially Paris, bringing with them new French fashions and a flamboyant style of military dress. The early nineteenth century rambler was a highly visible figure, proactive in his occupation of space.

This chapter focuses primarily on *Life in London*, one of the most popular of these early nineteenth century rambling texts. The author was Pierce Egan (1772–1849) and the illustrators George Cruikshank (1792–1878) and Robert Cruikshank (1789–1856). *Life in London* describes the rambles of three young males as they explore London in 1821. The three men are Corinthian Tom, a young Londoner, bachelor, member of the aristocracy, with an inheritance and a London residence – Corinthian House; Robert Logic, Tom's drinking companion, an Oxford student, also with an inheritance, living at the Albany chambers for bachelors; and Tom's cousin, Jerry Hawthorn, a fine sportsman and drinker, who comes from the same class background but lacks credibility as a male due to his rural origin. Through rambles around London, involving various drinking and sporting activities, *Life in London* tells of Jerry's initiation into urban lifestyle and manhood. Rambling played an integral part in producing a public display of heterosexual, upper class masculinity. The rambler represented the shared features of a new kind of urban masculinity – the mobility, visuality and urbanity of a young, heterosexual, middle to upper class male consumer.

The rambler's mobility represents an attempt to establish the public realm of the city as a place for men. The rambler's aim was to partake in a world of pleasure – heterosexual sexual pleasure. Contemporary magazines concerned with sex and whoring described themselves in terms of rambling.[14] The pursuit of women was an important aspect of rambling. All the women whom the rambler encountered in the public spaces of the city were represented in terms of their sexuality and described as "cyprians." The word is defined as "belonging to Cyprus, an island in the eastern Mediterranean, famous in ancient times for the worship of Aphrodite or Venus," goddess of love, as "licentious, lewd," and, in the eighteenth and nineteenth centuries, "applied to prostitutes."[15]

The term cyprian described women occupying public space as prostitutes, whether or not they were exchanging sex for financial benefit. The cyprian was a stimulus to the rambler. A spectacle – an object of display – her body was the site of the ramblers' desire and gaze. Corinthian Tom's partner in *Life in London* was the alluring and beautiful cyprian, Corinthian Kate. The rambler's desire for, and pursuit of, these female sexual commodities defined his urban masculinity and heterosexuality. *Life in London* can be described as a mapping of prostitution, in that all the places of public leisure visited were spaces where cyprians displayed themselves and picked-up clients. Homes of cyprians, such as Corinthian Kate's apartments, were also represented, as were the most exclusive brothels – the "nunneries" of King's Place in west London's St James's. But in *Life in London*, although the ramblers pursued, flirted, drank with cyprians and spent money on them,[16] their rambles never took them to a brothel.

In 1828 a sequel was published, *Finish to the Adventures of Tom, Jerry and Logic in their Pursuits through Life in and out of London*.[17] This rambling text also mapped prostitution but in a very different way. Here the spaces of prostitution represented are those where sexual transactions took place: from the nunnery, or the closed residential private brothel, to the lodging house, or low and public brothel, to the street. Corinthian Kate, a figure of desire in *Life in London*, is represented as a figure of disgust in *Finish*. Her decline marks a shift in attitude between the two rambles, from a ramble which celebrates city life and the pleasures of drinking, gambling and whoring to a ramble which moralises about the damaging effects of urban living. In *Finish* the ramblers suffer for their pleasures, through debt, disease and death. Corinthian Kate takes her own life. Only Jerry survives, who leaves the city to marry Mary Rosebud and live in the country.

MOBILITY

> CORINTHIAN TOM'S unceasing Anxiety to mix with the World uncontrolled.[18]

> The society we know, our own culture, is based upon the exchange of women. Without the exchange of women, we are told we would fall back into the anarchy (?) of the natural world, the randomness (?) of the animal kingdom. The passage into the social order, into the symbolic order, is assured by the fact that men, or groups of men, circulate women among themselves.[19]

In contemporary urban discourse, we are obsessed increasingly by figures who traverse space – flâneur, spy, detective and prostitute. For the rambler, mobility was a critical aspect of his masculinity and public urban identity. His mobility was both social and spatial – his dominant class position allowed him to mix with a variety of social classes and to move freely between the exclusive clubs, opera houses, assembly rooms in the west of London and working-class taverns and other leisure spaces in Covent Garden's Holy Land and further east in East Smithfield. The juxtaposition of the scene in Allmax, a tavern in the east, and Almack's exclusive assembly rooms in the west, represents the rambler's mobility – the ability to experience both sides of the city – the prerogative of the dominant upper- or middle-class male.

In *Life in London* the idealised figure of the corinthian represents the mobility of the rambler. Corinthian Tom was the archetypal corinthian, a gentleman with property in the form of land and money, known for his elegant manner, fashionable

14.3 George and Robert Cruikshank, "*Tom* getting the best of a Charley" from Pierce Egan, *Life in London*

14.4 Abstract

clothes and sportsmanship.[20] In social rank, the corinthian was "the highest order of swell," where swell refers to a "well-dressed" man.[21] This hierarchy, like "the super-eminence of that order of architecture," was determined by decoration, "superlative articles of dress."[22] But unlike the swell whose identity was determined only by dress, a crucial aspect of the corinthian's identity was his class. Class defined the corinthian's leisure time and gentlemanly attitude, as well as his character, politeness, generosity, good humour and, most importantly, his sportsmanship. Corinthians were "sporting men of rank and fashion" – first class boxers, fencers, hunters and drivers.[23]

Sport represented the possibility for male bonding within a class society. Boxing, in particular, by prioritising the ideal qualities of English manhood and creating patriotic unity, appeared to cut across class and political boundaries. Boxing publications were accompanied by images of the stylised heads and torsos of working class bruisers, whose sporting physiques were compared to the celebrated beauty of the classical Greek hero.[24] But as well as representing idealised physical attributes, pugilism also promoted admirable social aspects of masculinity – sportsmanship, courage, gallantry, calmness, tolerance, fair-play and honour. For men of different classes, sport and associated leisure activities, such as drinking, offered opportunities for male bonding.[25]

Sporting societies, such as the Pugilistic Society and the Four-in-Hand coaching club, established shared social codes, including sporting rules, dress, language and manners.[26] Such codes, although adopted by upper-class men as an essential aspect of fashionable sporting masculinity, originated as integral parts of lower-class culture. A contemporary etching described how "a modern man of fashion" should "dress like a coachman," "study boxing and bull baiting" and "speak the slang language fluently."[27] The flash lingo or "the canting or slang language" was the language of working-class criminals.[28] However, given its close links to cockney or vernacular London language, its use represented urban identity, and flash dictionaries, rambling tales and boxing treatises often published by the same publishers, sometimes as two volume sets,[29] were aimed at upper-class men, students and sporting men.[30]

The corinthian represented an idealised version of the rambler, as an upperclass male, who mixed with different classes through socialising, while retaining his own hierarchical relation. The corinthian column in the frontispiece of *Life in London* represents this ideal social order. At the top of the column are the "ups" or "the flowers of society," the King and the nobles; next are the merchants or "respectables;" at the bottom are the "downs" or "the mechanicals, the humble labourers and the human vegetables." The ramblers – Tom, Jerry and Logic – are positioned at the centre of the column, drinking.[31]

Structured around social and spatial contrasts, the ramble represents a culturally diverse journey ranging from high culture to popular culture, from grand interiors to dark streets. The most striking juxtapositions are between the east and the west, represented as two different class zones. From the seventeenth century onwards, the city and the eastern districts surrounding it were commercial and industrial zones, inhabited by the working class mostly in slums, including a large number of immigrants, most numerously the Irish. The west was populated by members of the aristocracy, nobility and wealthy bourgeois class who moved out of the city westwards to new residential squares, first to Covent Garden and Soho and later to St James's and Piccadilly. In search of pleasure, the ramblers moved freely between the clubs, opera houses, theatres and arcades in the west of London and the places where "real" life was to be found – the leisure spaces of the working class, from Covent Garden's Holy Land to the taverns of St Giles and East Smithfield. The rambler's desire and ability to mix with a variety of social classes and experience both the west and east of the city represented an important part of his urban identity – his social and spatial mobility.

In the eighteenth and nineteenth centuries, as London developed into an important centre of consumption, the role of streets became increasingly important as zones of trade, commerce, administration and entertainment. A number of improvements in lighting, paving and drainage facilitated the movement of people and goods and also provided a social space for visual display and consumption.[32] The architect John Nash's work in the first decades of the nineteenth century in the fashionable, commercial and residential areas around Piccadilly focused on celebrating urban movement.[33] His urban designs combined classical and romantic elements of town-planning, treating urban elements, streets, buildings and the flow of traffic like landscapes.[34] Regent Street, designed with promenading and walking in mind, was nick-named "Corinthian Path," indicating its high class and fashionable status. The amount of traffic on streets, both vehicular and pedestrian, created a need for adopting distinctive styles of public urban behaviour, such as the fast and aggressive driving of wheeled vehicles or walking on the right hand side of the street.[35]

Moving was also a defining feature of the cyprian. Cyprians were described as "lady birds" having "lightness and mobility of spirit" or "energy of body and spirit." The names of cyprians spotted by ramblers in the park corresponded to birds, such as the Sparrow Hawk and the White Crow.[36] Their mobility defined in terms lightness and flightiness referred to their moral constitution – their "moral frailty" – as well as their ability to move. Movement for women held moral connotations, for example, although female magazines encouraged their readers to walk as a suitable form of female exercise, it was only under certain controlled conditions: moderately, in the early morning, with company. Walking in the public streets, especially lingering rather than hurrying, and wearing revealing or conspicuous clothes, was suggestive of a woman's immorality.[37]

The cyprian was an urban peripatetic – a nymph of the pavé.[38] Her mobility in the public places of the city was a cause of concern. Her link to the street, as streetwalker or nightwalker, associated her with the lowest class of prostitute. Whereas the movement of the rambler, his active engagement in the constant pursuit of pleasure, was celebrated as urban exploration, the mobility of the cyprian was represented as the cause of her eventual destruction. Her movement was transgressive, blurring the boundaries between public and private, suggesting the uncontrollability of women in the city. The cyprian body was perceived as disorderly, because as a moving female public body, it flouted patriarchal rules for women's occupation of space.

In Irigaray's essay "Women on the Market," the circulation of women among men is what establishes the operation of society. As mothers, wives, daughters, virgins and prostitutes, women are objects of exchange among men; they are commodities.[39] Irigaray's conception of woman-as-commodity – the object of physical and metaphorical exchange among men – is critical to any understanding of the gendering of space through movement, and of the threat caused by the self-determined movement of women in public space. In patriarchy, men are distinguished from women through their relationship to space. In terms of ownership, men own space and women as property; whereas women are owned as property, confined as and in space. In patriarchal relations of exchange, men move through space and subjects of exchange; whereas women are moved through space between men as sexual commodities.

In Irigaray's symbolic order, women have three positions: the mother who represents pure use value, the virgin who represents pure exchange value, and the prostitute who represents both use and exchange value. Mothers are the place and sign of use value, they are private property, excluded from exchange, "reproductive instruments marked with the name of the father and enclosed in his house." Virgins are the place and the sign of exchange value, of social relations between men, "simple envelope veiling[s]." Once these envelopes are violated, women are relegated to the status of use value; they become the private property of one man, and are removed from exchange among men. Virgins are entrapped as and in private property. The prostitute, however, does not fall into the binary opposition of use and exchange value – she is both.

According to Irigaray's work, by taking herself to market and exchanging herself, the prostitute mimics male discourse, in so doing, she disrupts the male economy, exposing the exchange of women at its foundation. For some critics, it is the "ambiguous unity in the prostitute of use and exchange value which positions her as a speaking subject."[40] Motivated by the desire to sell herself, the cyprian's position as a self-perpetuating, moving subject establishes her as a threat to patriarchal ideologies controlling the circulation of women among men. In patriarchy, the ownership and exchange of property, including women, is controlled by defining boundaries and identifying thresholds which are permanent, closed and fixed around women. Female subjects and spaces which operate within, but also escape, the controlling mechanisms of private property and ownership in patriarchal capitalism and are represented in terms of spatial metaphors of disorder.

Descriptions of bodies of prostitution – disorderly due to their mobility – resonate with descriptions of spaces of prostitution as disorderly in terms of the fluidity of their boundaries and thresholds. The thresholds of buildings other than family homes, known to be occupied by women, such as shops, brothels and theatres, were represented as sites of danger and intrigue. The threshold – the place where the boundary is pierced – where passage occurs from outside to inside represented not only the material transition from exterior to interior, from known public territory to unknown private territory, but also the metaphor of sexual penetration. In particular, the threshold of the brothel was connected with suspicion. It was because entrances to brothels were hidden or tucked away, rather than on display, that men could be accosted, decoyed or lured inside.

The presence of cyprians at the entrance lured men over the threshold to take a "peep at the *Curiosities*" within.[41] The procuress, on the other hand, was represented as a repulsive figure at "the mouth of her cavern,"[42] guarding the entrance, using various deceits to entrap innocent people. If the threshold to the brothel, the place which allowed movement in and out, was considered problematic, a covered hole, a trap or snare, in a similar way, so was the cyprian body. In pornographic rambling tales, the spatial metaphors of "closet," "slit" and "catacomb" were used as forms of titillation,[43] but the terms "hole," "pit" and "ditch" were also used to describe the sexually immoral or public woman in religious tracts.[44] The more promiscuous the woman, the deeper and more open the hole.[45] The cyprian body was perceived as an open body occupying the public realm. Punctured, but not necessarily exposed, it created a treacherous topography, a trap one could fall into – "a serpentine allurement."[46]

The seduced or penetrated body of the cyprian was an open and disorderly medium requiring regulation. The two laws which indirectly controlled prostitution in public space did so through the ordering of disorderly spaces and disorderly bodies. The Disorderly Houses Act of 1752, still not updated in the early nineteenth century, and used to prosecute brothel owners, expressed concern for unregulated public spaces – disorderliness here was the source of "irregularity and crime."[47] Women's movement on the street was controlled through the Vagrancy Acts, updated in 1822 and 1824, which defined "prostitutes" and "nightwalkers" who were "wandering in public streets" as "idle and disorderly."[48] Disorderly spaces and bodies were also associated with class trouble, fear of revolution and disputes over property ownership. Such concerns were represented through the various solutions muted to control prostitution, which invariably involved the incarceration of the female body in places for punishment and/or rehabilitation.

From *Life in London* to *Finish*, the decline of the prostitute body and spaces of prostitution are represented in terms which categorise a shift from order to disorder, from contained to fluid, from private to public, from closed to open and from home to street. The more controlled the boundary of a brothel the more respectable it was thought to be. The cyprian's home, in this case Corinthian Kate's private and elegant apartments in the west of London, represent the most regulated and controlled spaces of prostitution.[49] Those further east in Covent Garden, such as bagnios or lodging houses and late night drinking venues, were considered less regulated and more open to crime. For example, in *Finish*, Jerry is robbed in one low brothel or lodging house in Covent Garden,[50] and in another the building catches on fire almost killing him and the cyprian he is with (fire is a recurring motif signifying hell and danger in rambles).[51] Corinthian Kate fares no better. Forced to leave the apartments paid for by Tom, she is found by the ramblers in a state of inebriety and disease under Covent Garden Piazza – an open exposed place. Her figure and face are shown diseased and bloated from alcohol and syphilis.[52] The squalid room in a lodging house brothel in the east, where Corinthian Kate dies, a place where individuals picked up their own clients in the street and brought them back to the house, is represented as open socially and in terms of its decaying physical fabric and burning materiality.[53]

VISUALITY

> The Rambler in the public streets,
> Admires at everything he meets . . .
> Ladies you'll find of every class,
> In shape, just like the hour glass[54]

[T]he duplicity of the veil's function . . . used to cover a lesser value and overvalue the fetish[55]

14.5 George and Robert Cruikshank, "*Jerry* in training for a Swell" from Pierce Egan, *Life in London*

14.6 Abstract

Scopophilia, what Sigmund Freud called the desire to look, is stimulated by structures of voyeurism and narcissism, both of which derive pleasure in looking. Voyeurism is a controlling and distanced way of looking in which pleasure is derived from looking at a figure as an object. Narcissistic pleasure is produced by identification with the image and can be considered analogous to Jacques Lacan's mirror stage – just as children form their ego by identifying with the perfect mirror image, so spectators derive pleasure from identification with the perfect image of themselves in others.

Laura Mulvey has argued that various kinds of visual pleasure are constructed through relations of sexual difference, structured by the gendered unconscious rather than the conscious. For example, in the work of Freud, the fear and anxiety of castration which arise in the boy child as a result of looking cause him to invent fetish objects to stand in for the mother's lack of phallus. Here looking is active and gendered masculine, while being-looked-at is passive and feminised. This model of the male gaze and the female spectacle, although binary in nature and over simplified, provides a useful starting point for thinking about the gendering of space through looking.[56] In the first instance, it positions the rambler as an active "looking" male subject. Representations of the male gaze are integral to the construction of urban masculinity. The rambler's precedent, the London spy, is represented as a voyeur, and his successor, the Parisian flâneur, is associated with a "mobile, free, eroticized and avaricious gaze."[57] Rambling is connected with visual pleasure, with narcissism and voyeurism, with the desire to look.

For the rambler, looking was connected to exploring and to knowing. *Life in London* provided a "complete cyclopedia" – a new kind of book for a new kind of city – a text which allowed readers to "see life."[58] By adopting a "camera obscura" view of the city, Egan's rambler became a voyeur, possessing "the invaluable advantages of SEEING and not being seen."[59] The camera obscura position allowed the viewer to gain visionary control, to frame the object like a picture. On a visit to a low life tavern, a site of potential danger, the ramblers donned disguises which served to distance them from the scene in a voyeuristic manner.[60] On a visit to Newgate, the reality of the scene – prisoners preparing to die – was suppressed by adopting a panoramic and distancing view, tending towards a surveillant and categorising gaze.[61] Similar elements of spectacular and detached observation were created at this time in other cultural forms, such as Nash's schemes for urban improvement, panoramas and dioramas as new popular forms of entertainment, and the social caricatures of graphic artists.

The rambler and other figures in the ramble, such as the dandy, also demanded visual reciprocity. The rambler as a dandy had a narcissistic body – one associated with its own surface – a surface which made social position apparent through body position and gesture, and the display of materials or ornaments.[62] Fashion played an essential role in the construction of male urban identity in the early nineteenth century. Rambling tales laid great emphasis on the difference between town and country through ways of dressing.[63] In the eighteenth century, court hierarchies of dressing had been rejected in favour of simple and practical styles, derived from the dress of the sporting country gentleman. The John Bull outfit consisted of everyday riding clothes – a top hat, a simple neckcloth, a small coat (cut away in the front), a waistcoat, breeches fitting into riding boots and a stick, later modified to suit urban lifestyles and a city aesthetic.[64] In *Life in London*, on arrival in the metropolis, Jerry, the country relative, must first undergo an "elegant metamorphose," discarding his "rustic habit" for fashionable top-boots, white cord breeches, a green coat with brass buttons and a neat waist coat.[65]

The adoption of simple styles made it possible to obscure social rank through dress, and so increasingly subtle codes were used to establish exclusivity. Beau Brummel, the archetypal dandy, rejected finery for a sparse and precise style of dress and an obsessive attention to detail – cleanliness, cut and fit.[66] The socially aspiring attitude of the dandy who, in order to reject bourgeois notions of thrift and hard work, sought to emulate the leisured life of the aristocracy, posed a class threat. By representing his interest in fashion and display as ridiculous, the dandy was marginalised as a "fashionable non-descript."[67] His attention to surface effect, a characteristic usually associated with the feminine, was considered unmanly and his appearance was described in terms of exaggerated female forms, such as waists pinched-in with stays.[68] Alternatively, in relation to the highly decorated masculinities preceding him, the dandy's sleek and unadorned appearance has also been interpreted as a highly erotic version of "unpainted masculinity."[69]

The social ritual of dressing in the correct urban fashion was an important first step in the process of initiation for new ramblers. This set of activities took place in the chambers of the urban bachelor with a tailor in attendance. Dressing was followed by an afternoon parade around St James's to purchase new commodities and display self and possessions.[70] Bond Street and St James's Street catered for the male consumer, with gun shops, booksellers, theatre ticket agents, sporting prints exhibitions, hatters, tailors, cravats, hairdressers, perfumers, jewellers and other expensive tradesmen.[71] Other urban locations visited by ramblers within St James's included chambers, hotels, sporting venues, coffee houses, clubs and taverns, all of which played an integral part in producing a public display of heterosexual, upper-class masculinity. The narcissistic aspects of the rambler, represented through the dandy, reflected an intense preoccupation with developing an urban aesthetic and style which opposed those of the corinthian. For the corinthian, fashion was displayed through social mobility, whereas the dandy's most renowned social art was one of exclusivity, "cutting" or ignoring acquaintances in the street.[72] Unlike the corinthian who mixed with both classes and moved from east to west in search of pleasure, the dandy's social exclusivity required him to remain in the west.[73]

The rambler, as a narcissistic spectator, derived pleasure from identifying the perfect image of himself in others and required sites for looking at other men. The rambler also desired spaces to display his leisure time and money, his "conspicuous consumption," to other men and women. Possibly the most fashionable places of display for upper-class young men were the ground floor bow windows of the clubs on St James's Street. Membership of these clubs was extremely select and the famous "Bow Window at White's," built out over the entrance steps in the centre of the front facade in 1811, was inhabited as a space of high fashion by a circle of dandies, including Brummell.[74] From the bow windows, men could show off their exclusivity to those in the surrounding rival clubs and display status and leisure time to the street. When Crockford's club opened in 1828, the ground floor rooms also possessed windows. These were carefully distinguished as "bay" windows or observatories, from which to "look out" and "survey" the street, in distinction to White's' "bow" window, a place in which to be looked at.[75] The bow window was a place for dandies and ramblers to look out and to be looked at.

Although we have seen that "looking" and "being-looked-at" are, in certain cases, reciprocal positions which can both be adopted by one sex, psychoanalytic theories of the male gaze and the female spectacle tend to allow us to consider women only as looked at objects on display. The cyprian body was the site of the ramblers' desire and gaze – an object of display in the public spaces in the city. Rambling texts represented female identity in terms of surface spectacle.

The displayed surface of the body is composed of a close relationship between clothes and the fleshy body. In the early nineteenth century, the issue of "covering" was connected with a number of gendered themes around decency. A correct amount and kind of covering represented feminine decency in terms of honesty and modesty, whereas an incorrect covering represented indecency in terms of dishonesty and immodesty. Clothing was expected to be neither too revealing nor too obscuring of the body that lay beneath. To cover too little was immodest, to cover too much was dishonest. Both transgressions were connected with excess, extravagance and with prostitution. An excess of flesh represented exposure and wantonness, and an excess of clothing in the form of decoration represented artifice and vanity.

Strict rules governing the appropriate amount and kind of covering to be worn were recorded as "fashion" in women's magazines.[76] Fashionable clothing for women of the upper classes in England in the first two decades of the nineteenth century was a highly minimal costume adopted from post-revolutionary Paris, inspired by the democratic politics of Greek culture. The gowns were full length, of a semi-transparent white fabric, worn with minimal undergarments and stockings. Sparse, revealing and décolleté, the waist was raised to draw attention to the breasts. The material was dampened so that it clung to the body like drapery, representing the body as a sculptural form.[77] But fear of French politics meant that by the end of the second decade of the nineteenth century, nakedness was connected with political radicalism. The exposure of the breast and the transparency of the gown were considered immoral.[78]

In rambles, cyprians were associated with surface value and considered to be kept for "*empty shew* than *real use*."[79] In *Life in London*, the display of breasts by females in the street and in the theatre and assembly rooms represented them as cyprians.[80] Cyprians were also distinguished by the excessive display of gaudy dresses and decorative headwear and jewellery. Cyprians were believed to be motivated by "allure,"[81] and by "principles of lust, idleness, or avarice."[82] Their desire to "dress-up" above their class in order to attract rich clients connected them with wearing deceitful coverings. Similarly, since their occupation could often not be distinguished through their surface appearance, cyprians' clothes also represented deceitfulness. Evidence that some cyprians, dress-lodgers, did not own their clothes but rented them from brothels,[83] and that others would pawn their clothes in hard times, substantiated suspicions concerning the dishonest quality of cyprian dress.[84]

In rambling texts associations were made between the pleasures of viewing the city through the controlling and framing techniques of the camera obscura and viewing the female body. Similarly, associations were also made between the surface of buildings and femininity as "to-be-looked-at-ness." The connection between gambling and deceptive appearance featured in descriptions of Crockford's club as a common gaming house "masquerading" as a respectable subscription house in order to create an aura of respectability.[85] The extravagance of the interior decoration, including the use of glass, mirrors and chandeliers, was considered to be falsely seductive and interpreted by anti-gamblers as part of a plan to seduce the gambler and encourage the play of unrealistically sums of money.[86] Gambling hells were described as: "temple[s] of ruin, indolence, and guile" and gambling as "an abandoned prostitution of every principle of hallow and virtue."[87]

The issue of display took on a special relevance in relation to the role of actresses and dancers whose bodies were uncovered/exposed on public stages.[88] On stage, the aspects that a woman usually kept private were made visible, and such visibility, in terms of the overlapping of public and private, was connected to indecency and immorality.[89] Madame Vestris, a performer best known for her travesty roles, provided a focused example of public display. Playing male figures, dressed in breeches and skin tight trousers, she displayed to the audience her legs, buttocks, hips and thighs.[90] For audiences largely consisting of young men, the display of Vestris' legs was the focus of attention.[91] The leg of the travesty dancer provided a metaphor for the transgressive eliding of public and private spheres in terms of covering and display, where the display of a female leg on a public stage was read as an act of exposure and wantonness.

The omnibus boxes on stage at the Italian Opera House in St James's formed a focus for the visual pleasure of the male ramblers and patrons of the ballet, providing privileged vantage points for the close scrutiny of the predominantly women dancers and singers. In these boxes, as in the foyers of theatres, men were represented holding spy glasses to their eyes.[92] In an etching of the green room at the Italian Opera House in a rambling text, the focus was also on visual display. Here the ramblers represented were engaged in watching and sketching the dancers, using eye glasses, while the dancers surveyed their own bodies and dancing techniques in the large mirrors.[93]

Two other public female figures encountered by the rambler, conflated with cyprians and associated with surface and display, were female shoppers and shop-girls. Through their "conspicuous consumption" – the items bought, the clothes worn and the amount of leisure time spent shopping – the female shopper was a visual indication of male wealth and status.[94] But the commonly held male view of the female shopper was that she was overly concerned with her appearance and therefore trivial, superfluous, overindulgent and extravagant – a "dollymop" or amateur prostitute.[95] Shopgirls were also considered to be obsessed with their appearance and to have a desire for "finery" beyond their means. Such women were assumed to supplement their incomes with prostitution – to be "slygirls."[96] The connection of shopgirls and female shoppers with cyprians was closely bound up with issues of surface display, where inappropriate or excessive covering, represented through a fascination with dress and decoration, was considered deceitful. Such surfaces were represented as immoral in their ability to mask what lay beneath: in this case class difference.

If we take traditional models of psychoanalysis where the gaze is constructed through the development of the male subject, it is possible for a female spectator "to look" only if she is identified with an active male, or to consider the construction of female identity in relation to being looked at. For Joan Rivière, woman *is* masquerade, the display or performance of femininity,[97] but for other feminists masquerade theorised this way is an alienated or false version of femininity.[98] Irigaray's work utilises the operations of masquerade and mimicry as conscious subversive, destabilising and defamiliarising strategies for flaunting spectacle and speech. Irigaray's theory of "mimicry" shows how, when working within a symbolic system with predetermined notions of feminine and masculine, where there is no theory of the female subject, by deliberately assuming the feminine style assigned to them, women can uncover the mechanisms which exploit them.[99]

In emerging discourses around the threat of female presence in public space, male ambivalence (simultaneous feelings of fear and desire towards female sexuality) placed emphasis on the looked-at nature of the surface, on the tension between display, what was being revealed, and secrecy, what remained hidden. Places occupied by women, such as the bow windows of shops in arcades and boxes at the opera, were represented as sites of intrigue and deceit. The presence of women in both these places presented a threat to patriarchal ideologies concerning women and property. From the late eighteenth century, the great majority of opera box subscribers were women.[100] Arcade shops were also private spaces often owned by women.

Such places provided women with sites from which to display their property-owning status to the street. Male fears of female owned spaces resulted in the representation of both opera box and shop bow window as sites of intrigue.

A critical aspect of gendered identity is played out through spatial relations of movement and vision. Men and women represent their social and gendered relations of equivalence and dominance through positions as spectators and objects of sight, and through free movement and viewed containment in public arenas. The rambler and the cyprian, precursors to the Parisian flâneur and prostitute, are gendered representations of urban space in early nineteenth century London. Thinking about the dialectical relation between identities and spaces, representations and constructions, allows an analysis which pays greater attention to the complexity and fluidity of gendered space. By paying greater attention to the fluidity of urban movement, the figures and spaces of the ramble are a starting point for considering the gendering of public space through the pursuit of pleasure. It is through this complex series of gendered looks and moves that relations of consumption, display and exchange are played out in a way in which the patterning of gendered space is far more complicated than the continuing debate around the separate spheres suggests.

References

1   Luce Irigaray, *This Sex Which is Not One* (Ithaca, NY: Cornell University Press, 1985), pp. 170–91.

2   Amateur, *Real Life in London* (London: Jones and Co., 1821–2), pp. 198–9.

3   Griselda Pollock "Modernity and the Spaces of Femininity," *Vision and Difference: Femininity, Feminism and the Histories of Art* (London: Routledge, 1988), p. 79.

4   *Oxford English Dictionary* (*OED*), CD-ROM, 2nd edition (1989).

5   Nathaniel S. Wheaton, *A Journal of a Residence During Several Months in London* (Hartford CT: H. and F.J. Huntington, 1830), p. 119.

6   Eric Partridge, *A Dictionary of Slang and Unconventional English* (London: Routledge and Kegan Paul, 1964), p. 958.

7   Francis Grose, *A Classical Dictionary of the Vulgar Tongue* (London: S. Hooper, 1788), n. p.

8   The semi-narrative structure first appears in Edward Ward, *The London Spy* (London: J. Nutt and J. How, 1698–9).

9   See, for example, R. King, *The Complete London Spy for the Present Year 1781* (London: Alex Hogg, 1781).

10 Amateur, *Real Life*.

11 Pierce Egan, *Life in London* (London: Sherwood, Neely and Jones, 1820–1).

12 William Heath, *Fashion and Folly: or the Buck's Pilgrimage* (London: William Sams, 1822).

13 Bernard Blackmantle, *The English Spy* (London: Sherwood, Jones and Co., 1825).

14 See for example, *The Rambler's Magazine* (London: R. Randall, 1783–9); *The Ranger's Magazine* (London: J. Sudbury, 1795); *The Rambler's Magazine* (London: J. Mitford, 1820); *The Rambler's Magazine* (London: Benbow, 1822); *The Rambler* (London: T. Holt, 1824); *The Rambler's Magazine* (London: J. Mitford, 1828).

15 *OED*; Partridge, *Dictionary*, p. 284.

16 Egan, *Life*, pp. 48–9.

17 Pierce Egan, *Finish to the Adventures of Tom, Jerry and Logic in their Pursuits through Life in and out of London* (London: J. S. Virtue, 1828).

18 Egan, *Life*, p. 72

19 Irigaray, *This Sex*, p. 170.

20 Egan, *Life*, chs 3 and 4, pp. 43 and 53.

21 Pierce Egan, *Grose's Classical Dictionary of the Vulgar Tongue* (London: Sherwood, Neely and Jones, 1823), n. p.

22 John Badcock, *Slang: a Dictionary of the Turf* (London: T. Hughes, 1823), p. 57.

23 Charles Hindley, *The True History of Tom and Jerry* (London: C. Hindley, 1890).

24 See for example, Pierce Egan, *Boxiana* (new series) (London: George Virtue, 1828–9).

25 Among the accoutrements every rambler should own is a flagon. See Egan, *Life*, title page.

26 Egan, *Boxiana* (1818), p. 28; Jacob Larwood, *The Story of the London Parks* (London: Francis Harvey, 1872), v. 8, pp. 282–4.

27 See T. Rowlandson, "Three Principal Requisites to form a Modern Man of Fashion," (London: n. d.).

28 Grose, *A Classical*, n. p.

29 See, for example, George Andrewes, *The Stranger's Guide* (London: J. Bailey, 1808); George Andrewes, *A Dictionary of the Slang* (London: G. Smeeton, 1809); Badcock, *Slang*; John Badcock, *A Living Picture of London, for 1823* (London: W. Clarke, 1828); Egan, *Boxiana*, Egan, *Grose's*; Egan, *Life*; Smeeton, *Flash*, Smeeton, *The Art of Boxing*; George Smeeton, *Doings in London* (London: Smeeton, 1828).

30 See Egan, *Grose's*, title page and preface, pp. xxv–xxviii.

31 Egan, *Life*, pp. xiii–xiv and 22–4.

32 The London Lighting Act of 1761 and the Westminster Paving Acts of 1761 systematised street lighting and paving to a certain extent.

33 See, for example, Hemione Hobhouse, *A History of Regent Street* (London: Queen Anne Press, 1975), pp. 72–3.

34 See, for example, John Summerson, *John Nash: Architect to King George IV* (London: George Allen and Unwin, 1935), pp. 204–5.

35   Badcock, *Living*, pp. 47–8.

36   Blackmantle, *Spy*, v. 2, pp. 18–9.

37   *Belle*, (July 1806), p. 314.

38   Smeeton, *Doings*, p. 91.

39   Irigaray, *This Sex*, pp. 170–91.

40   Shannon Bell, *Reading, Writing and Rewriting the Prostitute Body* (Bloomington and Indianapolis: Indiana University Press, 1994), p. 91.

41   Egan, *Life*, p. 167.

42   Amateur, *Real*, v.1, p. 524.

43   *Rambler's Magazine* (London: J. Mitford, 1828), v.1 n. 1, p. 32. and v. 2 n. 1, p. 212.

44   Guardian Society, *Report of the Provisional Committee of the Guardian Society for the Preservation of Public Morals providing Temporary Asylums for Prostitutes* (London: James Low, 1816), p. 33.

45   *A Letter to the Right Rev. the Lord Bishop of London containing a statement of the Immoral and Disgraceful scenes which are every evening Exhibited in the Public Streets by Crowds of half Naked and Unfortunate Prostitutes* (London: Williams and Smith, 1808), pp. 12–13.

46   William Hale, *Considerations on the Causes and the Prevalence of Female Prostitution* (London: E. Justing, 1812), p. 35.

47   See "An Act for the Better preventing Thefts and Robberies, and for regulating Places of Publick Entertainment, and Punishing Persons Keeping Disorderly Houses," 25 George II, cap. 36, n. 4 (1752), *Statutes at Large, 23 George II – 26 George II (1750–2)* (Cambridge: Charles Bathurst, 1765), v. 20, pp. 375–80.

48   See "An Act for Consolidating into one Act and Amending the Laws relating to Idle and Disorderly Persons, Rogues and Vagabonds, Incorrigible Rogues and other Vagrants in England," 3 George IV, cap. 40 (1822), *Statutes at Large, 3 George IV (1822)* (London: His Majesty's Statute and Law Printers, 1822), v. 62, pp. 133–42; and "An Act for the Punishment of Idle and Disorderly Persons, and Rogues and Vagabonds, in that part of Great Britain called England," 5 George IV, cap. 83 (1824), *Statutes at Large, 5 George IV (1824)* (London: His Majesty's Printers, 1839), v. 64, pp. 281–9.

49   Egan, *Finish*, p. 250.

50   Egan, *Finish*, pp. 214–21.

51   Egan, *Finish*, pp. 337–43.

52   Egan, *Finish*, pp. 294–331.

53   Egan, *Finish*, pp. 311–15.

54   *Rambler's*, v. 1 n. 3 (March 1822), p. 109.

55   Luce Irigaray, *The Speculum of the Other Woman* (Ithaca, NY: Cornell University Press, 1985), p. 116.

56   See, for example, Laura Mulvey, "Visual Pleasure and Narrative Cinema," Laura Mulvey (ed.), *Visual and Other Pleasures* (London: Macmillan, 1989), pp. 14–26.

57 See, for example, Janet Wolff, "The Invisible Flâneuse: Women and the Literature of Modernity," *Theory, Culture and Society*, v. 2 n. 3 (1985), pp. 36–46; Pollock, *Vision and Difference*, p. 79.

58 Egan, *Life*, pp. 23–4.

59 See Chapter 2 entitled "A Camera-Obscura View of the Metropolis, the Light and Shade attached to 'seeing Life,'" Egan, *Life*, p. 18.

60 See "TOM and JERRY '*masquerading it*' among the *cadgers* in the *Back Slums* in the Holy Land," Egan, *Life*, p. 346.

61 Egan, *Life*, p. 282.

62 Arthur W. Frank, "For a Sociology of the Body: an Analytic Overview," Mike Featherstone, Mike Hepworth and Bryan S Turner (eds), *The Body: Social Process and Cultural Theory* (London: Sage, 1991), pp. 36–102; and Pierre Bourdieu, *Distinction: a Social Critique of the Judgement of Taste* (London: Routledge and Kegan Paul, 1984), p. 190.

63 Amateur, *Real*, v. 1, p. 102.

64 James Laver, *Dandies* (London: Weidenfeld and Nicolson, 1968), pp. 10 and 153.

65 Egan, *Life*, pp. 145–8.

66 Faired Chevianne, *A History of Men's Fashion* (Paris: Flammarian, 1993), p. 9.

67 Egan, *Grose's*, n. p.

68 See, for example, Robert Cruikshank, "Dandies Dressing" (1818); Richard Dighton, "The Dandy Club," (1818); George Cruikshank, "The Dandies Coat of Arms," (1819); George Cruikshank, "Monstrosities," (1822).

69 Elizabeth Wilson, *Adorned in Dreams* (London: Virago, 1985), p. 180.

70 See, for example, Amateur, *Real*, v. 1, p. 102; Blackmantle, *Spy*, v. 2, p. 253; Egan, *Life*, p. 213; Captain Gronow, *Reminiscences* (London: Smith, Elder, 1862), pp. 74–9; Heath, *Fashion*, plate 14; Felix MacDonogh, "A Morning Ride in a Noble-Man's Curricle," *The Hermit in London* (London: Henry Colburn, 1819), v.2, pp. 35–42.

71 Captain Gronow, *Recollections and Anecdotes* (London: Smith, Elder, 1863), pp. 136–7.

72 See, for example, M. Egerton, "The Cut Celestial," "The Cut Infernal" and "The Cut Direct" (1827).

73 The dandy, Beau Brummell, once apologised for having been seen as far east as Charing Cross. See Eileen Moers, *The Dandy: Brummell to Beerbohm* (Lincoln, NB: University of Nebraska Press, 1978), p. 66.

74 Gronow, *Reminiscences* (1862), pp. 46 and 62.

75 See Robert Cruikshank, "Exterior of Fishmongers-Hall, St James's Street, with a view of a Regular Break down," showing "Portraits of the Master-Fishmonger and many well known *Greeks* and *Pigeons*," Blackmantle, *English*, v. 1, p. 373, plate 24.

76 *Belle*, (July 1806), p. 231; *Belle*, (July 1809), p. 43.

77 *Belle* (February 1806), p. 64.

78 *Belle* (February 1806), pp. 16 and 20.

79 *Rambler's*, v. 1 n. 4 (April 1822), p. 161.

80 Egan, *Life*, p. 173.

81 Mary Wilson, *The Whore's Catechism* (London: Sarah Brown, 1830), p. 76.

82 Hale, *Considerations*, p. 4

83 Amateur, *Real*, v. 1, p. 571.

84 Amateur, *Real*, v. 1, pp. 566–7.

85 Deale, *Crockfords or Life in the West* (London: Saunders and Otley, 1828), v. 1, p. 72.

86 Deale, *Crockfords*, v. 2, p. 253.

87 Heath, *Fashion*, plate 21.

88 Anon., *Memoirs* (1836), pp. 7–8.

89 Tracy C. Davis, "Private Women and the Public Realm," *Theatre Survey*, v. 35 n. 1 (May 1994), pp. 65–71.

90 *The Drama or Theatrical Pocket Magazine*, v. 3 n. 7 (December 1822), p. 316, King's Theatre Archives (1826), Theatre Museum, London.

91 Anon, *Memoirs of the Life of Madame Vestris* (London: privately printed, 1830), p. 63.

92 Gronow, *Reminiscences* (1862), p. 179.

93 See Robert Cruikshank, "The Green Room of the King's Theatre, or Noble Amateurs viewing Foreign Curiosities," Blackmantle, *English*, v. 1, p. 225, plate 11 and pp. 208–9.

94 Thorstein Veblen, *The Theory of the Leisure Class* (Harmondsworth: Penguin, 1979).

95 Hilary Evans, *The Oldest Profession* (London: David and Charles, 1979), p. 116.

96 Dorothy Davis, *A History of Shopping* (London: Routledge and Kegan Paul, 1966), p. 125.

97 Joan Rivière, "Womanliness as Masquerade," *International Journal of Psychoanalysis*, v. 10 (1929), pp. 303–13.

98 See, for example, Mary Ann Doane, "Film and the Masquerade: Theorising the Female Spectator," *Screen*, v. 23, ns 2–4 (September–October 1982), pp. 74–87.

99 Irigaray, *Speculum*, pp. 113–7; Irigaray, *This Sex*, p. 84.

100 Box 2482, King's Theatre Archives, Theatre Museum, London.

Chapter 15
The construction of identity: Virginia Woolf's city
Barbara Penner

Virginia Woolf had a lifelong fascination with London, making the city – which she once called "the passion of her life"[1] – the subject of countless diary entries, letters, essays and fictional works. It is not surprising, then, that Woolf figures prominently in literary studies of female writers in the city, nor that Elizabeth Wilson refers to her in the conclusion of *The Sphinx in the City*. In Wilson's assertion of the city as an important site of emotional and political freedom for women, Woolf and her fourth novel, *Mrs Dalloway*, seem to provide invaluable evidence of how the female response to modern urban life is more positive than that of men. Wilson states:

> In *Mrs. Dalloway*, Virginia Woolf exulted in the vitality of a summer's morning in London
> . . . Acknowledging the unstable and uncertain nature of personal identity, she does not
> find this alarming, as did Kafka and Musil . . . Mrs. Dalloway and [Dorothy Richardson's]
> Miriam Henderson are not estranged. For them urban life offers not only adventure,
> but reassurance. The city is an enveloping presence in their work, and they seem to find
> its vast amorphousness maternal or even womblike. Instead of disintegrating, they are
> held by it.[2]

Upon a closer reading of this paragraph, a strange ambiguity becomes apparent: just whose experience is Wilson describing? She seems to perceive Virginia Woolf and Mrs Dalloway as interchangeable: for instance, it is Woolf, rather than Mrs Dalloway, whom Wilson describes as "exulting" in the vitality of London in the novel. This approach leads to some confusion when Wilson's discussion of Mrs Dalloway and Miriam Henderson ("For them urban life offers not only adventure, but reassurance"), mentions "their work," presumably referring now to Woolf and Richardson. It is unclear to whom the vast amorphousness of the city appears "maternal or even womblike" – the authors, the characters, or both?

In response to canonical accounts of city life and modernity which privilege male experience, Wilson's thesis is that women have experienced the modern city differently to men, and her efforts in *The Sphinx in the City* to provide an alternative history of their experience is of particular significance to feminist scholarship. In order to locate evidence of female experience, Wilson has relied heavily upon a variety of non-traditional sources, including journalistic, autobiographical and literary ones, asserting that they "all contribute on equal terms to a 'discourse' about the city."[3] But the potential complexity of her textual analysis here is greatly diminished by its dependence on two underlying assumptions: first, that there is necessarily some sort of correspondence between an author's view of the city and that of the fictional character created; and second, that both fiction and personal writing can be read as if they were objective documents of female experience. While it does not annul the overall value of her history, Wilson's reductive reading of Woolf and *Mrs Dalloway* effectively underlines one of the larger problems facing feminist critics and historians: namely, how do we use and interpret cultural representations of women in our work in a way that does not ignore their specificity? Gillian Beer sums up the difficulty this way: "Representations [of women] rapidly become representatives . . . the authentic voice of a group."[4] How do we avoid the common trap of treating representations as if they reveal to us some sort of authoritative, essential female experience?

A number of key feminist critics from a variety of fields – such as literary criticism, cultural studies and art history – have addressed this problem.[5] In particular, the literary critic Toril Moi and the historian Joan W. Scott have produced important discussions of the dangers of readings which assume that texts can yield or illuminate a "true" experience for readers. Moi, for instance, roundly attacks the notion that a text can be read as the unitary vision or expression of an author, observing that with this interpretation literature is reduced to autobiography, "a mere window on to the self and world."[6] Scott warns of the pitfalls of using the evidence of experience as the starting-point for an alternative historical analysis, noting that this often naturalizes difference as a self-evident fact, rather than establishing it as "that which one seeks to explain."[7] Both Moi and Scott strongly reject the notion that "an author, thought of as a single and unchanging consciousness, should straight-forwardly describe her experience in order that a reader, thought of as a passive receiver, can possess it too."[8]

Instead, Moi and Scott argue that a successful textual reading is one which acknowledges the instability of language and identity (not just of the fictional characters but of the author, reader and historian/critic as well) and challenges the notion of a causal relationship existing between experience and meaning.[9] Specifically, Scott, based on her belief that subjectivity, identity and experience are all constituted discursively, calls for what she terms a "literary" reading which attempts to "historicize" experience by attending to "the historical processes that, through discourse, position subjects and produce their experiences."[10] Scott emphasizes that these discursive processes are complex, competing and historically variable, transforming identity into a "contested terrain" where many factors, such as sex, class, race and age intersect.

In this chapter, I offer a more detailed rereading of Woolf and *Mrs Dalloway*, closer in spirit to the interpretation proposed by Moi and Scott. Rather than mining

Woolf's personal writing and her fiction for proof of the distinctiveness of women's urban experience, I consider the way that they represent the production and reproduction of difference within the city. Does the London represented in Woolf's work "contain" female experience and identity as Wilson suggests? Or does it take a more active part in forming and dispersing them, generating the myriad representations of gender – the "thicket of self-refutation"[11] – which we will find at the heart of *Mrs Dalloway*?

STREET HAUNTING IN LONDON

On 26 May 1924, after moving back to London from the suburban isolation of Rodmell, Woolf wrote in her diary:

> One of these days I will write about London, and how it takes up the private life and carries it on, without any effort. Faces passing lift up my mind; prevent it from settling, as it does in the stillness in Rodmell.[12]

Few prominent writers, male or female, have acknowledged their creative debt to a city so publicly: Woolf often claimed that London was essential to her activity as a writer, serving as a major stimulus for her work. Later, in the same diary entry, Woolf mentions how, after working, she would dart outside to "refresh her stagnancy" walking in the streets of London.[13] These urban rambles provided Woolf with more than literary inspiration: she also saw them as a means of shedding her gendered identity and achieving the androgyny she felt was crucial to the creative mind.

Woolf clearly articulated this idea in a little known essay of 1927 called "Street Haunting: a London Adventure," in which she guides the uninitiated through the pleasures of rambling the winter streets of London. She recommends rambling in the early evening between four and six, when the darkness and lamplight bestow a certain "irresponsibility" which enables us to "shed the self our friends know us by and become part of that vast republican army of anonymous trampers, whose society is so agreeable after the solitude of one's own room."[14] In an extraordinary passage, she explains how individual identity can be suspended when one passes through the streets at this hour:

> The shell-like covering which our souls have excreted to house themselves, to make for themselves a shape distinct from others, is broken, and there is left of all these wrinkles and roughnesses a central oyster of perceptiveness, an enormous eye.[15]

This omniscient eye floats smoothly downstream, through the streets, watching the anonymous passers-by, looking through a window to the privacy of a drawing room, observing and recording not only the urban scene but also the stories, imaginings and memories that it stirs. Woolf's rambler happily window-shops, has brief encounters in stores with strangers and meditates on the infinite, split nature of the self which is compelled to unity only "for convenience's sake."[16]

At this point, Woolf's anonymous rambler bears a certain resemblance to Walter Benjamin's *flâneur*. For, like the *flâneur*, Woolf rambles not only for pleasure but also for acquisition, using the scenes, images and people she encounters en route as a source for her critical and creative works: it is not insignificant that Woolf's "pretext" for her twilight ramble is the need to buy a pencil. As she observes, "London itself perpetually attracts, stimulates, gives me a play, a story and a poem without any trouble, save that of moving my legs through the streets."[17] Indeed, descriptions of the city from Woolf's diary often resurfaced in published pieces, just as the *flâneur*'s impressions of the urban spectacle reappeared in *feuilleton* and magazine articles.

The striking difference between Woolf's account and that of a flâneur, however, is that there is a notable absence of sexuality or of physical contact – such as the brush of strangers passing – on Woolf's streets. In fact, Woolf's title "Street Haunting" evokes the image of a disembodied, gender-neutral presence which hovers above the corporeality of city life. This lack of a specific gender is not accidental, for Woolf repeatedly emphasized the need for androgyny in writing as a means of seeing beyond the boundaries of the gendered self. By casting off one's individual identity, she argues, one might "give oneself the illusion that one is not tethered to a single mind but can put on briefly for a few minutes the bodies and minds of others."[18] Woolf attempts to escape her particular social position (as a white, privileged, lesbian woman) by pursuing in her imagination the various objects, events and people she encounters on her twilight rambles, effectively embarking on a series of fictional voyages which allows her to "put on" a host of different subjectivities – from a dwarf, to a washerwoman, to a publican.[19] Like Sally Munt's lesbian *flâneur*, the experience of strolling through the city becomes for Woolf analogous to the experience of wandering through one's mind in the production (and consumption) of literature: her physical and fictive urban experiences become entwined in their representation.[20]

However, the city does not always permit this escape from identity. In fact, Woolf often represents it as being the place where women are forced to confront the patriarchal nature of the public realm and the enormous difference between the male and female status. Woolf felt that the difference of female status was caused in large part by women's limited access to power within the public realm (i.e. within academia or government), a dilemma which was dramatized by the physical barriers she encountered on her walks. There is the famous scene in *A Room of One's Own* when Woolf's thoughts are interrupted as she walks through Oxbridge University by a beadle telling her that she cannot walk on the lawn which is reserved for the all-male students and dons: she is later denied entry to the university library. Woolf also describes a similar sense of exclusion in certain "public" spaces in London:

> Again, if one is a women one is often surprised by a sudden splitting off of consciousness, say in walking down Whitehall, when from being the natural inheritor of that civilization, she becomes, on the contrary, outside of it, alien and critical.[21]

Whitehall, Westminster, St James's – these are identified by Woolf as ideological spaces of patriarchal power where she becomes profoundly aware of her gendered identity.

A more ambiguous image of Woolf's relationship to the city emerges. On many levels, Woolf obviously did respond to the city with "joy and affirmation," praising the spirit of London and the possibilities it offered for liberation, both from the isolation of suburbia and the constraints of gender. But, despite the autonomy it offered, Woolf felt that the city was also where women's position as "outsiders" within the patriarchal order was continually being reinforced. While she felt that the city offered an escape from one's individual identity, she also underlined that this freedom was illusory and brief, disappearing the moment one returned to the private realm: a situation which, surprisingly, she did not decry, but rather depicted as reassuring. As she wrote at the end of "Street Haunting," "as we approach our own doorstep again, it is comforting to feel the old possessions, the old prejudices, fold us round, and shelter and enclose the self which has been blown about at so many street corners."[22] The temporary thrill of her ramble over; it is in the home, rather than in the city streets, where Woolf's identity is gathered up and contained once more.

MRS DALLOWAY'S LONDON

As many of Woolf's personal experiences in the city closely parallel those of various characters throughout *Mrs Dalloway*, it is undeniably tempting to view the latter's experiences as being little more than autobiographical sketches. A literal interpretation, conflating the author's lived experiences with her fiction, is further encouraged by the fact that Woolf draws such a precise physical portrait of London at a very particular moment in time. The action of *Mrs Dalloway* unfolds over the course of a single day in June 1923, following the central characters as they move through the city – Clarissa Dalloway as she prepares to host a party that night, her former lover Peter Walsh who has just returned from India, and Septimus Warren Smith a First World War veteran who has gone mad. The characters' routes are described in such detail that they can be traced on a map of London (in fact, my edition of *Mrs Dalloway* includes a map of

"Mrs Dalloway's London" for that purpose).[23] What, other than a desire to record the city she loved so much, could account for the precision of Woolf's description?

Upon closer inspection of the text, however, an alternative interpretation presents itself, one where London functions as more than a descriptive foil for the characters and is an active agent which positions them within the patriarchal order. At a most basic level, for instance, the characters in *Mrs Dalloway* are often introduced by reference to where they live in London – for example, Mrs Dalloway is from Westminster, the mothers in Regent's Park are from Pimlico, Mrs Dempster is from Kentish Town – information which was meant to immediately locate them within the class structure for a contemporary reader.

On a deeper level, it can also be argued that the monuments and buildings that Woolf describes are not chosen randomly but are symbols for certain ideas which, Jeremy Tambling asserts, Woolf meant to critique. Tambling's argument is particularly interesting because it challenges the tradition of interpreting *Mrs Dalloway* as a "domestic" novel, remarkable mainly for its "stream-of-consciousness" writing style. Tambling attempts to demonstrate that Woolf was motivated not only by aesthetic concerns, but by the desire to reflect critically on specific political and social issues of her time, such as the First World War, British imperialism, the medical establishment and sexual identity.[24]

In support of his claim that Woolf's choice of buildings and spaces is highly symbolic, Tambling analyzes the route which Peter Walsh takes after visiting Clarissa Dalloway in Westminster. Walsh walks down Victoria Street, past Westminster Abbey, the Houses of Parliament, and up Whitehall (where he glares at the statue of the Duke of Cambridge and contemplates his own former socialist leanings). He is overtaken by marching boys in uniform going to lay a wreath at the Cenotaph (which, like the tomb of the Unknown Warrior contemplated later by Miss Kilman, is a new monument to the War) and goes on to Trafalgar Square, facing statues of the war heroes Nelson, Gordon and Havelock. The spaces through which he passes represent and glorify imperial state power, arousing pride and a sense of belonging in Walsh, almost despite himself.

> Coming as he did from a respectable Anglo-Indian family which for at least three generations had administered the affairs of a continent (it's strange, he thought, what a sentiment I have about that . . .), there were moments when civilization . . . seemed dear to him as a personal possession.[25]

In Trafalgar Square, Walsh spots an attractive girl and pursues her in a state of excitement, envisioning himself as an adventurer, a "swift and daring" buccaneer. He contemplates whether or not the anonymous object of his desire is married and if she is "respectable," and notes the redness of her lips. He pictures them meeting, sharing an ice, projecting qualities onto the beautiful stranger so that "she became the very woman he had always had in mind." The imaginary dalliance ends when the girl enters her home in one of the little streets off Great Portland Street and Walsh, pleased with his escapade, continues on to Regent's Park.

It is clearly no coincidence that this sexual pursuit takes place just after Walsh has been contemplating the most potent symbols of Britain's military might. The connection between male sexuality and official power is made even more explicit in a scene at the end of the novel when Clarissa remembers how the respectable Hugh Whitbread once forced Sally Seton to kiss him in the smoking-room at Bourton "to punish her for saying that women should have votes."[26] Throughout *Mrs Dalloway*, Whitbread is presented as a character who represents and maintains the status quo: Lady Bruton, an otherwise formidable woman, turns "gratefully" to him when she finds herself incapable of writing editorial letters to *The Times*, aware of the "futility of her own womanhood" because she does not have a command of political letter-writing, as Whitbread does.[27] Clearly, Hugh Whitbread violates Sally Seton in order to remind her – as he does Lady Bruton – of her position outside the Establishment. As such, he functions like Drs Holmes and Bradshaw who continually reinforce official definitions of "sanity" or "propriety" throughout the novel. Dr Bradshaw, the medical establishment's representative, accomplishes this by promoting "Proportion" and "Conversion" as values which are vital not only for maintaining the health of an individual, but also the collective health of the nation. His argument connects the discourses of medicine and war, as can be seen in the description of "Conversion" as an allegorical goddess figure who was, "even now engaged – in the heat and sands of India, the mud and swamp of Africa, the purlieus of London . . . – in dashing down shrines, smashing idols, and setting up in their place her own stern countenance." "Conversion" and "Proportion" are set up as twin pillars which, by promoting health, duty and self-sacrifice, support the glory of imperial Britain; they become significant features of the ideology of nationalism and imperialism which upholds and advances the power of the state, like the commemorative or triumphal statues and architecture Walsh passes on his walk.

But the central emblem of Westminster's power is Big Ben, whose chimes are heard throughout *Mrs Dalloway*. The chiming of the hours serves as a continual reminder of the regulation and order imposed on everyday life in London by governing authorities: a symbol of what Paul Ricoeur calls "monumental" time.[28] Hearing the chimes – like seeing the sky-writing aeroplane above or the royal motorcar passing – momentarily unifies the individual characters as they pursue their own thoughts and lives in the city, making them aware of their participation in a collective urban experience. Mrs Dalloway, for example, after hearing Big Ben boom out, begins a string of meditations on life and London:

what she loved was this, here now, in front of her; the fat lady in the cab. Did it matter then, she asked herself, walking towards Bond Street did it matter that she must inevitably cease completely; all this must go on without her; did she resent it; or did it not become consoling to believe that death ended absolutely? But that somehow in the streets of London, on the ebb and flow of things, here there, she survived, Peter survived, lived in each other, she being part, she was positive, of the trees at home; of the house there, ugly, rambling all to bit and pieces as it was; part of people she had never met; being laid out like a mist between the people she knew best, who lifted her on their branches as she had seen the trees lift the mist, but it spread ever so far, her life, herself.[29]

Big Ben emphasizes the linearity and unity of official time – its "presentness" – in contrast to the continual shifting between present and the past which characterizes the individual characters' thoughts throughout *Mrs Dalloway*. It also stands as a symbol of permanence, counteracting the fluid, transient nature of the self and experience in the novel.

The self is in a continual process of construction in *Mrs Dalloway*. In fact, Woolf stated that her objective was to "build up" Clarissa Dalloway's identity in each scene through her encounters with people and places[30] – an approach which lays great significance on the spaces and experiences of everyday life. It is these encounters which give Mrs Dalloway's character shape: as Tambling observes, "Mrs. Dalloway exists in the interstices between people and places and her character rises from contact with these things."[31] Mrs Dalloway is produced by her physical environment and cannot be understood independently of it. For this reason, Mrs Dalloway feels the impossibility of saying of herself, "I am this, I am that" and describes herself as being "laid out like a mist" in the streets of London.[32]

Understanding London and the experience it represents is crucial, then, to understanding the aspects of individual and collective identity described in the novel: the city becomes a site for exploring the changing nature of experi-ence and identity. We have already seen how this occurs in Peter Walsh's walk, and how the contact with symbols of imperial London inspire a nostalgic pride in him signalling that, even though he claims to feel alienated from the world of Hugh Whitbread, the older Peter has become much more "Establishment" than even he recognizes.

The physical features and boundaries of the characters' immediate environment define and circumscribe their behaviour. Leaving those boundaries – either in action or thought – opens up a space or gap where the characters are individually able to resist or subvert the existing order which, as represented by the city of Westminster, is overwhelmingly patriarchal, bourgeois and heterosexual in nature. Perhaps the most obvious example of resistance is Elizabeth Dalloway's daring bus trip down the Strand where "Dalloways did not go:" she feels like a "pioneer," exploring territory "so different from Westminster."[33] Impressed by the serious and busy air of the Strand, she begins to contemplate having a profession as either a doctor or a farmer and meditates on the possibilities open to a woman of her specific class and generation.

Another more subtle example of the possibility for resistance is found in the scene when Clarissa, in her bedroom in Westminster, recalls her adolescent love for Sally Seton and their kiss in the moonlight at her family's country house, Bourton. This rapturous scene of female sexual awakening is extremely significant because it occurs in the country. This is not a random choice for, throughout the novel, Bourton is consistently presented as a pastoral female world, removed in both time and space from the ideological and gendered space of marriage, heterosexuality and culture in Westminster. Ironically, the connection between the natural world and freedom from the constraints of normative gender roles is ultimately reinforced by Elizabeth Dalloway's bus-ride: while her voyage might be read as a celebration of the opportunities provided for women in the city, we learn that what really has motivated Elizabeth's trip is a desire to escape from the oppressive presence of Westminster, her society hostess mother, and the feminine identity which is being thrust upon her by society. In fact, Elizabeth quite clearly equates personal freedom with the country:

> People were beginning to compare her [Elizabeth] to poplar trees, early dawn, hyacinths, fawns, running water, and garden lilies; and it made her life a burden to her, for she so much preferred being left alone to do what she liked in the country, but they would compare her to lilies, and she had to go to parties, and London was so dreary compared with being alone in the country with her father and the dogs.[34]

Though Woolf was well aware that it was a traditional literary convention to relegate women to pastoral and natural settings, she does not challenge the binary opposition of city/country, culture/nature, public/private and the association of the latter terms with women in *Mrs Dalloway*, perhaps in order to highlight female alienation from human-made culture or from their own sexuality. The female characters in the novel – particularly Clarissa, Lady Bruton, Lady Bradshaw and the older Sally Seton – are seen as participating in ultimately enforcing the patriarchal system, playing out their gendered roles in society in a similar way as Mrs Ramsay in *To the Lighthouse*.[35] Their collusion in the system is such that they feel no profound sense of loss or regret: when Clarissa remembers how her kiss with Sally Seton is broken up by a jealous Peter Walsh, for instance, she reflects that in spite of this, she really owed Peter a great deal because he taught her what the word "civilized" meant. (The strong suggestion of Clarissa's repressed homosexuality would also seem to counter Wilson's claim that Mrs Dalloway is not "estranged.")

It is undeniable that, as Wilson observes, many passages in *Mrs Dalloway* do pay tribute to city life. Clarissa and Elizabeth both discuss their love of the bustle, the noise and the excitement of the city streets. Walking in London is presented as a release from the demands of domesticity, and Clarissa anticipates her morning walk as an adventure: "What a lark! What a plunge!" While this quotation is often offered as unequivocal proof of Clarissa's appreciation of the city, however, a closer inspection reveals that its meaning is somewhat less obvious. Meaning in *Mrs Dalloway* is often established through the repetition of certain words or phrases, and "plunge" is used throughout the novel in a variety of contexts: at the beginning of the novel, Clarissa recalls "plunging" into the open air of Bourton when life seems full of promise; and again, at the end of the novel, Clarissa uses the word "plunge" in contemplating Septimus Smith's suicide ("But this young man who had killed himself – had he plunged holding his treasure?").[36] The word "plunge" expresses the "pregnant ambiguity" which underlies all scenes and events in the novel.[37] Though the city is the site of great possibility where identity is fluid and young women like Elizabeth Dalloway may one day become doctors, it is also a place which "swallows up many millions of young men called Smith."[38]

While it impresses with its "communal spirit,"[39] it also makes many keenly aware of their "outside" status, particularly the female characters who find things in London "queer" and feel "exposed" among so many strangers. Septimus Smith's newly immigrated war-bride, Rezia, in despair over her husband's madness, wants to cry out, "I am alone; I am alone!"[40] For all her class privilege, even Mrs Dalloway is aware of a darker undercurrent on her walk: "She had a perpetual sense, as she watched the taxicabs, of being out, out, far out to sea and alone; she always had the feeling that it was very, very dangerous to live even one day."[41]

Moreover, any freedom or resistance that one may find walking in the streets of London seems only to be transitory. After Mrs Dalloway's walk to buy flowers, she returns to her house like "a nun who has left the world and feels fold round her the familiar veils and the response to old devotions." Like Woolf, Mrs Dalloway welcomes this familiarity: far from feeling trapped, she feels herself "blessed and purified." Unlike Woolf, however, Clarissa gratefully attributes the restoration of a sense of self, "to Richard her husband, who was the foundation of it."[42] In one of the most comic-tragic scenes of the novel, Elizabeth gives up meditating on her future in the Strand to go home to dress for her mother's party where she is compared to a poplar, a river and a hyacinth by Willie Titcomb – a sign that, despite her own reluctance, she is being situated in the symbolic order which defines woman as metaphor, as other, like the allegorical statues of imperial Britain.

HOSTESSES, GODDESSES AND POPLARS

Moi has pointed out that one of the greatest difficulties which feminists confront in reading Woolf's fiction is that it represents few overtly "feminist" characters or single, unified subjects: hence the tendency, Moi argues, for critics to label Woolf's fiction as "feminist" based on what is known of her life, rather than on her representations of female characters. Similarly, in *The Sphinx in the City*, *Mrs Dalloway* is attributed with a positive response to the city, seemingly based on what is perceived to be Woolf's response to it. But *Mrs Dalloway* should not be read as a mouthpiece for Woolf's views, for to do so is to misunderstand both the repressed (and repressive) role of the Westminster society hostess – Clarissa Dalloway is no closet feminist – and the highly ambivalent nature of her relationship to the city.

I would argue, however, that it is precisely because of these multiple points of view and the varying – often contradictory – representations of modern city life they make possible that Woolf's work is of such potential value to feminist historical analysis. With her detailed and attentive explorations of the ways in which characters – both male and female – are shaped by patriarchal society, particularly within the public spaces of the city, Woolf's writing can allow the construction of a highly sophisticated understanding of the relationship between identity and urban life.

What is required from those writing a history of difference is a reading of experience, as represented in personal or fictional accounts, which is equally sensitive to the process of subject formation: one which avoids generalization and in Scott's words is alert to the "complex and changing discursive processes by which identities are ascribed, resisted, or embraced." In this rereading of experience in Woolf's personal writing and *Mrs Dalloway*, the focus is not on uncovering identity; rather, it is on considering the ways in which identity is constructed and how the city participates in this process. It recognizes how in Woolf's work identities emerge through repeated contact with the external world – the built environment, people on the street, language and everyday objects. While the fluidity of this process allows for some small personal resistance to normative social roles, the characters' experiences are seen as being circumscribed by their position within the social structure: characters, from Mrs Dalloway to Hugh Whitbread to Rezia Smith, are continually being positioned according to the major axes of gender, sexuality, class, age, and nationality. Identity and experience are at once individually and collectively inscribed.

Although the exultation Wilson describes is a feature of female urban experience in some cases, fear and alienation are equally present. Rather than being the "maternal or even womblike" space as Wilson claims, in both Woolf's personal writing and her fiction the city is very deliberately defined as the space of patriarchal/imperial ideology, and it is through encounters with this ideology – as embodied in Westminster – that women are inscribed and reinscribed by their gender to become hostesses, goddesses and poplars.

ACKNOWLEDGEMENTS

I would like to thank Iain Borden, Charles Rice, Michael Hatt and Jane Rendell for their feedback and encouragement. I would especially like to thank Amelia Gibson and Katharina Ledersteger-Goodfriend, with whom many of the ideas in this chapter were initially discussed and developed.

References

1   Quoted in Susan Merrill Squier (ed.), *Women Writers and the City: Essays in Feminist Literary Criticism* (Knoxville, TN: University of Tennessee Press, 1984), p. 3.

2   Elizabeth Wilson, *The Sphinx in the City: Urban Life, the Control of Disorder, and Women* (London: Virago, 1991), p. 158.

3   Wilson, *Sphinx in the City*, p. 10.

4   Gillian Beer, "Representing Women: Re-presenting the Past," Catherine Belsey and Jane Moore (eds), *The Feminist Reader: Essays in Gender and the Politics of Literary Criticism* (London: Macmillan, 1997), p. 78.

5   For a general introduction and overview of many of the key issues involving women and representation, see Frances Bonner, Lizbeth Goodman, Richard Allen, Linda Janes and Catherine King, *Imagining Women: Cultural Representations and Gender* (Cambridge: Polity Press, 1992).

6   Toril Moi, *Sexual/Textual Politics: Feminist Literary Theory* (London: Routledge, 1985), p. 8.

7   Joan W. Scott, "The Evidence of Experience," James Chandler, Arnold I. Davidson and Harry Harootunian (eds), *Questions of Evidence: Proof, Practice, and Persuasion across the Disciplines* (Chicago: University of Chicago Press, 1994), p. 370.

8   Su Reid, "Introduction," Su Reid (ed.), *Mrs Dalloway and To the Lighthouse* (London: Macmillan, 1993), p. 12.

9   Though I draw some broad comparisons between Moi's and Scott's views, it should be clear that their criticism is generated by different theoretical aims and concerns. Moi, in her introduction to *Sexual/Textual Politics*, specifically targets the humanist conception of self lurking behind many Anglo-American feminist readings of Woolf and contrasts it to the more fluid readings of self and of language encouraged by French theorists like Julia Kristeva. On the other hand, Scott, in "The Evidence of Experience," criticizes

"historians of difference" who aim to challenge conventional histories but, by giving a foundational status to experience and ignoring how it is constituted through discourse, have diminished the critical thrust of their histories. Scott's proposed reading, following Foucault, instead places much greater emphasis on the use of discursive analysis.

10 Scott, "Evidence of Experience," p. 369.

11 Marianne Hirsch, "The Darkest Plots: Narration and Compulsory Heterosexuality," Margaret Homans (ed.), *Virginia Woolf: a Collection of Critical Essays* (Englewood Cliffs, NJ: Prentice Hall, 1993), p. 198.

12 Virginia Woolf, *The Diary of Virginia Woolf. Vol. 2, 1920–24* (Harmondsworth: Penguin, 1981), p. 301.

13 Woolf, *Diary of Virginia Woolf*, p. 302.

14 Virginia Woolf, "Street Haunting: A London Adventure," *Yale Review*, v. 24 (1927), p. 49.

15 Woolf, "Street Haunting," p. 50.

16 Woolf, "Street Haunting," p. 56.

17 Dorothy Brewster, *Virginia Woolf's London* (London: George Allen and Unwin, 1959), p. 113.

18 Woolf, "Street Haunting," p. 62.

19 This idea was developed with Katharina Ledersteger-Goodfriend and Amelia Gibson.

20 See Sally Munt, "The Lesbian *Flâneur*," David Bell and Gill Valentine (eds), *Mapping Desire: Geographies of Sexuality* (London: Routledge, 1995), and in Iain Borden, Joe Kerr, Jane Rendell with Alicia Pivaro (eds), *The Unknown City: Contesting Architecture and Social Space* (Cambridge, MA: MIT Press, 2000). Wilson also fully acknowledges the possibilities which the imagination opens up in our experience of the city, suggesting that cities might be more usefully understood by women as being "settings for voyages of discovery." Wilson, *Sphinx in the City*, p. 11.

21 Quoted in Hirsch, "Darkest Plots," p. 196.

22 Woolf, "Street Haunting," p. 62.

23 Virginia Woolf, *Mrs Dalloway* (Oxford: World Classics, 1992), pp. xl–xli.

24 Jeremy Tambling, "Repression in Mrs Dalloway's London," Reid (ed.), *Mrs Dalloway and To the Lighthouse*, p. 58.

25 Woolf, *Mrs Dalloway*, p. 71.

26 Woolf, *Mrs Dalloway*, p. 238.

27 Woolf, *Mrs Dalloway*, pp. 142–3.

28 Rachel Bowlby, "Thinking Forward through Mrs Dalloway's Daughter," in Reid (ed.), *Mrs Dalloway and To the Lighthouse*, p. 149.

29 Woolf, *Mrs Dalloway*, pp. 10–11.

30 Quoted in Elizabeth Abel, "Narrative Structure(s) and Female Development: the Case of Mrs Dalloway," Homans (ed.), *Virginia Woolf*, p. 94.

31   Tambling, "Repression in Mrs Dalloway's London," p. 63.

32   Woolf, *Mrs Dalloway*, p. 10.

33   Woolf, *Mrs Dalloway*, pp. 178–80.

34   Woolf, *Mrs Dalloway*, p. 176.

35   Moi, *Sexual/Textual Politics*, pp. 13–15.

36   Woolf, *Mrs Dalloway*, p. 242.

37   J. Hillis Miller, "*Mrs Dalloway*: Repetition as Raising of the Dead," Reid (ed.), *Mrs Dalloway and To the Lighthouse*, p. 53.

38   Woolf, *Mrs Dalloway*, p. 110.

39   Woolf, *Mrs Dalloway*, p. 198.

40   Woolf, *Mrs Dalloway*, p. 30.

41   Woolf, *Mrs Dalloway*, p. 10.

42   Woolf, *Mrs Dalloway*, p. 37.

Chapter 16
Thick time: architecture and the traces of time
Jeremy Till

Start with Kant. The proclamation on space and time in the early pages of the first *Critique* demands a response:

> it is therefore not merely possible
> or probable
> but *indubitably certain*

(you cannot deny the force of these words)

> that space and time, as the *necessary* conditions of all inner and outer experience,

(you can no longer take these terms space and time for granted)

> are merely subjective conditions of all our intuition.[1]

And here starts the epistemological revolution. Kant has argued that space and time are not properties of objects, but are conditions of the mind. You have them as pure forms of *a priori* intuition – and in relation to the conditions of space and time "all objects are mere appearances." Start with Kant. Lots have, and so did I. But not to explain Kant. I am no philosopher. My purpose is to solicit philosophers, and in particular philosophers of time, to help me think an aspect of architecture. Philosophy is often used and abused by architectural thinkers and doers. Architecture is sometimes used and abused by philosophers. The two enter into an unholy alliance, each satisfying the other's vanity. Physical constructs propped up by mental tropes; mental constructs illustrated though physical form. Foundations, structures, grounding, constructs . . . these words and many more build bridges between architecture and philosophy. It is in language that each finds an analogy with the other, whether that language is one of stability and order or of slippage and ambiguity.[2] It is an analogy based around structure and form (or their lack) at the inevitable expense of content and intent. When best executed, these analogous mechanisms allow each discipline to argue with each other in a stimulating manner,[3] even if that argument remains within self-referential and isolated circles. At worst the analogy is used instrumentally to direct the actions of architecture. It is more than coincidence that the publication of the philosopher Gilles Deleuze's book, *The Fold*, was accompanied by a rash of folded buildings led by Peter Eisenman's Columbus Convention Center. The tactics of philosophy are used to direct the form making of architects – and if those tactics have a subversive edge in the undermining of traditional philosophical institutions then it suits those avant-garde architects to analogously claim that subversion as a principle of their own work. Dangerously, the work is also often claimed as "political," but this is in fact an ineffectual game within the politics of form which too easily ignores the redolent politics of space and its occupation.[4]

In contrast to an approach which attempts to construct causal links between philosophy and architecture, I prefer to first acknowledge and then exploit the very distinctness of the two disciplines. For me, the most constructive feature of philosophy is the conceptual distance that it can open up between ways of thinking and objects of enquiry. In many cases this distance results in a retreat to noumenal empires, intellectual citadels removed from grounded experience of the world. However, in other cases this distance allows a productive reinscription of the object of enquiry. Philosophy provides the luxury of setting a space to think unburdened by instrumental demands; there is no need for a direct result. However, this is not to say that such thinking cannot structure intent and then action. It is in this mode that I attempt to employ some philosophy of time – to help me understand something more about the production of architecture. My intent is not to legitimise an architectural speculation by resorting to philosophical gravitas, nor to scatter uprooted quotations in the hope that they will rub dignity into the surrounding sentences. To repeat, I am no philosopher and this is not a discourse on the philosophy of time (no Bergson, no Heidegger). I am an architect who sometimes finds the intellectual space away from the demands of architecture a useful and necessary place from which to speculate on the next set of actions.

The making of architecture never follows the simple linear route that the idealists or determinists would have us believe. It is, rather, a constant set of negotiations – between internal intents and external forces, between certitude and chance – in which different modes of working and thinking continuously overlap. It is in this spirit that I approach writing about architecture, deliberately mixing history, criticism, anecdote and unsupported speculation. Buried within it all is the work of certain philosophers, sometimes brought consciously to the surface but more often lying within as a latent force guiding the direction of the text. In accepting the spirit of chance, I am not bothered in the knowledge that this chapter would have been quite different if I had packed, say, Heidegger and Marx rather than Joyce and Lefebvre in my summer holiday suitcase. Writing about architecture should never aspire to be fully prescriptive or definitive because the production of architecture in its very contingency resists the imposition of direct prescription. This chapter makes no claim to proposing a theory. To do so would only maintain the false distinction between theory and practice, a distinction which proposes that there can be theories of architecture which might administer the practice of architecture. Instead my hope is to suggest a way of thinking which is theoretical and practical at the same time.

FROZEN TIME

> Can't bring back time. Like holding water in your hand.
> James Joyce, *Ulysses*

Back to Kant. Prompt a way of thinking to react with or against

> that space and time, as the necessary conditions of all inner and outer experience.

For Kant, as with others before and after, space and time are essential conditions of experience, and with this status they are raised to become central philosophical categories. Space and Time. Time and Space. Dependently joined and so when artificially separated always wanting.

Of the two categories, it is space which architecture has most commonly appropriated into its own discourse, often in a manner which conflates space as a philosophical category with space as an architectural phenomenon. Space in architecture is often thought of, thought through, as abstract matter, there to be pushed and pulled in accordance with the genius of the architect. The standard words of architectural discourse give it all away – layered space, folded space, negative space – all these determine space as a kind of formal stuff. In this abstraction, space is detached from its historical and social constitution and thereby divorced from its essential connectedness with time. It is an abstraction that is inscribed in the chosen methods of architectural representation, the plan and section, described by one philosopher/architect as "absolutely barbarous things for measuring space because they do not measure time."[5] Architectural space, in the purity of its formal and conceptual genesis, is emptied of all considerations of time and is seen as a formal and aesthetic object. Time is frozen out or, rather, time is frozen. But this act is not an oversight, a mere forgetting of time. More it is an active defence against "the terror of time."[6]

Le Corbusier knew exactly what he was doing in arranging loaves and fishes into miraculous domestic arrangements in the photographs of the early villas. Freeze life, freeze time, control time. It is a control which attempts to banish those elements of time which present a challenge to the immutable authority of architecture. Time is defeated by removing from it the most dangerous (but also of course most essential) element, that of flux. Conditions of cyclical time (seasons, night, weather) or linear time (programmatic change, dirt, ageing, social drift) are either denied or manipulated to organise Karsten Harries' "defence against the terror of time . . . to abolish time within time."[7] Contemporary production of architecture thus presents the paradigm of architecture captured at an idealised moment of conception. Take those pictures of buildings caught perfectly before people, dirt, rain and history move in; since the beginning of the twentieth century it is these pictures which have framed a history of architecture in both its production and reproduction – a history, in which architecture is seen to be a stable power, existing over the dynamic forces of time.

It is in the rhetoric and work of the hi-tech movement that these attitudes to the control of time can be identified most clearly. As we shall see, the hi-tech protagonists in a pincer movement deny cyclical time on the one hand and control linear time on the other. Whilst these actions follow modernist tenets, they are, in the hi-tech movement, provided with an additional and decisive weapon: that of technology.

In order to defeat the cyclical time of days, seasons and years, shiny, hard, immutable surfaces are employed to shrug off the effects of weather, dirt and accident. One of my favourite photographs is of two full-size prototype panels hanging from a crane in the barren landscape of the London Docklands. One panel is made of stainless steel, the other of granite; otherwise they are identical. In front stand the clients and architects of the future Canary Wharf tower; they are here to choose between the two materials. They look as if they are shuffling their feet with indecision, but in fact the choice must be clear. Leave the granite for the ground hugging neo-classical stuff below. This is a tower which defies nature's forces (wind, gravity, seasons); it has to be clad in radiant steel. Later, there is that moment when the building is under construction and the panels still covered in blue plastic; a shrink wrapped tower. I announce my yearning to have the job of peeling back that tight layer to reveal the glorious, shiny tower beneath. "Fetishist," my friends say. "Exactly," I respond – because only through the fetish of the surface is the illusion of the control of cyclical time maintained. There is here a debt to Corbusier's *Law of Ripolin* ("there are no more dirty, dark corners . . . on white walls these accretions of dead things from the past world would be intolerable; they would leave a stain")[8] but technology has moved on, whitewash has given way to metals and plastics. In this progression, we lose the connection that Le Corbusier made between the visual purity of the whitewash and the moral purity of the whitewashed spaces ("whitewash exists wherever people have preserved intact the balanced structure of a harmonious culture").[9] The hi-tech surfaces are justified in terms of their technological and aesthetic prowess rather than their social resonances.

In the reduction of hi-tech to an aesthetic, the main emphasis is not so much that the buildings should *actually* deny cyclical time, but that they should *look* as if they could. It is clear that these hi-tech boys (for so they are) have never done the cleaning; any common sense would tell them that the shinier the surface the more apparent the dirt, the tarnish, the changes. It was when cleaning cradles hunched over the top of buildings became an aesthetic in their own right that the problem became most absurdly apparent.[10] The cleaning cradles, or the spectacle of trained mountaineers clambering in specially developed suckered boots over I.M. Pei's Louvre Pyramid with polishing cloths, are essential in maintaining the *illusion* that architecture can stand outside the ravages of time. In fact they are just signals of the ensnarement of technological determinism, in which technology has moved from being a means to an end to being an end in its own right, one technology (the cradle) attempting to solve a condition created by another technology (the shiny surface) without questioning the efficacy of technology in the first place.

Behind the surfaces, environmental systems are used to master the effects of diurnal and seasonal cycles. Heat, light and coolth are deployed to contrive an even sense of time over and above external rhythms, building management systems operating unseen in the background to maintain constancy. The contemporary fashion for presenting hi-tech buildings as computer-rendered nocturnal images brings with it a covert sense that these buildings and their technologies (representational and real) are even capable of standing in the face of that oldest dread of all, that of night.

When it comes to the linear time of history, the technology of hi-tech architecture is used to control time. In the late twentieth century the progressive claims of hi-tech and the reactive claims of the traditionalists are two sides of the same coin, joined by an attitude that architecture can reify a particular condition of time, and in this reification freeze it. The traditionalists' abrupt appropriation of past architectural figures attempts to summon up in an instant an aesthetic, and with it the values attached to that aesthetic. Just add people to these perfected images and the hope is that they will assume the virtues of that frozen moment in time. Princely Poundbury is the most explicit example of an attempt to conjoin moral and aesthetic values, conveniently forgetting the feudal systems which developed those values in the first place while busily worrying over the civic choice of lampposts. But like all instant mixes ("just add water") the result can never match the complexity of the original, particularly when the original is subject to all the dynamics of time. Time, as Joyce reminds us, is too slippery to recreate. ("Can't bring back time. Like holding water in your hand.")

Where the traditionalists yearn fruitlessly for the instant of a lost age, the hi-tech movement is, they tell us, summoning up an instant of the immediate future. This is indicative of a more general tendency of nineteenth and twentieth century modernity, namely its ability to see itself in specific relation to other epochs. Modernity is not merely placed "in a linear sequence of chronological time," but assumes a transcendence over the past and with this "a reorientation towards the future."[11] One of the results of this rupturing is that time is divided into discrete epochs, each of which becomes available for isolated representation, torn from a dynamic continuity. For hi-tech architecture, this time is one of a historicist lineage of progress, a determinist series of discrete moments, the next one of which architecture assumes the right to express in a gesture of formal and technological progression.

There is much talk of buildings expressing the spirit of the age, and technology is employed to do this job. Technology is deployed as an emblem of newness; progress is announced through the development of ever more refined joints, ever more complex systems, ever more shiny surfaces. In much hi-tech rhetoric this projection towards a reified future takes on a crusading cant; it becomes a moral necessity for architecture to stand for the next epoch. In fact such representation is simply an aestheticisation of frozen time. Thus the architect Jean Nouvel can state that "the capacity for capturing or freezing the values concealed in a specific moment" is "the power of architecture." But this power is illusory. However much one burnishes the surface, sharpens the technique – actions that are becoming increasingly frantic as we approach that great moment of time, the millennium (now that is a big one to freeze) – time slips in round the back to disrupt those static perfections.

When Bruno Schulz implores "don't tamper with time," he might be speaking directly to these cryonic architects.

> Keep off time, time is untouchable, one must not provoke it! Isn't it enough for you to have space? Space is for human beings, you can swing about in space, turn somersaults, fall down, jump from star to star. But for goodness' sake, don't tamper with time.[12]

And yet architects persist in denying this irrepressible force, believing that time can be held within architecture either technically or representationally. Of the canonic hi-tech buildings, it is perhaps the Beauborg Centre designed by Renzo Piano and Richard Rogers that has most majestically tried to fly in the face of time. Just 20 years after its completion, the building is now closed for restoration, shrouded in the manner of the great cathedrals; a fitting tribute to a magnificent old new building. When shrouds are lifted from the cathedrals, there is a sense of certainty that what will be revealed is a restoration; restoration to the original historic state and restoration to a better condition. With Beauborg, the expectation of what should be revealed is less certain. The collapse of the restorative time scale to 20 years confuses our sense of where the building stands in time. The confusion is heightened by the intentional model of time that is built into Beauborg; it is meant to be able to accommodate change, announcing its flexibility brashly through the aesthetic of frame and parts. And so when the shroud is dropped, would it be more authentic to reveal a completely different set of forms within the overall frame or should a heritage notion of authenticity force a return to the building's primal state?

The answer may be found in the reaction to a previous modification. When Gae Aulenti took the flexibility rhetoric at face value and moved in a container for the modern art collection, the building and its supporters fought back. Aulenti's enclosed spaces and fixed white walls were seen as a betrayal of the openness and transparency of the host building. The attack and its implications were ruthless; the building may be flexible but only in a certain kind of way. Of course issues of style were at stake as well, but what becomes apparent is not so much that the building is really flexible but that it is seen to be flexible. Beauborg thus represents a single moment in time, reifying the condition of flux that was seen to be the identifying feature of the contemporary world in which the building was conceived. This reinforces an iconic reading of Beauborg, fitting it neatly into a genealogy of monumentalist time in which buildings are suspended above the passage of real time.

Yet when the shrouds come down, one thing is for sure: Beauborg will be cleaner. And another thing is equally sure: that cleanliness will invoke a feeling of helplessness in that there is a certainty that time will once again rush in to upset the hygienic image of renewedness.

There is always a tension between what architecture thinks itself to be and what it actually is. In the case of Beauborg and the times it is meant to hold, but is manifestly held by, this tension stretches – but never breaks – the building. It remains magnificent not because of its original iconic status, but despite it as time surges up to reformulate the building. However, in order to accept this reformulation not as an affront to the authority of architecture but rather as something positive, one has to reverse an equation: not to see time as held in architecture but to see architecture in time. In this latter spirit, I am secretly hoping that when those shrouds come down, they will have put a few of those pipes into sensible square ducts.

THICK TIME

> Hold to the now, the here, through which all future plunges to the past.
> James Joyce, *Ulysses*

Back to Kant. For the last time. He starts his explanation of time in *Critique of Pure Reason* with the words: "Time is not an empirical concept derived from any experience."[13] These words fly in the face of what we perceive to be a common sense notion that time is a condition of the world, understood through experience of the world. Kant, however, argues against the idea that "time inheres in things." For him, time is not a property of objects but a form of intuition – with regard to time, the intuition of an object is "not to be looked for in the object itself but in the subject to which the object appears." It is the autonomous subject who brings representations of time to the world and not vice versa. Because the subject "really has representations of time and determinations of it," time can be represented "prior to objects and therefore *a priori*." Time, for Kant, is thus a "form of knowledge" which comes prior to our experience of the world. The rational mind actively constitutes the temporality of the world and its objects.

Any attempt to lay the precision of Kant's arguments over the rough carcass of architecture is doomed to clumsy failure and I would be the last to find causal links between Kantian notions of time and the conceit of modernist architects in freezing time. But, however subliminally, a powerful legacy of the Enlightenment endures, the legacy of the rational subject asserting prior knowledge over experience of the world. A legacy of a strange power of mind over matter. In its degraded form (without the firm hand of Kant to guide us), this power of mind over matter transpires as a conceit, but it is a conceit that has allowed the architect to maintain an illusion of buildings existing *over* time in the bitter face of the reality of time. To overcome this conceit demands a reversal of the Kantian equation – to dismiss any *a priori* notions of time and accept that our knowledge of time is a product of our experience of time in an acknowledgement of time as a condition which "exceeds and precedes all constitutive activity of the self."[14] One's experience of the world is radically affected by different modalities of time. In this light, time (in all its guises) is apprehended not as an abstraction to be intellectually ordered but as a phenomenological immediacy to be engaged with at a human and social level. Bodies, and the buildings that they inhabit, exist within time, and so an understanding of the temporality of human existence – of time as lived – provides clues as to how to approach the temporality of architecture.[15]

It is the work of a novelist rather than a philosopher that most acutely describes time as lived and the impossibility of placing it into a neat set of categories. In *Ulysses*, James Joyce weaves threads of epic time (the time of the Homeric Gods), natural cyclical time (the rivers, the shifting sands), historical cyclical time (the repetitive sense of Ireland's identity), linear historical time (the particular chronological response to colonisation), personal time (Joyce's own life reinscribed in the pages), fuzzy time (memories snatched), focused time (the endless newspapers), their future time, my future time (when will I finish it?) . . . and so on and on. The relationship of these threads is always restless, so that no one temporal modality predominates over the others. It is not, as is implied in many phenomenological philosophies of time, a matter of the present being held in the thrall of the past, but of the two coexisting in a coincident, continually evolving relationship – a present in which the anticipation of the future is always at hand ("Coming events cast their shadows before them," muses Bloom). *Ulysses* invokes a sense of time not as a series of successive slices of instants,[16] but as an expanded present.[17] Thick Time. It is a present that gathers the past and holds the future pregnantly, but not in an easy linear manner ("Hold to the now, the here, through which all future plunges to the past").

Time in *Ulysses* is revealed through the literary device of the epiphany, "the moment in which the soul of the commonest object seems to us radiant" in a sudden "revelation of the whatness of the thing."[18] These epiphanies in all their immediate ordinariness, but eventual complexity, give to *Ulysses* a concentration on the everyday as the place of extraordinarily productive potential. Time, for Joyce, inheres in the commonplace objects and situations of Dublin (a reversal, remember, of Kant's argument that time does not inhere in things). Joyce's time, as he follows Bloom, Dedalus and their friends through the streets of Dublin, is the time of the everyday, but it is by no means ordinary, summoning up as it does the richness of multiple and coincident modes of time. Normally, everyday time is seen to be subsumed by more ascendant temporal modes – thus the linear time of progress in its concentration on the iconic, the one-off, has no place for the quotidian. Joyce's triumph is to contextualise these other modes of time through the everyday. In *Ulysses* other times are seen through, and thereby reformulated by, everyday time.

Joyce's time elides with the philosophical readings of everyday time. In these, what is stressed is the way that everyday is subject to constant repetitions and cycles,[19] but is also open to randomness and chance. The everyday is the result of "a myriad repetitive practices,"[20] and thus accumulates traces of the past, but in its very incompleteness is always accessible to reformulation and thus orientated towards the future. It is thus the place where "the riddle of recurrence intercepts the theory of becoming."[21]

It is the anticipation of action that most clearly identifies the thick time of the everyday. The traditionalists are swayed by the siren chants of repetition and the progressivists caught within the tramlines of linear history; in both cases the next step is implicitly given and, in the end, uncritical. In thick time, however, there is an openness to action which in gathering the past and projecting the future, is necessarily interpretative of both conditions.

Everyday time is thick time, that time of the extended present which avoids mere repetition of past times or the instant celebration of new futures. Thick time is where the interception of recurrence and becoming provides the space for action.

TRACING TIME

In this short journey from abstracted notions of time to grounded, messy readings of the everyday, space has slipped unnoticed into argument. I could not have kept it out. Space and Time. Time and Space. Dependently joined and so when artificially separated always wanting (each other).

Ulysses is also the story of a city, Dublin, whose stones, waters, sands and airs spatialise time. And so, following Joyce, I will let time enter my spaces, but only that thick time of the everyday. It is a time which will disrupt the iconic, perfected autonomy of the frozen building, not just in terms of weather and dirt, but in terms of those repetitive, habitual actions so overlooked by architects clinging to illusions of a detached monumental time. It is a time which accommodates all those smoking travellers who, on each occasion that they return to Paris, ride to the top of the Beauborg escalators (together with all those non-smokers). They stub their cigarettes out in the raised perforated pipes which by now have long lost their heating function and become extended ashtrays – pipes which have become one of many traces of habitual actions which have imploded[22] any notions of the canonic to reveal a reading of Beauborg as the ultimate building of the everyday.

Of course, this thick time has always been around, secreting into those gaps left by the delusion of abstracted, static, spaces existing beyond the tides of time. Secreted but not secret, because these redolent spaces are now legible for interpretation of those past actions, those traces of time that have passed through. Temporised space is thus revealed as a socially constituted construct.

And the debt is repaid. In spatialising time, architecture and the city restores a thinking to time: that most volatile of conditions is given presence in space and through this can be read in all its coincident forms. This reading occurs in an expanded present where the past can never be rested as a perfected moment of tradition ready for restitution. In thick time, the architect of the here and now casts a critical eye to the previous spatial configurations of control and domination while at the same time formulating the redemptive potential of a possible future. Through its grounding in an extended present, this spatial future will not be disturbed by the influx and flux of time, but will sustain all those conflicting conditions (of occupational change, of "weathering as completion,"[23] of indeterminate manoeuvres, of habitual actions) that everyday time brings with it.

POSTSCRIPT: DIRTY TIME

I want to end with a story. I like stories. They bear retelling. Stories have a levity which allows adaptation to the time of telling, as opposed to histories which still bear the weight of fixed authority.

The story is of James Joyce. He spends Christmas, the last before he dies, in Switzerland. His host is the architectural writer Sigfried Giedion. The manuscript for *Space, Time and Architecture*, is complete, holding time in images and words. (This much is true, even history; it is December 1940.)[24]

16.1 De Bijenkorf Department Store, Rotterdam (1955–7); architects Marcel Breuer and A. Elzas
Jeremy Till

The author of unstable time sits with the documenter of frozen time. They discuss moving to some neighbouring new houses designed, all white and neat, by Marcel Breuer. Joyce is resistant to the move, pointing to the "fine walls and windows" of the traditional house they are sitting in, fire blazing. At the same time he mocks the Swiss fixation with cleanliness and order – a fixation that both Giedion in his writing and his compatriot Breuer in his buildings express through the triumphant power of modernism to banish time and stains.

"You don't know how wonderful dirt is," says Joyce to Giedion.

It is as if these words were transmitted to Breuer.
As an ageing man, carrying the traces of time,
Breuer builds the De Bijenkorf Department Store in Rotterdam.
Dirty, thick, time.

References

1　Immanuel Kant, *Critique of Pure Reason* (London: Macmillan, 1929), p. 86 (emphasis added).

2　These ideas are developed in Jeremy Till, "The Vanity of Form," *Journal of Architecture* (forthcoming).

3　The most brilliant recent example is that of Mark Wigley, *The Architecture of Deconstruction: Derrida's Haunt* (Cambridge, MA: MIT Press, 1995).

4　This point is well made in Mary McLeod, "Everyday and 'Other' Spaces," in Debra Coleman, Elizabeth Danze and Carol Henderson (eds), *Architecture and Feminism* (New York: Princeton Architectural Press, 1996), p. 5, and in Mary McLeod, "Architecture and Politics in the Reagan Era: From Postmodernism to Deconstruction," *Assemblage*, n. 8 (February 1989).

5　Paul Virilio, "Gravitational Space," interview, Laurence Louppe (ed.), *Traces of Dance* (Paris: Editions Dis Voir, 1994), p. 35.

6　Karsten Harries, "Buildings and the Terror of Time," *Perspecta*, n. 19, (1982) p. 64.

7　Harries, "Buildings and the Terror of Time," p. 65.

8　Le Corbusier, *The Decorative Art of Today* (Cambridge, MA: MIT Press, 1987), p. 188.

9　Le Corbusier, *Decorative Art*, p. 190

10　Most famously in the Lloyds Building, London (1986), architects Richard Rogers Partnership.

11　Peter Osborne, *The Politics of Time: Modernity and Avant-Garde* (London: Verso, 1995), p. 9.

12　Bruno Schulz, *Sanatorium under the Sign of the Hourglass* (London: Picador, 1987), p. 131.

13　Kant, *Critique of Pure Reason*, p. 74. All subsequent quotes are from pp. 74–8.

14　Osborne, *Politics of Time*, p. 45.

15　While the most famous phenomenological exposition of time remains Heidegger's *Being and Time*, the more immediately relevant for my purposes is Paul Ricoeur, *Time and Narrative, Vol. 3* (Chicago: University of Chicago Press, 1985), with its thinking through the tension between the individual time of the soul (in all its phenomenological richness) and the universal time of the world (in all its cosmological significance). See especially pp. 12–23. Ricoeur's important exposition shows how historical time, as narrative, has mediated this tension. See also Osborne, *Politics of Time*, pp. 45–8.

16　A definition first proposed by Aristotle and persistent ever since.

17　See Stephen Kern, *The Culture of Time and Space, 1880–1918* (London: Weidenfeld and Nicolson, 1983), p.86.

18　James Joyce, quoted in Richard Ellmann, *James Joyce* (Oxford: Oxford University Press, 1983), p. 83.

19　"The everyday is situated at the intersection of two modes of repetition: the cyclical, which dominates in nature, and the linear, which dominates in processes known as 'rational.'" Henri Lefebvre, "The Everyday and Everydayness," *Yale French Studies*, v. 73 (1987), p. 10.

20 Osborne, *Politics of Time*, p. 196.

21 Henri Lefebvre, *Everyday Life in the Modern World* (New Brunswick, NJ: Transaction Books, 1984), p. 18.

22 See Jean Baudrillard, "The Beauborg Effect," Neil Leach (ed.), *Rethinking Architecture* (London: Routledge, 1997), pp. 210–18.

23 Mohsen Mostafavi and David Leatherbarrow, *On Weathering* (Cambridge, MA: MIT Press, 1993), p. 45.

24 The story is retold in Ellmann, *James Joyce*, p. 740. The dirt quote is also "true." Giedion's *Space, Time and Architecture* was based on the Norton lectures at Harvard 1938–9, and first published in 1941. One of many examples of Giedion's attitude to time, and in particular its aestheticisation through the rationality of architecture, is his description of the staircase at the Werkbund as "like movement seized and immobilized in space." See also Jeremy Till, "Architecture in Space, Time," *Architectural Design*, special issue on "Architecture and Anthropology," (October 1996), Claire Melhuish (ed.), pp. 9–13.

Chapter 17
The use of fiction to reinterpret architectural and urban space
Katherine Shonfield

This chapter revises the interpretation of architectural and urban space by questioning the supremacy of technical pronouncements on the city and its architecture. The strands of a theoretical position run through three elements. The first is that apparently natural or objective characteristics of space can be interpreted in terms of the activities of capitalism, particularly the pursuit of profit. The second is that the quest for purity, expressed by taboos against pollution, permeates architectural and urban practice. And the third is that fictions, particularly in film and the novel, can be used in a number of ways to elucidate unseen workings of architecture. I set out not only to make connections across a range of scales, from the architectural detail and the interior, to city strategy, but also to promote ways of thinking about space that transgress the imposition of this text's own categories. The paradox is that imposition of structure is necessary to comprehend and undertake such liberating and creative transgression.

The text shifts between one theoretical technique for deciphering space and another. At times one or the other, or both, disappear from view. At other times all three approaches are brought into play. In teaching modern architectural history, the work from which this chapter springs, I have had recourse to all of the views. Here, I try to indicate what the interconnections and disjunctures between the three views could be. To begin, however, I first want to outline the relevance of each theoretical approach one by one.

CAPITALISM

The division of labour
In David Harvey's view, the operations of the division of labour, that is, the tendency of capitalism to divide production into a growing number of separated tasks, cannot be understood without recognition of that other fundamental *spatial* division, also imposed and necessary to the capitalist system: the division between the place of work and the place of residence.

[This] means that the struggle of labour to control the social conditions of its own existence splits into two seemingly independent struggles. The first, located in the workplace, is over the wage rate, which provides the purchasing power for consumption goods, and the conditions of work. The second, fought in the place of residence, is against secondary forms of exploitation and appropriation represented by merchant capital, landed property and the like.[1]

The division of labour has a major impact not only on the material production of space but also on the scientific and technical understandings which the state needs to call upon in order to impose its spatial will.

It was no accident, therefore, that the tightening of the monetary, spatial, and chronological nets in the latter half of the nineteenth century was accompanied by the rise of distinctive professions each with its own corner on the knowledge required to give coherence to those nets . . . the power of engineers and managers, economists and architects, systems analysts and experts in industrial organisation, could not be taken lightly. It became powerfully embedded in key state and corporate functions as planning became the order of the day. Intellectual conflicts over the meanings of money, space, and time had and continue to have very real material effects. The conflict over modernity and design in architecture, for example, is more than a conflict over taste and aesthetics. it deals directly with the question of the proper framing of the urban process in space and time.[2]

Ideology

More particular to contemporary marxism is the view I hold in this chapter, after both Henri Lefebvre and David Harvey, namely that architecture, its constructions and urban strategies are accepted within society via a set of ideas and assumptions which *conceals* the fact that architecture is an economic product, and subject to economic interests. So the division of labour carries with it "a dissolving and disintegrating ideology that meets the requirements of the market and the social division of labour by promoting fragmented intellectual skills."[3] The architectural impact of this notion is summarised by Walter Benjamin in his description of the rift between home and work in mid-nineteenth century Paris:

For the private citizen, for the first time the living-space became distinguished from the place of work. The former constituted itself as the interior. The office was its complement. The private citizen who in the office took reality into account required of the interior that it should support him in his illusions.[4]

The ideological role of the interior – that it should support illusions – was a kind of spatial compensation for clearly experienced exploitation at work. Because the mechanisms of economic exploitation are more obvious at work, this direct ideological-concealing role of the interior is only possible once the two places – work and home – have been divided in space.

But while spatial constructions may act ideologically, in the specifically marxist sense that they represent ideas and ideals that both serve the interest of the economic class in power and conceal the workings of that interest, this does not mean their form is under current ideological control. The imposed boundaries of the past may come back to haunt the present. So Benjamin writes that

> the urban process . . . appears as both fundamental to the perpetuation of capitalism and a primary expression of its inner contradictions now expressed as produced external constraints. Capitalism has to confront the consequences of its urban structurations at each moment in its history. The reduced second natures become the raw materials out of which new configurations of capitalist activity . . . must be wrought.[5]

The version of marxism assumed here is dialectical: that there is a volatile and active interchange between ideas, the structures that represent those ideas (art as much as the legal system) and the economic climate that prevails. With Lefebvre, I contend that "it cannot be sufficiently emphasised that it is impossible to reduce marxist thought to economism."[6] Hence the use here of the ideas of both pollution and fiction in varying relationship to the economic shapers of urban architecture.

PURITY AND POLLUTION TABOOS

The horror film *The Fly* was first made in 1958 and then remade in 1986.[7] In both versions the theme is the same: a scientist called Brundle attempts to develop a new form of transportation that entails dematerialising the body into atoms, and reassembling it in another place, using a device called a "teleport." The experiment goes fine until a fly enters the teleport by mistake. As a consequence, the genes of the scientist and the fly become muddled up and he is transformed into a hybrid – Brundlefly. The defined and delineated classes of man and fly are thereby transgressed and the result is successfully revolting. In the later version of the film, to make matters worse, the scientist has sex with a reporter, who subsequently dreams that she has given birth to a grub.

The anthropologist Mary Douglas, in trying to identify the genesis of pollution taboos, states that "Dirt is matter out of place."[8] What is so vividly repulsive is not the grub itself, but the fact that it is present in the body of a woman – that is, *out of place*.

This taboo is against transgression between established classes: it is Douglas' explanation of Jewish dietary law as defined in the Old Testament book of Leviticus. She rejects the commonly held functionalist explanation of these taboos, which tells us, for example, that shellfish are forbidden because they are more liable to deterioration than fish. Rather, the argument she uses to explain Leviticus' list of rules is that animals whose characteristics straddle two classes – such as those that both swim and walk on land, like crabs – are the ones condemned as abominable, dirty and hybrid:

> These shall ye eat that are in the waters: whatsoever hath fins and scales in the waters, in the seas, and in the rivers them shall ye eat. And all that have not fins and scales in the seas, and in the rivers, of all that move in the waters . . . they shall be an abomination unto you . . . All fowls that creep, going upon all four, shall be an abomination unto you.[9]

In Douglas' thesis, matter is classified in terms of identifiable and clearly delineated *form*, in order to establish what is polluted and taboo. "Pollution dangers strike when form has been attacked."[10] *Social well-being (purity) is identified quite literally in the form or the edge of form defined in a "sea of formlessness."*[11] The sea of formlessness is the unclassifiable, against which form must defend itself. Douglas goes on to distinguish three kinds of social pollution, which vary according to the vulnerability of the defining edge (the line which delineates the pure form under threat): "the first is danger pressing on external boundaries the second, danger from transgressing the internal lines of a system; the third, danger in the margins of the lines."[12] Extrapolating from Douglas' explanation, Leviticus' forbidden creatures have in common with Brundlefly the characteristics which make them dirty and abominable. They straddle two classes; their edges are unclear and difficult to delineate; they do not have identifiable form which can be categorised; and they cannot be reduced to an original set of parts or classes.

From these principles, we can, paradoxically, arrive at a number of categories ourselves which allow us to class the formal consequences of pollution taboos.

Smearing

As Douglas herself vividly makes clear in her citation of Jean-Paul Sartre's essay on viscosity, the transgressor has identifiably formal characteristics. As the line is so very important in delineating a clear edge against trespass, it follows that the viscous, things which do not of themselves respect edges, and which are difficult to put a line around, but which are not yet flows, is to be resisted.

> The viscous is a state half-way between solid and liquid. It is like a cross-section in a process of change. It is unstable, but it does not flow. It is soft yielding and compressible . . . it attacks the boundary between myself and it.[13]

Classification and ordering

The Leviticus example demonstrates the authority of the class. To systematise things in this way we need clearly identifiable characteristics. As we have seen, characteristics which straddle two classes will define the object as polluted and dirty. In buildings, architecture and the city we would expect to see a virtue made of the delineation of *boundary*. Following from this is rationality.

Rationality

This way of ordering the world via sets of identifiable characteristics is considered rational; indeed we appeal to reason in order to convince ourselves and others that we are correct in our terms of classification. The guarantee of rationality is in turn associated with capability of the object which we want to classify being reduced to a set of original parts.

Original parts or elements

The original parts that we can, so-to-speak, boil things down into are, by virtue of the fact that they cannot be further reduced, pure and clean. Great store is set by the authentic. If you are uncertain of something's parentage, you can be sure it is a bastard.

Specialisation

If there is unassailable virtue attached to the reduction of an object into parts, it follows that specialisation – whether in ideas or objects – is a good thing.

Classicism

Classicism is therefore understood as a style which imposes purity of part, category and order, via a set of rules which depend on the imposition of absolute boundary, in the form of the firm delineation of architectural elements.

The decorative

The decorative is that which undermines or challenges the firmness of category and delineating boundary. It fuzzes edges, and renders the clear impure and muddy.

Even without the benefit of these extrapolations on the theme that "dirt is matter out of place," the struggle against dirt lends itself unusually easily to the transgression of established genres, intellectual disciplines and spheres of interest, and to the transgression between common metaphor and material description. Who, for example, is really sure whether the expression *ethnic cleansing* is literal or figurative? In matters urban, the power of the *metaphor* of dirt in the city was the spur for the great revisionist movements of the nineteenth and twentieth centuries. Again it was at one and the same time a crusading metaphor and literally true: dirt and pollution caused untold disease. Indeed, Jonathan Raban has written that the *idea* of dirt "subsumes the sheer imaginative cumbersomeness of the city which makes us . . . incapable of distinguishing its parts from its whole,"[14] and that in relation to England, "the single feature of the city which has adhered most strongly to writers minds is its dirt, and dirt is one of the few objects whose moral connotation is as definite and public as its physical characteristics."[15] Dirt, then, significantly subsumes the *categories and orders* of the city, by being in some overriding way true. François Maspero describes how in 1935 Aubervilliers in the Parisian suburbs was a "chemical town" and "land of death," "a concentration of 'dirty industries' considered undesirable inside the walls of Paris."[16] Louis Chevalier has shown how an area of the city which is designated an anomaly (i.e. which does not readily fit in one category or another) and unfitting to the desired urban order, not only is designated dirty, but literally begins to acquire dirt and collect things-out-of-place – the material symptoms of the thing we call urban neglect.

> Beyond the specific filthiness of les Halles there was the filth of Paris, of which les Halles was the recipient . . . their neighbourhood was the dump where Parisians threw everything they no longer wanted . . . One found the strangest things, transported from who knows what part of Paris, thrown in the streets around the markets.[17]

The overarching activity of architecture and building construction can be described as the assertion of *order*.

FICTION

Since Sigmund Freud's *The Interpretation of Dreams* in 1900, the status of interpretation itself has changed. The importance of the dream becomes *precisely what you remember*, nothing more. The elusive whole which memory itself imagines it can retrieve becomes secondary, a mythic, almost ancestral realm. And so interpretation, the text, is the primary site of discourse.

What happens when we accept that architecture does tangibly exist, not as a pristine, impervious whole, but in the perception of the beholder? If fictional representations of the architecture and the city are understood as the architectural equivalent of the dream record, then their entire status can change. This does not mean that literary codes are directly applied to spaces – because, as Lefebvre says, this would reduce the space "to the status of a *message* and the inhabiting of it to the status of a *reading*."[18] But, currently, fictions are accepted at best as interesting parallel commentaries to mainstream architectural history. This official history uses the vocabulary of specialist knowledge – formal, constructional and so on – to present the profession's assertions in unassailable terms. By contrast, the modern fictive voice starts from the admission that its narrative is personal and one among many.

The following analytical possibilities exist in using fiction to decipher space.

Allegory

Highlighted in Christine Buci-Glucksmann's discussion of Benjamin's own interest in the fictional form of allegory is the possibility that "reality exists independently of the languages by which it is made available so that its real nature remains ineffable and hidden. This hidden quality of reality can only be . . . expressed by symbol, by allegory or parable."[19]

Narrative

The *story* of how a space is used, as an adjunct to character and action, reveals an unspoken history of the role of space within the city. Space can be a character acting independently within the narrative itself. The play on "Her" in the title of Jean-Luc Godard's film *Two or Three Things I Know about Her* (1966), to refer directly both to the city of Paris and to the many headed prostitute subject, makes this deliberately clear.

Structural pattern

The everyday experience of living in the modern city is so disjunctive and meaningless that the habitual condition of living can be described as the fictional imagination's attempt to describe a pattern.

> To live in a city is to live in a community of people who are strangers to each other. You have to act on hints and fancies for they are all that the mobile and cellular nature of city life will allow you. You expose yourself in, and are exposed to by others, fragments, isolated signals, bare disconnected gestures, jungle cries and whispers that resist all your attempts to unravel their meaning, their consistency.[20]

This is such a common, consciously recognised experience that the fictional structuring of the city through pattern is a characteristic of most of the great novels of the nineteenth and twentieth centuries. Unlike architecture and construction, fiction is acceptable as a form of structuring the large scale experience of the city in even the most technical of publications.[21]

A related paradox of the both/and variety defines the fictive voice, and it is again inherent to the notion of transgression: simultaneously with its implicit multiplicity, for the duration of the narrative, the single fiction has absolute authority. For the post-structuralist this is doubly paradoxical in that it reintroduces the pleasures of structuralism's all-seeing eye. The use of fiction within architectural theory assumes that the reader can, as when watching a film, voluntarily suspend their own disbelief. Thus far-reaching structural connections can be understood at one and the same time as fictional and, for the duration of the argument, be accepted as absolutely true.

Fiction has a peculiarly transgressive role in challenging the primacy of the specialist: in this sense, a combination of the two structuralist approaches, taboo and marxism, might *explain* the rise of the specialist, but it takes the active operation of fiction to *subvert* her/him. The transgressive role of fiction entails:

- that, like feminism, it enfranchises insights and experiences of architecture and urbanism of the non-expert (as manifest in films and novels)
- that specialist knowledge is subjected to a wider structure which does not privilege such information, but which instead allows its consideration on the same terms as the insights of the non-expert
- that, vice versa, the raising of the cultural commentaries of fiction beyond the level of the aperçu is to be seriously considered on a par with such specialist knowledge.

A number of CROSS-OVERS between the three deciphering methods – capitalism, pollution taboo, fiction – can operate.

A modified structuralism

The notion of a fiction modifies the implicit universality and truth which accompany both the idea of pollution taboo and the notion that causes in human affairs are ultimately driven by economics. These ways of structuring events can, themselves, be thoroughly exploited, but at the same time be treated as fictions, as texts "up for" interpretation.[22] As such, it allows their thorough exploitation, but it is nevertheless possible to "try them out," as you might try a novel or a film. This is useful because the drawback to the rejection of structuralism's claims to objective truth is that it has left us with the impression that statements we make about architecture and the city can at best only ever be partial or fragmentary. Attempts to get at an overall theory that "explains" things are out of favour; there is a fashion for the flash of insight, the little observation. The possibility of furthering understanding by making bold connections between apparently disparate circumstances is denied. One consequence for matters urban is that, in default of an overriding theory, once again decisions get given over to the specialist, and problems are confirmed as subject to technical expertise rather than to general knowledge.

Thus an intentionally paradoxical way of looking at the world can thread through explorations of architecture and the city. Structural connections are confidently assumed, but they may be treated on a par with a kind of fictional coincidence: they sustain the story, and allow us to follow the argument.[23] But how can you assert the necessity of structure while examining the potential of moments where it is deliberately challenged? This dilemma, it seems to me, is familiar to marxists. Lefebvre, writing immediately following the massive transgression of space, social and political structures of the May 1968 events in France,[24] articulates that "a serious concern with spontaneity implies at the same time a delineation of spontaneity. This must be done in the name of a theory which pure spontaneity tends to ignore."[25] Elsewhere, he cautions against the static nature of structuralism, citing Herbert Marcuse on linguistics. He points to "linguistics' . . . particularly dangerous role. Operating in the reified world of discourse, it purges thought and speech of *contradictions and transgressions*."[26] The play of action in the world – here with transgressive and challenging implications – and its analysis in terms of structural connections is to be thought of as a kind of mini version of the dialectic. It is a two-way interaction between economic forces and the superstructures of society – art, politics, ideas – which drive progress on a macro scale.

Form and theoretical and physical structures

This interaction, between structure itself and challenges to its own categories and edges, is not just a theoretical theme here. It is a formal theme too. In the work of the Baroque architect Bernardo Vittone, there is a relationship between the physical, delineated structure of his churches and the spatial and material methods he uses to literally challenge and transgress the viewers' rational expectations of that structure. This is apparent in his development of the double-skinned vault. At his chapel at Vallinotto in Piedmont, Italy, Vittone constructs a structural inner skeleton which supports a dome, and which also works as a windowed canopy onto a series of outer vaults depicting pictures of heaven.

The inner skeleton is an entirely visible comprehensible structure, whereas the structure of the outer vaults is obscured completely. The inner skeleton acts as a structure of reason through which worshippers' view heaven floating above: in a nifty reversal of expectations, it is the illusion of heaven which is illuminated, via a hidden window admitting the real light of earth, while the inner earth-bound structure remains dark. It is through the clear delineation of this inner containing structure that, paradoxically, the illusion of heaven above us is made apparently *more real*. In this work of Vittone's there is literally a base structure – the inner skeleton – and a superstructure – the outer vaults. The one is literally down-to-earth, while the other depicts possibilities beyond the earthly, beyond the immediate material reality of the inner vault. The possibilities of the one cannot be "read" without the other – they work dialectically. To achieve this, the purity of delineated architectural

17.1 Chapel at Vallinotto, Piedmont: interior view; architect Bernardo Vittone

17.2 Chapel at Vallinotto: section; architect Bernardo Vittone, engraving by Instruzioni Diverse

categories, its clearly defined visible elements of dome, column, wall and window, are deliberately transgressed. The section shows that you cannot see where domes are supported by columns, where columns meet the earth, or where a window begins or ends.

It is particularly in the field of *formal*, physical identification of transgression that use of Douglas' definitions of pollution taboos is fruitful. Any designer or builder experiences the decisions they make on an immediate, material level. However restricted, a surprising number of choices do exist in the working day concerning this rather than that shape, component or material. What I offer to the reader here is a way of interrogating the specific details of architectural and urban *form* illuminated by *non-formal* issues – cultural, economic and political. Architecture is a practical subject, massively loaded with meaning for culture at large: this is acknowledged as a matter of course by everyone other than those, like surveyors, in whose professional interests it is to ignore such uncomfortable complexity. My intention is to bring the two aspects, the practical specifics and cultural meaning, to bear on each other. This is very difficult; making simply passing references to the cultural in formal analysis, and vice versa, is much easier. To read Harvey's examination of the building of the Sacré Coeur in Paris is a real disappointment because it does not address the specific spatial or material qualities of that place;[27] to read architectural theorist Colin Rowe's detailed examination of the formal properties of Le Corbusier's entry for the Palace of the Soviet's competition,[28] a piece which ignores the entire political context of this clearly loaded project, is equally frustrating.

One of the reasons why the work of the marxist Benjamin is so important is that he is able to focus on an identifiable figure through which to muse on the workings, veils and manifestations of capitalist interests. With characteristic compression he says:

> Ambiguity is the *figurative* appearance of the dialectic, the law of dialectic at a standstill. This standstill is Utopia, and the dialectical image therefore a dream image. The commodity clearly provides such an image: as fetish. The arcades, which are both house and stars, provide such an image. And such an image is provided by the whore, who is seller and commodity in one.[29]

Benjamin's work on the arcades points the way: its space is not just a product, for it also is a fetish. It seeks to cover up something else; it is ideological. Benjamin implies that the arcades' very *ambiguity* – both "house and stars" – is the reason why this particular architectural commodity is especially fruitful ground for unravelling the capitalist dialectic.

In this context, the films *Alfie*[30] and *Darling*[31] provide material for examining the architectural minutiae of the 1960s interior: the side-board and the padded wall. The schism Benjamin speaks of between home and work is at the outset gendered. Woman is established in the home, the man at work; the association of the woman with the interior, the fixed decorative, is set up. This division is dependent on physical changes to the city: in Paris the Haussmann road projects, in London the suburban railway system – the fate of the interior is inextricably bound up with, first, the world outside it, and second, with the situation of women in time and space. Once post-war economics dictate that women *en masse* go to work in the office, the character of the interior changes. New system building erases the decorative interior in the home: it becomes depicted as merely the other side of the wall. Effectively it becomes part of the urban scene, the world outside: a place where the *flâneur* Alfie can move in and out at will, sampling different women, like a fantasy flow diagram.

17.3 Flow diagram by Gordon Cullen from *MHLG Homes for Today and Tomorrow*
By kind permission of HMSO

In the context of women at work, the decorative attaches itself to women themselves: the painted dolly bird pictured against stark walls becomes a kind of peripatetic interior. At the site of utter exclusion of female power, the executive suite and boardroom, the decorative again breaks free from the surface of the woman's body and into the interior beyond. While the home and working office beyond become an efficient machine, the boardroom becomes feminised: a romanticised version of the home, dependent as all romanticism on a sense of loss. Grained timber panelling abounds; walls are soft and padded; the subversively anti-modernist hidden storage space makes a surreptitious come-back. One object in the boardroom interior becomes purely iconic: the side board or credenza.

In *Sabrina Fair*,[32] it is a remnant from an idealised kitchen: a feminine magic carpet object that can magically span the rift between office and home. Audrey Hepburn, visiting the successful but unfulfilled executive Humphrey Bogart in his executive suite, dons an apron and magically conjures up a wholesome meal from its unpromising urban cocktail contents. The boardroom, site of the harshest economic decisions, veils itself as the place where all is right with the world: the rift between home and work, the universal characteristic of developed capitalism, is healed. In *Sabrina Fair*, the home comes to the office and cures it of its barren unwholesome character.

17.4 John Schlesinger, *Darling* (UK, 1965)

Fiction, meaning and architecture

The importance of fiction, and in particular film, is that its own intent to tell a story – even in the widest possible sense – means that its use of "practical" architecture is inevitably self-consciously loaded with meaning. I am struck by the way a film-maker will commonly spend much longer determining how the artefacts of architects, and other urban designers, are to be filmed, than was originally spent designing the artefacts themselves in the first place. In Roman Polanski's films *Repulsion*[33] and *Rosemary's Baby*,[34] the role of detail is crucial both to the entire action of the film and to the viewer's saturation in the fictional meaning the producer is trying to convey. In these two films, the litany of illegitimate piercings of the skins of the heroine's respective apartments acts both as a metaphor for the violation of the female body, and as crucial incidents in forwarding the narrative. In *Repulsion*, the camera traces the onslaught of a minute series of cracks in the plasterwork of Catherine Deneuve's apartment. At the film's climax, the walls begin to literally smear the edge between Deneuve and themselves. In *Rosemary's Baby*, the corridor is worryingly ambiguous: neither in Rosemary's flat nor in the neighbouring flat, a hidden door allows a devastating penetration of Rosemary herself and her apartment by the devil worshippers next door. In each film the indeterminate, impure edge has overwhelming and nightmarish consequences.

17.5 Roman Polanski, *Repulsion* (UK, 1965)

It is not just the film-maker who encapsulates this sophisticated architectural sensibility. Importantly, the viewer's comprehension of the viewer of architectural clues is assumed, and by the evident success of the films I have used as examples here, we can conclude that the assumption is right.

Form and politics

So the notion of transgression subsumes both the formal and the political. But what kind of relationship really exists? Is it conceivable that a complete correspondence could occur between a virtually total visualisation (i.e. a visual logic carried to the extreme) and a "logic of society" – the strategies inspired by a state bureaucracy?[35]

The purport of Douglas' *Purity and Danger* is that the political – the assertion of power in a particular society – has a formal expression in the excluding characteristics of pollution taboos. In an important passage, Douglas points out that:

> Pollution dangers strike when form has been attacked. Thus we would have a triad of powers controlling fortune and misfortune: first, formal powers wielded by persons representing the formal structure and exercised on behalf of the formal structure; second, formless powers wielded by interstitial persons; third, powers not wielded by any person, but inhering in the structure, which strike against any infraction of form.[36]

What does this mean for architectural production? If we observe a concerted reassertion of clear rules, both in the sense of a structure within a design, and a structure to apply to that design, we should look for two things. First, for the attack on form against which this reassertion of architectural rules reacts, and second, for the formal structure under defence. "Formal structure" here has the meaning of a societal structure, whose interests are expressed by those who most vociferously assert the need for a recall to order.[37]

So, for example, one might interpret the Brutalist hegemony in post-war British architecture as follows. Form was perceived as under attack by a decorative free style associated with the buildings and designs of the 1951 Festival of Britain.[38] This coincided with an economic need to industrialise the building industry, leading both to the standardisation and to the specialisation of components – in Douglas' terms, the purification of form.[39] Politically, the onset of the Cold War lead to (a) a literal reassertion of physical boundary at the macro-scale – the Iron Curtain, the Berlin Wall – and (b) a need to distance all cultural communities, including the architectural, from the politics and aesthetics of Socialist Realism and instead to project honesty and transparency.[40] On a broader cultural level, the taste for the uncompromising, brutally honest warts-and-all approach was personified in the figure of the Angry Young Man and the Technicolor-rejecting, slice-of-life films of the British New Wave. In architecture, the formal structure under defence was the purity of pre-war Modernism: the terms of exclusion inherent in Brutalism – against colour, decoration, uncertainty of line, hybrid materials – were the reassertion of architectural rules in the face of the Anything Goes aesthetic of the immediate post-war decade.

At the scale of marxist spatial analysis of the city and landscape, the formal coincidence of political and "pure" interests directly connects the development of capitalism to burgeoning specialisation and fixed delineation. This applies both to space, and to the professional and technical tasks associated with the control of space, such as architectural design. The drawing of *immovable lines* around fixed edges was a necessary prerequisite "for the development of unambiguous definition of property rights in land. Space thus came to be represented, like time and value, *as abstract, objective, homogenous, and universal in its qualities*."[41] The regular delineation of space – whether at the micro scale of a component, as in the post-war building industry, or at the macro scale of the city – smoothes the way to the commodification of space allowing it to be bought or sold as other products. "Builders, engineers, and architects for their part showed how abstract representations of objective space could be combined with exploration of the concrete malleable properties of materials in space."[42] For Harvey, the general consolidation of space as universal is ultimately driven not by the tendency towards classification and delineation, but by the forces of capitalism's own expanding tendency to commodify everything.[43]

Once this universal parcelling out of defined space is established, a number of accompanying formal consequences pertain. These work in parallel both with space's delineation, and also with its categorisation, attendant on the growing division of labour. Ambiguity of function is cast out. In a powerful and dense passage which deserves quotation in full, Lefebvre describes the social and professional manifestations of what he calls spatial abstraction – the result of this quasi-universal containment of space – coupled with space's atomisation into functions:

> Euclidean space . . . is literally flattened out, confined to a surface . . . The person who sees and knows only how to see, the person who draws and knows only how to put marks on a sheet of paper, the person who drives around and knows only how to drive a car – all contribute in their way to the mutilation of a space which is everywhere sliced up . . . the driver is concerned only with steering himself to his destination and in looking about sees only what he needs to see for that purpose; he thus perceives only his route, which has been materialised mechanised and technicised and he sees it from one angle only that of its functionality: speed, readability, facility . . . The reading of space that has been manufactured with readability in mind amounts to a sort of pleonasm, that of a *"pure" and illusory transparency*. Space is defined in this context in terms of the perception of an *abstract subject*, such as the driver of a motor vehicle, equipped with a collective common sense, namely the capacity to read the symbols of the highway code, and with a sole organ – the eye – placed in the service of his movement within the visual field. Thus space appears solely in its reduced forms. Volume leaves the field to surface and any overall view surrenders to visual signals spaced out along fixed trajectories already laid down in the "plan." An extraordinary – indeed unthinkable, impossible – confusion gradually arises between space and surface, with the latter determining a spatial abstraction which it endows with a half-imaginary, half-real physical existence. This abstract space eventually becomes the simulacrum of a full space . . . Travelling – walking or strolling about – becomes an actually experienced, gestural simulation of the formerly urban activity of encounter, of movement among concrete existences.[44]

By contrast, during the events of May 1968 in the Paris region, self-consciously transgressive political activities burgeoned: in particular the established intellectual categories were rejected, in part by virtue of their uncritical reflection of the economic divisions of labour.[45] This then impacted to explode the spatial abstraction of the city.

> During those days the dichotomies between activity and passivity, between private life and social life, between the demands of daily life and those of political life, between leisure and work and the places associated with them, between spoken and written language,

between action and knowledge, all these dichotomies disappeared in the *streets, amphitheatres and factories* . . . Horrified and impotent, the adherents of norms witness the sequence of transgressions. They are unable to conceive of the initial transgression: the crossing of the border that "normally" separates the political and non-political areas, and the ensuing emancipation.[46]

Like the division of labour itself, these acts had their formal spatial expression. A key catalyst of the events was the demand at Nanterre for *libre circulation*. Nanterre, where Lefebvre taught, is a post-war Parisian suburb, a university by the motorway made of anonymous concrete blocks. Danny Cohn-Bendhit, like a latter day Alfie, led the protests in favour of free circulation. What was being demanded was the right to freely circulate in and out of the bedrooms of female students: the transgression of literal, physical boundaries in the name of freedom.

Structural truth

A belief in structural truth is inextricably bound up with the spatial battle against matter out of place. To be structurally honest it is not enough to know that an arch rests on a column, or that this element supports that one: you have to see it to believe it. Such visual transparency requires the absolute delineation of the structural components, and therefore has direct consequences for the final appearance of a building. If there is any fuzziness or bastardisation or transgression at the junction between two parts, how will anyone see for sure that you are being honest? Notwithstanding the economic imperatives of an industrialising building industry, structural honesty in and of itself demands specialist components. One specialist component not only must be guaranteed absolutely distinguishable from another, but also must not trespass on the other's specialist role.

The British Brutalist movement connected the apparently unrefined qualities of materials, used in their original, irreducible condition, with an attempt to "face up" to the realities of the conditions of post-war life, and "drag a rough poetry,"[47] in Peter Smithson's words, out of these conditions of the everyday. The assumption is that covering up brute reality, whether social or cultural, is equivalent in the realm of building construction to covering up pure undefiled materials and elements. Hence the act of revealing, still at a *constructional* level, acquires for architects a moral authority at a *cultural* level. For the philosopher Theodor Adorno, writing in *The Jargon of Authenticity*, "the more earnestly the jargon sanctifies its everyday world . . . the more sadly does the jargon mix up the literal with the figurative."[48] This mix-up between the literal and figurative, observed in relation to the idea of dirt, emerges in the related field of structural truth. As Lefebvre observes:

> The oddness of this space . . . is that it is at once homogeneous and compartmentalised. It is also simultaneously limpid and deceptive; in short fraudulent. Falsely true – "sincere," so to speak; not the object of a false consciousness, but rather the locus and medium of the generation (or production) of false consciousness.[49]

Rationality and irrationality

Another "take" on the tension between structure and transgression concerns the notion of rationality and irrationality. This related pair of dualities is, at first sight, less a formal issue and more to do with the self-conscious expression of ideas. Yet there are moments in the rhetoric of architectural production when reason is overtly appealed to. Architects working in the eighteenth century could hardly escape the pervasiveness of *soi-disant* Rationality, while the contemporary building component industry is wedded to the accepted formal demonstrations of rationality – numbering systems, specialisations, categories within categories. Architects have to regularise their activities and submit themselves to accepted rationalities in the fields which affect them, in particular those legal and financial. In the broader spatial terms which affect city scale, Lefebvre observes that:

> A classical (Cartesian) rationality thus appears to underpin various spatial distinctions and divisions. Zoning . . . which is responsible – precisely – for fragmentation, break-up and separation under the umbrella of a bureaucratically decreed unity, *is conflated with the rational capacity to discriminate*. The assignment of functions . . . "on the ground," becomes indistinguishable from the kind of analytical activity that discerns differences. What is being covered up here is a moral and political order: the specific power that organises these conditions, with its specific socio-economic allegiance, seems to flow directly from the Logos – that is from a "consensual" embrace of the rational. Classical reason has apparently undergone a convulsive degeneration into technological and technocratic rationality; *this is the moment of its transformation into its opposite – into the absurdity of a pulverised reality*. It is on the ground too that the state-bureaucratic order . . . simultaneously achieves self-actualisation and self-concealment, fuzzying its image in the crystal clear air of functional and structural readability.[50]

The "Her" of Godard's *Two or Three Things I Know about Her* addresses both the various prostitute protagonists and the city of Paris herself. While in the Polanski films the violation of the heroine's bodily surface and the surface of her apartment interior work in synchronicity, in the Godard film the parallel analogy refers to the rupture at urban scale. So "the absurdity of pulverised reality" is, specifically, the building in the 1960s of the giant Périphérique ring road around Paris: a constructional project which renders, in terms of technological rationality, the previous spatial connections of the city nonsensical. In the face of the onslaught of bulldozers, the prostitute, draped in the colours of the tricolour, tells us that she dreams "she has been torn into a thousand pieces." Like a visual illustration of Lefebvre's spatial abstraction, Godard's depiction of the new city of Paris is an architect's model of orthogonal blocks, created from the packaging of international commodities. In opposition to this classical rationality, a closing image of Godard's film is a bunch of flowers thrown over the delineation of the Paris region: edgeless, undelineated and uncategorised.

17.6 Jean-Luc Godard, *Two or Three Things I Know about Her* (France, 1966)

Of the three theoretical approaches presented here, two (marxism and the structuralist analysis of pollution taboo) use the apparent paradox of rational systems to unearth the irrational in human activity. Only fiction does not assert that its role is to systematise an otherwise irrational world. Yet the thrust of both marxism and Douglas' structuralist work is not just to unearth the irrational; what gives it teeth is the way in which it systematically demonstrates the irrational outcomes of apparently quite rational systems. The aim of the marxist analysis of the apparently rational circulation of capital is to demonstrate the irrational dysfunctional outcomes of market economics – crises of over-production, world recessions and so on. In a kind of equivalence, Lefebvre suggests above that, with the development of capitalism, classicism undergoes a degeneration which transforms it into a kind of remorseless a-logicality, precisely by the operation *ad absurdum* of its system of logic.

17.7 Moore Barracks, Shorncliffe, Kent: exterior view (1969); architects Westwood, Piet and Partners

This remorseless a-logicality is to be read at micro as well as macro level. Buildings replete with what Lefebvre calls "structural readability" can nevertheless become logistically dysfunctional. The architectural rules of purity, legibility and honesty promoted by Brutalism dictate that elements should not be covered up, and that structural function be clearly expressed. At Moore Barracks in Shorncliffe, Kent, designed by architects Westwood, Piet and Partners, the concrete slab of the floor is unambiguously visible in contrast to the non-structural brickwork that forms the external wall. The published details were praised for their honesty.

> The external skin of brickwork is non-structural. The continuous clerestory allows this to be expressed by sloping back the face of the stub columns.[51]

17.8 Moore Barracks, Shorncliffe, Kent: section (1969); architects Westwood, Piet and Partners

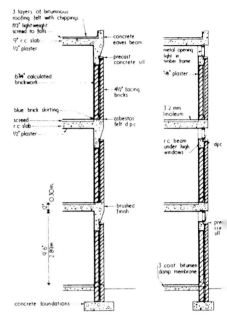

This "expression" is employed to make the following points: (1) the concrete is structural (2) we can see this because it sits on another element of the structure (the inner face of the cavity wall), and (3) it eschews contact with potentially polluting Non-Structure – the external brickwork skin – so it slopes its face to make absolutely certain that we can see it is resting *behind* the external face and *on* the inner one. This building itself may not leak; however, we could well imagine that, when it rains, water runs down the sloping face of the concrete slab columns and, aided by capillary action, straight on to the inner skin of the cavity wall which though structural is nevertheless inside and therefore could reasonably be expected to remain dry. A system of logic operating *ad absurdum*?

For Douglas, too, it is not sufficient to refer to hygiene as the rational source of pollution taboos: she unearths a complex system of taboos against intrusions which bring no objective harm whatsoever. This is why, as Bryan Turner has said,

> From the point of view of an alternative history of capitalism it is the irrational violence of passions and the destructive energies of human sexuality which are important . . . This perversity of human rationalism is probably best captured by the ambivalent figures of Benjamin's Angel and Baudelaire's prostitute, by the *flâneur* and the bohemian, rather than the penny-pinching, rationally organised, capitalist entrepreneur.[52]

Turner notes that the arch-chronicler of human rationality, the sociologist Max Weber, argued that the "origins of capitalist rationality lay not in a rational world view, but, on the contrary, in the deeply irrational impulse of salvation within the terrifying theology of Calvin. In short, the roots of modern rationality lay in religious irrationality."[53] But the totality of religious experience, after all, appeals to both reason (this is inherent both in any moral code and in the patterns of institutional organisation) and, at one and the same time, to the suspension of reason: witness the belief in normally incredible happenings such as the Resurrection and Assumption of Christ. The Baroque is a period of particular interest in this context. Its overt Counter Reformatory mission can be understood as a conscious intent to bypass reason by appealing, as decreed by the Council of Trent, to all five senses in order to seduce the errant Protestants back to the true church. The example of Vittone's work cited above, poised between the Enlightenment and the Baroque, serves as an archetypal and masterly simultaneous expression of reason – the transparent logic of the inner skeletal structure – and divine experience which transgresses reason's earth bound rules – expressed in the structural mystery of Vallinotto's outer shells.

This subversive quality of the Baroque is not only architectural: Buci-Glucksmann in *Baroque Reason* makes clear that the idea of *progress* is challenged by the Baroque. She associates the idea of "progress" in modernity with the "great classical form," of a fulfilled meaning of history corresponding to reality, of Truth as a system and of the Subject as identity and centre. In opposition to this, the Baroque presents from the beginning quite a different, "post-modern" conception of reality in which the instability of forms in movement opens onto "the reduplicated and re-duplicable structure of all reality: enchanted illusion and disenchanted world."[54] Progress is inherent in the marxist analysis of capital, in that inevitable economic crisis will worsen until a properly rational system of production and distribution, i.e. communism, replaces it. That this rejection of progress is not, however, incompatible with a marxist outlook is indicated by Buci-Glucksmann's citation of Benjamin's own understanding of the opposition of the two world views, Classicism and the Baroque: "By its very essence Classicism was not permitted to behold the lack of freedom, the imperfection, the collapse of the physical beautiful nature."[55]

The fiction itself, as an analytical tool, operates as a form of *baroque reason*. It runs counter to the two systematic approaches of marxism and the structural identification of the operation of pollution taboo. It is without the burden of overt rationality, whether of form or content, and without the need to assert truth or progress.

My contention with these few examples is to propose that culture at large evidences an untapped spatial and architectural understanding. The site of this understanding is in its fictions. The power of this comprehension is that it itself transgresses imposed categories of specialisation, expertise, professional and political restricted practices. The pity of it is that it remains untapped, both by those very professions and the public who for the most part persist in seeing their own spatial engagement as subject to a "superior" comprehension. By moving fictional insight to centre stage, it may yet be possible to both kick the technical off its pedestal and reveal its own fictional origins, and to argue for the constructive exploitation of the analysis and insight of the fictions of film and the novel in public discussion of the city's future.

References

1   David Harvey, *Consciousness and the Urban Experience* (Oxford: Blackwell, 1985), p. 38.

2   Harvey, *Consciousness and the Urban Experience*, p. 32.

3   Henri Lefebvre, *The Explosion: Marxism and the French Revolution of May 1968* (New York: Monthly Review, 1969), p. 119.

4   Walter Benjamin, *Charles Baudelaire: a Lyric Poet in the Era of High Capitalism* (London: Verso, 1983), p. 167.

5   Benjamin, *Charles Baudelaire*, p. 273.

6   Lefebvre, *Explosion*, p. 53.

7   Kurt Neumann, *The Fly* (USA, 1958); David Cronenberg, *The Fly* (USA, 1986).

8   Mary Douglas, *Purity and Danger: an Analysis of the Concepts of Pollution and Taboo* (London: Routledge, 1966), p. 35.

9   Leviticus 11:9, 10, 20, quoted by Douglas, *Purity and Danger*, p. 41.

10   Douglas, *Purity and Danger*, p. 104.

11   Douglas, *Purity and Danger*, p. 104.

12   Douglas, *Purity and Danger*, p. 122.

13   Douglas, *Purity and Danger*, p. 38.

14   Jonathan Raban, *Soft City* (London: Hamish Hamilton, 1974), p. 25.

15   Raban, *Soft City*.

16   François Maspero, *Roissy Express* (London: Verso, 1992), p. 177.

17   Louis Chevalier, *The Assassination of Paris* (Chicago: University of Chicago Press, 1994), p. 212.

18   Henri Lefebvre, *The Production of Space* (Oxford: Blackwell, 1991), p. 7 (emphasis in the original).

19   Turner goes on to say: "This problem is fundamental to the work of Benjamin, whose theory of language has often been neglected in favour of exegesis of his aesthetic theories." Bryan S. Turner, "Introduction," Christine Buci-Glucksmann, *Baroque Reason: the Aesthetics of Modernity* (London: Sage, 1994).

20   Raban, *Soft City*, p. 7.

21   See, for example, Brendan O'Leary's "British Farce, French Drama and Tales of Two Cities: Reorganisations of Paris and London Governments 1957–86," *London Public Administration*, v. 65 (Winter 1987), pp. 369–89.

22   Something of this approach informs Buci-Glucksmann's interpretation of Benjamin's own interpretative methodology : "In the dialectical image the past of a given epoch is always 'the past of always.' But it presents itself as such only in the eyes of a particular epoch – the one in which humanity, rubbing its eyes, recognises precisely this dream image for what it is. At that moment the historian's task is the interpretation of dreams . . . Faced with the fine totalities of classicism, or with a Marxist Weltanschaung aesthetic,

Benjamin therefore emphasises quite a different scanning of history to bring out an archaeology of modernity at its crucial turning points: the seventeenth-century baroque, the nineteenth century of Baudelaire (and not Balzac), the literary avant-garde of the twentieth century." Buci-Glucksmann, *Baroque Reason*, p. 46.

23 See, for example, how each character, artefact and space of Charles Dickens' novel *Our Mutual Friend* links up with the one character of John Harman, who remains invisible except in providing this structural connection, in much of the text.

24 Henri Lefebvre taught at the suburban university of Nanterre, where the "events" were sparked off. The events involved mass demonstrations student strikes, general strikes and the immobilisation of transport. They were regarded by libertarians and marxists as a time on the brink of revolution.

25 Lefebvre, *Explosion*, p. 74.

26 Lefebvre, *Explosion*, p. 29 (emphasis added).

27 Harvey, *Consciousness and the Urban Experience*, p. 221.

28 Colin Rowe, "Transparency: Literal and Phenomenal," *The Mathematics of the Ideal Villa and Other Essays* (Cambridge, MA: MIT Press, 1982), p. 160.

29 Benjamin, *Charles Baudelaire*, p. 171.

30 Lewis Gilbert, *Alfie* (UK, 1966).

31 John Schlesinger, *Darling* (UK, 1965).

32 Billy Wilder, *Sabrina Fair* (USA, 1954).

33 Roman Polanski, *Repulsion* (UK, 1965).

34 Roman Polanski, *Rosemary's Baby* (USA, 1968).

35 Lefebvre, *Production of Space*, p. 312. Though admitting such coincidence is improbable, Lefebvre does say that Brasilia seems to be an example.

36 Douglas, *Purity and Danger*, p. 104.

37 Lionel Esher, *A Broken Wave: the Rebuilding of England 1940–1980* (London: Allen Lane, 1981), p. 60.

38 For Reyner Banham, the external boundaries of what the profession understood as "architecture" were under threat both from the Festival Style, but also from widespread local authority architecture of the immediate post-war years, "a style based on a sentimental regard for nineteenth century vernacular usages, with pitched roofs, brick or rendered walls, window boxes, balconies, pretty paintwork, a tendency to elaborate woodwork detailing and freely picturesque grouping." He goes on: "The younger generation, viewing these works, had the depressing sense that the drive was going out of Modern Architecture, its pure dogma being diluted by politicians and compromisers who had lost their intellectual nerve." Reyner Banham, *The New Brutalism* (London: Architectural Press, 1966), pp. 12–13.

39 See Brian Finnimore, *Houses from the Factory: System Building and the Welfare State* (London: Rivers Oram Press, 1989).

40 Banham indicates that the young Brutalists reacted against the London County Council's architects' department Communist caucus who were promoting the decorated, debased modernism of the post-war years as the British version of Socialist Realism. Banham, *New Brutalism*, p.13.

41 Harvey, *Consciousness and the Urban Experience*, p. 13.

42 Harvey, *Consciousness and the Urban Experience*, p. 13.

43 "[A]ll manner of other conceptions of place and space – sacred and profane, symbolic, personal , animistic – could continue to function undisturbed. It took something more to consolidate space, as universal, homogeneous, objective and abstract in most social practices. That 'something' was the buying and selling of space as a commodity." Harvey, *Consciousness and the Urban Experience*, p. 13.

44 Lefebvre, *Production of Space*, p. 313 (emphasis added).

45 This transgression extended to established intellectual categories:
"The movement at first concentrated on specifically economic objectives: buildings, credits, employment, market restraint, imperatives of the division of labour. These old demands – inadequately but forcefully taken over by the bureaucratic trade-union and political apparatus – were soon superseded. The movement began to raise questions of ideology and 'values.' The question of specialised knowledge came to the fore. This type of knowledge – fragmented. departmentalised – is condemned by the most perceptive students . . . in addition, the students violently attack the form of education, which they accuse of masking the deficiencies of content by high-handedly imposing both ideology and fragmented knowledge." Lefebvre, *Explosion*, pp. 110–11.

46 Lefebvre, *Explosion*, pp. 115–16 (emphasis added).

47 Banham, *New Brutalism*, p. 12.

48 Theodor Adorno, *The Jargon of Authenticity* (London: Routledge and Kegan Paul, 1973), p. 33.

49 Lefebvre, *Production of Space*, pp. 50–1 and 310.

50 Lefebvre, *Production of Space*, p. 317 (emphases added).

51 *Architects' Journal* (26 February 1969), pp. 565–82.

52 Turner, "Introduction," Buci-Glucksmann, *Baroque Reason*, p. 34.

53 Turner, "Introduction," Buci-Glucksmann, *Baroque Reason*, pp. 17–18.

54 Buci-Glucksmann, *Baroque Reason*, p. 134.

55 Walter Benjamin, *The Origin of German Tragic Drama* (London: New Left Books, 1977), p. 176.

Index

Page numbers in *italics* refer to illustrations